Maintaining Upgrading and Troubleshooting

IBM PCs, Compatibles, and PS/2 Personal Computers

Mark Minasi

COMPUTE! Books
Radnor, Pennsylvania

To Sheila, for the support, the help, and the love.

Editor: Pam Plaut
Cover design: Anthony Jacobson
Copyright 1990, Mark Minasi. All rights reserved.

Copyright 1987, Iomega Corporation. Reprinted excerpts of installation manual/user's guide for the Iomega PC250 Host Adapter Card used in this book.

Copyright 1987, Hewlett-Packard Company. Reprinted excerpts form the HP ScanJet User's Guide used in this book.

Printed in the United States of America

10 9 8 7 6 5 4 3 2 1

Library of Congress Cataloging-in-Publication Data
Minasi, Mark.
    Maintaining, upgrading, and troubleshooting PCs and compatibles.
    including the PS/2 / Mark Minasi.
        p.   cm.
    ISBN 0-87455-230-3
    1. Microcomputers.   I. Title.
    QA76.5.M531445   1990
    004.165—dc20   89-85954
                                                        CIP

The author and publisher have made every effort in the preparation of this book to ensure the accuracy of the information. However, the information in this book is sold without warranty, either express or implied. Neither the author nor COMPUTE! Publications, Inc. will be liable for any damages caused or alleged to be caused directly, indirectly, incidentally, or consequentially by the information in this book.

The opinions expressed in this book are solely those of the author and are not necessarily those of COMPUTE! Publications, Inc.

COMPUTE! Publications, Inc., Post Office Box 5406, Greensboro, NC 27403, (919) 275-9809, is part of ABC Consumer Magazines, Inc., one of the ABC Publishing Companies, and is not associated with any manufacturer of personal computers.

dBase, dBase III, and *dBase III Plus* are registered trademarks of Ashton-Tate. DOS is a registered trademark of International Business Machines Corp. *Lotus 1-2-3* is a registered trademark of Lotus Devopement Corp. The Mace Utilities a registered trademark of Paul Mace Software, Inc. *MultiMate* is a registered trademark of MultiMate International/Ashton-Tate. *PC Tools* is a registered trademark of Central Point Software. *SideKick* is a registered trademark of Borland International, Inc. The Norton Utilities is a registered trademark of Peter Norton Computing, Inc. *WordPerfect* is a registered trademark of WordPerfect Corp. *WordStar* is a registered trademark of WordStar International Corp.

Contents

Why This Book? • Who Is This Book For? • Terminology • Structure of This Book • Safety Notes and Cautions

Top-Level PC Taxonomy: Chips and Buses • The Next Step: PC Features

General PC Disassembly Advice • PC/XT/AT-Specific Disassembly Hints • Disassembling the PS/2s

The System Board/Motherboard • Central Processing Unit (CPU) • Main Memory • Buses: PC, AT, ISA, Micro Channel, EISA and More • System Clock • Numeric Coprocessor (Math Coprocessor) • Power Supply • Keyboard • The Notion of a Controller • Display and Display Adapters • Floppy and Hard Disk Controller and Disk Drives • Printer Interfaces • Modems and Communication Ports • System Clock/Calendar • Other Strange Boards • Some Identification Hints • Model Identification Revisited: Specifics of Particular Machines

Heat and Thermal Shock • Magnetism • Stray Electromagnetism • Avoiding Water and Liquids • Summary: Making the PC Environment "PC Friendly" • A Sample Preventive Maintenance Program

Chapter 6. Troubleshooting Problems: What to Do When Something Goes Wrong 77

General Troubleshooting Rules • Troubleshooting Steps • Check for Operator Error • Is Everything Plugged In? • Check the Software • Memory Resident (TSR) Problems • What Am I Doing Differently? • Check External Signs • Run Diagnostic Programs • Under The Hood: Troubleshooting Step 7 • Documenting Trouble Calls

Chapter 7. Installing New Circuit Boards (Without Creating New Problems to Troubleshoot) 93

Configuring New Circuit Boards • Board Installation • Board Testing • Installing Motherboards

Chapter 8. Repairs with Circuit Boards and Chips 119

Fix or Replace Boards? • How Do You Find the Bad Board? • Night of the Living Data: Making a Dead Machine "Undead" • Finding and Replacing Bad Chips

Chapter 9. Semiconductor Memory 130

Reading Memory Chips: Size, Access Time, and Wait States • Reading Memory Error Messages • Other Causes of Memory Errors • Tips on Installing Memory Chips

Chapter 10. Power Supplies and Power Protection............. 146

Components of the Power Supply • Power Supply Connections • Maintenance • Upgrading the Power Supply • Troubleshooting the Power Supply • Protecting the PC from the AC • The Grandaddy of Power Problems: Lightning

Chapter 11. Hard Disk Drive Overview and Terminology 169

Disk Structure: Hardware and Software • Disk Performance • Hardware: The Controller and the Drive

Chapter 12. Hard Disk Drive Installation 183

Hard Disk Hardware Installation • Hard Disk Software Installation

Foreword

Here it is—available to all PC owners for the first time. The book you need to select, assemble, upgrade, and repair everything in the PC line from the original IBM PC to the PS/2s to "no-name" PC clones.

Whether you have a machine at home or 1,000 at the office, this book can make you more effective as a PC repair person. If you are a PC user, and repair is only an occasional activity, you'll find this book an entertaining and informative way to cut down on trips to the repair shop as well as a guide for confidently choosing and installing upgrades from memory boards to disk drives.

And if troubleshooting is what you're after, it's discussed on virtually every page in this book. The approaches are always geared to finding the lowest cost, fastest, most effective answer to your problems. There's even information on how to bring a dead machine back to life. Again, step-by-step instructions lead you through system resurrection.

Do you think you'll never understand how the components of your machine work? Now you'll find out—in plain English. Upgrade your older machine to newer technology, learn what utilities will give you the most value for your money, configure new circuit boards, work through RS-232 cable design even if you don't know how to use a screwdriver, and install and set up new hard disk and floppy disk drives.

Stop wasting time and money on nonfunctional PCs. Author Mark Manasi shows you how to increase your productivity almost instantly.

Acknowledgments

This was a big task. I couldn't have done it without some essential help. I'd like to thank several people in particular.

Sheila Walsh read everything I wrote to make sure it would make sense to normal humans. She calmly insisted that obscure parts be rewritten, even when I was at my most ursine. She even tactfully ignored me when I was fed up with rewriting and just yelled, "If they're too dumb to understand *that*, they're not *allowed* to read the book!" Such comments were only the product of late nights and long hours, however, and I eventually saw things her way. (One might say I was then at my most "ursinine.") The text is much better for her suggestions, and I appreciate her tenacity. She also pointed out stylistic errors in pictures and tables, and cleaned up nearly 50 tables in this book. On top of that, she ran errands for me and made me eat when I forgot to. Rarely have I worked with an assistant who assists so well.

Rob Oreglia, one of the partners at Moulton Minasi & Co., patiently explained the details of electrical ground, do's and don'ts about surge protectors, and has, in general, kept me on the straight-and-narrow about facts that I otherwise might have let slip. Rob's insistence on actually *reading the documentation* (an obsession I lack, sadly) when he sets out on a project has taught me a few things and gotten me out of a few corners. Rob advised me heavily on Chapter 10, "Power Supplies and Power Protection," and designed the AT memory error message maps in the Memory chapter. Rob also took the pictures in this book and did a very nice job; I think you'll agree.

Scott Foerster, another partner and a true techie guru, came to MM & Co. after having first run a repair department at a Computerland back in the early 80s, and then teaching computer and electronic design and troubleshooting at a community college for several years. Scott has shared dozens of troubleshooting tips over the past few years tips with the rest of us who teach the troubleshooting classes, and we're all grateful for his suggestions. Scott knows this stuff right down to the soldering irons. When I write stupid things at four a.m. like "Set your voltmeter to AC current and test to see if you're getting 120 volts," Scott catches it. Thanks, Scott.

Pete Moulton cofounded MM & Co. with me. As a sideline to his teaching and consulting, he installs PC systems for big and small companies. He's got more war stories than you can hear in the time it takes to drink *several* pints of your favorite ale, and they have enriched this class. (Don't order Pete a beer, however—he drinks red wine.) The "Rules of Troubleshooting Almost Anything" in the beginning of Chapter 6 are derived from one of Pete's lectures.

Sharon Wells has assisted me both in real-life PC repairs and in troubleshooting seminars since 1987. She's always full of suggestions, comments, and forceful opinions about what will and won't work in the book. She's read a lot of the text over the last two years, provided insights, and generally helped separate the wheat from the pile of chaff that is information about the PC troubleshooting business.

Thanks to the other MM & Co. staff I haven't yet mentioned in descending order of seniority: Susan Porter, Mike Sola, Beverly Johnson, Jodie Miller, and Pam Ritondale. Ditto for our associates Paula Longhi, Bob Deyo, Hank Stanton, Terry Keaton, Dave Stang, and Brock Meeks.

There are now quite a number of companies offering PC troubleshooting seminars, but ours was the first. So when I looked for a seminar house to sponsor a PC troubleshooting seminar, the only folks who would take a chance on it were Julie, John, and Doug at Data-Tech Institute. They were brave enough to give it a shot and savvy enough to market it so it became a success. To the DTI folks, thanks very much.

Thanks to the following companies for allowing me to reproduce some of their materials in this book:

Hewlett-Packard Printer Division (for LaserJet inserts)
Hewlett-Packard Office Automation (for ScanJet inserts)
Iomega Corporation (for Bernoulli Host Adapter inserts)

Thanks to the U.S. Weather Service for the lightning map in the power supply section.

A few of the graphics are derived, in part, from Micrografx Clip Art, quite a nice collection. One needn't acknowledge the creators of clip art that's been paid for, but MGX makes nice stuff and is worth the look.

Thanks also to the various companies who assisted in assembling the table of hard disk drive specifications:

Seagate
Data Technology
Western Digital
Various contributors to BBSs around the land.

And whoever else I missed.

Chapter 1
Introduction

Why This Book?

I wrote this because I've always wanted to teach a five-day PC troubleshooting class. But that's not why I got *started* writing this, so let me start at the beginning.

Imagine you're using your PC one day. All of a sudden, the floppy drive light goes on for no apparent reason, the system reboots itself, and "601" appears on the screen. Nothing else happens—the machine refuses to do any more. You turn it on and off again, and it does the same thing. What now? Call the serviceman? The local PC expert? Open the yellow pages?

The above disk disaster happened to me in 1982, shortly after PCs arrived on the scene but after the warranty on my PC ran out. I had an all-IBM machine, but since some of the parts came from a dealer who wasn't an authorized IBM dealer, IBM wouldn't even talk to me. So I went to a service department of a large computer store chain seeking help. I looked at their hourly rates and *knew* from their high prices that they must have known

what they were doing, so I confidently left my machine with them. They kept the machine for two months, said they couldn't find anything wrong with it, and charged me $800.

The problem, of course, persisted. I was scared. I had just spent some big bucks for this computer, plus $800 on some non-repairs, and it still didn't work. So I figured, "what the heck, I can't make it any worse" and took off the top.

What I saw was that the drive was connected with a ribbon cable to a circuit board that I later found was called "the floppy controller board." The controller board was new, the drive was new (the repair shop had already replaced them)—but what about the cable? You guessed it. For $35 I bought a new cable from a local computer supply place, and the problem went away forever.

I found out that I wasn't the only person with PC repair needs. In 1987, 7 out of 10 PCs suffered a breakdown of some kind. Each problem took an average of five days to fix, and the fix cost an average of $257.* Even if you pay a maintenance company lots of money to keep your machines in shape, you should still do whatever repairs you can. That's because the high cost of machine failures isn't the cost of the machine—it's the cost of the lost work time, as employees must wait in line to use machines or forgo the services of a PC altogether. You might have to wait four hours for a service person, only to find that the fix is a simple five-minute operation. Result: four hours of lost employee time.

Emboldened by my success, I read what few references existed about microcomputer repair, and I tried fixing a lot of things. Some things got fixed, some got "smoked." I asked a lot of questions, made a lot of mistakes, and finally got to the point where at the worst I didn't do any damage, and usually I met with success.

I'd like to accelerate you to that point with this book (although you'll still "smoke" the occasional device—everybody does). Once I figured out how simple it is to fix PCs, I developed a series of seminars on PC repair that my co-workers and I conduct in the U.S., Canada, and Europe. These two- to three-day seminars have been popular due to the significance of the topic and the fine work of the marketing companies handling them, Data-Tech Institute and Frost & Sullivan, Ltd.

But I've always wanted to teach a five-day class.

You see, a five-day professional seminar really doesn't sell. The seminar would cost too much to run, we would have to charge too much for it, and no one would come because companies

can't afford to let their people (particularly their PC support staff) stay away five consecutive days. So we trim the less important stuff, do fewer exercises, and rush like crazy to get out in two or three days. It drives me crazy not to be able to cover the topics with the thoroughness they deserve. Worse, the classes unanimously say they've had a great time and learned a lot, but that they desperately needed an extra day or two.

So, welcome to the five-day class.

This book won't teach you to fix all problems. Not all problems can be fixed—for instance, leaving a hard disk out in the rain will probably render that erstwhile data storage medium usable for little more than a paperweight. Nevertheless, even if you've never opened up a PC or installed an expansion board, this book can help.

I'll also help with terminology. Part of your job might involve talking to technical types. Some of those folks are good at talking to ordinary mortals, but there are some (and I'm sure you know a few of them) who can't seem to speak a single sentence without a liberal sprinkling of TLAs (Three-Letter Acronyms). A thorough reading of this book will enable you to speak fluent "PC-ese," and the index will provide you definitions of most PC terms.

You'll also see a fair amount about installation in this book. Installation of new equipment often brings headaches: how to do it, why it doesn't work once installed, testing the new equipment, ensuring that it doesn't adversely affect already-installed equipment. You'll also learn how to take a tired old PC and soup it up for better performance.

Who Is This Book For?

I'm writing this for the needy and the curious. Some of you need to under-

---

* According to a survey from the Business Products Consulting Group of Centerport, NY, as reported in the 12 January 1988 *PC Week*. The results were based on a survey of 500 business users. Besides, it was about time for a statistic.

stand the machines you depend upon so much, so you can better keep them in top shape. Others might just wonder what's going on under the hood. Whoever you are, dig in and try something!

So don't let that useful little gray box on your desk control you when it goes down—take control of it. (Remember who's supposed to be boss.) Even if you never take the machine apart, you'll still learn a lot about what goes on under the hood of your machine, and how to make it work faster and live longer.

Terminology

There are so many machines, it's hard to know how to refer generically to PCs. Here are the informal conventions used in this book: *PC* in this text includes all PC compatible machines—the XT, XT clones, the AT, AT clones, and the 386 and 486 machines, unless otherwise specified. *XT* refers to XTs and XT clones—8088 based machines. *AT* refers to 286, 386, or 486 machines in general. I don't refer to IBM machines in particular unless specified otherwise. *PS/2* refers to the micro channel PS/2s (the 50 through the 80) and does not include the 25 and 30.

My goal in developing this book is to include material of use to "techies" as well as to those who have never even opened up a PC. I'm not going to try to make an electrical engineer out of you; I'm not one myself. All it takes to do most PC maintenance is a screwdriver and some patience. I've made every effort to keep the jargon to a minimum and to define unusual PC terms as they're used.

Structure of This Book

First, you'll take a minute to survey the machines out on the market and look at the features that separate one type of PC from another. Then you'll look under the hood and see what's inside a PC. Next, you'll step back and examine some preventive maintenance techniques and troubleshooting approaches. Finally, you'll look in detail at circuit boards, hard and floppy disks, printers, and other PC essentials.

Safety Notes and Cautions

Before we get started, a few words of disclaimer:

This text mentions many products. I'm not endorsing these products. Where they are noted, they've been of value. However, manufacturer quality can vary, and goods can be redesigned.

In general, it's pretty hard to hurt yourself with the PC, short of dropping it on your toe. But there are a few exceptions:

Power Supply. There's a silver or black box with a fan in it in the back of your machine. It's the power supply; it converts AC from the wall socket into DC for the PC's use. You can't miss the label that says in five languages, "If you open me, I'll kill you." Don't open it. In fact, let me reiterate:

> **Don't open the power supply or the monitor. Under the wrong circumstances it could kill you.**

- There's always somebody who doesn't pay attention to the important stuff, but **PAY ATTENTION TO THIS.** If you open the top of the power supply while the machine is plugged in, even if the power is off, you could get a full

120 volts through you if you touch the wrong things. Even if it's not plugged in, there are power-storing devices called *capacitors* that can give you a good shock even after the machine has been unplugged and turned off. The same, by the way, goes for monitors.

It's certainly safe to *replace* a power supply, although when doing such a replacement, again be double sure it's unplugged before removing the original one. More important, why go into the power supply in the first place? The only possible user repair imaginable is to replace the fuse in the box; don't even think of trying that unless you know how to discharge large capacitors safely.

- Another power supply item: Never connect a power supply to the wall socket and turn it on *when it isn't connected to a PC motherboard*. Only turn on a power supply when the motherboard power connectors are in place. Called "running it without a load," some of the power supplies will literally explode if you run them like this.
- Unless it's an emergency procedure, back up your data before doing anything drastic. What if something goes wrong and the machine never comes back on?
- You can damage circuit boards by removing them while the power's on. Don't do it. Turn the machine off before removing a circuit board.

The rest of the things you'll find in the PC are safe, but don't ignore the above warnings.

Chapter 2
PC Models: How They're Different, How They're Similar

The book has already referred to *XT-type machines* versus *AT-type machines,* not a fair thing to do to the troubleshooting novice. Here's where I make amends. In some ways, all PC-compatibles are the same. From the lowliest 256K floppy-only PC to the mighty PS/2 Model 70-A21, they all run DOS. *Lotus 1-2-3* version 2.1 runs on just about everything. But look closer, and soon they start to appear pretty different.

Top-Level PC Taxonomy: Chips and Buses

Let's start out differentiating machines by two things: their *software compatibility* and their *hardware compatibility*. Software compatibility is determined by the kind of processor chip used. We'll discuss processors in some more detail a bit later in the book, but for now just understand that you'll see either the 8088/8086/80188/80186 family, composed of a number of very similar chips; the 80286, which is a newer and more powerful chip that constitutes a family in itself; or the 80386/80386SX/80486 family, the newest and most powerful part of the Intel lineup of CPU chips.

Hardware compatibility refers to the question, "Can I take a circuit board, put it in the computer and make it work?" The XT, PC, and AT share a common *bus*—the connector used to attach expansion boards to the computer's main circuit board (called a *motherboard*). Expansion boards, like memory or I/O boards, that work in a PC will generally work just fine in an AT. The PS/2 line, however, uses a newer and completely incompatible bus called the *Micro Channel Architecture*. PS/2 expansion boards don't work in PCs, and vice versa. Please note that when I say *PS/2*, I'm referring to the *real* PS/2s—the models 50 through 80. The 25s and 30s aren't completely PS/2 machines.

So there are four basic processor chip families and two basic bus types (there are variations within each group, but you'll see them later). There are, then, eight PC types. You can see some examples in Table 2-1.

The Next Step: PC Features

Buses and chips are the big stuff, but you might be saying, "That's not all there is to it—I've heard of megahertz, BIOS

Table 2-1. Types and Examples of PC Compatible Computers

| Processor Chip | Computer Bus Type: | |
	PC (ISA) Bus	Micro Channel Architecture (MCA)
Intel 8088, 8086, 80188, 80186	IBM PC, XT, Portable, PC Jr, XT/370, PC/3270, PS/2 Model 30, Model 25	None in Category
NEC V20, V30	Compaq Deskpro, Portable	
	Toshiba T1000, T1100+, T1200	
	Zenith Z171, 181,183, 151, 158, 159, Eazy PC	
	AT&T 6300	
	Leading Edge Model D	
	Hyundai Blue Chip	
Intel 80286	IBM AT, XT286, AT/370, AT/3270, PS/2 Model 30-286	IBM PS/2 Model 50
	Compaq Deskpro 286	IBM PS/2 Model 50Z
	Zenith Z248,LP286,SuperSport 286	IBM PS/2 Model 60
	AT&T 6300+	
	Toshiba 1600, 3100, 3200	
	AST Premium/286	
Intel 80386, 80386SX, 80486	Compaq Deskpro 386, 386S	IBM PS/2 Model 55
	Zenith Z-386	IBM PS/2 Model 70P
	AT&T 6386	IBM PS/2 Model 70
	AST Premium/386	IBM PS/2 Model 80
	ALR FlexCache 20	Tandy MC5000

type, video boards, and other things. Just what are they, and how do they fit in?" The answer is that they're indeed important; we'll get to them in various parts of the book. Not to leave you hanging, however, there's a brief mention of the big PC features in Table 2-2. I don't want to minimize the importance of, say, the video board, but you don't commit yourself to a long-term decision about video when you buy most machines. Virtually any video board can be added to most machines later, as a nice stereo system can be added to virtually any car. (Why the weasel wording about "most" machines? A few machines—the AT&T 6300, the Leading Edge PC, and Zenith's LP286 and Eazy PC come to mind—incorporate the video function right on the main circuit board, or *motherboard*, which makes video upgrade difficult or impossible.)

Table 2-2. What Makes PCs Different?

Feature	Brief Description	Typical Examples
CPU type	The CPU determines how much memory the system can address, what kind of software it can run, and how fast it can go.	8088 80286 80386 80486
Bus Type	The bus determines what kind of expansion circuit boards will work in the machine. All of the common buses here are compatible in varying degrees with each other except Micro Channel, which is not. ISA (Industry Standard Architecture) is the new name given to the old bus most machines use. Micro Channel was introduced in 1987 by IBM for their PS/2 machines. EISA (Extended Industry Standard Architecture) is the non-IBM manufacturer's answer to Micro Channel.	PC Bus (8 bit ISA) AT Bus (16 bit ISA) Proprietary 32 bit 16 bit Micro Channel 32 bit Micro Channel EISA
BIOS Manufacturer	BIOS (Basic Input/Output System) is the low-level system software that determines your machine's compatibility.	IBM Compaq Phoenix Award
CPU Speed	Megahertz (Mhz) roughly measures system speed. If all other things were equal, a 10 Mhz machine would be faster than a 5 Mhz machine. (All other things usually aren't equal.)	4.77 Mhz (PC speed) up to 33 Mhz (some 386s attain this)
Video Board	The video board affects what kind of software you can run and how quickly data gets onto the screen. You can easily change it, and the oldest PC can use anything from a monochrome board up to a VGA or 8514. Video boards get better by: • Offering more colors • Being able to show more dots on the screen • Being faster	Monochrome Adapter (MDA) Color/Graphics Adapter (CGA) Hercules Graphics Card (HGC) Enhanced Graphics Adapter (EGA) Professional Graphics Controller (PGC) Video Graphics Array (VGA) 8514 High Resolution Adapter
Parallel Port	The parallel (printer) port can serve as a high-speed bidirectional interface on some computers. Some manufacturers tout this feature, but it isn't very important.	Unidirectional Bidirectional

Table 2-2. *continued*

Feature	Brief Description	Typical Examples
Serial Port UART	The UART is the main chip around which a serial port or internal modem is built. You need a 16450 to run OS/2. The PS/2 Models 50Z and 70 have a slightly different chip than either 8250 or 16450, which will keep some communications software from running. Can be changed on many systems.	8250 16450 PS/2 Model 50Z, 70
Amount of Memory	There are several kinds of memory: conventional, extended, and expanded. They all solve different problems. Some software won't run without a particular amount and/or kind of memory.	640K, and so forth
System Clock/ Calendar	Again, not terribly important. Machines with built-in clocks usually have DOS support to directly read or modify the time and date. Some must run a separate program.	Built-in on motherboard Added on expansion board
Hard Disk Interface	The method the hard disk controller (a circuit card in the system) uses to talk to the hard disk. Affects speed. Can be easily changed in most systems.	ST506/412 ESDI SCSI
Hard Disk Encoding Scheme	Method used to squeeze more data onto a track (an area on a hard disk). Can easily be changed.	MFM RLL ARLL
Keyboard Type	IBM originally put a keyboard control chip in the keyboard for the PC and XT. They moved it to the motherboard for the AT, so you must know which kind of keyboard interface you have. Most clone keyboards have a switch allowing them to swing both ways.	XT type AT type
Floppies Supported	The kind of floppies your machine supports. Can fairly easily be changed.	5.25″ 360K 5.25″ 1.2M 5.25″ 720K (unusual) 3.5″ 720K 3.5″ 1.44M
Number of Expansion Slots		3 to 10
Configuration method	Computers won't work until you tell them about themselves, or configure them. It's either done with physical switches or software.	Switches Configuration (CMOS) memory

Table 2-2. *continued*

Feature	Brief Description	Typical Examples
Number of interrupts (IRQ levels) supported	Affects the number and type of expansion boards in a system.	8 or 16
Number of DMA (Direct Memory Access) channels supported	Affects the number and type of expansion boards in a system.	4 or 8
Printer Control Language	Tells your printer how to underline words, put pictures on the page, and change typefaces.	Epson codes HPPCL (LaserJet commands) PostScript Others

Don't let that table make your head spin and convince you to go back to simpler work, like high-energy physics. All those things are included in the table because you'll hear about them in the PC repair business. All these issues (and much more, as they used to say in the great days of radio announcing) are covered later on.

That's half of PC identification. There's more, but it will make more sense after we've gotten under the hood, so I'll leave that for "Model Identification Revisited" in the next chapter. Now that you have some idea of the kind of machine you have and where it fits into the PC universe, let's open it up and take a look inside.

Chapter 3
Disassembling the PC

Never been inside your PC? Step inside. . . .

Maintenance, upgrades, and troubleshooting sometimes require disassembly of the PC. That's sometimes—most problems can be solved without taking the hood off the machine, so avoid becoming trigger-happy with your electric screwdriver. Here's some advice to safely take your machine apart so you can get it back together again.

General PC Disassembly Advice

1. **Make sure you have adequate workspace.** You'll need a lot of room—most of a tabletop would be good. To reduce the potential for static electricity, raise the air humidity to 50 percent or so, use a commercial antistatic remedy, or just touch something metal before you touch any PC component. (See Chapter 5, "Avoiding Service: Preventive Maintenance" for more ideas on handling static electricity.)

   At this point, cowardice and practicality form a marriage of con-

venience. If the machine is still in the warranty period, take a look at the warranty to see if you void it by disassembling the computer. If you can make the problem an SEP (Somebody Else's Problem), then by all means do. If you're sure a printer is dead right out of the box, don't try to fix it—just send it back.

2. **Keep the small parts organized.** Get a cup to store screws and small pieces of hardware. If you just leave the screws on the table, you'll eventually end up accidentally sweeping the screws off the table and onto the floor, where they'll roll down a sewer grate or under the heaviest object around. I knew a guy who kept the screws in the vent atop the power supply, the one just above the fan. One day he forgot they were there and turned the machine on. Power supply fans can *really* sling screws around!

   As there will be at least two kinds of screws (ones to hold on the case tend to be a different size from the rest of the screws in the system, and Seagate 200-series hard disks generally require short screws), it's not a bad idea to steal a page from car mechanic books and use an egg carton. It has a bunch of compartments, and you can label each one. Remember, the plan here is to end up without any spare parts.

3. **Back up the configuration.** If you're disassembling an AT-type machine (386s and 486s are included here), your machine stores a small bit of vital configuration information in a special memory chip generally miscalled the *CMOS chip* that's backed up with a battery. You're probably going to end up removing the battery, so the system will complain about not being configured when you reassemble it. That means you'll have to run your machine's SETUP program to reconfigure the system once it's back together. SETUP will be covered later, but it's basically going to ask you how much memory you have, what kind of floppies you use, and it'll want a number from 1 to 47 to describe your hard disk type. You can figure out all this for yourself, but why go to the trouble? Just run the SETUP program before disassembly. It'll tell you what your current configuration is. Just write that down and then remember to park your hard disk before shutdown.

Load the SETUP information.

Set the DATE and TIME with DOS, reboot, and the system will be fine.

4. **Protect the hard disk.** Does your machine have a hard disk? Your computer should have come with a program to park the heads of the hard disk. Parking the heads protects the drive, and we'll talk more it in the hard disk chapters. Run that program to park the heads. If your drive was an expensive one, it might be an auto-park model that doesn't require parking. Check the documentation, if available. By the way, you can't hurt an auto-park drive by running a parking program, so if you're unsure, go ahead and run a parking utility.

5. **Turn the PC and associated peripherals off.**

6. **Remove the monitor from atop the PC and set it aside.** If you don't have much workspace, it's not a bad idea to put the monitor on the floor, with the tube facing the wall so you don't kick in the tube accidentally.

7. **Remove the top carefully.** On the back of the PC there are five (two on pre-1983 PCs) screws. Remove them and put them in the cup. Don't knock the cup on the floor yet; wait for more, smaller screws and hardware. Slide the cover forward and set it aside carefully—don't rip the thin ribbon cables when you remove the top. Also,

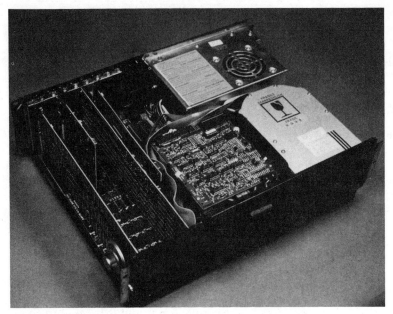

IBM XT with cover removed.

Figure 3-1 Removing a PC's Cover (Rear View)

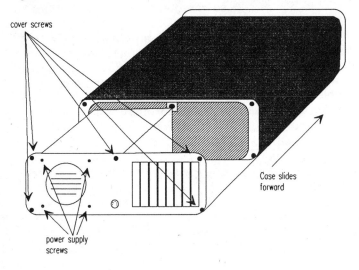

Figure 3-2 Where Things Are in an XT or AT-type Chassis (Front View)

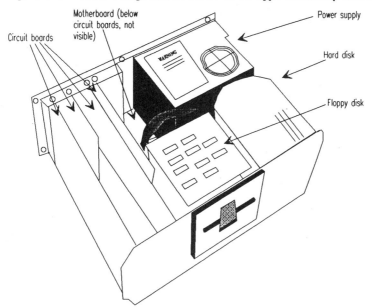

it's very easy to break one of the little wires. Just a nick can make your floppy or hard disk (the peripherals that use these cables) misbehave. I once saw a cable that had received the "rip the top open and scratch the cable" treatment cause floppies to read and write fine, but refuse to format.

If you've never done it before, take this opportunity to put your name on the inside of the case. This is a small extra bit of security. By the way, the most important screw in the back is the top center screw—it holds the weight of the monitor. In normal usage, it's best to ensure that all five screws are in place. However, if you're going to be lazy, the one screw you must have in place is the center screw.

By the way, should you need to replace the case screws on most PC-type systems, they're type 6-32, $\frac{3}{8}$-inch screws. The circuit boards

and drives are secured with type 4-40, $\frac{3}{8}$-inch screws.

8. **Diagram!** Ensure that you have some paper and pen so you can diagram what you disassemble. In what order were the boards? When you unplug something, it might not be simple to see how to reconnect it unless you have a good diagram. If there's no distinct marking on a cable, use a marker to make one. These machines aren't library books; it's okay to write on them. Remember, the game plan is that you should leave the machine the way you found it. You might not be able to fix the system, but you certainly don't want to leave it any worse than you found it. If you're new in computers, pay special attention to these items:

- *Ribbon cables.* They're flat cables connected to upright pins on circuit boards, and there's a definite "correct" way to put them on a

13

connector. Put them on backwards, and your PC could
smoke. Note that the ribbon cables have a dark line on one side.
Does that go up on the board?
Down? Toward the speaker?
Toward the power supply? (Note
I don't say *left* or *right*—those directions can get you in trouble.)
Make sure to note the current
position of the cables in your diagram.

- *Board and cable placement.* In general, it doesn't matter to the computer in which slot you put a
board. But certain boards might
be in particular places to ease
routing cables. You should be
able to tuck cables out of the way
when reassembling; take note of
how it's done on your diagram
before you take the machine
apart.

- *DIP switches.* After you remove a
board, it never hurts to make a
note of the DIP switch settings.
I've spent 20 minutes setting a
DIP switch bank only to find that
I've set the wrong bank, messing
up a perfectly good configuration
and making my reassembly task
all the more difficult. Besides,
there are "DIP switch gremlins"
who move the switches when
you're not looking. (Honest,
there *are*—I don't have kids or
cats, and I can think of no other
explanation.)

- *Motherboard connections.* Once
you've got the box open, you'll
see the main circuit board or
motherboard. It will have a number of things connecting to it:

  - Power supply connections.
  They're often two white plastic
  connectors labeled P8 and P9.
  Mix them up when you reassemble the machine, and poof!
  goes the system.

  - Speaker connection. This connects the *timer* (which generates
  the sound signal) to the speaker. It's generally a connector
  with yellow and black wires.

  - Keylock connection. On systems with front panel keylocks,
  a set of wires (two on some
  systems, four on others) connects the motherboard to the
  keylock. Fail to reconnect it,
  and the keylock feature won't
  work.

  - Turbo switch/light. Many
  "turbo" clones have a front
  panel switch to speed up or
  slow down the computer. There
  might also be a light to indicate
  whether the machine is operating at high speed (turbo mode)
  or not.

- *Brackets and braces.* On an AT,
you'll see small metal tabs
screwed into the case to hold the
drives in place. Before you remove them, notice if they're
identical or if they vary in size.
Ensure you can return them
where you found them. Newer
ATs have a *keeper bar* across the
front of the drive. Diagram it, or
you'll play "how does this fit?"
when trying to reassemble.

Another problem child is the
later (1986–87) XT with IBM-supplied half height drives. An upright steel clip holds the two
drives together so they can be
supported adequately by the
older XT case, which features
screw holes for a single full-
height drive. You might think it's
obvious when you disassemble it
where it goes back in place, but
you won't think that when you
put the machine back together.

9. **Caution when removing boards
and drives.** If you're going to re-

move a circuit board or drive, detach all connectors to it. Be very careful about forcing anything open or off. Remove the board's retaining screw (put the screw in the cup, remember) and grasp the board front and back with two hands. Rock the board back and forth (not side to side!) and it will come out. Don't touch the gold edge connectors on the bottom part of the board—keep finger gunk off the edge connectors.

Summary: Disassembly Hints

- Always ask yourself: "Is this trip necessary?"
- Work with sufficient space.
- Don't force things. Stop and look.
- Be careful when removing the top that you don't rip cables.
- Park the hard disk.
- Back up the configuration or document DIP switch settings.
- Diagram!
- Keep screws and other small things organized.
- Detach cables and connectors before removing devices or boards.

PC/XT/AT-Specific Disassembly Hints

Most desktop machines these days look fairly similar inside. They have a power supply, drives, expansion boards, and a motherboard. XT- and AT-type machines are very similar here except for the way their drives are mounted. You can vary these steps, but here's one basic approach to disassembling these specific machines.

1. After removing the cover, again note in a diagram which boards are in which slots.
2. Remove the circuit boards. Ensure that you can differentiate the boards—is there a marking, a connector, an unusual chip that will allow you to separate one board from another? I've said it before, but remember that you must be able to replace any connector cable.

   By the way, that means you should note what connectors are not attached to anything. For example, if you have a hard disk in your machine (not a hardcard), you'll have a board in your machine called a hard disk controller. It's easy to pick out—it's the circuit board with ribbon cables running from it to the hard disk. Your hard disk controller probably has two

Figure 3-3 Removing a Circuit Board

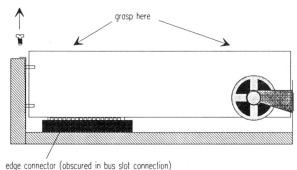

grasp here

edge connector (obscured in bus slot connection)

Figure 3-4   Hints for Differentiating Circuit Boards

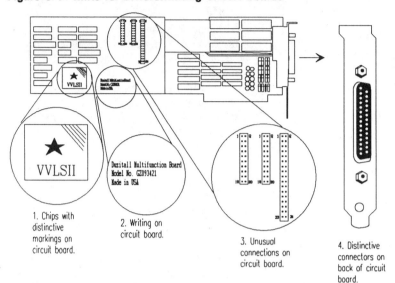

1. Chips with distinctive markings on circuit board.

VVLSII

Duzitall Multifunction Board
Model No. GZ093421
Made in USA

2. Writing on circuit board.

3. Unusual connections on circuit board.

4. Distinctive connectors on back of circuit board.

(on most XTs) or three (on most ATs) such ribbon cables connected to it. Find it, and then take a look at where the ribbon connectors attach to the circuit board; notice there are three (four on an AT) connectors but only two cables (three on an AT). The point here is, if you don't notice the connectors without cables during disassembly, you could look at the cables when reas-

sembling and spend a lot of time wondering what to connect to them. (This isn't gospel—your XT controller could actually have three cables, or your AT controller have a full complement of four.)

3. Once the boards are out, it's easier to get to the drives. Drive mounting is one of the few places where the XT-type and AT-type machines differ. With both drives, however,

P10 power connector on floppy disk.

Figure 3-5 Floppy Data and Power Connection for an AT-Type Machine

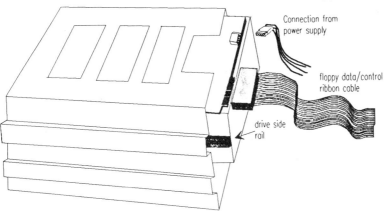

you'll see the same cable connections: separate power and data/control cables for floppies, and separate power, data, and control connections for hard disks. Let's consider these cables first, and then look at XT- and AT-specific removal problems.

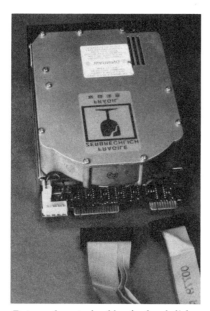

Data and control cables for hard disk.

The power cable is a four-wire, milky white plastic connector running from the power supply to the floppy. On IBM machines, it's generally labeled P10, P11, or P12. Remove it from the drive's circuit board carefully, as the connector tends to be a bit balky about coming loose from some drives, and now and then I see some would-be Hercules end up breaking the connector right off the floppy altogether. Just grasp the power connector and gently rock it side to side. It will come loose.

Next, you'll see a ribbon cable or two on the backs of the drives—one ribbon for floppies, two for hard disks. Diagram and remove them. Now you're ready to remove the drives.

XT-type machines generally secure drives with holes predrilled in the chassis. The XT chassis was designed for two full-height drives, but half-heights have been popular for years. Some XT-type manufacturers have responded by drilling holes that can accommodate either half-height *or* full height drives. Others have kludged up a solution

17

Removing mounting screws from the XT hard disk.

wherein two half-heights are joined with a bracket to form a single unit; then the (full-height) unit is screwed into the chassis that only accommodates full-height drives.

Most XTs only secure their drives with screws on one side of the chassis. That's not wonderful, but nearly all XT-type manufacturers do it. IBM tried to shore up drives on the last batch (1986–87) of their XTs with an extra screw into *the bottom*. (Imagine my surprise after spending ten minutes trying to figure out why the drive didn't come out like all the others I'd taken apart over the previous five years.)

Once you've removed the screws, pull the drives out through the front of the chassis. Be careful not to "behead" any of the little components on top of the floppy drive's circuit board. The exception to the "pull it out through the

front" rule comes from IBM. I just mentioned the 1986–87 XTs: Be careful if you come across one of these machines. They're IBM XTs with two IBM-supplied half-height floppy drives. Your first clue is that there are two half-height floppy drives with asterisks (*) embossed on the front bezel. Now pick up the chassis and look underneath

Pulling floppy drive from computer chassis.

18

Figure 3-6 Removing AT Drive Tabs

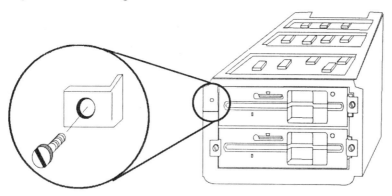

the drives. Are there two screws (or screw holes, if someone disassembled it previously but was too lazy to put them back)? Take these bottom screws out. These drives won't come out the front. Instead, locate and remove a thin rectangular piece of plastic fitted around the front plates of the drives. Remove it. Now the two drives come out of the system together *from the back.*

AT-type machines use a somewhat more elegant approach to drive mounting. Plastic rails mount on the side of the drive, sort of like the rails on the sides of desk drawers. The chassis includes "drive bays" that mate to the rails. The drive then slides in and out of the chassis like a drawer out of a desk.

Now, having the drives slide around like drawers might not be the neatest thing around, so the drives are secured with metal tabs and screws. Once you've unscrewed the tabs, the drives come right out. Some systems make all the tabs a bit different from each other, again to ensure that you know which tabs go back in which locations.

4. Remove the power supply. By now its drive connections are detached, so you needn't worry about them. There are two motherboard connectors, however, usually labeled P8 and P9, that must be detached. Note that P8 is toward the back of the machine, and P9 toward the front. Then remove the four screws in the back of the chassis that hold the power supply in place. Finally, you must push the power supply forward to disengage it from two clips built into the chassis.

5. Finally, the motherboard comes out. Again, the motherboard is the circuit board lying flat in the bottom of the case. It's about the only thing left in the system by now, so you need only remove the speaker and keylock connections and take out a couple of screws.

You'll see from one to five (depending, again, on whether it's an IBM or a clone PC, XT, or AT) small plastic connectors with a few wires attached to them on the motherboard. Most systems have a speaker cable with yellow and black wires. On IBM ATs, the speaker connection has the black wire to

19

Figure 3-7 Power Supply Connections

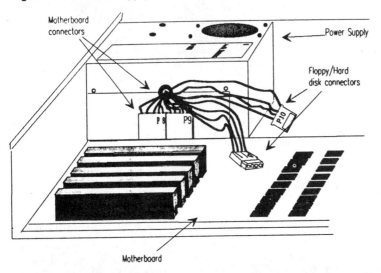

Removing XT power supply mounting screws.

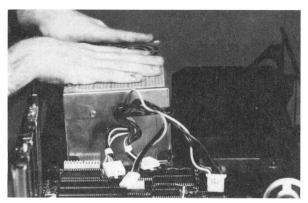

Pushing XT power supply forward.

the front of the case, yellow toward the back. AT-type systems generally have a keylock connector. The keylock has four wires: two blacks, a green, and an orange. The green wire goes toward the front of the box, the black one toward the back.

You could remove the battery from the motherboard (assuming it has one), but if possible try to remove the motherboard with the battery attached. This saves you the

XT power supply with mounting clips.

Figure 3-8 XT Motherboard View with Detail Showing Connection Points

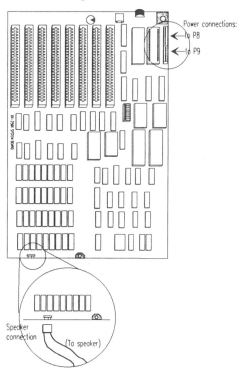

trouble of reconfiguring the system when you reassemble.

The motherboard is now only held down by two screws. Remove them.

They're held off the metal case with some plastic spacers. *Only remove the screws—* not the spacers. The board slides over and out of the case.

Figure 3-9 AT Motherboard View with Detail Showing Connection Points

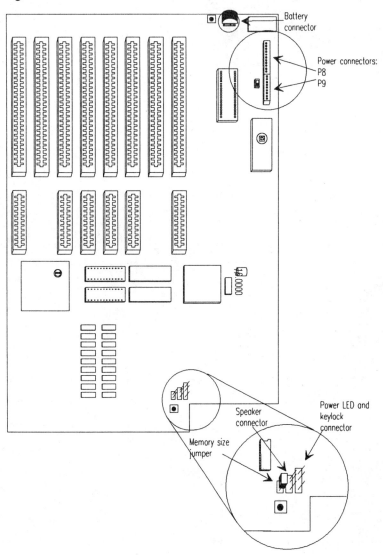

Figure 3-10 How to Remove a Motherboard

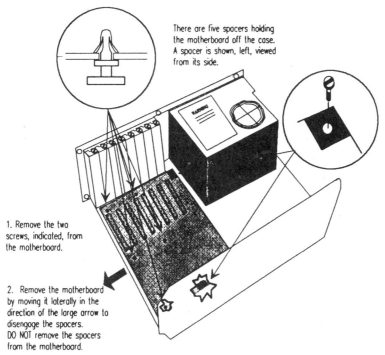

There are five spacers holding the motherboard off the case. A spacer is shown, left, viewed from its side.

1. Remove the two screws, indicated, from the motherboard.

2. Remove the motherboard by moving it laterally in the direction of the large arrow to disengage the spacers. DO NOT remove the spacers from the motherboard.

Removing motherboard mounting screws.

Disassembling the PS/2s

Each model in the PS/2 line is disassembled differently, but here's how to take apart the most common ones: Model 50, Model 50Z, and Model 70.

1. Take the cover off. Note the lack of cables—less diagramming to do. The Model 50 is organized into a "two story" arrangement with the drives and the fan on the top floor, and the speaker, power supply, and motherboard on the bottom floor. We'll remove the speaker, clean off the second floor, and then remove the second floor altogether.

2. Find the speaker/battery module. It will pull up and off, but there's a catch on the bottom of the module that holds it in place. Push in the catch, then pull up. On other PS/2 models there's a four-wire connection to the side of the speaker; remove it. By the way, while you have the speaker off notice two pins sticking out of the side. If you have a PS/2 password you want to get rid of, just turn the machine off, short the two pins, and turn it back on. The password goes away. (You short the two pins by putting a jumper on them and squeezing them so they touch, or else putting a metal object like a screwdriver between them so there's an electrical connection.) Unfortunately, some of the newer PS/2s don't have the two pins. Instead, on those models there's a multiwire connector that goes from the speaker assembly to the motherboard. Remove the motherboard connection and reconnect it backwards. This will eliminate the password.

3. Remove the floppies. Each one has a catch on the bottom. Just pull it up and the drives slide out. On the

60 and 80 there is, in addition, a black spring lever you must pop up; you'll hear a "click." Then remove the drive by pulling up on its catch and sliding it out.

4. Remove the hard disk. The Model 50's hard disk slides left and right like a sled on skids. It's held in place with two plastic stays. Press the stays down with one hand, and push the drive over the stays while they're flattened. The drive will come right out.

5. Remove the hard disk controller. It's the board where the hard disk was attached. Just grasp it by the big blue handles, and rock it up and out.

6. Find the small plastic "crowbar" tool near the speaker in the case. It's used to pop up the white plastic snaps that hold the second floor in place. Pop the two snaps up on the fan, and the fan comes out.

7. Pop up the several snaps on the second floor, and remove the second floor. Now the motherboard is exposed.

8. To remove the motherboard on the 50, you must remove the power supply at the same time. There are several screws in back of the case that hold the power supply to the case, a few that secure the interface connections to the case, and several that hold the motherboard down on the case. Remove them, and remove the power supply and the motherboard at the same time. Then you can detach the motherboard from the power supply.

Reassembly Hints. When reassembling machines, just reverse the order of disassembly. Plan ahead. Don't be afraid to pull some things out and start over if you're in a corner. The important thing is to *take your time*. Here are a few tips on putting your computer back together.

Connecting Cables and Edge Connectors: The Pin 1 Rule. Expansion boards in the PC are often controller boards for external devices like disk drives or displays. Cables connect the boards to the displays. A common short cable type is a ribbon cable.

Most ribbon connectors are symmetrical with respect to one or more axes. They could plug in one or two ways. Plugging in a connector upside-down will usually damage the device, or the controller board, or both. Most cables are *keyed*—a connector is modified so it cannot be plugged in incorrectly. However, some are not, and so the following bit of information is valuable.

A ribbon cable consists of many small wires laid out flat in parallel to form a flat cable, hence the "ribbon" name. One of the wires on the extreme outside of the cable will be colored differently than the others. For instance, ribbon cables are usually blue, white, or gray. The edge wire's color is often darker, like dark blue or red. This wire connects to pin 1 of the connector. This information has saved me more times than I care to recount. I learned it after incinerating a hard disk. (If you're going to make mistakes, you might as well learn from them.)

How do you find pin 1 on the circuit board? Many are stenciled right onto the board, which is very nice. Others only label pin 2, as pin 1 is on the back of the board. So look for a 1, and if you can't find it use 2. If you can't find either, turn the circuit board over. Notice the round blobs of solder where chips are secured to the circuit board. These are called *solder pads*. On some circuit boards, all of the solder pads are round except for pin 1's—it's square. Take a look at the

figure, which illustrates two ways of finding pin 1.

You'll find pin 1 on the circuit board of a hard or floppy disk, on disk controllers, or anywhere a ribbon cable connects to a circuit board.

Like most other convenient rules, there are exceptions. You might not find any indication of pin 1. Not all boards are labeled. Sadly, there are no Pin 1 Police. That's why diagrams are so important.

Common Reassembly Mistakes. In general, all you need to do a good reassembly is patience and a good diagram. But here's what people tend to do wrong. Most of this stuff isn't fatal to your system in the long term, but it'll make you sweat until you figure it out. And if you take it to a repair shop to get it "fixed," the repair people will know who caused the problem.

- **Forgetting to reconnect P8 and P9.** This isn't actually common (thank goodness), but it's important. If you forget to connect the motherboard power connectors P8 and P9 to the motherboard, the power supply may actually explode when you turn the machine on.
- **Bad motherboard seating.** Pay special attention when reseating the motherboard on its plastic spacers. Notice that the spacers are designed with a top disk and a bottom disk, and a bit of space between. Then notice that that the motherboard has raised metal slots with a *V* shape. The spacers are supposed to sit so the *V* is between the upper and lower disk. Get a flashlight and check the spacers. Another way to test motherboard seating is to insert a circuit board; if it doesn't fit right, your motherboard is probably seated wrong.
- **Reversed data or control cables.** "Let's see, which side *does* this blue

Figure 3-11 How to Find Pin 1 on a Circuit Board

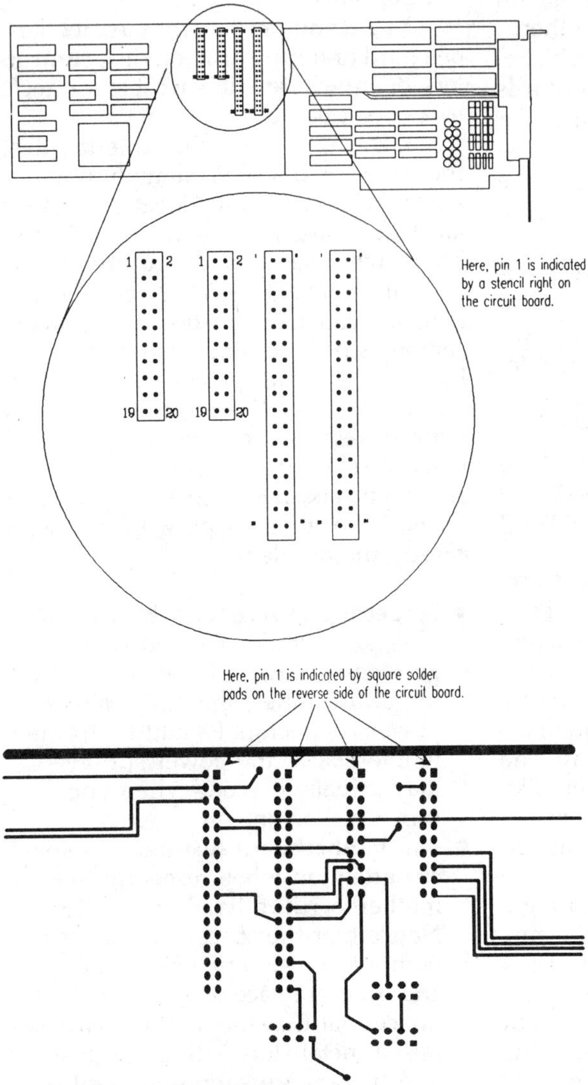

Here, pin 1 is indicated
by a stencil right on
the circuit board.

1 2   1 2

19 20   19 20

Here, pin 1 is indicated by square solder
pads on the reverse side of the circuit board.

line go on?'' Very common. If you don't diagram carefully, you could find yourself having trouble trying to figure out how a ribbon cable connects to a drive. If you didn't diagram carefully, use the Pin 1 Rule to help you.

● **Mishandled boards.** Don't stack boards; lay them out separately. Occasionally, rough handling can scratch and remove a circuit board trace. This can be repaired by soldering a short (as short as possible!) wire across the cut in the trace. If unsure, since traces can be faint or thin to begin with, use your ohm-meter. Set to low ohms (Rx1 on the dial), and then put the probes on either side of the suspected cut. The meter should read 0 if everything's okay.

- **Forgetting to attach power.** This one's good for a heart attack. You forget to attach that milky white four-wire P10, P11, or P12 power connector to the hard disk, and—auggh!—you get "disk boot failure."

- **Neglecting to plan cabling.** Tyro troubleshooters stuff the cables any which way to get them in the box. Then, the next time they open the box, the cables pop up and get caught on the tab for the center screw. Cables rip and bend, teardrops flow, you get the picture. Stuffed cables also impede airflow in the case and heat up the inside of the machine.

Put the drives partway in, attach their cables, and then look and ask: How can I route these cables so they'll be out of the way? Sometimes the best way is to move the drives around, so don't hesitate to be creative. For example, most XTs with one full-height floppy drive and one full-height hard drive would be better configured with the floppy on the outside (that is, to the right of the hard disk, as seen from the front) rather than vice versa, which is the norm. You can sometimes rearrange the boards to facilitate cable placement.

- **Forgetting the speaker connection, keylock connection, battery.** The first two are minor, the last annoying. Forget to reconnect the battery, and you won't be able to configure the system.

- **Panicking when it doesn't power up immediately.** I've seen students do this sometimes. They can't get the computer to boot up, so they tear it apart again, ripping cables and forcing boards out before removing their screws. Stay calm. No matter how important the machine is, you cannot fix it by rushing.

Peculiarities of Particular Models. That's useful advice in general, but here are some strangenesses you'll see in particular computers:

- **Backplane design.** Many but not all compatible computers don't have a motherboard per se but put the CPU on expansion boards. In fact, that's all there is on one of these machines—expansion slots. For example, when you open a Z-248, Zenith's popular 286-based system, you find only a board with slots and a battery after you've removed the expansion board. What *would* be the motherboard is divided, like the old kingdom of Gaul, into three parts: the *backplane board*, with the battery; the *CPU/Memory* board, with the CPU, memory, ROM, and some other chips; and the *I/O card* with the keyboard controller, diagnostic LEDs, and more chips. Zenith's not the only one to use the backplane approach. Kaypro, Wyse, and Telex have all used it at one point.

The *raison d'etre* for this seems to have been flexibility. You could change from a 286 to a 386 CPU by just replacing the CPU/memory and I/O boards. A nice idea, but what's so hard about replacing a motherboard? Besides, for what Zenith charges for the upgrade kit you can buy a brand new AST 386 computer. It's also annoying in that it forces you to buy parts from Zenith, rather than allowing use of generic motherboards for replacements. Zenith and Kaypro seem to concur.

Their most recent computers have a more traditional motherboard.

- **Hidden motherboards.** Open up an AT&T 6300 or 6386, and at first glance you seem to have stumbled on a backplane machine: no motherboard, and only slots. But look further—none of the expansion slots have a CPU. The trick is to turn the box over and remove a bottom panel. You'll see a large motherboard, one that includes a few extra functions. The 6300 motherboard includes serial and parallel ports and the floppy controller right on the motherboard, rather than on separate boards as in other machines. This is both a blessing and a curse. It's a blessing because it saves you slots. It's a curse because it means that when the floppy controller fails you, you must buy a whole new motherboard rather than changing a $29.95 floppy controller board (as you can do in an XT clone).

- **Workaholic motherboards.** Some compatible machines incorporate several functions that ordinarily would be found on expansion boards, like video, parallel and serial ports, and floppy controllers right on the motherboard. My personal preference is toward less motherboard integration, as that means there are several cheap boards in a system rather than one expensive board. In fairness, I should say on the positive side that integration can reduce chip count and increase reliability. The devil's deal, then, is that you get a computer that's more reliable but will cost more money to fix when it does fail.

  The most prominent offenders in this category are the PS/2 machines (more about them later). Another is the Zenith LP286: It puts an entire computer on the mother-

board, including hard disk controller, video, parallel, serial, and floppy. You want 8514 video or SCSI disk controllers? No can do, unless you can figure out how to disable the on-board resources. In defense of Zenith, though, they picked Cadillac components—1:1 hard disk controller and VGA video paired up with a 0 wait state 10 Mhz 286 make it a computer with a nice response. Just don't try to fix it.

- **Kooky keyboards.** The AT&T machines all use a keyboard with a D-shell connector rather than the more common DIN connector.

- **Strange video.** The AT&T machines insist on a nonstandard graphic board. In text mode, they respond like a normal PC, but they support a graphic standard used only by AT&T. Thankfully, the 386 machines (the 6386s) also support EGA. Some of the video monitors use a female 25-pin connector just like the parallel port. Plug the printer into the video or vice versa, and you can literally smoke either the port or the peripheral.

Most compatibles, like Compaqs and ASTs, follow the IBM structure pretty closely. There are, however, some that are a bit off the beaten path. Here, then, is some extra advice on two common compatibles, the AT&T 6300 (an XT-type machine) and the Zenith Z-248 (an AT-type machine).

AT&T Disassembly Steps. The 6300's not bad, once you know what to expect.

1. Remove the top. Take out the circuit boards in the usual way, except for the large board on the outside edge of the motherboard. It's the video board and requires some extra work (it's usually the last

thing you remove from the system).

2. Remove the two large power cables that connect to the video board. Make sure you know which cable goes to which connector.

3. Disconnect the drives from power (white cables) and data (ribbons). Then look under the bottom drive. You'll see a metal tongue. Pull up the end of the tongue with a screwdriver. Then a cradle containing both drives can be pulled forward and out.

4. Turn the machine upside down. Remove the bottom panel to expose the motherboard. Remove its retaining screws. Remove and note the ribbon connections from the upper part of the computer. The motherboard will now only be secured with the edge connectors from the video board. Slide the motherboard away from the connectors, and set it aside.

5. Turn the machine back rightside-up. Remove the backplane board, the one with the slots. Again, you'll do this with the video board still in place.

6. Remove the metal panel protecting the video board. It's held in place with several screws.

7. You can now remove a few screws and the video board comes off.

Zenith Z-248 Disassembly Hints. The Zenith is pretty close to most AT-like machines, with a couple of exceptions.

- The power supply has only one connection line, not two as in most compatibles.
- The drives are contained in a *cradle* that must be removed before the drives can be serviced or replaced. Note a black phillips screw on the outside front of the chassis, just below the drives. Remove this. You'll also notice a horizontal metal tab sticking out of the chassis right below where the screw was. Tap that with the back of a screwdriver to loosen the cradle. Now notice the metal box—the cradle—containing the drives. Pull it toward the back of the Z-248, and it'll come right out. Then the drives can be removed by taking out the side screws.

Two very important words of caution about the Zenith hard disks:

- Notice that the hard drives are secured with short screws. Keep them. If you put regular $\frac{3}{8}$-inch screws into the side of the common Seagate ST225, ST238, or ST251, you'll damage the drive.
- With these Seagate drives, DO NOT install all four screws. The drive won't work. Only use three.

Now you're ready for open-PC surgery. Here's what you can expect to see inside.

Chapter 4
Inside the PC: Pieces of the Picture

Now that it's in pieces, let's see what you've got . . .

The PC is a modular device. This modularity makes problem determination and repair much more tractable than, say, repairing your TV. Also, your PC lacks the large *capacitors* that make the TV dangerous to fool around with even when unplugged. If the problem's so bad that you have to open the machine to fix it (remember that most PC problems involve broken software or "broken" users, not hardware), many repairs just involve finding and replacing the faulty component. Also, being able to go to a strange machine and identify the components impresses the heck out of a skeptical audience, such as those folks who question your troubleshooting abilities. So Step 1 is to identify what's in the box.

A PC is composed of just a few components:

- System Board or Motherboard, containing:
  - CPU (Central Processing Unit)
  - Bus
  - Expansion Slots

- Planar Memory
- System Clock
- Numeric Coprocessor
- Keyboard Adapter (Interface)
- Power Supply
- Keyboard
- Display and Display Adapter
- Floppy Disk Controller and Floppy Disk Drives
- Hard Disk Controller and Hard Disk Drive(s)
- Multifunction Board, containing:
  - Printer Port
  - System Clock/Calendar
  - Serial Port (RS-232C port)

The System Board/Motherboard

Since their creation in 1974, microcomputers have usually included most of their essential electronics on a single printed circuit board called the *motherboard*. The IBM PC and compatibles are no exception (save those that put the CPU on an expansion board, like Kaypro, Zenith, and Wyse), but IBM chose to use a different term. Rather than calling this main circuit board a motherboard, Big Blue calls it the *system board*. I'll use both terms interchangeably in this

30

Figure 4-1 Motherboard Detailing Significant Areas

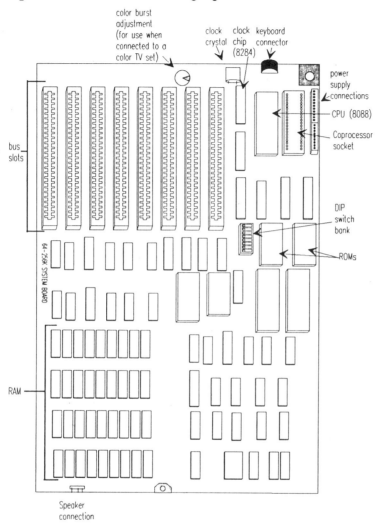

text. The PC compatibles are no exception, but, again, some models (Kaypro PC, Telex 12xx, Zenith Z-15x, and old Zenith Z-248 computers) use the backplane approach.

The Z-248 backplane is a pain, but Zenith included a neat diagnostic feature: six LEDs labeled *CPU, ROM, RAM,* *INT, DSK,* and *RDY.* Turn the machine on, and all six LEDs light. The CPU does a quick self-test, and its LED goes out. The system then checks and extinguishes LEDs for ROM, RAM, interrupts, and the disk controller. Finally RDY goes out once DOS has loaded correctly.

31

Figure 4-2 AT Motherboard Detailing Significant Areas

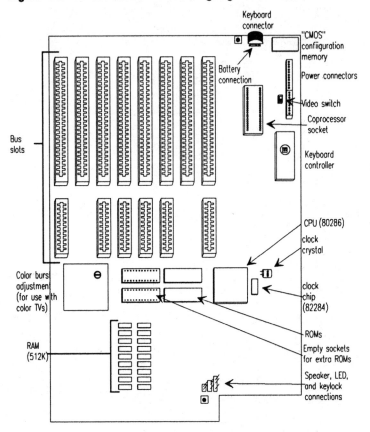

The newer PS/2 machines have yet another name for the motherboard: the *planar board*.

Central Processing Unit (CPU)

The "heart" of the PC is a microprocessor chip created by Intel Corporation or some other company they have licensed. Intel has designed and created many microprocessors over the years, but the ones that interest us are the 8088, 80286, 80386, and 80486.

CPU performance determines, in part, computer performance. CPUs vary in several ways that affect their performance. These ways are introduced in Table 4-1. Take a minute now and look over this section so you'll understand where a lot of PC limitations come from later.

CPU Speeds (megahertz). Computers run to the beat of a clock, like a beginning piano player plays to the beat of a metronome. If you set the metronome too fast, the beginner will become confused and the music won't come out right. Similarly, if you set the clock rate of a CPU too high, it will malfunction. You won't damage the chip; the computer just won't function properly. Part of the design of a computer like the PC includes determining a clock rate.

Table 4-1. CPU Properties

Property	Describes	Units	Range
CPU Speed	How many operations can be done per second?	Mhz	4.77 Mhz–33 Mhz
Microcode Efficiency	How many steps are required, for example, to multiply two numbers?	clocks	varies
Word Size	What is the largest number that can be handled in one operation?	bits	16 bits–32 bits
Data Path	What is the largest number that can be transported into the chip in one operation?	bits	8 bits–32 bits
Maximum Memory	How much memory can the chip use?	MB	1 MB–4,096 MB

CPU clocks generally "tick" more than a million times per second. A clock that ticks at exactly one million times per second is said to be a one Megahertz clock, abbreviated 1 Mhz. The Apple II used a 2 Mhz clock. The original PC and XT use a 4.77 Mhz clock. The AT originally used a 6 Mhz clock, and later IBM offered a version that ran at 8 Mhz. Clone makers offer computers with clock speeds up to 33 Mhz. All other things being equal, a faster clock means faster execution and better performance.

Table 4-2, "Typical Computer Speeds for IBM Computers," lists some clock rates for some true Blue models.

Word Size. Any computer can be programmed to manipulate any size number, but the bigger the number, the longer it takes. The largest number the computer can manipulate in one operation is determined by its *word size*. This is either 8, 16, or 32 bits.

Think of it this way: If I asked you, "What is 5 times 6?" you would answer, "30" immediately—you did it in one operation. If I asked, "What is 55 times 66?" you would do a series of steps to arrive at the answer. Fifty-five is larger than your word size. Five isn't. That's one reason

why a 386, with 32-bit registers, is faster than a 286, with 16-bit registers.

Data Path. No matter how large the computer's word size, the data must be transported into the CPU. This is the width of the computer's "loading door." It can be 8, 16, or 32 bits. Obviously, a wider door will allow more data to be transported in less time than will a narrower door. Consider, for example, an 8 Mhz 8088 versus an 8 Mhz 8086. The only difference between the 8088 and the

Table 4-2. Typical Computer Speeds for IBM Computers

Computer	Speed (Mhz)
PC	4.77
XT	4.77
AT	6 or 8
Model 25/30	8
Model 30-286	10
Model 50, 60, 50Z	10
Model 55	16
Model 70	16 to 25
Model 80	16 to 20

8086 is that the 8088 has an 8-bit data path, the 8086 a 16-bit data path. Now, both the 8088 and the 8086 have 16-bit registers, so a programmer would issue the same command to load 16 bits into either one; the command *MOV AX,0200* will move the 16-bit value 200 hex into a 16-bit register called AX. That will take twice as long on the 8088 as the 8086 because the 8086 can do it one operation, while the 8088 takes two. Note what's going on—although they're both 8 Mhz computers, the 8088 machine computes more slowly for some operations.

Memory Address Space. This talk of megabytes always confuses some so let me digress for a minute. *Megabytes* is a unit of storage size, just about the amount of space needed to store a million characters. We use it to talk about the size of *primary memory* or RAM, the kind of memory that goes in expansion boards and that *Lotus* can run out of if you've got a large spreadsheet, as well as *secondary memory*, which is on disk drives. When most people say *memory* they're talking about primary memory, meaning chips or RAM. Folks usually just say *disk* when that's what they mean, rather than secondary memory.

Disk is also not volatile, which means when you shut it off it retains its data. Remove power from a memory chip (which happens whenever you turn the machine off), and it forgets whatever it contained; that is *volatile* memory. That's why you have to save your work to disk before shutting off the machine.

But the fact that both disks and memory get measured in megabytes confuses people. I'll say, "I work with a 386 with four megabytes of memory," and they'll think, "what good is *that*? Even *I've* got 20 megabytes on my XT." I was talking about primary memory— four megs of RAM. I didn't say anything at all about how much hard disk space I have. *They* were thinking of hard disk

space and didn't tell me how much memory their XT has. (Probably 640K, a little over one-half of a megabyte.) End of digression.

You can't just keep adding memory to your PC indefinitely. A particular chip can only *address* a certain size of memory. For the oldest chips, this amount was 65,536 bytes—a 64K memory. The original PC's CPU can address 1024K, or one megabyte (MB). Other, newer chips can address even more. The 80386 and 80486 can address gigabytes (billions of bytes).

Details on CPU Chips. In some cases, you'll have to remove and replace these chips in order to upgrade or fix a problem. Here is some more background about them. As we've seen, several CPU chips are used in the PC market. They're all based on a line of chips from Intel called the *iapx86* family. Table 4-3, "CPU Specifications and Applications," summarizes their characteristics.

Some of these chips are more or less powerful. Some can actually allow you to improve the throughput of your existing PC. For instance, if you have a PC or PC clone, you can replace your 8088 chip with a V20 chip and see about a 5 to 20 percent increase in performance. The upgrade cost is only about $20.

The 8088. The 8088 is older and less powerful than the 80286 and is used in the PC. It comes in what is called a *40 pin DIP package*, which means a rectangular plastic case with two rows of 20 pins. *DIP* stands for Dual In-line Package. Older 8088's are called 8088-1, as they can only run at low speeds (5 Mhz or slower). *Turbo PC/XT* clones may run at 6.66, 7.16, or 8.0 Mhz. To do this, they use the 8088-2, which is rated at up to 8 Mhz. The 8088 is the equivalent of about 29,000 transistors.

The 80286. The 80286 is a newer chip, designed by Intel in 1981. Its package is a square of plastic called a *PGA*, or Pin Grid

Table 4-3. CPU Specifications and Applications

Maker	Model	Max Speed (Mhz)	Size (bits)	Path	Memory (MB)	Examples of Computers Utilizing Chip
Intel	8088	8	16	8	1	IBM PC, XT, Portable
Intel	8086	8	16	16	1	PS/2 Model 30, Compaq Deskpro
Intel	80C86	8	16	16	1	Toshiba 1100+
Intel	80186	16	16	16	1	3Com 3Server3, Tandy 2000
NEC	V20	10	16	8	1	Kaypro 2000
NEC	V30	10	16	16	1	NEC Multispeed, Kaypro PC
Intel	80286	20	16	16	16	IBM AT, PS/2 Model 50,60
Intel	80386DX	33	32	32	4096	Compaq Deskpro 386, PS/2 Model 70,80
Intel	80386SX	20	32	16	16	Compaq 386S
Intel	80486	25	32	32	4096	Apricot 486

Array package. It also comes in a cheaper package called a *PLCC*, or Plastic Leaded Chip Carrier. The PGA package has an inner and an outer square of solid pins; the PLCC arranges thin tinfoil-like legs around its perimeter. The 286 packs a lot more power into a small package than the 8088 does: the 80286 is the equivalent of about 130,000 transistors in about the same volume. Because of this, the 80286 runs hotter and may require extra cooling provisions such as *heat sinks*, small

Figure 4-3   Chip Package Types

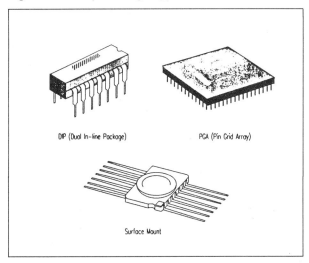

DIP (Dual In-line Package)   PGA (Pin Grid Array)

Surface Mount

metal caps of metal cooling fins that fit on top of a chip and enable the chip to better dissipate the heat it generates.

The 80836DX and 80386SX. The 80386 or, as it's officially called by Intel, the 80386DX is a powerful member of the iapx86 family. Introduced in 1985, the 80386 comes in a PGA package and is the equivalent of about 250,000 transistors. It incorporates a wealth of programming features, including the ability to multi-task DOS programs with the help of a "hypervisor" program like DeskView/ 386 or VM/386. Its 32-bit data path speeds data access, although to date few expansion boards except memory boards use this full 32-bit capability.

The 386SX is identical to the 386DX except that it has a 16-bit data path to allow it to be more easily incorporated into AT-type hardware designs (recall that the AT's 286 has a 16-bit data path also).

The 80486. The newest member of the iapx86 family, the 80486, is sort of an upgraded 386. It combines a tuned-up 386 with two chips that speed up a 386 system: the 385 cache controller and the 387 numeric coprocessor. The microcode is larger and faster—there are the equivalent of 1.25 million transistors in this chip—so a 25 Mhz 386 with a 385 and a 387 will execute only half as many instructions per second as a 25 Mhz 486.

Better yet, the 486 chip is actually cheaper than a 386, 385, and 387 together, so theoretically 486 computers could be cheaper than 386 machines. Time will tell.

Main Memory

Memory used to be easy to understand. Computers (pre-PC) all had something like 1K, 4K, 16K, 32K, 48K, or 64K. Then the PC came along with bigger numbers—up to 640K of memory! Larger numbers, but no more confusing.

Now there's *extended, expanded, LIM,* and *conventional* memory, to say nothing of ROM. Why so many kinds of memory? Mainly because of unfortunate planning: nobody ever thought the PC would need more than 640K of memory. Here's a look at how memory works.

The PC, like all computers, must have *main memory.* Main memory is high-speed memory the CPU can read from or write to. "High speed" here means less than a microsecond to read/write. The other name for such memory is *RAM* or Random Access Memory, a particular kind of chip on circuit boards. (Again, don't confuse it with disk drives, which are sometimes called *secondary memory,* because they also store data but at rates that are hundreds of thousands of times slower than main memory. Hard disks take longer than a millisecond to respond to requests.)

Memory is easy to pick out on a circuit board. It's packaged either as a *bank* of eight or nine small chips, or it's a mini-circuit board with several square chips mounted on it called a *SIMM* for Single Inline Memory Module. Memory is always organized into banks, either eight or nine discrete chips, or a SIMM. Most motherboards have room for four banks of memory. Some of the newer machines have no memory on the motherboard at all but instead have a large circuit board with room for megs and megs of memory. As each SIMM is the equivalent of nine chips, SIMMs make replacing bad memory easier but repair options less flexible—changing one chip is a lot cheaper than changing nine.

The familiar first 640K of a PC's memory is called *conventional memory.* It's supplemented by reserved areas containing *ROM,* Read Only Memory. 286 and later machines can address memory beyond that called *extended memory.* Also a small but important number of applications can use special memory called

Figure 4-4 SIMM (Single Inline Memory Module)

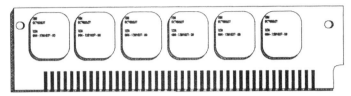

expanded memory or, as it's also known, *LIM memory.* Let's look at these in turn.

Conventional Memory. PCs can use 640K of main memory when running DOS and DOS programs. This first 640K is called *conventional memory* and is located on the motherboard and/or expansion boards. *K* refers to 1024, so for example, 64K equals 64 × 1024 65,536 *bytes* of data. Each byte can hold the equivalent of about one character. A picture called a *memory map* is a common way of depicting memory usage, so let's use it to show what goes in the conventional 640K. I'll build one as we go through the various kinds of memory.

Figure 4-5 is a map of how my system uses memory when I'm working with *Lotus 1-2-3* version 2.1.

The map shows decimal memory addresses and hex addresses. Read it from the bottom up. Lower on the page is a lower address. The bottom 1K is an area reserved by a piece of software called the BIOS that I'll explain soon. DOS (this is PC DOS 3.3) then takes up the next 53K. An additional 15K are taken up with *TSRs* (Terminate and Stay Resident programs). You probably use these every day in your work. The program to use your IRMA board, if you've got one—you know, the one that connects you to the mainframe when you hit both Shift keys—is one example. Borland's *SideKick* is another. I use two small utilities named RELOCATE and VKEYRATE to speed up my screen and keyboard response time, and a third called DOSEDIT

Figure 4-5 Example Memory Map for Conventional 640K

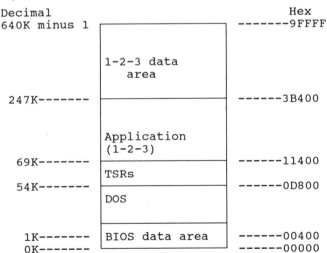

that remembers the last 20 commands I've typed so if I make a mistake I can recall a previous command, edit it, and resubmit it to the PC. These programs are examples of TSRs: they load and essentially "attach" themselves to DOS, extending the system's abilities and, unfortunately, its size.

The next 178K is taken by the 123.EXE program itself. The remainder is then available for *1-2-3* worksheets. The top address is *640K minus 1* rather than *640K* because we started counting at *zero*, not one.

Memory can be physically located either on the motherboard, an expansion board, or, more likely, on both. The original PCs had an old system board called the PC-1. The PC-1 motherboard could only accommodate 4 banks of 16K memory chips, so only 64K memory could be put on it. In 1983, IBM changed the PC motherboard so, among other things, four rows of 64K memory could be put on it, for a total of 256K. The third recent motherboard was introduced in 1986, allowing two banks of 256K chips (512K total) and two banks of 64K chips (128K total) for a grand motherboard total of 640K. Virtually all clones available since 1985 have allowed 640K on the motherboard. The most recent IBM XT-type motherboard is on the IBM Model 30, a faster new XT-type machine. Many 286- and 386-based clones allow up to four megabytes right on the motherboard. Again, only the first 640K is conventional memory, the kind easily usable by DOS. The remainder is either configured as extended or expanded memory, covered in the following pages. The old crop of PC and AT designs will be around for quite a while, so staying with them won't be much of a handicap. (As a matter of fact, as of late 1989 there are 35 million PCs of all kinds, 27 million of which are XT-type machines.)

For those millions of PCs without the room on the motherboard for 640K, supplemental memory has to come from expansion boards like Q/Cor's Quadboard or AST's SixPakPlus. The IBM term for main memory on the system board, by the way, is *planar memory*.

The Reserved Memory Area: ROMs and Buffers. The careful reader will have noticed that the original PC's CPU, the 8088, can address one megabyte (1024K) yet PCs only use 640K. Why?

In addition to the BIOS data area and the space taken up by DOS, the PC needs to steal from the CPU's memory address space for the following:

- Video memory
- Small amounts of memory called *buffers* or *frames* used by some expansion boards
- Special memory containing system software called *ROMs* (Read Only Memory)

Back in 1981, IBM reserved the area from 640K to 1024K in the PC's memory address space for these purposes. Here are some details on the three uses for the addresses.

Video Memory. Video memory is memory used by video boards to keep track of what's to be displayed on the screen. When a program puts a character or draws a circle on the screen, it's actually making changes to this video memory. IBM set aside 128K for video memory, but most video boards don't actually need or use that much memory space. Table 4-4, "Typical Video Memory Requirements," shows the common video boards and their memory capacities.

Memory Address Space Used differs from *Total Memory on Board* for the EGA and VGA because these video modes use a technique called *paging* that allows them to put lots of memory on the video board. Lots of memory means better vi-

Table 4-4. Typical Video Memory Requirements

Board	Memory Address Space Used	Total Memory on Board (K)	ROM on board
Monochrome Display Adapter (MDA)	B0000–B1000 (4K)	4	none in memory address space
Color Graphics Adapter (CGA)	B8000–BC000 (16K)	16	none in memory address space
Enhanced Graphics Adapter (EGA)	A0000–BFFFF (128K) (B0000–B1000 can be disabled)	256	C0000–C4000 (16K)
Video Graphics Array (VGA)	A0000–BFFFF (128K) (B0000–B1000 can be disabled)	256	C0000–C6000 (24K)

deo without taking up a lot of the CPU's total 1024K memory address space. (I'll explain *ROM on board* in the next section.)

Note that the EGA and VGA can be convinced to disable memory usage from B0000 to B1000, the addresses the MDA uses. That's so your system could run two monitors. Why run two video boards and monitors? Some debugging systems let you test-run your program with program output going to the CGA, EGA, or VGA monitor while displaying debugging information on the MDA.

ROM (Read Only Memory). Another kind of memory exists that cannot be altered but only read, so it's called Read Only Memory or ROM. This is memory someone (usually the computer manufacturer) loads just once with a special device such as a PROM blaster, an EPROM programmer, or the like. You can read information from ROMs, but you can't write new information. (Well, you *can* write the information, but the ROM will ignore you. Think of ROM as a chip that can give advice but not take it.)

Why have a memory chip you can only store information in once? Well, unlike normal RAM, it has the virtue of not losing its memory when you turn the machine off—techie types would say it's *nonvolatile.* You use ROM to store software that won't change. In essence, you can say that ROM contains the software that tells the system how to use a circuit board.

ROMs are found on expansion boards like EMS, LAN, or EGA cards. It's also found on the system board. The ROM on the system board contains a piece of software called *BIOS,* the Basic Input/Output System. DOS doesn't communicate directly with your hardware but issues commands through BIOS. That's why the BIOS is so important: it determines in large measure how compatible your PC compatible is.

As you'd expect, IBM's BIOS is the standard of compatibility. Back in the early 80s, the first cloners developed BIOSes that conformed in varying degrees to the IBM standard, so the question "Does it run *Lotus 1-2-3* and Microsoft *Flight Simulator?*" was the acid test of compatibility. Nowadays, two companies, Phoenix Software and Award Software, derive large incomes from their main business of writing compatible BIOSes for clone makers. This has simplified the business of cloning considerably.

I've said that ROM contains software. As you know, software changes from time to time. Occasionally a problem can be fixed by "upgrading the ROM"—getting the latest version of the ROM-based software from the manufacturer. Probably the worst offenders here are 3278 terminal emulation boards like the IRMA board from Digital Communications Associates. (The newer IRMA 2 doesn't use ROM but loads its software from disk.)

For this reason, you've got to know exactly what ROMs are in the computers you're responsible for maintaining. In a maintenance notebook keep track of the serial numbers or dates on the labels pasted on the backs of the ROMs in your PCs. Whenever you install a board, note any ROM identifying marks. It will save you having to pop the top to find out about ROM when you call for service.

ROMs can usually be identified because they're generally larger chips—24 or 28 pin DIP chips. They're socketed (so they can be easily changed), and often have a paper label pasted on them with a version number or some identifier printed on it. (IBM BIOS ROMs don't carry paper labels on most PCs, XTs, and ATs but do on later machines.) ROMs are

memories, albeit inflexible ones, and so require a place in the memory addresses in the reserved area from 640K to 1024K.

Buffers and Frames. Some boards need a little memory space reserved for them. A LAN board, for example, might require 8–16K of storage space used to buffer LAN transmissions. A LIM board (described a little later) needs 16K to 64K of "page frame" memory space to buffer transfers into and out of LIM memory. Those memory pieces must fit somewhere in the reserved area from 640K to 1024K in the PC memory address space.

Before we leave this section, let's add reserved areas to our memory map.

Extended Memory. Not content with the 8088/8086, Intel began in 1978 to develop processor chips with power rivaling that of minicomputers and mainframes. One thing early micros lacked that more powerful computers had was larger memory address spaces. So from the 80286's introduction in 1981 onward, Intel chips could address megabytes and megabytes. An 80286 can actually talk to or *address* 16 megabytes. An 80386 or 80486 can address four *gigabytes* of RAM. The term for normal RAM above the 1MB level is *extended memory*.

Figure 4-6 Memory map of the first 1024K

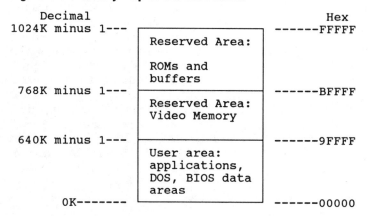

```
      Decimal                                          Hex
1024K minus 1---   +--------------------+      ------FFFFF
                   | Reserved Area:     |
                   |                    |
                   | ROMs and           |
                   | buffers            |
 768K minus 1---   +--------------------+      ------BFFFF
                   | Reserved Area:     |
                   | Video Memory       |
                   |                    |
 640K minus 1---   +--------------------+      ------9FFFF
                   | User area:         |
                   | applications,      |
                   | DOS, BIOS data     |
                   | areas              |
   0K-------       +--------------------+      ------00000
```

But there's a catch. In order to use this extra memory, the 286 and later chips must shift to a new processor mode called *protected mode*. Protected mode has lots of virtues, but one big flaw: when a chip is in protected mode, it's incompatible with an older 8088 or 8086. Here's why.

Most early CPUs used in microcomputers were more glorified calculator chips than computers—the 4004, 8008, 8080, 8085, 8086, 8088, 80188, and 80186. Intel intended for the 80286 to have some powers that were mainframe-like; in particular it would be able to talk to more memory and to protect that memory.

Mainframes run multiple programs at the same time, which is called *multitasking*. Basically, the memory space of the computer gets parceled out to the applications ("Okay, text editor, you get 120K, and database, you get 105K, and spreadsheet, you get 150K—no, you may *not* have more!"), and everyone's expected to stay in their places. But what about the odd program that accidentally strays from its area? If the text editor stretches a bit, it overwrites the database's area—what to do?

That's why mainframes have memory protection. The CPU has hardware built into it that keeps track of what application gets to use what memory. If an application tries to reach out of its space, the protection hardware senses this and stops the application, probably by ending the program and informing the user. The 286 and later chips have this memory protection. These chips can also address memory beyond 1024K, but only while in protected mode. Again, the 8088, 8086, and earlier chips cannot under any circumstances address memory beyond 1024K, and so cannot ever have extended memory.

Basically, programs that run while in protected mode don't try to do *anything* with memory without first re-questing memory blocks from the operating system; then they stay in their places.

And that's the problem.

This whole notion of first asking the operating system's permission before using memory is totally unknown in the DOS world. Programs pretty much assume they're the only program in the system, so they just take whatever they want without asking for it. So for the 286 to have memory protection, it would not only have to be a *different* chip, it would have to be an *incompatible* chip—incompatible with DOS and DOS programs, in particular.

Now, designing and releasing a new chip that was totally incompatible with any previous Intel offerings would be suicidal. So Intel gave the 286 and subsequent chips split personalities: When they boot up, they act just like an 8088, except faster. They can talk to 1024K, and no more. (This is the 8088 emulation mode or, as the documentation calls it, the *real mode*. Why is it called real mode? I don't know—maybe it was real hard to program.) With a few instructions, it can shift over to protected mode and talk to lots of memory beyond 1024K. But, again, once the 286 or later chip is in protected mode, it can't run programs designed for real mode—DOS and DOS programs, that is.

You might be wondering, why don't they just write an operating system that uses this protected mode? They have—that's the whole idea of OS/2. So memory beyond 1024K on a 286 or later machine is mainly unusable to DOS. I say "mainly" because there are a few programs that, thanks to some snazzy programming, can make use of the memory beyond 1024K. Probably the best-known of this class of programs is *Lotus 1-2-3* version 3.0; earlier versions can't use extended memory. This need for extended memo-

Figure 4-7 Memory Map of the First 1024K and 384K of Extended Memory

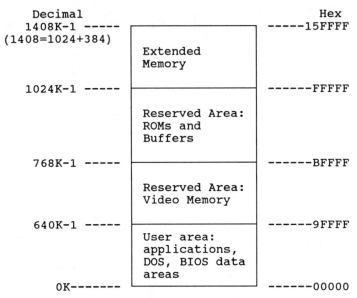

```
    Decimal                                              Hex
   1408K-1 -----    ┌──────────────────┐    -----15FFFF
(1408=1024+384)     │                  │
                    │  Extended        │
                    │  Memory          │
                    │                  │
   1024K-1 -----    ├──────────────────┤    ------FFFFF
                    │                  │
                    │  Reserved Area:  │
                    │  ROMs and        │
                    │  Buffers         │
                    │                  │
    768K-1 -----    ├──────────────────┤    ------BFFFF
                    │                  │
                    │  Reserved Area:  │
                    │  Video Memory    │
                    │                  │
    640K-1 -----    ├──────────────────┤    ------9FFFF
                    │  User area:      │
                    │  applications,   │
                    │  DOS, BIOS data  │
                    │  areas           │
       0K-------    └──────────────────┘    ------00000
```

ry explains why 8088-based machines cannot run *1-2-3* version 3.0.

As XT-type machines are based on 8088/8086 chips, they cannot have extended memory. ATs and 386-based machines can. When you see your computer count up to 1024K, 2048K, 4096K, or the like during the power-on self test, you've got some extended memory. Most common is a 286 with 1024K of memory. This is divided into two sections: The first 640K is addressed from 0 to 640K and is thus conventional memory. The remaining 384K gets moved above the 1024K mark, getting addresses from 1024K to 1408K. As it's addressed above 1024K, this 384K is extended memory. (Why break it up? Why not just address the memory as 0 to 1024K? Recall that the reserved area from 640K to 1024K must not have user memory in it.) Here's how it would look on our memory map in Figure 4-7.

EMS, LIM, Paged, Expanded Memory. Most PC users eventually come to feel that 640K of memory, the most DOS will allow, is insufficient for most needs. But, as we've seen, extended memory is mainly useless under DOS. So what can be done?

Spreadsheets are a very popular application for the PC, but most spreadsheets on the market have the flaw that the entirety of their data must be in main memory. Thus, a data file of a megabyte or two is impossible for a spreadsheet under DOS.

Lotus, Intel, and Microsoft (LIM) got together and developed a standard for a product that bypasses the DOS limitations through *memory paging.* Up to 32 megabytes of paged (it's also called expanded) memory can be installed in a PC. It's sometimes known as the *Expanded Memory Standard (EMS).*

Basically, the LIM memory isn't viewed by the system as memory. All the

Figure 4-8   Memory Areas

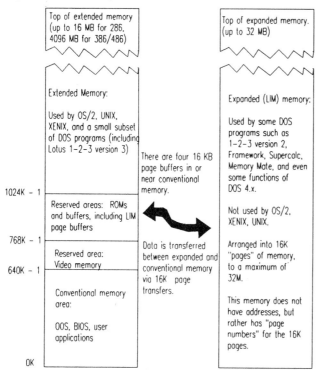

Top of extended memory (up to 16 MB for 286, 4096 MB for 386/486)

Top of expanded memory. (up to 32 MB)

Extended Memory:

Used by OS/2, UNIX, XENIX, and a small subset of DOS programs (including Lotus 1–2–3 version 3)

1024K – 1

Reserved areas: ROMs and buffers, including LIM page buffers

768K – 1

Reserved area: Video memory

640K – 1

Conventional memory area:

OOS, BIOS, user applications

OK

There are four 16 KB page buffers in or near conventional memory.

Data is transferred between expanded and conventional memory via 16K page transfers.

Expanded (LIM) memory:

Used by some DOS programs such as 1–2–3 version 2, Framework, Supercalc, Memory Mate, and even some functions of DOS 4.x.

Not used by OS/2, XENIX, UNIX.

Arranged into 16K "pages" of memory, to a maximum of 32M.

This memory does not have addresses, but rather has "page numbers" for the 16K pages.

PC knows is that there are 16K-sized pages of storage available. LIM can support up to 2,000 of these pages, hence the 32MB maximum size. LIM boards allocate 64K of memory, enough space for four pages, somewhere in the reserved area between 640K and 1024K, so a program can manipulate up to four pages at a time. LIM is manipulated, then, by pulling in a page from LIM memory to the memory in the reserved area, reading and/or modifying the page frame, and possibly writing the page frame back to the LIM memory. This memory is called a *page frame*, and moving data to and from LIM and page frames is called *paging*.

We can now finish our memory map by adding expanded memory off to the side of the normal memory column, as in Figure 4-8, "Memory Areas."

Perhaps you're wondering if all this paging takes time. It does, so LIM memory is slower than conventional memory. LIM gets around DOS's 640K limitation, but at a cost of speed. Even if you're willing to accept the speed cost, this isn't a panacea: Remember that only software written specially for the paged memory can use this memory. There are only a few applications that do this; Lotus is the best known. Two common examples of this kind of memory board are the Intel AboveBoard and the AST RamPage cards.

The Old Memory Switcheroo: Making Extended Look like Expanded. I know this has been confusing, but it's about to get worse, so buckle up. So far

I've made the extended versus expanded barrier sound like an unbridgeable one, but that's not so.

- Many 286 memory boards are reversible for extended or expanded. These are good buys, as you might need expanded today and want to be able to use extended later. Some machines, like Zenith's LP286, allow you to configure memory beyond 640K as any combination of extended and expanded.
- 386 computers have the ability to make extended memory act like expanded memory. This conversion requires a program to emulate LIM memory, so (of course) such a program is called a *limulator*. Good examples are *386-to-the-Max* from Qualitas and *QEMM386* from Quarterdeck. Many 386 vendors offer such a program free, as Compaq does with its CEMM program. Their addresses are:

Qualitas
7101 Wisconsin Ave. 1386
Bethesda, MD 20814
(301) 907-6700

Quarterdeck Office Systems
150 Pico Blvd.
Santa Monica, CA 90405
(213) 392-9851

- In general, limulators for 286s aren't a good idea, as full LIM 4.0 powers can't be emulated and the 286 isn't built to limulate. But All Computing in Toronto offers a solution: the ChargeCard 286. Priced at $400, the ChargeCard gives your 286 the power to limulate, as well as adding an extra 90-odd K to DOS memory.

That ends our tour around memory. Let's review:

- Conventional Memory:
  - Available to all PCs
  - Limited to 640K
- Extended Memory:
  - Only possible with ATs or 386-based machines
  - Impossible with XTs or PCs
  - Of very little value under DOS
  - Used by OS/2, XENIX
  - Used by *Lotus 1-2-3* version 3.0
- Expanded Memory:
  - Also called LIM (Lotus-Intel-Microsoft) memory
  - Can be used with PCs, XTs, ATs—any PC machine
  - Useful under DOS *with programs that can use it,* such as *Lotus* versions 2.1 and 2.2.
  - Generally can't be used by OS/2

The only problem remaining is how to keep them apart. I always remember extended versus expanded by pronouncing the latter *exPanded*, so I can remember that it's *Paged*.

Buses: PC, AT, ISA, Micro Channel, EISA and More

What Is a Bus? The CPU must talk to memory, expansion boards, coprocessor, keyboard, and the like. It communicates with other devices on the motherboard via metal traces in the printed circuit. But how can expansion boards be connected to the CPU, the memory, and so on?

Some computers, like the earlier Macintosh line, didn't allow easy expansion. To expand a 128K or 512K Mac, the circuit boards had to be partially disassembled or modified in ways not intended by the original developers. Installing a hard disk actually involved disassembling the computer, soldering connections onto the Mac motherboard, and reassembling the machine. Making modifications difficult puts the user at the mercy of the modifier, as virtually all such modifications are done at the expense of the manufacturer's warranty and service agreement, if any. You don't have to do such brain surgery on a PC, thankfully. PCs have expansion slots that allow easy upgrade. (Today's Macs also have expansion slots, thankfully.)

Another disadvantage of the old Macintosh approach is that average people couldn't do the modifications themselves. This would be like your having to cut a hole in the wall of your house to find a main power line every time you wanted to use an appliance. Without standard interface connectors, you'd have to find the power line and then splice the appliance into it to get power for the appliance.

This scenario, as we know, is silly, since we have standard outlet plugs. Any manufacturer who wants to sell a device requiring electrical power needs only to ensure that the device takes standard US current and add a two prong plug. "Upgrading" my house then (adding the new appliance) is a simple matter: just plug and play. Many computers adopt a similar approach. Such computers have published a connector standard: Any vendor desiring to offer an expansion board for a particular computer need only follow the connector specifications, and the board will work in that computer. From the earliest computers such a connector has existed. First called the *omnibus connector*, as it gave access to virtually all important circuits in the computer, it quickly became shortened to *bus*, and so it has remained.

So a bus is a communication standard, an agreement about how to build boards that can work in a standard PC. For various reasons, however, there aren't one but *four* different such standards in the PC world, and a few oddballs in addition.

The First PC Bus. The first microcomputer, the Altair, had a bus that was a standard in the industry for years and is still used in some machines; it was called the S-100 or Altair bus. The Apple II used a different bus. The PC introduced yet another bus with 62 lines.

The 62 lines mentioned above are offered to the outside world through a standard connector. These connectors are called *expansion slots*, as expansion boards must plug into these slots. There are five on the PC and eight on the XT and AT.

The most common are the simple 62 line slots found on the original IBM PC and XT. As those machines were based on the 8088, and the 8088 has an 8-bit data path, eight of the 62 wires are data lines. That means this bus is eight bits wide, so data transfers can only occur in eight-bit chunks on this bus. Expansion slots on a computer with this bus are called *8-bit slots*.

The AT (ISA) Bus. When developing the AT, IBM saw it had to upgrade the bus. One reason was because the 80826 is a 16-bit chip, as you recall. They certainly could have designed the AT with an 8-bit bus, but it would be a terrible shame to make a 286 chip transfer data eight bits at a time over the bus rather than utilize its full 16-bit data path. So it would be nice to have a 16-bit bus. On the other hand, there was backward compatibility with the PC and XT to think of. So IBM came up with a fairly good solution: They kept the old 62-line slot connectors and added another connector in line with the older 62-line connector to provide the extra eight bits and some other features as well. Slots with both connectors are called, as you'd expect, *16-bit slots*. Most AT and 386-type machines have at least two of the older 8-bit slots for purposes of backward compatibility.

As the 16-bit slots are just a superset of the 8-bit bus, 8-bit boards work just

Figure 4-9   XT Versus AT Bus Slots

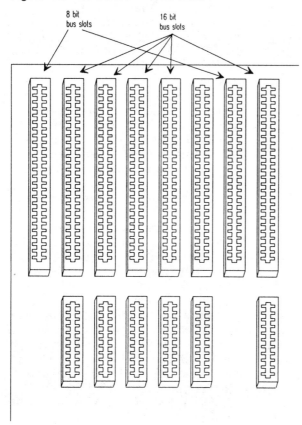

Figure 4-10   PC Board with 8-bit Connector

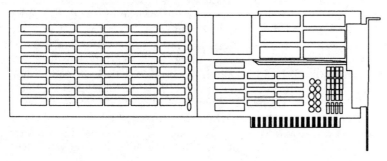

Figure 4-11   PC Board with 16-bit Connector

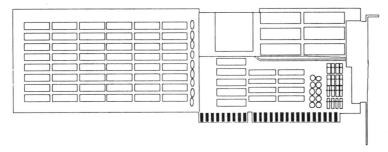

Figure 4-12   8-bit Board with Skirt

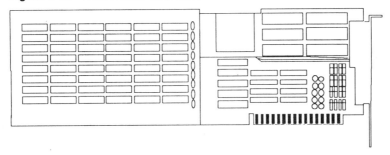

Figure 4-13   ISA Board and MCA Board

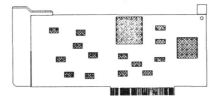

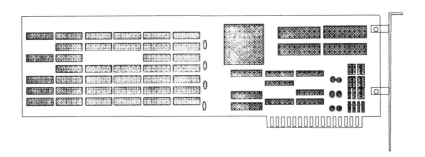

fine in 16-bit slots. If you have an AT-type machine, you might have noticed that it has not only 16-bit slots but also the older 8-bit connectors. If the 16-bit slots can use 8-bit boards, why have any 8-bit slots on an AT-type machine at all? The answer isn't an electrical reason but a physical one. Some older 8-bit boards have a "skirt" that extends down and back on the circuit board, making it physically impossible to plug it into a 16-bit connector.

Lately the trade press has taken to calling the AT bus the *ISA* or Industry Standard Architecture bus.

Just How Fast Is that Bus? The AT bus is tough to get to run at high speeds. It's noisy and tends to be pretty unworkable above 10 Mhz. Many circuit boards won't even work properly when forced to operate above 8 Mhz. So how do companies offer 33 Mhz computers with the old AT bus?

The answer is that they don't run the bus at the full CPU rate. Up to 8 Mhz, most clones run the bus at the same rate as the CPU—a 6 Mhz computer runs the bus at 6 Mhz. Above 12 Mhz, Compaq started offering machines that ran the CPU at one rate—12 Mhz—and the bus at 8 Mhz. Everybody copied the idea, so there are a lot of machines running at 12 Mhz and above with buses creeping along at a mere 8 Mhz. This is good because you can put a regular old LAN board into your 33 Mhz Zenith and use it as a server without having to spend $20,000 dollars for a mythical 33 Mhz LAN board. This does, however, have its drawbacks.

The big drawback is that some boards should run at CPU speed, like memory boards. If you have a 12 Mhz 286 clone (with an 8 Mhz bus), buy an extended memory board, and pop it into one of the computer's 16-bit slots, then you'll have extended your memory, but all memory accesses on that board *will be at 8 Mhz, not 12 Mhz.*

Beware the 10 Mhz Bus! You might have noticed that I talked about machines with CPU speeds up to 8 Mhz having buses running at the same rate as the CPU, and machines over 12 Mhz running buses at 8 Mhz, skipping over the 10 Mhz machines.

Most 10 Mhz machines with AT-type buses seem to be designed with the philosophy, "Well, we really *ought* to go to the extra trouble and expense to run the bus at a different speed [8 Mhz], but 10 is close enough, isn't it?" So most 10 Mhz machines run the bus at 10 Mhz.

That means 10 Mhz computers actually have the fastest buses in the PC/ISA world!

Most boards run fine at 10 Mhz, but some will give you some trouble, in particular IBM's 8-bit Token Ring board and many video boards. Recall that video boards need memory. As very few video board makers get praised for the speed of the memory chips they choose for their video boards, most video board memory is selected assuming that the board will be plugged into a slot running no faster than 8 Mhz.

The result is that most of the time the board runs fine. But sometimes you get a video failure on bootup. The answer is to buy a video board with fast memory on-board. Headlands Technology (Video 7) and Paradise make video boards that seem to handle 10 Mhz buses just fine.

The bottom line: Be careful with what you put into 10 Mhz slots. If a board seems to fail, lower the speed (there's usually a turbo switch) and then reboot. If the problem goes away, it may have been caused by the 10 Mhz bus slots. The answer probably is to replace the board with a faster one.

Buddy, Can You Spare 32 Bits?
When Compaq introduced the first 80386-based desktop, it wanted to exploit the 32-bit power of the 386 chip. They included a new 32-bit slot, mainly for use with memory. Some 386 clones have adopted this, but it's not a very significant part of the market. It seems that each vendor has developed its own 32-bit "standard." Intel has one it's been pushing, AT&T has another, Micronics a fourth, and so on. This is really not a standard, but expect to see a strange 32-bit slot of some kind on a 386 motherboard for a memory board.

Not too many vendors are pushing their proprietary slots very hard any more, as they're all looking ahead to the new EISA standard (see a couple of sections ahead).

The PS/2 Bus: Micro Channel Architecture (MCA). IBM changed the rules again on April 2, 1987, when they announced the PS/2 line. In order to facilitate faster data transfer within the computer and to lower noise levels, the PS/2 Models 50 to 80 (*not* the 25 or 30) have a new bus called the *Micro Channel Architecture (MCA)* bus. It's completely incompatible with the old bus. Expansion boards made for the PC, XT, or AT won't operate in the PS/2 line. Be sure when you buy expansion boards that you know what kind of machine they're destined for, and buy ISA or MCA as appropriate.

MCA is neat because it's cleaner, as I said before, so it should be able to transfer data at higher speeds than the current ISA machines. It also includes something called *Programmable Option Select*, or *POS*, that allows circuit boards to be a lot smarter about how they interact with the computer. For one thing, DIP switch and configuration problems lessen considerably. We'll talk more about POS in the section on configuration of new boards.

EISA (Extended Industry Standard Architecture). MCA is a pain because IBM has locked it up six ways to Sunday, patent-wise. Companies can't clone the MCA without paying a Draconian *five percent of their gross* to IBM as fealty (oops, that's supposed to be "royalties") for use of MCA. Five percent of gross is probably more than most companies are making as *profits*. For the five percent, you don't even get the plans for MCA. First clone-makers are supposed to spend hundreds of thousands of dollars figuring out how to clone MCA—IBM offers no help—and then they get to pay Big Blue the five percent.

So Compaq talked eight other compatible makers (the usual guys—Tandy, AST, Zenith, AT&T, and some others) into forming a joint venture to respond to MCA—they're called the *Gang of Nine*. It would have MCA's good features without sacrificing compatibility with the old AT (ISA) bus, and presumably it would cost less than five percent of profits. At this writing (fall of 1989) I've seen some prototype EISA machines, so they could be commonplace by late 1990.

It won't be a smooth road for EISA, however. Compaq has retained a lead role in EISA development and legal control similar to IBM's. It remains to be seen whether the Gang of Nine will be the only ones allowed to make EISA machines, or whether EISA technology will be offered to third-tier outfits like CompuAdd for a reasonable price. If Compaq is seeking merely to create a subset of the market it can control as IBM does, EISA will probably die on the vine. It's not clear that building a proprietary bus is a great plan, anyway: MCA is still actually *hurting* IBM sales so far, even two and a half years after its introduction. In 1988, Apple beat IBM for the first time in many years in "number of micros sold" (Apple sold 1.24 million machines, IBM 1.22 million). It wasn't because

Apple did better—it was because the PS/2s have hurt IBM's sales more and more as time goes on.

EISA will have a full 32-bit data path, POS-like features, and speeds to about 20 Mhz. That means memory probably will still require its own proprietary slot for faster machines; MCA has the same problem.

System Clock

The system clock mentioned before is the "metronome" for the computer system. It's implemented on the PC on a chip called the 8284A. The 8284A is located near the 8088 on the system board. The AT-class machines don't have an 8284 but an 82284.

The clock chip is easy to find, if your machine has such a chip (some manufacturers, like Compaq, blend the chip in with some others, so there's no discrete chip). Just find the crystal and the CPU. The clock is often between the two of them.

You'll need to find the clock chip to install a reset switch in a PC later in the book.

Numeric Coprocessor (Math Coprocessor)

Next to the 8088 on a PC or near the 80286 on an AT is an empty socket. From 1981 to 1983, IBM wouldn't say officially for what the socket on the PC was intended. But then they announced what everyone already knew: It was for the Intel 8087, a special purpose microprocessor. The 8087 is a microprocessor that's only good for one class of tasks: floating-point numeric operations. If you do a lot of floating-point calculations (calculations with numbers that have decimal points), *and if the software that you use is written to take advantage of an 8087*, such a chip is a good investment. The classic program people think of is *Lotus*, but most spreadsheets,

CAD/CAM, or engineering applications can benefit. An 8087 costs under $100 at this writing, a 287 runs from about $200, and a 387 from about $500. The 486 actually includes floating-point instruction support right on the chip, so there's no such thing as a 487.

Some programs insist on a coprocessor. The latest version of AutoCAD, for example, refuses to run on a machine without a coprocessor. I can't stress how important a coprocessor is for some applications. I used to use a CAD program called Generic CADD—a nice cheap CAD package that would use a coprocessor, if present. I did a bunch of work on a turbo XT (9.54 Mhz) with an 8087 coprocessor, then moved to a 386 *without* a coprocessor. The 386 was actually slower when it came to screen redraws. (Now my 386 has a coprocessor, and it runs blindingly fast.) Transcendental operations (sines, cosines, logarithms, and the like) can be 20 times faster on a coprocessor than on the CPU.

You need to know two things about coprocessors: which go with what processor, and what speed to buy.

Matching Processors and Coprocessors. Intel markets three coprocessor chips:

Table 4-5. Coprocessor Chip Information

Chip	Maximum Speed (Mhz)	Package Type	Typical CPU
8087	10	DIP	8088/8086
80287	12	DIP	80286
80387DX	33	PGA	80386DX
80387SX	20	PGA	80386SX
80486	25	PGA	80486

In general, the 8088 and 8086 go with the 8087, the 80286 goes with the 80287, and the 80386 goes with the 80387. There are, however, occasional exceptions. Early in the 386 game, several companies released motherboards based on the 386 with a 287 coprocessor. The reason is simple: The 387 wasn't out yet. (In some senses, the decision to use the existing and known 287 was a good one. Intel tried to beat everyone to the punch with their first 386/387 motherboard. Unfortunately, the board was released before Intel finished the 387. Subsequent changes to the 387 made the Intel motherboard's 387 socket useless.) Generally, hybrid 386/287 motherboards run the 287 at 6 to 10 Mhz. A 386 running by itself at 16 Mhz can often outperform an 8 Mhz 287! Therefore, when shopping for 386 machines, don't bother even considering motherboards with only 287 sockets.

Matching Coprocessor Speed to CPU Speed. The coprocessor is an independent CPU, and as such can be run at any speed within the chip's limits. The decision of how fast a coprocessor *actually* runs is made by the board designer. How do you know how fast a coprocessor you need? There are two simple rules:

- For anything but an AT or AT clone, coprocessor speed should be equal to or greater than processor speed.
- For an AT or AT clone, coprocessor speed should be equal to or greater than *two thirds* of processor speed.

AT designs with slower coprocessors are unfortunate, as a coprocessor running at two-thirds processor speed is often worse than no coprocessor at all. Why do designers do it? The answer is that IBM started it with the AT. Slower coprocessors are cheaper. Designers, wanting to be compatible, aped the IBM decision. Note that not all 286 machines have this problem—IBM runs the Model

50/60 coprocessors at the full 10 Mhz of the processor.

Power Supply

U.S. line current is 120 volts Alternating Current (AC). The PC, like most digital devices, is set up to use Direct Current (DC) at 5 and 12 volts. The conversion process is done by a *power supply*. The power supply is the silver or black box to the right rear side of the PC. Power supplies are rated by the amount of power they can handle: 63.5-watt power supplies are used on PCs, 130-watt power supplies on XTs, and 200-watt power supplies on ATs. Your power supply determines in part how long your computer components last. A good power supply costs less than $200. Chapter 10 discusses selecting, replacing, and installing a power supply. The power supply can't always cope with environmental conditions, so the chapter also discusses add-on products: surge supressors, spike isolators, and uninterruptible power supplies.

Figure 4-14   Power Supply

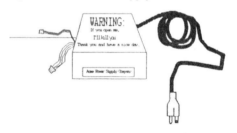

The power supply is easy to find in the system: It's the silver or black box in the back of the chassis that has a label on it that in five languages says, "If you open me, I'll kill you."

Keyboard

The PC is useless without an input device, and the keyboard is the input device used by most of us. The keyboard is subject to a number of hazards, however, and needs maintenance—and sometimes replacement. The PC's keyboard actually contains a microprocessor of its own called the Intel 8041, 8042, or 8048. Taking apart a keyboard isn't hard; reassembling one is. Attacking both those problems, and discussing alternative and replacement models, is the subject of Chapter 19, "Keyboards."

The Notion of a Controller

From here on in this chapter you'll see add-in boards of various kinds. Most are *controllers* of some kind. All peripheral devices, whether internal or external, need something to communicate between them and the computer. Sometimes these are called *controllers, interfaces, ports,* or *adapters.* For example, a hard disk needs a hard disk controller. Controllers mainly exist for these reasons:

- To isolate the hardware from the software.

    Western Digital's WD1002 XT-type hard disk controller is as different from IBM's original XT-type controller as a Corvette is from a Chevette, yet 99 percent of the software written to work with the former works just fine (or better) with the latter. The underlying hardware is much better and a lot different, so you'd imagine there would be big compatibility problems; but the hardware has been housebroken to respond to CPU requests in the same manner (although faster) as the old Xebec-designed IBM controller. Ditto video controllers designed by ATI or Paradise: they respond to the same software as IBM's original CGA, EGA, or VGA, but are cheaper and generally work faster. Using controllers with well-defined

interfaces makes building compatible hardware possible.

You can understand the value of well-defined interfaces and modularity by looking at an automobile. Perhaps (if you're my age) you learned to drive in an old 60s car or, if you're my Dad's age, in a car from the 40s. Both of us now drive cars designed and built in the 80s. The old 1967 Country Squire station wagon was a radically different car from the Honda I now drive. The Hudson my dad drove in the 40s is an even more radical difference from his current Toyota truck. But despite our education on different cars we're both as well prepared to drive an 80s car as someone who's only driven 80s cars, because the *interfaces* are the same. Because I interact directly not with the car but with the dashboard gauges and controls, I don't need to know the innards. If somebody stole into my back yard tomorrow and replaced my internal combustion engine under the hood with an engine that runs on air, I wouldn't know the difference.

- To handle speed matching.

    Most peripherals are considerably slower than the CPU in transferring data. Even the hard disk, for example, is thousands of times slower than the CPU. Most microcomputers (like the PC) have been designed to control everything in their systems, but that's not necessary. A company named Cogent Data Systems makes a hard disk controller for AT-class machines with memory and a microprocessor right on it: The main CPU just makes a request of the hard disk controller, and then (with the right software) goes off to handle something else while waiting for the controller to do the job. Eventually, the controller informs the CPU that it's finished with the data request, and that the controller has already transferred the data into the CPU's memory. Truthfully, the "speed matching" benefits of controllers haven't been really exploited in the PC world yet, as intra-PC "distributed computing" doesn't really exist—yet.

- To convert data from the CPU's format ($\pm$ 5 volts, digital, and so on) to whatever format the peripheral uses (for example, something called *Modified Frequency Modulation* for a hard disk).

The CPU speaks its own electrical language to other chips on the motherboard. But it's a language without too much power—a CPU wouldn't be able to "shout" loudly enough to be heard any appreciable distance on a LAN. Devices like video monitors need signals massaged into forms they can utilize. Again, controllers serve this function.

A typical system will have a keyboard controller, a video controller, ones for the floppy and hard disks, and interface controllers for parallel and serial ports.

A Common Misconception. Many think a controller must be on a board all its own. Not at all. The keyboard controller is generally not a board, but just one chip on the motherboard. The hard and floppy disk controllers are usually on separate boards in XT-type machines, but on the same board on most AT-class machines. As we've seen, many of the newer machines put the video, hard disk, floppy disk, parallel, and serial controllers *all* on a single board—the motherboard.

Let's take a quick look at the common controllers in the system.

Display and Display Adapters

The PC, like most computers, uses video Cathode Ray Tube (CRT) technology to display information for user reception. To allow the computer to communicate with a display monitor, a display adapter must be inserted into one of the PC's expansion slots. Several display adapters are available:

- The IBM Monochrome Display Adapter (MDA) and compatibles.

    Offered really out-of-this-world (for 1981) text on a microcomputer screen—sadly, however, no graphics.
- The Hercules Monochrome Graphics Adapter and compatibles.

    One company took the MDA and added graphics. Most programs don't support the Hercules graphics (which is a shame, as they're pretty good for the price), but some of the biggies like *1-2-3* do.
- The IBM Color/Graphics Adapter (CGA) and compatibles.

    Introduced with the MDA for use with games, the CGA offered lousy text and lousy graphics.
- The IBM Enhanced Graphics Adapter (EGA) and Compatibles.

    It was really annoying that people with Commodore 64s had better games than PC owners. A lot of that was due to the lousy graphics. To allow better games on the PC (no, that's not really true), IBM introduced the EGA in 1984. It was very expensive at first—over $1,100 for the board and monitor—but now an EGA system with monochrome monitor that shows you colors as shades of gray can be assembled for under $300. The EGA offers good text and good graphics.
- The IBM Professional Graphics Adapter and compatibles.

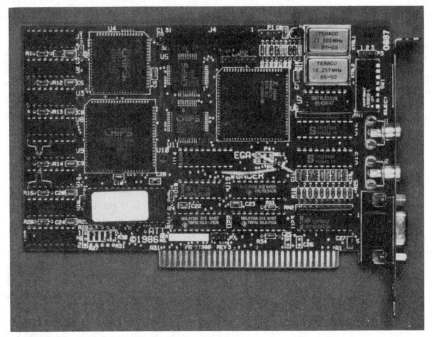

EGA board.

The PGA was a $3,000+ package IBM offered as a more powerful alternative to the EGA in 1984. It never caught on.

- The IBM Video Graphics Array.

Sporting PGA-quality graphics, the VGA made its appearance in 1987 with the PS/2s. The graphic and text quality are better than EGA, but not so much that one is tempted to throw away a $400 EGA monitor and $150 EGA board to embrace VGA. Not so much a revolution as just simple evolution. A nice board, nonetheless, and preferred over EGA if you're upgrading from CGA or MDA.

- The IBM Multi Color Graphics Array.

A cut-down version of VGA for the Models 25 and 30.

- The IBM 8514/A Very High Resolution Graphics Adapter.

Does some nifty stuff, including allowing you to see two 80 × 25 screens right on one monitor. The screens are in Squint-O-Vision, but it's awfully nice for debugging or desktop publishing. At the moment, however, it's a bit rich for most of our tastes—$3,000 for the monitor and board.

- Non-IBM High Resolution Graphics Adapters.

Each adapter may service one or more types of displays. The major families of displays are the following:

- Monochrome TTL Monitors
- Composite Video Monitors
- RGB Monitors
- High Resolution RGB Monitors
- Multiscan Monitors

I have no intention of telling you how to open up and attempt to service one of these monitors—it's dangerous and not particularly cost effective. However, some simple maintenance and troubleshooting techniques can be done with the monitor cover in place. I'll discuss them in the chapter on displays and display adapters.

Floppy and Hard Disk Controller and Disk Drives

The floppy disk drive is an essential peripheral. Since it's a peripheral, it requires an interface card. This card is called a *floppy disk controller board*. These will, in general, not give you many problems. They do fail, however, so you need to know how to recognize and address this.

The much more fertile ground for failure lies in the floppy disks and floppy disk drives themselves. Floppy drives can require speed adjustment, head alignment, and head cleaning. Speed adjustment and head cleaning can be done simply and cheaply. Alignment can require some specialized equipment and

isn't always cost effective, but it will be discussed later.

Beyond adjustment is the problem of compatibility among drive types. There are two kinds of $5\frac{1}{4}$-inch floppies, two kinds of $3\frac{1}{2}$-inch floppies, and Zenith makes a laptop that uses 2-inch floppies. Nowadays, I don't even consider outfitting a machine without a $3\frac{1}{2}$-inch drive. The floppy chapter talks about floppy installation and includes a section on installing $3\frac{1}{2}$-inch drives in older XT and AT type machines (it's fairly simple).

Hard disks are a godsend if you've been using floppies, because they store more data and are faster, but they bring their own host of problems. Hard disk (IBM calls them *fixed disk*) controllers can develop problems, or they may contain the key to better hard disk performance. There are a lot of options in hard disk controllers these days, and we'll examine them.

Some hard disk failures, like precipitous drops in speed or loss of data, can be addressed at either the controller or the drive level. Problems like head crashes can be avoided with some simple techniques explained in the chapter on hard

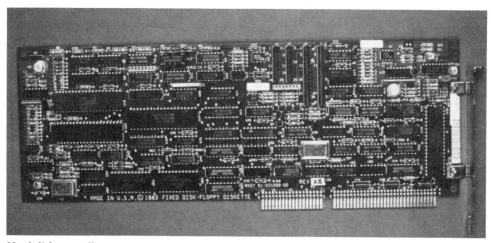

Hard disk controller.

disks. Even the ultimate disaster—a reformatted hard disk—can be reversed in some cases.

We tend not to think of certain boards, like parallel ports or video boards, as AT-specific or XT-specific. The hard disk controllers, unlike most other types of circuit boards, have radically different designs. In general, they're not interchangeable.

Printer Interfaces

Despite the "Electronic Age" and the "Paperless Office," we still don't believe something is true until we see it on paper. Would you *really* believe you had gotten that promotion until you received the letter? You don't use E-mail for that kind of stuff. Printers and plotters produce this *hard copy* output for us. As should be familiar by now, such devices require an interface, generally a *Centronics parallel port* or an *RS232C serial port*. In the case of the parallel port, the interface usually poses few or no problems. Serial ports can be troublesome sometimes, but inexpensive diagnostic tools described in "Modems and Communications Ports" (later in this chapter) can quickly isolate problems.

Printer ports have names DOS can understand. DOS calls the first printer port on a PC *LPT1*, or *Line PrinTer 1*. Also, DOS supports LPT2 and LPT3.

The actual printer is the greater source of failures. Printers employ a large number of moving parts. Some dot matrix and laser printers are very reliable, while some daisy wheel printers can offer no end of problems. The chapter "Printers and Plotters" examines printer maintenance. Worse yet, as printers get more powerful, their software gets more complex. It's a shame so many people fail to exploit the full power of their computers simply because *WordPerfect* or *Word* isn't programmed to do the exploiting. "Printer Software

Troubleshooting" introduces you to the world of escape codes and Hewlett-Packard's LaserJet Printer Control Language (PCL) to let you unlock the power of your PC printer.

Modems and Communication Ports

The other common printer interface is the serial port. It's more commonly used, however, for *modems*—MODulator/DE-Modulators. Modems allow computers to communicate remotely with other computers via phone lines. Virtually all modems use serial ports, also known as a *comm port*, an *RS232* or *RS232C*, or the new official name that no one seems to know or use, the *EIA 232D port*.

The DOS names for the communications ports are COM1 and COM2. DOS 3.3 will also allow COM3 and COM4, but they're limited in their usefulness (more on that in "Modems and Communications Ports" (Chapter 4).

RS232 is a source of many cable problems. Either the wrong cable is configured, or environmental problems (electronic noise) cause communication errors. Data communications troubleshooting is an entire book in itself—several books, in fact—but we cover the essentials in "Modems and Communications Ports."

System Clock/Calendar

The system clock/calendar keeps the date and time even when the unit is turned off. The AT-type machines are designed to include the clock right on the motherboard. XT-types don't have it, so they must get by with the help of add-on boards. The vast majority of the time, the only problem from the clock will be with (1) the battery or (2) the software to use it.

The battery causes problems, of course, when it runs down and no longer keeps time. Replacement is no problem,

IBM RS-232 adapter.

save for some clock/calendar boards that solder the battery on the board. You have to wonder if the people who designed those boards want to be able to charge you $120 three years later to replace the battery.

The other clock problem is how to change the time and date, and how to get the time and date from the clock/calendar board into DOS's time and date?'' Again, on AT-type machines it's a piece of cake—DOS directly supports it. But XT-type machines need a separate program, like SETCLOCK, ASTCLOCK, or PWRUPCLK, to name a few I've seen. The only trouble is that the programs tend to get lost. If you're a support person, become packrat-like when you see disks with programs to support various boards. Nobody else will know where these disks are, so it's up to you.

By the way, don't confuse this with the clock that raps out the beat that the PC dances to—the one I mentioned a few pages back based on the 8284 or 82284 chip. They're different circuits. The CPU clock doesn't run when the power is off to the PC. The clock/calendar, on the other hand, has a battery to allow it to run even when the system is off.

Other Strange Boards

That's about it for the commonly found boards. You might also see the following boards:

- **Mouse interface boards.** Some mice interface via the serial port, but others use their own special interface card. Such a mouse is called a *bus mouse,* as opposed to a *serial mouse,* which is attached with the serial port.
- **Local Area Network (LAN) boards.** If your company has a Token Ring

57

or Ethernet network, there's got to be a physical connection to the network. That's supplied by a LAN interface card. The most common ones you'll see are:

- Ethernet or its variation, StarLAN
- Token Ring
- ARCnet

- **3270 emulation cards.** Despite improvements in IBM's *SNA (Systems Network Architecture)* in the past few years, it's probably easiest to get your PC to talk to the mainframe by making it look like a dumb 3270 terminal, the familiar IBM "green screens" you see in offices around the world. *Dumb* in terminal parlance means it lacks stand-alone processing power. DCA (the IRMA guys), Attachmate, and others make a nice business filling this need. Plug one in your system and your PC can hook up to the same old coaxial cable that's been serving IBM mainframe users for years.

- **Tape controllers.** If you want to install a tape drive for backup to your system, you'll need a controller of some kind. Many tape drives can use the floppy controller, but it's not recommended—such tapes are painfully slow, and remember that you bought the tape to quickly back up the hard disk. Some tapes are internal, some external. I'd recommend external, because then you can buy a tape controller board for all of your machines, buy only a few of the expensive tape drives themselves, and let the users share the occasional use of a tape drive. (That's *occasional* only when compared to the frequency of use for the hard disk. Backups should be near-daily if you generate work of any importance at all. Yes, I know

it's a pain, but can you really afford to lose a whole day's work?)

- **Scanner interface cards.** Graphical and character scanners are becoming more and more popular, and with good reason—desktop publishing really shines with graphics. Today's audience demands lots of visuals. Scanners offer a way to add pictures to text in a computer-readable form. *Character scanners* allow easier entry of text in computer-readable form.

Some Identification Hints

The above descriptions look good on paper, but how can you actually disassemble a computer and hope to identify the parts? Here are a few hints.

- The power supply is, as we've said, marked prominently with a "do not open" label.
- The hard disk, if one exists, is likely to be a sealed box with air vents on the top and a circuit board on the bottom.
- The floppies should be self-evident.

The circuitry can be identified with some simple rules:

- RAM Memory is usually easy to spot—it's nine small chips in a row or column, often socketed. It may alternatively be in SIMM form.
- ROM Memory is usually a large chip or pair of chips in sockets, often with a label on the top indicating software version number.
- Note where boards are attached. The board that's attached with a ribbon cable to the floppy drives is probably the floppy controller. Ditto for the hard disk.

Figure 4-15 Hard Disk "Pin Cushion"

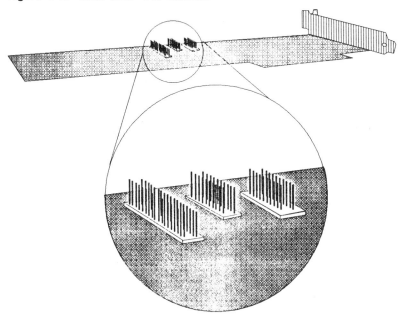

- Although the best way to find the hard disk controller is to just follow the ribbon cable from the hard disk back to a circuit board—that board is probably the controller—another method is the extremely unusual nature of the hard disk interface connectors. You see, the hard disk uses a single 34-pin connector and two 20-pin connectors right on the circuit board. These connectors mate directly to the ribbon cables mentioned before. They're quite hard to miss; in fact, the hard disk controller is the board you can find in the dark, because it looks like a pin cushion extends out from it.
- Note what kind of connectors you find on the back of a circuit board. A common connector type is the D shell, so called because it looks like a capital D. It may have 9, 15, 25, or 37 pins or sockets in it, so it could be referred to as a *male DB9* (nine pins in a D shell), *female DB25* (25 pins in a D shell), and so on. Table 4-6, "Common Connectors and Probable Uses," is a good reference to the connectors on expansion card backs you'll most likely see.
- Finally, there's the *process of elimination:* you know there's a hard disk controller board here somewhere, and you've identified everything but one board—good chance that's it. (This is, of course, a last-ditch method.)

Model Identification Revisited: Specifics of Particular Machines

Now that you've heard of clock/calendars, ROMs, and such, we're ready to

Table 4-6. Common Connectors and Probable Uses

Connector Type	Common Use
Male DB9	Serial Port
Male DB25	Serial Port
Female DB9	Video, either RGB or EGA color, or Monochrome TTL
Female DB15	Game/Joystick Port
Female DB25	Parallel Printer Port
Female DB37	External Floppy Port (IBM XT floppy controller usually)
Other common connectors:	
Female D shell, 3 rows, 15 sockets	VGA
BNC "push and turn"	3270 coax or LAN
Genderless "Boy George" connectors	IBM Token Ring
RJ11, RJ13, RJ45	Internal Modem, ARCNet, or Ethernet
Common combinations:	
Connector Type	Common Use
Female DB9, one RCA jack	Color Graphics Adapter
Female DB9, two RCA jacks	Enhanced Graphics Adapter

finish the PC differentiation that we started a couple of chapters back. Although the IBM XT and PC are very similar machines, they have a few differences that are apparent under the hood.

IBM PCs and XTs differ by:

- Number of slots: the PC has five, the XT has eight.
- Number of DIP switches: the PC has two banks of eight switches, the XT one bank of eight switches.

- Number of ROM chips: five for the PC, two for the XT. (Generally only one for XT clones. Strictly speaking, there aren't too many PC clones.) The PC has room for a sixth chip, but it's an empty socket.
- First bank of memory: As I've mentioned, the IBM XT and PC have four *banks* (nine-chip groups) of memory chips. The first bank *(bank zero)* is the most important, as is the memory where DOS loads itself. This first bank of memory is soldered onto the PC's motherboard, and socketed on the XT's motherboard. This might seem a subtle point, but it's not. If the first bank of memory is bad on the system board, the motherboard can't run DOS—you see, DOS isn't smart enough to load itself somewhere else if that first bank is bad. Result: bad memory in bank zero means a dead motherboard (in fact, a bad bank zero is the cause of over half of all "dead" motherboards).

I've already said the *big* differences between the XT machines and AT machines are in the bus and the processor.

Differences between XT-type and AT-type machines:

- Clock/calendar: AT-type machines have a built-in clock/calendar. XT machines generally need a separate board.
- Configuration: AT-type machines have only a few or no switches. XT machines generally have eight or more DIP switches for configuration.
- ROMs: The AT has two ROMs, and room for two more. XT clones usually only have one ROM on their motherboards.

Figure 4-16 Rear View of Common Adapter Boards and Probable Identification

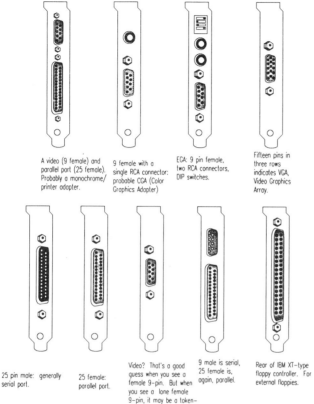

A video (9 female) and parallel port (25 female). Probably a monochrome/printer adapter.

9 female with a single RCA connector: probable CGA (Color Graphics Adapter)

EGA: 9 pin female, two RCA connectors, DIP switches.

Fifteen pins in three rows indicates VGA, Video Graphics Array.

25 pin male: generally serial port.

25 female: parallel port.

Video? That's a good guess when you see a female 9-pin. But when you see a lone female 9-pin, it may be a token-ring LAN board.

9 male is serial, 25 female is, again, parallel.

Rear of IBM XT-type floppy controller. For external floppies.

- Motherboard size: People often ask me, "Can I upgrade my XT-type machine by replacing the motherboard with an AT-type motherboard?" In general, AT-type motherboards are physically larger than XT motherboards and can't fit in XT boxes. (There are, however, a group of AT-type motherboards called "baby" AT motherboards. They do fit in XT boxes and are discussed later.)
- Maximum memory: XTs generally can't accommodate more than 640K of user memory. AT-type machines can have just under 16M of memory. 386-based machines could theoretically have 4096M of memory.

After considering the XT-type and AT-type machines, we have the PS/2s and PS/2-like computers. These machines generally have a smaller *footprint,* the space they take up on the desktop. They put on the motherboard functions like the video, hard disk controller, floppy disk controller, serial ports, and parallel ports that are on separate circuit boards on older machines. This is both a blessing and a curse, as we'll see later. Besides the actual PS/2s, machines like the Zenith LP286 fall into this category.

PS/2 and PS/2-like machines may have the following:

- Bus: Micro Channel bus slots.
- Memory: Older machines use a bank of nine small chips to comprise a bank of memory. PS/2-like machines tend to use the small "miniboards" of memory chips mentioned before called SIMMs (Single Inline Memory Modules).
- Smaller drives: Many of the PS/2-like machines only have space in their chassis for a $3\frac{1}{2}$-inch drive. If you want a $5\frac{1}{4}$-inch drive you've got to install an external $5\frac{1}{4}$-inch.
- Unusual drive interfaces: Earlier machines use an industry standard drive interface called ST-506/412. (Don't worry, you'll hear more about it later in the chapter on hard disks.) That's nice because you can buy any drive you like and put it into most PC compatible machines. PS/2-like machines (Compaqs; the Zenith LP286; and the PS/2 Models 50, 50Z, and 70) seem to be going in the direction of strange disk proprietary interfaces. What it means in English is that you've pretty much got to buy PS/2 drives from IBM, and Zenith LP286 drives from Zenith.

Chapter 5
Avoiding Service: Preventive Maintenance

The most effective way to cut down your repair bills is by good preventive maintenance. Some of this is common sense. However, many misconceptions exist in the PC community about what does and does not make good maintenance sense. A few factors endanger your PC's health:

- Heat and dust
- Magnetism
- Stray electromagnetism
- Water and corrosive agents

Heat and Thermal Shock

Every electronic device carries within it the seeds of its own destruction. More than half of the power given to chips is wasted as heat, and heat destroys chips. One of an electronic designer's main concerns is to see that an electronic device can dissipate heat as quickly as it can generate it. If not, heat slowly builds up until the device fails.

You can help your PC's heat problem:

- Install an adequate fan.
- Ensure that you're using the proper size power supply.

- Run it in a safe temperature range.
- Keep the insides dust-free.

The second point—ensuring that your power supply is sized correctly—is taken up in the chapter on power supplies. The others are discussed below.

Removing Heat with a Fan. Some computers, like the Atari 520 or the Commodore 64, don't require a fan, as enough heat dissipates from the main circuit board all by itself. But the PC will surely fail without a fan.

When designing a fan, engineers must trade off quiet operation for cooling power. The fans in the power supplies of most XT-type machines don't seem to do a very good job in either category— they're noisy, and the temperature inside the case of an operating PC or XT can be 30 degrees Fahrenheit warmer than the room outside. ATs are generally cooler, with case temperatures around 15 degrees warmer inside than outside— the phrase is "15 degrees over ambient." The fan is needed to transport away the heat being generated by the circuit boards, drives, and power supply. Lots of memory and large disk drives are contributing heat factors, as are internal modems (they seem to run fairly hot). One Deskpro 386-like computer I work with was 25 degrees warmer inside the case than outside. If I remove everything but the minimum memory, video, and disk controllers, there's only a 10 degree difference.

You can buy a better fan for your PC in one of two ways. Either get a new power supply containing a better fan or buy an extra "helper" fan.

One company, PC Power and Cooling Systems, specializes in improved power supplies for PCs. They sell a Turbo-Cool 150 for PCs and XTs, and a Turbo-Cool 200 for ATs and AT-like 386s. They're no noisier than the standard power supplies, yet have been measured to lower temperatures by as much as 35 to 40 degrees in some machines. Obviously, my 386 wouldn't be cooled by 35 degrees, since it's only 25 degrees over ambient; the best a fan can do is to lower the temperature inside the machine to the surrounding temperature. However, installing a PC Cooling Systems fan cooled my machine from 25 degrees over ambient to only 4 degrees over ambient.

PC Power and Cooling System's address is:

PC Power and Cooling Systems
31510 Mountain Way
Bonsall, CA 92003
(619) 723-9513

PC Cooling Systems also makes add-in "helper" fans for PCs. These are very thin fans that fit inside the case between the case and the chassis. They cost $65 for PCs and XTs, and $75 for ATs.

Safe Temperature Ranges for PCs. Electronic components have a temperature range within which they're built to work. IBM suggests that the PC, for instance, is built to work in the range between 60 to 85 degrees. This is because, although the circuit boards can run as hot as 125 degrees, a typical machine might be as much as 40 degrees hotter *inside* the case than outside it. 125 − 40 = 85 degrees, the suggested maximum temperature.

Obviously, if you've got a good fan, the acceptable range of room temperatures expands considerably. If you have a really good fan, the temperature inside the machine would be the same as that outside. You don't want the inside of the PC to get any higher than 110 degrees— hard disks fail at that point, although, again, circuit boards can function in higher temperatures than that. (So my floppy-only laptop can function in the Gobi Desert, although I've not had the chance or inclination to try it yet.)

Since the temperature inside the PC is ambient plus some constant, there are two ways to cool the inside of the PC: lower the constant with a good fan or lower the ambient temperature. Keep the room cooler and the PC will be cooler.

Heat aids the corrosion process. Corrosion is a chemical process, and chemical processes roughly *double* in speed when the temperature of the process is raised by 10 degrees Centigrade (about 18 degrees Fahrenheit). Chips slowly deteriorate, the hotter the faster.

How do you measure temperature and temperature changes in your PC? Simple—get a digital temperature probe. Radio Shack markets one for around $15, catalog number 63-842. There's also one available from Edmund Scientific:

Dual Function Digital Lab Thermometer
$40—Catalog # E36,987
Edmund Scientific Company
101 E. Gloucester Pike
Barrington, NJ 08007
(609) 573-6250

The easy way to use the probe is to tape it over the exit vents by the fan's power supply. An indoor/outdoor switch lets you quickly view the PC's inside temperature and ambient temperature.

Duty Cycles. It was stated before a device should get rid of heat as quickly as it creates it. Not every device is that good, however. Devices are said to have a *duty cycle*, a number expressed as a percentage that is the proportion of the time a device can work without burning up. For example, a powerful motor might have a 50 percent duty cycle. This means it should be active only 50 percent of the time. A starter motor on a car, for example, must produce a tremendous amount of power. Powerful motors are expensive to produce, so instead cars use a motor that can produce a lot of power for a very short time. If you crank the engine on your car for several minutes at a stretch, you would likely damage or destroy the car's starter motor. Floppy disk drive motors are a similar example: Run a floppy motor continuously and you would likely burn up the motor. Hard disk motors, on the other hand, run continuously and must be designed with a 100-percent duty cycle. Disk stepper motors for PC hard disks aren't designed to run continuously. Thus, it's okay to leave your hard disk turned on 24 hours a day, but probably not acceptable to make it read or write data constantly.

Duty cycle is used to describe active vs. nonactive time for many kinds of devices, although it's (strictly speaking) incorrect. Some desktop laser printers, for example, won't run well if required to print continuously.

Thermal Shock. Because a PC is warmer inside than outside, changes in room temperature can become multiplied inside a PC.

This leads to a problem called *thermal shock*. Thermal shock comes from subjecting components to rapid and large changes in temperature. It can disable your computer due to expansion/contraction damage. The most common scenario for thermal shock occurs when the PC is turned on Monday morning after a winter's weekend. Most commercial buildings turn the temperature down to 55 degrees over the weekend. Your office may contain some of that residual chill early Monday morning. Inside the PC, though, it still might be 55. Then you turn the machine on. Within 30 minutes the PC has warmed up to 120 degrees. This rapid, 65-degree rise in temperature over a half hour brings on thermal shock.

This is one argument for leaving the PC on 24 hours a day, 7 days a week. (You'll see some more reasons to do this soon.) The temperature inside the PC will be better modulated. By the way, you can't leave portable PCs on all the time, but be extra careful with portables to avoid thermal shock. If your laptop has been sitting in the trunk on a cold February day, be sure to give it some time to warm up before trying to use it. Also, let it warm up in a *dry* place, or water vapor will condense on the cold platters. Water on the platters is a sure-fire way to reduce your drive's life.

Sunbeams. Another heat effect is caused by sunbeams. Direct sunlight isn't a good thing for electronic equipment. A warm sunbeam feels nice for a few minutes, but sit in one for an hour and you'll understand why PCs don't like them. Direct sunlight is also, of course, terrible for floppy disks. Find a shadowy area or use drapes.

Dealing with Dust. Dust is everywhere. It consists of tiny sand particles, fossil skeletons of minuscule creatures that lived millions of years ago, dead skin, paper particles, and tiny crustaceans called dust mites that live off the other pieces. Dust is responsible for several evils.

First, dust sticks to the circuit boards inside your computer. As it builds up, the entire board can become coated with a fine, insulating sheath. That would be good if the dust was insulating your house, but thermal insulation is definitely a bad thing for computers. You seek, as you have seen, to minimize impediments to thermal radiation from your computer components. To combat this, remove dust from inside the computer and from circuit boards periodically. A good period between cleaning is a year in a house and six months in an office. A simpler approach is to use the "while I'm at it" algorithm—when you need to disassemble the machine for some other reason, clean the inside while you're at it. A can of compressed air can assist you. Just as effective for the case and bracket assemblies is a dust-free cloth wetted with a little water and ammonia (just a few drops). Don't use the cloth on circuit boards; get a can of compressed air and blow the dust off.

This should be obvious, but when you blow dust off boards, be aware of where it's going: If you can have the vacuum cleaner nearby, or take the board to another area, you'll have better luck. *Please* don't hold the board over the PC's chassis and blow off the dust with compressed air—all it does is move, not *re*move, the dust.

The second dust evil is that it can clog spaces, such as:

- The air intake area to your power supply or hard disk
- The space between the floppy disk drive head and the disk

To combat the floppy drive problem, some manufacturers offer a floppy dust cover you put in place when the machine is off. The sad part of this is that you really need the cover when the machine is on. The reason is that CRT displays have an unintended, unpleasant, unavoidable (the three *U*s) side effect: They attract dust. Turn your screen on, and all the dust in the area drops everything and heads straight for the display. Part of the particles get side-tracked and end up in the floppy drives.

Some vendors say the way to cut down on dust in floppy drives is to close the drive doors. This is wrong for two reasons: First, the door isn't dust-tight. Second, double-sided drives should be stored with the doors open. This is because the heads don't touch each other and so cannot damage each other when the drive doors are open. Obviously this is a moot point for half-height drives, which don't allow you to close the doors unless a floppy is in the drive.

A place that creates and collects paper dust is, of course, the printer. You should periodically vacuum or blow out printers, away from the computer (remember, dust goes somewhere when blown away).

By the way, another fertile source of dust is ash particles. Most of us don't burn things indoors unless we're smokers. If you smoke, don't do it near the computer. A study by the U.S. government Occupation Safety and Hazard Administration (OSHA) estimated that smoke at a computer workstation cuts its life by 40 percent. That's $1,200 on a $3,000 workstation.

Magnetism

Magnets, both the permanent and electromagnetic type, can cause permanent loss of data on hard or floppy disks. The most common magnetism found in the office environment is produced by electric motors and electromagnets. A commonly overlooked electromagnet is the one in phones that ring or chirp (rather than beep). The phone forces the clapper against the bell by powering an electro-magnet. If you absentmindedly put such a phone on top of a stack of floppy disks and the phone rings, you'll have unre-coverable data errors on at least the top one. Your stereo speakers can do the same thing to floppies.

Don't think you have magnets around? How about:

- Magnets to put notes on a file cabi-net
- Paper clip holders with magnets
- Word processing copy stands with magnetic clips
- Magnetic screw extractors

Another source of magnetism is, be-lieve it or not, a CRT. I've seen disk drives refuse to function because they were situated inches from a CRT. X-ray machines in airports similarly produce some magnetism, although there's some controversy here. Some folks say, "Don't run floppies through the X-ray machine—walk them through." Others say the X-ray device is okay but the metal detector zaps floppies. Some people claim to have been burned at both. Per-sonally, I walk through an average of three to four metal detectors per week carrying $3\frac{1}{2}$-inch floppy disks and have never (knock wood) had a problem.

Airport metal detectors should be sufficiently gentle for floppies. Magne-tism is measured in a unit called *gauss*—a power of 25 gauss is required to affect a 360K floppy, more for denser floppies. Metal detectors *in the U.S.* (notice the stress) emit no more than 1 gauss. I'm not sure about Canada and Europe, but I notice that the fillings in my teeth seem to set off the metal detectors in the Ot-tawa airport.

What about preventive mainte-nance? For starters, get a beeping phone to minimize the chance of erasing data inadvertently. Another large source of

magnetism is the motor in the printer; generally, it isn't shielded (the motors on the drives don't produce very much magnetism, in case you're wondering).

Mainly, go on an antimagnet cru-sade. Magnets near magnetic media are disasters waiting to happen.

A sad story: A large government agency's data center bought a hand-held magnetic bulk floppy eraser. (I'm not sure why—they weren't a Secret shop, and thus did not have the need.) The PC expert in the shop tested it on a few junk floppies, turned it off, and then forgot about it. The next day he remembered that he had left it on top of a plastic floppy file drawer. This meant that the eraser, even though turned off, was about an inch from the top of the flop-pies. He spent the next day testing each of the floppies, one by one. Most were dead. The data center got rid of the bulk eraser. I'm not sure what they did with the PC expert.

Stray Electromagnetism

Stray electromagnetism can cause prob-lems for your PC. Here, I'm just referring to any electromagnetism you don't want. It comes in several varieties:

- Radiated Electromagnetic Interfer-ence (EMI)
- Power noise
- Electrostatic Discharge (ESD)—static electricity

Electromagnetic Interference. EMI is caused when electromagnetism is ra-diated or conducted somewhere you don't want it to be. I discuss two com-mon types—crosstalk and RFI—in the next two sections.

Crosstalk. When two wires are physi-cally close to each other, they can trans-mit interference between themselves. This doesn't mean short circuits—the in-sulation may be completely intact. The problem is that the interfering wire contains electronic pulses, which produce magnetic fields as a side effect. The wire receiving interference is touched or crossed by the magnetic fields. Magnetic fields crossing or touching a wire produce electronic pulses as a side effect. (Nature is, unfortunately, amazingly symmetrical at times like this.) The electronic pulses created in the second wire are faint copies of the pulses—that is, the *signal*—from the first wire. This interferes with the signal we're trying to send on the second wire.

Crosstalk isn't really a problem when applied to power lines, although I've heard of cases where the alternating current in power lines creates a hum on a communications line through crosstalk. The larger worry is when bundles of wires, such as data cables, are stored in close quarters.

There are five solutions to crosstalk:

- Move the wires farther apart (not always feasible).
- Use twisted pairs; varying the number of twists reduces crosstalk.
- Use shielded cable. The shield reduces crosstalk—don't even think of running ribbon cables for distances over six feet.
- Use fiber optic cable—it's photonic, not electromagnetic, so there's no crosstalk.
- Don't run cables over the fluorescent lights. The lights are noise emitters.

Radio Frequency Interference. *Radio Frequency Interference (RFI)* is high frequency (10 Khz+) radiation. It's a bad thing. Sources are:

- High speed digital circuits, like the ones in your computer
- Nearby radio sources
- Cordless telephones and keyboards

- Power-line intercoms
- Motors

Worse yet, your PC could be a *source* of RFI. If this happens, the FCC police come to your place of business and take your PC away. (Well, not really, but they will fine you. More on this later.)

RFI is bad because it can interfere with high speed digital circuits. Your computer is composed of digital circuits. RFI can seem sinister, because it seems to come and go mysteriously. Like all noise, it's an unwanted signal. How would you go about receiving a *wanted* RF signal? Simple—construct an antenna. Suppose you want to receive a signal of a given frequency? You would design an antenna of a particular length. (Basically, the best length is one-quarter of the wavelength, so a 30 meter wavelength is best picked up by a 7.5 meter antenna. It's not important to know that. To learn more about antennas, pick up an amateur radio book.) Now suppose there's some kind of RFI floating around. You're safe as long as you can't receive it. But what if your computer is connected to its printer with a cable that, through bad luck, happens to be the correct length to receive that RFI? The result: printer gremlins. Fortunately, the solution is simple: shorten the cable.

Electric motors are common RFI-producing culprits. I recently saw a workstation in Washington where the operator had put an electric fan on top (to cool the operator, not the workstation). When the fan was on, it warped the top of the CRT's image slightly. Electric can openers, hair dryers, electric razors, electric pencil sharpeners, and printers all are candidates. Sometimes it's hard to determine whether the device is messing up the PC simply by feeding back noise onto the power line (corrected by putting the devices on separate power lines), or whether it's troubling the PC with RFI.

Your PC also *emits* RFI, which can impair the functioning of other PCs, televisions, and various sensitive pieces of equipment. By law, a desktop computer cannot be sold unless it meets Class B specifications. The FCC requires that a device three meters from a PC must receive no more than a specific number of RFI (Table 5-1).

Table 5-1. Permissible RF Output (FCC Class B specification)

Frequency	Maximum Field Strength (microvolts/meter)
30–88 Mhz	100
89–216 Mhz	150
217–1000 Mhz	200

RFI became an issue with personal computers when the PC came out, because IBM had shielded its PC line and sought to make life a little tougher on the clonemakers. By pushing the FCC to get tough on PCs, IBM got a bit of a jump on the market. Unfortunately for IBM, getting Class B certification isn't that hard, and most clones qualify these days. Clonemakers now say their machines are *FCC Class B Certified*. This has caused the reverse of IBM's original intent, as the FCC certification seems to be a mark of legitimacy. In reality, FCC certification doesn't necessarily indicate good design, quality components, or compatibility.

Protecting your PC from the devices around it, and the devices from your PC, are done in the same way. If the PC doesn't leak RFI, it's less likely to pick up any stray RFI in the area. Any holes in the case provide entry/exit points. Use the brackets that come with the machine to plug any unused expansion slots. Ensure that the case fits together snugly and correctly. If the case includes cutouts for interface connectors, find plates to cover the cutouts or simply use metal tape.

A simple AM radio can be used to monitor RFI field strength. A portable Walkman-type radio is ideal, as it has light headphones and a small enough enclosure to allow fairly local signal-strength monitoring. A cheap model is best, since you don't want sophisticated noise filtering. Tune in an area of the dial as far as possible from a strong station (lower frequencies seem to work best), and you'll hear the various devices produce noises. The system I'm currently using has an XT motherboard, a composite monitor, an external hard disk, and a two-drive external Bernoulli box. The quietest part of the system is the PC: the hard disk screams and buzzes, the Bernoulli makes low frequency eggbeater-like sounds, and the monitor produces a fairly pure and relatively loud tone.

The PC sounds different, depending on what it's doing. When I type, I hear a machine gun-like sound. When I ask for a text search, the fairly regular search makes a *dee-dee-dee* sound.

Power Noise. Your wall socket is a source for lots of problems. They basically fall into a few categories:

- Overvoltage
- Undervoltage
- Transients—spikes and surges

Also, there's one power problem *you* **cause:**

- Power-up power surges

Let's consider the last first, then the others.

Power-Up Power Surges. I'd like to discuss one power-related item here: user-induced power surges. *What* user-induced power surges, you say? Simple: Every time you turn on an electrical device you get a power surge through it. *Some of the greatest stresses electrical devices receive is when they are turned on or off.* When do light bulbs burn out? Think about it—generally, it's when you first turn them on or off. One study showed that when a device is first turned on, it draws up to 4 to 6 times its normal power for less than a second. It's called *inrush current* in the literature of electricity. (The 4 to 6 figure is from page 27 of *Computer Electric Power Requirements* by Mark Waller, published in 1987 by Howard Sams.) For that brief time, your PC might be pulling 600 to 900 watts—not a prescription for long PC life.

What's the answer? Leave your PCs on 24 hours a day, 7 days a week. We've done it at my company for years. Either turn the monitor off, turn the screen intensity down, or use one of those annoying automatic screen blankers so an image doesn't burn into the monitor. Turn the printer off, too. Leaving the machines on also modulates temperature and reduces a phenomenon called *chip creep,* which I'll discuss in the next chapter.

What? You're still not convinced? Yes, it seems nonintuitive—most people react that way—but it really does make sense. First of all, consider the things you keep on all the time now:

- Digital clocks, which incorporate some of the same digital technology as microcomputers.
- Calculators. I've seen accountants with calculators that are on all the time.
- Mainframes, minis, and your phone PBX never go off.
- Televisions. Part of the TV is powered up all the time so it can "warm up" instantly, unlike older sets.
- Thermostats. The temperature regulating device in your home or business is a circuit that works all the time.

In addition to the things already mentioned, consider the hard disk. Many 10 and 20 megabyte hard disks were built to use low power motors so they could work with the underpowered PC power supply. You know from real life that it's a lot harder to start something moving than it is to keep it moving. (Did you ever push a car?) The cost, then, of these low-power motors is that sometimes they can't get started in the morning. At my company there's a 10MB disk that requires a "jumpstart" when it has been off overnight: If the thing doesn't want to work, you just remove it from the system, take off the hard disk's circuit board to expose the motor, and give the motor a spin. After a couple of spins, it can be reassembled, and it will start up fine. (Yes, we should throw it away, but we're cheap and stubborn.)

Here's the point: As long as we don't turn the system off, the hard drive works quite well, at least as well as old 10 meg hard drives work. This applies to hard disks in general—in fact, to anything with a motor. Yes, the motor's life is shortened when continuously on, but even then the expected life of the motor is beyond the reasonable life of a hard disk.

There's another reason you should keep the power on, as far as the hard disk is concerned. The initial power surge runs through *everything,* including the hard disk head. Let's suppose you don't park your hard disk head (more on that in the chapters on hard disks), so the head just ends up wherever it was when you turned the machine off. Now the surge goes through the head. It ends up blasting the data that happens to be sitting under the head with a "BLEAHHH!"—the surge "blurs" the data under the head. Finally, consider what happens when you don't turn the machine off at all: the head never crashes onto the platter, as happens when the machine is shut off normally.

A final word of caution. Leaving the machine on all the time is only a good idea if:

- Your machine is cooled adequately. If your machine is 100 degrees inside when the room is 70 degrees, it'll overheat when the room goes to 90 degrees on summer weekends when your building management turns off the cooling. Make sure your machine has a fan that can handle higher temperatures.
- You have adequate surge protection. Actually, you shouldn't run the machine at all unless you have adequate surge protection.
- You have fairly reliable power. If you lose power three times a week, there's no point in leaving the machines on all the time—the power company is turning them off and on for you. Even worse, the power just after a power outage is noise-filled.

Transient. This is any brief change in power that doesn't repeat itself. It might be an undervoltage or an overvoltage. *Sags* (momentary undervoltage) and *surges* (momentary overvoltage) are transients. Being brief, the transient can be of a high enough frequency that it slips right past the protective capacitors and whatever in your power supply and punches holes in your chips. (No, they're not holes you can *see*, at least not without some very good equipment.) Transients have a cumulative effect: The first 100 might do nothing. Eventually, however, enough chickens come home to roost that your machine decides, one day, to go on vacation. Permanently. We'll talk about protection against these things in Chapter 10.

Overvoltage. You're said to have an *overvoltage condition* when you get more than the rated voltage for a period greater than 2.5 seconds. Such a voltage measurement is done as a moving average over several seconds.

Chronic overvoltage is just as bad for your system as transient overvoltage: the chips can fail as a result of it.

Undervoltage. Summer in much of the country means air conditioners are running full blast, and the power company is working feverishly to meet the power demands they bring. Sometimes it can't meet the full needs, however, and so announces a reduction in voltage called a *brownout*.

Brownouts are bad for large motors, such as you'd find in a compressor for refrigeration. They make your TV screen look shrunken. And they confuse power supplies. A power supply tries to provide continuous power to the PC. Power equals voltage times current. If the voltage drops and you want constant power, what do you do? Simple—draw more current. But drawing more current through a given conductor heats up the conductor. The power supply and the chips get hot, and might overheat.

Surge protectors can't help you here. *Power conditioners* can—they use transformers to compensate for the sagging voltage. We'll discuss them in greater detail in the chapter on power supplies.

Electrostatic Discharge. ESD, or, as you probably know it, static electricity, is annoyingly familiar to anyone who has lived through a winter indoors. The air is very dry (winter and forced hot-air ducts bring relative humidity around 20 percent in my house, for example), and it's an excellent insulator. You build up a static charge and *keep it*. On the other hand, in the summer, when relative humidities might be close to 100 percent (I live in a suburb of Washington, D.C., a city built over a swamp), you build up static charges also, but they leak away quickly due to the humidity of the air. Skin resistance has a lot to do with dissipating charges. The resistance of your skin might be as little as 1,000 ohms when wet and 500,000 ohms when dry. (Fun fact courtesy of Jearl Walker's *Flying Circus of Physics,* published by Wiley, 1977.)

You know how static electricity builds up. Static can damage chips if it creates a charge of 1000 volts or more. If a static discharge is sufficient for the average person to notice it, it's 3000 volts.

Scuffing across a shag rug in February can build up 50,000 volts. This is an electron "debt" that must be paid. The next metal item touched (because metal gives up electrons easily) pays the debt with an electric shock. If it's 50,000 volts, why don't you electrocute when you touch the metal? Fortunately, the amperage—and the power—is tiny. (Power = voltage times current.) Different materials generate more or less static. Many people think certain materials are static-prone, while others are not. As it turns out, materials have a *triboelectric value.* Two materials rubbed together will generate static in direct proportion to how far apart their triboelectric values are.

Some common materials, in order of their triboelectric values, are:

Air	Cotton
Human Skin	Steel
Asbestos	Wood
Rabbit Fur	Hard Rubber
Glass	Nickel and Copper
Human Hair	Brass and Silver
Nylon	Gold and Platinum
Wool	Acetate and Rayon
Fur	Polyester
Lead	Polyurethane
Silk	Polyvinyl Chloride
Aluminum	Silicon
Paper	Teflon

Source: Robert Brenner, *IBM PC Troubleshooting and Repair Guide* (Howard Sams, 1985).

Once an item is charged, the voltage potential between it and another object is proportional to the distance between it and the other item on the table. For instance, suppose you charged a glass rod with a cotton cloth. The glass would attract things below it on the scale, like paper, and would attract even more forcefully things below paper.

Why does static damage PC components? The chips that largely comprise circuit boards are devices that can be damaged by high voltage, even at low current. The two most common families of chips are CMOS (Complementary Metal Oxide Semiconductor) and TTL (Transistor-Transistor Logic). TTLs are an older family that is faster switching—potentially faster chips (memories, CPUs, and such) could be designed with TTL. But TTL has a fatal flaw: It draws a lot of juice. TTL chips need much more electricity than CMOS chips, so they create more heat. So, while fast TTLs could be constructed, CPUs are tough because densely packed TTLs produce so much heat that they destroy themselves. (The 8088 is TTL inside, but the 80386 is CMOS.) One common family of TTL chips has ID numbers starting with 74, as in 7400, 7446, 74LS128, and the like. Actually, the *LS* in the middle of the ID means it's a variant on TTL called Low-power Schottky.

CPUs and memories are CMOS chips generally. CMOS has a lower theoretical maximum speed, but it runs on a lot less power. Sadly, that also means it's more subject to static electricity problems. TTL chips can withstand considerably more static than CMOS chips. CMOS chips can be destroyed by as little as 250 volts. Even if static doesn't destroy a chip, it could shorten its life. Static is, then, something to be avoided if possible.

Another effect occurs when the static is discharged. When the fat blue spark jumps from your finger to the doorknob, a small *ElectroMagnetic Pulse (EMP)* is created. This is the thing you've heard about that could cause a single nuclear explosion to destroy every computer in the country, except a lot smaller. It isn't too good for chips, either. I discharge my static buildup on something metal other than the computer's case. A metal desk or table leg is good. (A number of articles and books say, "Touch the case of the power supply." You *can* do this, but I prefer to use a table leg. The reason is simple: If I'm going to create an EMP, I want it as far from the chips in the PC as possible. The way these effects work, if you double the distance from the discharge to the PC, you divide its effects by *four*. By the way, touching the case of the power supply only makes sense if it's plugged in.)

For your computer, however, you might want something a trifle more automatic. The options are:

- Raise the humidity with an evaporative humidifier—ultrasonic ones create dust.
- Raise the humidity with plants, or perhaps an aquarium.
- Install static-free carpet.
- Put antistatic "touch me" mats under the PCs.
- Make your own antistatic spray (see below).

From the comfort point of view, I recommend the first option strongly. Your employees don't feel dried-out, and the static problem disappears. Raise humidity to just 50 percent and the problem will go away.

You can make inexpensive, homemade antistatic spray. Just get a spray pump bottle and put about an inch of fabric softener in it. Fill it the rest of the way with water, shake it up, and you've got a spray for your carpets to reduce static. Just spritz it on the rug; the rug will smell nice, and everyone will know you've been busy.

In a similar vein, a person from a temporary services agency once told me they tell their word processing operators to put a Bounce sheet under the keyboard to reduce static.

Technicians who must work with semiconductors all the time use a *ground strap* to minimize ESD. The idea with a ground strap is that you never create a spark (and therefore EMP) because you've always got a nice ground connection that's draining off your charges. A good ground strap is an elastic wristband with a metal plate built into it to provide good electrical connection, attached to a wire with an alligator clip. You put the clip on something grounded—the power supply case is the most common place—and fasten the strap around your wrist. Since you're connected to a ground, you continuously drain off your charges. A resistor in the ground strap slows down the discharge process a bit (from a microsecond to a few milliseconds), so you don't end up with one of the dangerous sparks we've discussed before. If you do a lot of board work in a dry place, ground straps are essential.

When you *must* handle electronic components, use these precautions:

- Reduce the amount of static you transfer to a chip with a ground strap, or remember the high-tech equivalent of knocking wood—touch unpainted metal periodically. One member of my staff has suggested to only handle chips while naked on a wooden floor. This would be an effective measure, provided your work environment is compatible with it.

- Don't handle components in areas having high static potential. For example, avoid carpets (unless they're antistatic) or low humidity environments. Don't wear an acrylic sweater when changing chips. Get leather-soled shoes. If your work environment allows it, you really can avoid static by removing your shoes and socks.
- Don't handle chips any more than necessary. If you don't touch them, you won't hurt them.
- Use the antistatic protective tubes and bags to transport and store chips.
- If possible, pick up components by their bodies. Don't touch the pins any more than is necessary.

Avoiding Water and Liquids

Water is an easier hazard to detect and avoid. You don't need any sophisticated detection devices. Shielding is unnecessary; you just keep the computer away from water.

Water and liquids are introduced into a computer system in one of several ways:

- Operator spills
- Leaks
- Flooding

Spills generally threaten the keyboard. One remedy recommended by every article and book I've ever read on maintenance is to forbid liquids near the computer. In most shops, this is unrealistic. Some people use clear flexible plastic covers on the keyboard, similar to ones Burger King uses on their cash registers. They're normal cash registers, but they have a plastic skin over them that allows the user to spill "special sauce" all over the cash register without harming it. With the plastic covers, they can just hose down the register. With a plastic cover, you could just hose down the keyboard. (Just kidding.)

SafeSkin is offered by Merritt Computer Products:

SafeSkin ($29.95)
Merritt Computer Products, Inc.
5565 Redbird Center Dr. Suite 150
Dallas, TX 75237
(214) 339-0753

They offer versions for the various odd keyboards in the PC world. On the other hand, should someone spill a Coke in a keyboard without one of these covers, all isn't lost so long as you act quickly! Disconnect the keyboard and flush it out at a nearby sink. Let it dry *thoroughly*, and it'll be good as new.

A similar disaster, flooding, sometimes occurs. Don't assume that flooded components are destroyed components. Disassemble the computer, clean the boards, and clean the contacts and edge connectors. You can buy connector cleaner fluids, or some people use a hard white artist's eraser. Do not use pencil erasers; a Texas Instruments study showed they contain acids that do more harm than good to connectors. Blow out crevices with compressed air. (If you *do* disassemble, clean, dry, and reassemble your computer, and find that it works, write the manufacturer a letter. They might put your face in an advertisement!)

Avoid floods by thinking ahead. Don't store any electrical devices directly on the floor where they'll be damaged when the floor is cleaned. Generally, flooding indoors is less than six inches deep. Be aware of flooding from improper roofing. When installing PCs, don't put one under the suspicious stain on the ceiling ("Oh, that—it was fixed two years ago. No problem now.").

Corrosion. Liquids (and gases) can accelerate corrosion of PCs and PC components. Corrosive agents include:

- Salt sweat in skin oils
- Water
- Airborne sulfuric acid, salt spray, carbonic acid

Your fear here isn't that the PC will fall away to rust. The largest problem corrosion causes is oxidation of circuit contacts. When a device's connector becomes oxidized, it doesn't conduct as well, and so the device doesn't function, or worse, malfunctions sporadically. Salt in sweat can do this, so be careful when handling circuit boards; don't touch edge connectors unless you have to. This is why some firms advertise that they use gold edge connectors: Gold is resistant to corrosion.

You don't believe you have detectable traces of finger oils? Try this simple experiment. Pour a glass of soda or beer into a very clean glass —preferably a plastic cup that has never been used before. There will be a noticeable "head" on the drink. (Diet soda seems particularly fizzy.) Now put your finger into the center of the head, just for a second. The head will rapidly dissolve, as the oils damage the surface tension required to support the head.

Carbonated liquids have carbonic acid, and coffee and tea contain tannic acids. The sugar in soda is eaten by bacteria that leave behind conductive excrement—like hiring some germs to put new traces on your circuit board. Generally, try to be very careful with drinks around computers.

Don't forget cleaning fluids. Be care-ful with that window cleaner you're using to keep the display clean. If your AT is on a pedestal on the floor, and the floor is mopped each day, some of the mopping liquid gets into the AT. Cleaning fluids are *very* corrosive.

Summary: Making the Environment "PC Friendly"

- Check power considerations (see Chapter 10, "Power Supplies and Power Protection."):
  - No heating elements (Mr. Coffee, portable heaters) in the same outlet as a PC.
  - No large electric motors (refrigerators, air conditioners) on the same line as the PC.
  - Some kind of power noise protection.
- Temperature ranges:
  - Maximum 110 F. (43 C.)
  - Minimum 65 F. (18 C.) This can be considerably lower as long as the computer remains *on* all the time.
- Control heavy dust. You can buy (from PC Power and Cooling) power supplies with a filtered fan that sucks in air through the *back*, rather than the usual approach of pulling it in through the front.
- Make sure there isn't a vibration source like an impact printer on the same table as the hard disk.
- Teach your users about:
  - Parking hard disks
  - Leaving the machines on all the time
  - Keeping cables screwed in and out of the way
  - Basic "don't do this" things in DOS, like formatting the hard disk
- Protect against static electricity.

A Sample Preventive Maintenance Program

While this chapter has discussed some PM concerns, I've mainly talked about environmental problems PCs face. The fact is, if you're a PC support person, you're probably too overworked to do actual preventive maintenance.

PM implies that you take a machine off a person's desk at regular intervals, perhaps as often as every six months, and move it to your "shop" to give it a good going-over so you can anticipate problems.

If you actually have the support staff to do this, here's the PM procedure I use. If you have only one machine, it's particularly important. These steps should take about two hours. Some of these things won't make sense yet, as they're discussed in later chapters. Don't worry about that. It will become clear once you've seen the rest of the book. I just wanted to collect the advice all in one place.

1. Pick up the PC at its worksite. Yes, this takes more time than if you have it delivered to your workplace, but you'll learn a lot. Examine:
   a) Are the connectors screwed in?
   b) Have screws disappeared from the back of the machine?
   c) What else is plugged into the PC's outlet? No Mr. Coffees?
   d) Is the PC on a rickety table?
   e) Is the PC near a window? Is it a direction that can get direct sun at some point in the day?
2. Ask if the machine is doing anything strange.
3. Ensure that the hard disk (if any) is backed up.
4. Park the hard disk and take the machine back to your shop.
5. Run the machine's diagnostics
6. Examine AUTOEXEC.BAT and CONFIG.SYS for any obvious problems—lack of BUFFERS command, for example.
7. Repark the head.
8. Disassemble the PC.
9. Clean the edge connectors with a connector cleaner and a lint-free cloth or a hard white artist's eraser.
10. Push the chips back into their sockets (discussed in the next chapter).
11. Use canned air to remove dust from circuit boards—don't forget the circuit board under the hard disk.
12. Reassemble the PC. Ensure that all of the cables are securely in place.
13. Rerun the diagnostics.
14. Ensure that all screws are present. If they're not, add screws.
15. Low-level format the hard disk with a nondestructive reformatter program like HOPTIMUM (Kolod Reasearch, *SpinRite* (Gibson Research), OPTUNE, or the like. (We'll discuss this in greater detail in the hard disk chapters.)

Chapter 6

Troubleshooting Problems: What to Do When Something Goes Wrong

Okay, suppose you dust out your PC fortnightly. You clean and adjust your disk drives semiannually. You have a robot that shoots anyone carrying food or drink who comes within 50 feet of your PC. But, one day, *WordPerfect* refuses to print your purple prose. How do you proceed?

General Troubleshooting Rules

These rules have kept me out of trouble for a long time. I know they'll be of use to you.

The answer to the question atop the page—"How do you proceed?"—is the topic of this chapter. I want very much to instill in you a philosophy of trouble-shooting, a philosophy built after much trial and even more error.

You've got to have confidence in yourself as a troubleshooter. Look, this stuff isn't that hard. My technical training is as a Ph.D. economist, I've got ten thumbs, and people pay *me* to fix machines—you can do it too. There's not that much to these machines. When it comes right down to it, the only thing you really can't replace for (at most) a hundred dollars or so is your data, and you can protect that with frequent back-ups.

If you don't go in there *knowing* you're going to win, you're going to get beaten—these machines can *smell* fear.

The Rules of Troubleshooting Almost Anything

Don't Panic
You Will Win
Write Everything Down
Do the Easy Stuff First
Reboot and Try Again
Remove Memory-Resident Programs
Draw a Picture

Separate the Problem into Components and Test Components
Never Guess
Trust No One: Documentation Sometimes Lies
Observe like Sherlock Holmes
Wish for Luck

My girlfriend, a black belt in Tae Kwon Do, tells me that an important tenet of that discipline is to "have an indomitable spirit." Sounds good to me—practice some Tech Kwon Do, and don't forget that indomitable spirit.

Your computer is affected by fluctuations in the power supply of a duration as brief as four milliseconds. That means if your power disappeared for only 1/200 of a second, you wouldn't see the lights flicker, the microwave would still work, and the TV wouldn't skip a beat—but several bytes of your computer's memory (not a lot of the memory, or you'd see a memory error message of some kind) would get randomized. The result is that a program that has always worked pretty well all of a sudden stops dead. You'll never find out why it locked up that one time in a thousand. Maybe everybody in the building was running their photocopiers at the same time. Maybe radiation from a solar storm assaulted your memory chips. It doesn't matter. The quick answer to this problem is just to start over.

Now, don't get too trigger-happy with the reboot if you're in the middle of an application. Try everything you can to make the machine respond and let you get back to DOS. If you reboot in the middle of an application, the application may have left files open, and any such files will be lost if you reboot before the application has closed them. (Such half-finished files lead to a phenomenon you might have seen called *lost clusters;* more on that in the hard disk chapters.) Memory-resident, or *TSR,* programs can interfere with system functions. It might just be that your drive E won't format because you've got your LAN software loaded. Don't ask me why—just try it. Remove all those pop-ups by rebooting without them, and see if the problem goes away. Software troubleshooting is just like hardware troubleshooting: Divide and conquer. Each piece of software you're running is a piece of the system, and you want to minimize the number of pieces you have to deal with. TSRs are the easiest part to remove.

I am, by nature, a lazy person. That's why I got interested in computers: they were machines that could free me from some drudgery. The *inexperienced* and lazy troubleshooter tries to save time by not making notes, by acting before thinking, and *swapping* when he ought to be *stopping.* . .to consider his next move.

What I've eventually figured out is that well-planned laziness is a virtue. An *experienced* lazy person looks ahead and says, "Oh, heck, what if I can't fix this thing? I don't want to create any more trouble for myself than necessary." So the lazy person keeps diagrams and writes down every action, to prevent tearing out hair while trying to put the thing back together.

The experienced lazy person does the easy stuff first. If it's a video, not a software, problem, there are four things that can be swapped: the motherboard, the video board, the cable, or the monitor. What gets swapped first? The easy thing does: the cable. I know a nonlazy troubleshooting type who was called one day about a *WordPerfect* problem:

"Mike (not his real name)," the caller said, "*WordPerfect* isn't printing with the new laser printer!"

Now, the experienced lazy person listens and says, "Gosh, how can I fix this without leaving my chair?" Personally, I'd zero in on the word *new* before laser printer. My next question would be something like, "What kind of printer did you have before the new laser printer?" (It probably was a daisy wheel.) "Have you ever seen *WordPerfect* print on this laser printer before?'' (Probably not.) "Have you reinstalled *WordPerfect* for the laser printer?'' (A confused "What?" is the most likely answer.)

Mike, on the other hand, attacked the problem by first swapping the motherboard on the PC that was attached to the laser printer. Yeah, yeah, we could observe that Mike's, umm, shall we say, "a couple sandwiches short of a picnic" when it comes to troubleshooting. But I see people do less extreme, but just as unnecessary, things all the time. Heck, I still do a lot of dumb things myself, like playing Macho Man with a screwdriver. But I hope to get better at remembering to be lazy when troubleshooting.

When you open up a machine, you expose the machine to a certain risk that you'll do something dumb to it. PC troubleshooting differs from, say, automotive troubleshooting in that the thing that's most commonly broken is the user. If you separate out the "broken user" stuff, like forgetting to turn it on and so forth, software is the next most common problem. Honest-to-God hardware problems are actually quite uncommon compared to user and software problems, which leads me to the seven specific troubleshooting steps.

Troubleshooting Steps

The lazy person makes the troubleshooting job tractable by breaking down problems into steps. Don't panic, be methodical, or you'll thrash helplessly about and get frustrated. Once you're frustrated, you're lost, and you start creating new problems.

Following is the method I use. It looks a lot like methods suggested by other people, but it's not the only method. You certainly don't have to use my method, but find one you like and stick to it. It's the "this will only take five minutes" repairs that get me in trouble.

(It's like when someone giving you directions says, "You can't miss it." You *know* you're in trouble then.) I'll assume for this discussion that you're interacting with someone else (the person with the PC problem), but you could just as easily interview yourself.

Before opening up the computer, do the following:

1. Check the nut behind the keyboard.
2. Check that everything is plugged in: power, monitor, phone lines, printer, modem, and so on.
3. Check the software.
4. Ask, "What am I doing differently?"
5. Check external signs, and make notes of them.
6. Run the diagnostics diskette.
   Only then, if you still haven't solved the problem,
7. Disassemble the machine, push the socketed chips back into their sockets, clean the connectors, and put the machine back together.

Check for Operator Error

Operator error is responsible for 93.3 percent of PC failures. (That's a made-up statistic, but it got your attention and probably isn't far from the truth.) There are lots of things an operator can do wrong. For example, when I used to teach hands-on *dBase III+* classes, I'd regularly see students looking bewildered at the screen, saying, "It didn't work." I'd ask, "Did you type in exactly what I told you to?" "Yes," they would reply. I'd look at the screen. Indeed, they did type in exactly what I told them to *this time*. Several commands back, however, they miskeyed something and ignored the resulting error message. These are intelligent people, they were just under some stress (having to pay attention to me *and* the computer), and they missed a detail. It's easy to do.

The language of computers confuses people. You've heard the stories about users doing goofy things: They're true. I've seen them. I once watched a user follow the *dBase III* 1.0 installation instructions to "Insert System Disk 1 in drive A and close the door." After inserting the disk in the drive, the user then got up (looking a little puzzled, I'll admit) and closed the door to the office. If I hadn't actually been there to see it, I probably wouldn't have believed it.

When teaching those same *dBase* classes, now and then I'd get this problem. A student was staring at the keyboard in puzzlement.

"What's wrong?" I asked.

"I'm looking for a key," he replied.

"Which one—I'll point it out," I offered.

"The 'any' key," he said, still puzzled. I looked at the screen. *dBase* was prompting, "Press any key to continue. . ." I had just finished my "pay attention to what the computer is doing" lecture, so this poor soul was trying his hardest to follow my directions. (Nowadays, there's an answer for the "any key" searchers. Egghead Discount Software sells an "any key" kit. It's a keytop sticker that says *ANY KEY*. You install it on, well, any key.)

Even worse, sometimes users will (horrors!) prevaricate slightly. "I didn't do anything. It just stopped working." Please note: I'm not one of those techie types whose motto is, "Assume the user is lying," but sometimes it happens. More often, it's not that they lie; they just don't know what's important.

People feel defensive calling a support person. You want to collect as much information as possible. If you make them feel defensive, they'll remember incorrectly or withhold information. Here's a trick telemarketers are told:

Smile when you're on the phone with someone. It works. (As Sam Kinnison says, "It creates the illusion that you care.") Being a support person can be wearing. There's a great tendency to feel that "these people must get up early in the morning to think up dumb things to ask," but you can't let it get you down. Remember, these folks can't be too dumb; after all, the same company that hired them hired you, too.

Another source of operator error is inexperience. The PC isn't the simplest thing in the world to master. The author of a book titled *Computer Wimp: 100 Things I Wish I'd Known Before I Bought My First Personal Computer* observes in that book that learning to use a computer system can be the most difficult learning endeavor a person can undertake in his or her post-school life. (Things like raising kids are undoubtedly tougher, but they're different kinds of learning experiences.) It doesn't take a genius to recognize that most PC hardware and software manuals aren't the easiest things to comprehend.

Is Everything Plugged In?

I know this sounds stupid, but we've all done it. A friend bought a Hayes Smartmodem 2400 and couldn't get it to work. It accepted commands all right but couldn't dial out. The phone line was tested with a regular phone and it worked fine. He was quite puzzled until he realized that he'd plugged the phone line into the *out* jack in the modem (intended to be connected to a phone line that would be shared between the modem and a phone), rather than the *in* jack. Another time, I ran the IBM diagnostic disk on my PC and kept getting *bad address mark* errors on my disk drives. I was all set to spend a lot of money for new drives until I realized that the scratch diskette I was using wasn't formatted. (The drives were fine.)

When you ask the user, "Is it plugged in?," be diplomatic. (Don't you hate when tech support people ask *you* that question?) But be firm.

- Is the PC plugged into some kind of multi outlet strip?
- Is the strip on? Did the user kick off the power switch?
- Can the user actually see that the power strip is plugged into the wall?
- Is the outlet on the wall switched?

I know of a large communications company that kept sending technicians to try to determine why a LAN server kept dying at strange hours of the night. They would set up the software at the user site, leave it running, and then eventually get called back to the site because, after a day or two, all kinds of files had been trashed. The techs would always ask, "Has this been turned off in the middle of an operation?" The users would shake their heads "no" solemnly and with annoyance—this tech guy wasn't going to weasel out of fixing the company's buggy software *that* easily, they thought. Finally this large company sent their SuperTech—the guy who'd seen it all. He looked over the server and listened to the users' story.

Now, this guy *knew* from the symptoms that the server was getting shut down improperly. So he looked for easy ways to turn the machine off accidentally. Noticing two light switches on the wall and only one fluorescent ceiling panel, he flipped both switches. You guessed it—the server was plugged into a switched outlet. The security staff, in making the rounds each night, was shutting off the lights.

- Are the peripherals plugged in? Are they plugged *into the computer?*

Not only is everything plugged in, but is everything in *tight*? Multiple-pin connectors slowly bend under gravity unless the mounting screws are tightened. As someone stretches his or her legs under the desk, a loose power cord can be moved enough to disconnect it, or to disconnect and reconnect it. Connectors on the floor take a lot of abuse.

Check the Software

Software problems arrive in several guises:

- Operator error
- Keyboard/screen/disk/timer conflicts with memory-resident software
- Software that doesn't clean up after itself
- Software that requires hardware that isn't connected or activated
- Buggy software

Memory Resident (TSR) Problems

Memory-resident software, like *SideKick, Metro, Prokey, Superkey,* and others are great. You don't have to exit *dBase* or *WordPerfect* to do a simple calculation, make a note, or enter an appointment in an electronic calendar. Just press a particular key combination and *SideKick* pops up. You do your work, then press Escape, and *SideKick* goes back to sleep. And those are just a few uses.

At least, that's the way it's supposed to work. Often it doesn't, however. Sometimes you press the key combination and the PC goes to sleep.

TSR programs are programs that load themselves into the system and then go to sleep and return control of the system to the user, *without removing themselves from memory.* They remain dormant until an outside condition of some kind wakes them up. They can be activated either by the timer that's built into the system or by some kind of device access (disk access, a keystroke, or certain characters being printed or displayed on screen).

Common kinds of TSR programs:

- Screen blankers. Called by the timer and lack of keystrokes, these programs shut down the video when the machine is waiting for the user.
- Popups like *SideKick* add some useful features like a phonebook or calculator to the system, making it available at any time. They're awakened by special keystrokes.
- Disk cache programs (covered later) silently monitor disk activity and try to anticipate what file the user will want next. They then preload the data from that file so the disk seems blindingly fast. They're invoked by disk activity.
- 3270 emulation and LAN programs. These must handle communications in the background. If they get busy, or try to get busy when the system is in the middle of something else, they can bring things to a grinding halt.
- Viruses are memory-resident programs that sit inside the system, sometimes waking with each disk access or timer tick, waiting for the right moment to do whatever their job might be. (Most likely that job is something destructive, although some viruses have been benign, just displaying messages of some political import.)

The problem arises because the software is awakened by some event like a keystroke or the timer. What happens if *two* different TSRs coexist in the system, and both try to monitor the keyboard, or the timer, or the disks? Often they can confuse each other, causing the system to either crash or misbehave. (For example, the disk cache program I used three years ago "misbehaved." Now and then it would lead the disk to tell me it had saved a file, when in actuality it had done nothing of the kind. Needless to say, I dumped that program pretty quickly.)

When odd things occur, software-wise, memory-resident applications are the first suspect. Reboot without the memory residents and try the operation again. (That's how I narrowed the problem down to the cache program.) If the problem goes away, try to reproduce the software failure and contact the manufacturer (see Chapter 21). Sometimes you can rearrange the "hot" keys in memory-resident applications. Other times rearranging the order in which you load memory residents solves the problem. When you find a workaround, make a note of it so you and your successors can save time later.

These conflicts are a major reason for OS/2, the new PC operating system. OS/2 creates multiple *virtual* PCs, each running a separate program. A program like *SideKick,* then, thinks it has its own machine and doesn't conflict with *WordPerfect*'s ability to get to the keyboard. This presumes that *SideKick* is written to play by the rules OS/2 lays down. Virtually no one played by the PC-DOS rules. How well OS/2 rules will be followed, only time will tell.

Poorly Terminated Software. Most software is fairly careful to restore your PC to its original state when it ends. Some, on the other hand, aren't so careful. Most software effects are fairly innocuous, like leaving the background of your display blue and the foreground yellow. The simple DOS command MODE BW80 will fix that. Perhaps you have both a color display and a monochrome display, and the software has left you in the color display: MODE MONO will fix that. Occasionally, software will disable Ctrl–Alt–Del (*Flight Simulator* is one example) or set the disk drives to nonstandard parameters. The only option then might be the big red switch or a soft reboot. (See Chapter 23 to see how to install a switch to do hardware resets.)

Other programs can leave a peripheral in a strange state. *DisplayWrite 4*, for example, doesn't reset the printer before terminating, so the printer could still be printing Times Roman when you try to print a DIR.

Hardware-Related Software Faults. For a while, you occasionally saw people writing in to computer magazines about a mysterious bug in the original Compaq Portable. For no reason at all, it would sometimes freeze up, and nothing would save it. Eventually the computer world figured out that the problem was sloppy fingers on the part of the operator.

The Compaq, like all PC compatibles and clones, has a PrtSc (print screen) key. Pressing Shift and PrtSc sends an image of the screen to the printer. If a printer isn't present, a PC does several retries and finally decides there's no printer attached. This is called *timing out*. The PC doesn't wait very long—just a few seconds. The Compaq, on the other hand, waits quite a long time. Thus, when the stray finger pressed Shift-PrtSc, the computer would wait and wait and wait for a printer to be attached. Actually, had the user waited a long enough, the computer would have come back.

A number of mysteries can be linked to software that doesn't recover well from disabled or nonexistent hardware:

- Trying to print to a nonexistent printer
- Trying to print to an Epson printer when a C. Itoh printer is attached

- Trying to print to a printer that is off line
- Trying to display graphics data on a monochrome monitor
- Running a program that assumes (generally for copy protection) that the PC is 4.77 Mhz speed, or that the floppy drive has 41 tracks
- Running a program that needs more memory than the PC contains

But here's my favorite hardware-induced software error. The PS/2s insist on being properly configured before they'll do any work for you. If they're configured wrong—if they boot up and find they have more or less memory than they expected, or more or fewer disk drives, or the like —they print a 162 error on the screen and wait patiently for an F1 to continue.

If you have an external floppy disk drive on a PS/2, it has its own power supply and power switch. If you forget to turn on the external floppy before booting up the PS/2, you'll get a scary-looking 162 error. Just turn the floppy drive on and reboot. Do *not* rerun the configuration program found on the Reference Diskette: Assuming the floppy is still off, it will sense there isn't an external floppy anymore and stop looking for it. Then when you do turn the external floppy on, the PS/2 won't talk to it. Argggh. (By the way, there are a number of PS/2 motherboards floating around that just plain won't hold a configuration for very long—that's another problem altogether.)

Faulty Software. Sometimes the problem is buggy software. Even the most popular programs can misbehave when faced with a full disk, insufficient memory, or some other situation the designer didn't anticipate or test.

Try to make the bug reproducible. If it's a suspected bug in a compiler product, trim off as much of the other code as possible while retaining the bug. Ideally, a program no longer than ten lines of code should demonstrate the problem. Then report it to the manufacturer and other users in your company.

What Am I Doing Differently?

When I worked in a large programming shop, junior people would often come to me for diagnostic advice on their code.

"This code worked before, but it doesn't now." "What did you change?" I'd ask. "Nothing," they usually replied. "Then why did you run it again?" I wondered.

There *has* to be something different. Otherwise, why are you running the software? Was some code changed? New data? A new machine? It's the first place to look. Did you add a memory board? Some early PC programs (Infocom games and early *WordStar*, in particular) would refuse to run if more than 512K memory was in the PC. "Illegal Operation," the Infocom games would complain, and reboot the PC. *WordStar* would say you didn't have *enough* memory! You'd think that adding memory couldn't cause problems, particularly if you had already checked the memory and found it error-free. In the case of the Infocom games, "Illegal Operation" isn't much of a hint about what's wrong. I barked up a lot of trees until I went back and examined the single change to the system: a memory upgrade.

If you have a problem like that, you've got to convince your system that it has less memory than it actually does. Probably the easiest way to do that is to load a VDISK of some size. *VDISK.SYS* is a program that comes with DOS. It fools your system into thinking some of your memory is in fact a very fast floppy disk. In the process, however, it steals that memory from DOS programs. Create a 256K VDISK on your 640K machine, and you end up with only 640K − 256K =

384K space for programs. You install it in your CONFIG.SYS like so:

device = vdisk.sys nnn

where *nnn* is the size of the VDISK. So, in my *WordStar* situation, I just ran a VDISK of 128K to bring the system memory down to 512K and then ran *WordStar*— no problem. By the way, both *WordStar* and Infocom have resolved these problems.

Hardware upgrades can conflict. Suppose, for example, you install an Intel AboveBoard paged memory board and a 3Com LAN board in the same PC. (This example isn't based on actual experienced problems. The boards were arbitrarily picked for the purposes of example.) Suppose the AboveBoard uses the same memory window as the LAN board. Most of the time, the AboveBoard is inactive: it's only called into action when you're working on a spreadsheet too large to fit into 640K. The LAN board, on the other hand, is used periodically to store and retrieve data, and to receive electronic mail. The user boots up alright, sees that the LAN works fine, and then starts working on *Lotus*. As long as the spreadsheet is small, there's no problem. Then the spreadsheet gets larger, and the spreadsheet program begins using the AboveBoard memory. Still no problem. *Then* disaster strikes: someone sends an electronic mail message. The LAN and the AboveBoard are active at the same time, and either the system freezes up, the LAN goes south, the spreadsheet is minced, or some combination of the above problems occurs.

Software upgrades can bring problems. Perhaps an application running under DOS 2.1 has just barely enough memory space to run: the extra 20-odd kilobytes required by DOS 3.2 makes it unable to work. A macro that required three minutes to run under version 2 of some spreadsheet might take two hours or not run at all under version 3.

One final story in this section. I was working with an early copy of OS/2 on a 386 clone. I hadn't booted OS/2 in several days, and I needed to get into OS/2 to run a program. I tried to boot, but I got a very scary looking error message. I tried again—no luck. I spent four hours (very late at night) swapping memory chips. No luck. Then I remembered I had enabled the video card's autoswitch capability the day before to run a DOS program. That couldn't be the problem, could it? But just in case. . .I flipped the switch back and tried again. Five minutes later, OS/2 was running my program, and I was kicking myself.

Check External Signs

If the computer has indicator lights, what do they indicate? Are all of the lights glowing on the modem? Does the printer indicate "ready?" Is the hard disk squealing or grinding? Does the monitor image look bent? Your drives and other peripherals produce hums, whirs, and clicks. After a while, these noises become familiar, and any variation in them signals a problem. Pay attention to these signs.

The first step in successful troubleshooting is in isolating the problem component. These signs may point the way.

It's very important to note any signs here. Note what lights are on and off, the positions of switches, and so on.

Run Diagnostic Programs

The IBM PC and AT come with diagnostic programs that can help pinpoint the problem (assuming, of course, that the computer is well enough to run them in the first place). Other computers do not. Various public domain diagnostic programs exist.

If you feel like spending money, third-party vendors make diagnostic products:

SuperSoft Service Diagnostics
$225 for 8088/8086-based PCs, $225 for 80286-based PCs
PO Box 1628
Champaign, IL 61820

Windsor Technologies, Inc.
PC-Technician
130 Alto Street
San Rafael, CA 94901
(415) 456-2200

PC-Technician runs on any clone or compatible; machine specific versions are available. Alternatively, IBM offers their Advanced Diagnostics for $175.

Truthfully, the programs aren't so valuable to locate errors. They mainly make you feel confident that there's nothing wrong with the PC. After all, what must be running in order to run these programs? Well, the system board must be running, the video must be working so you can see the screen, the keyboard must be active to accept commands, and the floppy must be able to load the program. So merely loading the diagnostic program (or any other program, for that matter) tells you some things about the system. When I talk to vendors I question the value (in a nice way, of course) of their software.

"Some of what you say is true, of course," admitted one author. "But to boot DOS requires over 64K of memory. Our program is self-booting and its first section loads in less than 16K of memory. That means that, in a case where you had a memory error between the first 16K and the first 64K, DOS would lock up when you tried to boot, but our diagnostic could run. Besides, the big value of a program like this is that a technician can go to a strange machine and get an overview checkup of the machine fairly quickly." So there you have the other side of the issue.

Running the IBM Diagnostic Programs. The IBM diagnostic disk is a bootable disk; put it in drive A and then reboot the system. It uses a simpler version of COMMAND.COM, so don't put it directly on your hard disk. This text won't dwell on running the diagnostic disk, as it's pretty simple—all menu driven. The IBM manual lacks some information on interpreting error codes, however, so a table of diagnostic error codes are presented in the section called "IBM Diagnostic Error Codes," later in this chapter.

For PS/2 50, 55, 60, 70, 75, 80, and 90 owners, there is hidden on the Reference Diskette a set of Advanced Diagnostics. If you buy the Advanced Diagnostics from IBM, you only get a (generally unnecessary) manual for $500. The program is activated from the Reference Diskette's Main Menu with the Ctrl-A key sequence. Just boot from the Reference Diskette, wait for the Main Menu to appear, and press Ctrl-A (*A* for *Advanced*).

The Power On Self Test (POST). One short diagnostic routine runs on the PC every time the PC is powered up. It does a memory test and checks to see that the basic important hardware exists. It's called the *POST*—Power-On Self Test, or, in the BIOS listing, *POD* (Power-On Diagnostics). The documentation given with the PC (at least, the documentation given with my PC) doesn't explain the error codes. Hopefully, you'll never see them. If you do, however, you'll want to know what they mean. They're shown in the section called "IBM Diagnostic Error Codes," later in this chapter.

The following description is taken from my reading of the assembly language listing for the PC-1 BIOS. It varies slightly for the AT and later PCs.

1. POST tests the 8088: registers and flags. If it fails, the system just halts.
2. POST computes and checks a checksum for the ROM. If it fails, the system just halts.
3. POST checks the DMA (Direct Memory Access) Controller, the 8237. If it fails, the system just halts.
4. Tests the 8259 interrupt controller. If it fails, the system does a long beep and a short beep, then halts.
5. Tests the 8253 timer: Is it running at the right speed? If it's not, the system does a long beep and a short beep. The code actually jumps to the same point as for the error message for the 8259, above. This is unfortunate, as it would have been nice if IBM could have added eight more bytes of code so the 8253 could have a different error message from the 8259.
6. Performs a checksum test on the BASIC ROM. If the ROM fails, there's long and short beep and halt. Again, this is a bit shortsighted. We can live without BASIC, so locking up the computer seems extreme.
7. Tests the video. If the 6845 video controller isn't present (which either means no video card or a defective 6845), one long beep and two shorts.
8. Asks installed adapters if they must initialize themselves. Common examples are hard disk controllers, EGA, and LAN adapters. If the boards respond *yes*, lets them initialize. When they finish, returns to BIOS startup.
9. Tests the CRT interface lines. If horizontal and vertical sweep don't appear, two longs and a short. If everything is okay, blinks the cursor on the PC.

10. Tests the memory and all system RAM.
11. Tests the keyboard. Stuck keys are detected here. Any keyboard problems are indicated by a 301 code on the screen followed by a short beep. The system is not halted.
12. Tests the cassette interface. If there are problems, shows code 131 and a short beep. Doesn't halt system.
13. Tests diskette adapter and drive A. Attempts to reset the drive and activate the drive motor. If problems appear, shows code 601 and does a short beep. Goes to Cassette BASIC.
14. Determines how many printers, serial ports, game ports, and so on are attached. Issues a short beep, loads the boot record, and transfers control to it.

ROM-Based Diagnostics. Some firms (Supersoft and Windsor Technology, in particular) offer a diagnostic tool that works even when the system won't boot. Such a tool is called a *ROM-based diagnostic.* Generally, you remove the BIOS ROM and replace it with a "miniboard" containing a ROM and some support electronics. This mini-board allows the diagnostic to boot the system and do chip-specific tests; it costs about $300. Separate ROMs are required for AT and PC class machines.

Award Software (the folks who write the AWARD BIOS some clones use) makes a plug-in diagnostic board called the "POST Card." Another company, Ultra-X, makes a similar product called RACER (Real-time AT/XT Computer Equipment Repair).

RACER $575
Ultra-X, Inc.
2118 Walsh Avenue Suite 210
Santa Clara, CA 95050

These tools are nice to have, but I'd caution anyone thinking of buying one: They're only of value if you intend to use the information they give. You have to be willing and able to remove and replace components on the system board, and here we're talking about soldering.

On the other hand, if such a tool is free, it might be handy. Zenith owners needn't hunt around for a diagnostic disk: Zenith diagnostics are built into the machine. Ctrl-Alt–Ins gets them going.

IBM Diagnostic Error Codes. Table 6-1 lists POST audio messages.

Table 6-1. POST Audio Messages

Signal	Probable Cause
No beep, nothing happens	Power supply bad or not plugged in
Continuous beep	Power supply bad
Repeating short beep	Power supply bad
1 long beep, 1 short beep	System board
1 long, 2 short beeps	Failure or lack of display adapter/cable
1 short beep, blank screen	Failure or lack of display adapter/cable
1 short beep, no boot	Floppy Drive Adapter Failure

Table 6-2. IBM Hardware Diagnostics/POST Messages

Code	Description	Code	Description
01x	Undetermined Problem Errors	4xx	Monochrome Monitor Errors
02x	Power Supply Errors	401	Adapter memory, horizontal sync frequency test, or video test failure
1xx	System Board Errors	408	User-indicated display attributes failure
101	Interrupt failure	416	User-indicated character set failure
102	Timer failure	424	User-indicated 80 × 25 mode failure
103	Timer interrupt failure	432	Parallel port test failed
104	Protected mode failure		
105	Last 804 command not accepted	5xx	Color Monitor Errors
106	Converting logic test	501	Color adapter memory, horizontal sync frequency test, or video test failure
107	Hot NMI test	508	User-indicated display attributes failure
108	Timer bus test	516	User-indicated character set failure
109	Direct Memory Access test error	524	User-indicated 80 × 25 mode failure
121	Unexpected hardware interrupts occurred	532	User-indicated 40 × 25 mode failure
131	Cassette wrap test failed	540	User-indicated 320 × 200 mode failure
161	AT Battery failure	548	User-indicated 640 × 200 mode failure
162	AT setup info incorrect (re-run SETUP)		
163	Time and date not set (run SETUP)	6xx	Diskette Drive/Controller Failures
164	Memory size error (run SETUP)	601	Adapter or drive failed POST
165	PS/2 does not know how to configure board	602	Diskette test failed: boot record not valid
199	User-indicated configuration not correct	606	Diskette verify function failed
		607	Write-protected diskette
2xx	Main Memory (RAM) Errors	608	Bad command diskette status returned
201	Memory test failed	610	Diskette initialize failed
202	Memory address error*	611	Timeout
203	Memory address error*	612	Bad NEC chip on diskette controller
		613	Adapter failed DMA test
3xx	Keyboard Errors	621	Bad seek
301	Keyboard error. If followed by a number, the number is the scan code of the key in question.	622	Bad CRC found
		623	Record not found
302	User-indicated error from keyboard test or AT keylock locked	624	Bad Address mark
		625	Bad NEC seek
303	Keyboard or system unit error	626	Diskette data compare error
304	CMOS doesn't match system		
		7xx	8087 or 80287 Math Coprocessor Errors

*See below how to decode these error messages

9xx	Printer Adapter Errors

Table 6-2. *continued*

Code	Description	Code	Description
1101	Asynchronous (RS232) Adapter Failure (COM1)	1532	Carrier Detect not on
		1533	Clear To Send not on
1201	Asynchronous (RS232) Adapter Failure (COM2)	1534	Data Set Read stuck on
		1536	Clear to Send stuck on
		1537	Level 3 interrupt Failure
13xx	Game Port Failure	1538	Receive interrupt results error
1301	Adapter test failed	1539	Wrap data miscompare
1302	Joystick test failed	1540	DMA channel 1 error
14xx	Printer Errors	1541	Error in 8273 error check or status reporting
1401	Printer test failed	1547	Stray interrupt level 4
1402	Dot matrix printer test failed	1548	Stray interrupt level 3
15xx	SDLC Adapter (Mainframe Connection) Failures	1549	Interrupt presentation sequence timeout
1510	Failure of 8255 port B	16xx	Terminal Emulation Errors (32xx, 5520, 525x)
1511	Failure of 8255 port A	17xx	Hard Disk/Disk Controller Errors
1512	Failure of 8255 port C	1701	POST error
1513	8253 timer 1 did not reach terminal count	1702	Adapter failure
1514	8253 timer 1 stuck on	1703	Drive failure
1515	8253 timer 0 did not reach terminal count	1704	Drive or Adapter failure: cannot be determined
1516	8253 timer 0 stuck on	1780	Drive 0 failure (drive C)
1517	8253 timer 2 did not reach terminal count	1781	Drive 1 failure (drive D)
1518	8253 timer 2 stuck on	1782	Adapter failure
1519	8273 port B error	1790	Drive 0 failure (couldn't read the LAST cylinder—probable misspecified drive)
1520	8273 port A error	1791	Drive 1 failure
1521	8273 command/read timeout		
1522	Interrupt level 4 failure	18xx	Expansion Chassis Failures
1523	Ring Indicate stuck on	1801	POST error code
1524	Receive clock stuck on	1810	Extender card failure
1525	Transmit clock stuck on	1811	Extender card failure
1526	Test Indicate stuck on	1816	Extender card failure
1527	Ring Indicate not on	1820	Receiver card failure
1528	Receive clock not on	1821	Receiver card failure
1529	Transmit clock not on	1812	Address or wait state failure
1531	Data Set Ready not on		
1530	Test Indicate not on		

89

Table 6-2. *continued*

Code	Description	Code	Description
1813	Address or wait state failure	2028	Receive clock not on
1819	Wait Request switch set incorrectly	2029	Transmit clock not on
19xx	3270 PC Communications Controller Failures	2031	Data Set Ready not on
		2030	Test Indicate not on
20xx	BSC Adapter (Mainframe Connection) Failures	2032	Carrier Detect not on
		2033	Clear To Send not on
2010	Failure of 8255 port B	2034	Data Set Read stuck on
2011	Failure of 8255 port A	2036	Clear to Send stuck on
2012	Failure of 8255 port C	2037	Level 3 interrupt failure
2013	8253 timer 1 did not reach terminal count	2038	Receive interrupt results error
2014	8253 timer 1 stuck on	2039	Wrap data miscompare
2015	8253 timer 0 did not reach terminal count	2040	DMA channel 1 error
2016	8253 timer 0 stuck on	2041	Error in 8273 error check or status reporting
2017	8253 timer 2 did not reach terminal count	2047	Stray interrupt level 4
2018	8253 timer 2 stuck on	2048	Stray interrupt level 3
2019	8273 port B error	2049	Interrupt presentation sequence timeout
2020	8273 port A error	21xx	Alternate BSC Adapter Failures
2021	8273 command/read timeout	2110– 49	Same as above, but with 21 prefix rather than 20
2022	Interrupt level 4 failure		
2023	Ring Indicate stuck on	2201	PC Wiring Cluster Adapter Failure
2024	Receive clock stuck on	2401	EGA Failure
2025	Transmit clock stuck on	2901	Color Dot Matrix Failures
2026	Test Indicate stuck on		Compact Printer Failures
2027	Ring Indicate not on		

Under The Hood: Troubleshooting Step 7

Assuming you've performed steps 1 to 6, you might actually have a circuit board problem. Many circuit board problems can be handled simply and without any fancy equipment. Step 7 just says:

- Take the PC apart
- Clean any connectors with an artist's eraser or connector cleaner
- Push all socketed chips back into their sockets
- Reassemble the PC

As we saw in Chapter 5 on preventive maintenance, edge connectors get dirty and make circuit boards fail. Sometimes "dead" boards will do the Lazarus trick if you clean their edge connectors.

If you examine most circuit boards, you'll see that most chips are soldered right onto the board. *Soldering* is a process where the chip is bonded to the printed circuits on the board by heating a mixture of tin and lead to the point where it's molten, and then allowing the tin/lead mixture to flow over the printed circuit and chip leg and finally solidify. Soldering is a great technique for mass-producing electronic components. The downside is that when you must fix soldered components, you must first desolder the components. This isn't much fun, and most people don't have soldering skills.

Not all chips are soldered to boards, however. Some are put in *sockets*. A typical board might have thirty soldered chips and four socketed ones. Chips are socketed either because they've been voted "most likely to fail;" or because the designer wanted to put off a decision till the last minute; or because the chip will likely have to be replaced periodically, because it contains software that changes over time—remember ROMs? So socketing chips makes our jobs as troubleshooters easier.

On the other hand, heating and cooling of systems make these socketed chips "creep" out their sockets, producing the *chip creep* mentioned in the last chapter. That's why you should push socketed chips back into their sockets when inspecting a board for whatever reason. One particularly persnickety tech I know actually takes the socketed chips out of their sockets, cleans their chip legs with connector cleaner, and *then* puts the chips back in the sockets.

This should be obvious, but let me point it out anyway. Don't push *soldered* chips. The best that it can do is nothing. The worst it can do is to damage a board, and maybe a chip. When you push socketed chips back into a board, be sure you're supporting the back of the board. If you just put a board on a table and

push down on the chips, you might end up bending and damaging the board.

I know advice like "take it apart, clean the connectors, push the chips back in the sockets, and reassemble" doesn't sound very dazzling, but, darn it, *it works!* Buying a board to replace a defective one is a pretty rare event for me as a troubleshooter, and I don't do much soldering. Besides, it impresses the people whose machines you're fixing; basically, all they see you do is touch the boards. Eventually, you'll get the reputation as a person who can just "lay hands upon the board and make it whole!"

Documenting Trouble Calls

If you're a professional troubleshooter (and even if you're not), one of the biggest favors you can do for yourself is to keep a log of trouble calls, problems, and solutions.

- It provides a record of your contribution to the organization.
- It can be used to justify requests for equipment or personnel.
- It allows you to track trends so you can anticipate future problems, either with particular individuals ("Mr. *X* calls us whenever he can't figure out how to turn the printer on.") or situations ("We can expect a call on files called *Y* from everyone with *WordPerfect*.").
- Documented problems and solutions can serve as an excellent training tool for new troubleshooters.

Whether you use a computerized database or just paper sheets, you should have a method for documenting trouble calls. Here are a few things that should be on each trouble report:

- Trouble report ID#
- Preliminary Information:
  - Who reported trouble?

- When was trouble reported?
- How was it reported (e-mail, phone, walk-in)?
- Related to previous trouble call? Trouble report ID#?
- Where was trouble reported?
- Specific complaint?
- Is this repeatable? Will your client be able to duplicate the problem before a technician's eyes?
- When did this first appear?
- What was done differently between before and after the problem appeared (if anything)?
- Does it occur periodically? When?

- On-site information:
  - Comments on PC environment: power, temperature, others
  - Technician's observation of trouble
  - Actions taken on-site
- If the PC was taken to the shop:
  - Date brought in
  - Actions taken
  - Result
  - PC returned to client? Date?
- Summary information/keywords:
  - Hardware, software, and/or user problem?
  - If software, what package(s)?
  - If hardware, what device(s)?

Chapter 7
Installing New Circuit Boards (Without Creating New Problems to Troubleshoot)

Circuit boards and chips are fairly reliable, so long as you keep them above water and don't subject them to the old 110 volt-torture test. Most boards you handle won't be defective boards. Much more often you'll be upgrading existing machines, like replacing a video board with a faster, more powerful one or adding a LAN board to a machine that isn't yet on your company's network.

Installing a new circuit board involves:

- Configuration. Make sure the board and the rest of the system communicate.
- Installation. Put it in the system and make sure the cables are all on correctly.
- Testing. Weed out the boards that either don't work or soon will stop working.

Installation looks scary the first time you see it, but it's really a snap once you wend your way through the terminology. Are you the kind of person who always flips past the part of the manual that talks about DMA, IRQ, ROM ad-dresses, and the like? Stick around. The concepts are easy (and essential). It's only the names that are off-putting.

Configuring New Circuit Boards

Most circuit boards are fully functional when you take them out of the box. But most circuit boards seem not to work when you install them in a PC. Why? The main reason is that the new board may *conflict* with existing boards or, more specifically, some resource on the board.

Configuration consists of:

- Resolving device conflicts
- Providing software support (BIOS and/or device drivers)

Configuration involves setting jumpers or DIP switches to select exactly what services the expansion board will provide. Typical configuration requirements:

- Tell an expansion board how much memory is on the board.
- Tell a serial port whether it's COM1: or COM2:.

DIP switches on expansion board.

- Tell a printer port whether it's LPT1, LPT2, or LPT3.
- Select DMA channels on a board (more on this later).
- Select IRQ lines on a board (more later).
- Select I/O address on a board (ditto).

In many cases, the board is preconfigured at the factory to the correct settings, but not always. It's hard for the manufacturer to know what the proper settings should be for four items: I/O addresses, DMA channels, IRQ lines, and ROM addresses.

Examples: Real-Life Configuration Conflicts. Getting down to brass tacks, here are a few examples of installation woes.

1. You install an internal modem in a PC with a floppy disk controller, color graphics board, and multifunction board. The modem refuses to work. A little testing shows that the serial port, which *used* to work, now doesn't work either. What do you do?
2. You install a multifunction board in a computer with a floppy disk con-

troller and a generic monochrome graphics card. The printer won't work. What do you do?
3. You install a Lotus/Intel/Microsoft expanded memory board in an XT, and you notice the next time you boot up that the clock/calendar has been reset to January 1, 1980. What do you do?

Each of these problems is caused by *resource conflicts*. Here's what caused them.

1. In the first case, both the serial port on the multifunction board and the modem sought to be recognized by the computer as COM1, Communications Port number 1. The basic PC can support two serial ports, named COM1 and COM2. A circuit board can call itself COM1 or COM2. But in this case, *two* circuit boards claimed to be COM1. As a result, neither would work. The answer is to convince one of the boards to be the other communications address, COM2.

   Before we go on to the next case, I hear you asking, "*How* do I convince one of the boards to be

COM2?'' The answer is the basis of configuration: You move a DIP switch or a jumper, or (on PS/2 machines) run a program to reassign the board's function from COM1 to COM2. (I'll have more to say about this in a minute, but I didn't want to leave you hanging.) On some boards, you have something that looks like a striped chip called a *jumper pack*. It's basically several wires in a chip package. You break some wires and leave others unbroken so as to enable or disable board functions. For example, IBM uses one on their RS-232 boards to select whether the board is COM1 or COM2. There are eight bands: four are broken, four left whole. To move from COM1 to COM2 or vice versa, remove the jumper pack, rotate it, and replace it.

Clue to Device Conflicts. If you've installed a new board and it doesn't work, don't just pull it out. Test the rest of the system. Does something that worked yesterday not work today? That's your clue

that (1) the board is probably not broken, but rather conflicting with something; and (2) you now know with what it's conflicting, so it's easier to track down exactly what you've got to change to make the thing work.

2. In the second sample problem, both the multifunction board and the monochrome graphics board had a parallel port, both trying to be recognized by the PC as LPT1 (parallel printer port 1). Again, we're faced with a scarce resource. The PC can only recognize three parallel ports: LPT1, LPT2, and LPT3. The answer is to either convince one of the ports to be LPT2 or LPT3, or perhaps to disable it altogether. You might choose to disable it if you had no need for two printer ports.

3. The third example is a bit more ''advanced'' a topic, but it illustrates the same problem. In this case, the expanded memory board and the clock/calendar tried to talk to the CPU chip via the same input/

IBM RS-232 board showing jumper pack.

Figure 7-1 Board Detail Showing Jumper

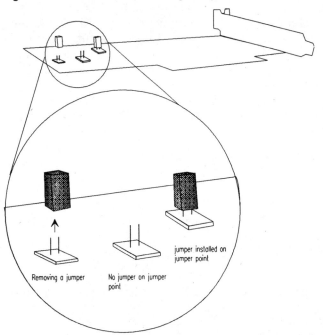

Removing a jumper

No jumper on jumper point

jumper installed on jumper point

output address, called an *I/O address*. The answer, as before, is to convince one of the boards to use a different I/O address. (Again, the answer to "how?" is coming.)

Resolving Device Conflicts. The simplest kind of installation problem is a conflict on the easy stuff, like COM1 or LPT1. In most cases, you can't have two video boards, as they'll stomp all over each other's video, ROM, and the like. You usually can't get away with two floppy controllers for the same reason. COMs and LPTs can conflict the same way, except you are allowed multiple COMs and LPTs.

You are *not*, however, allowed multiple COM1s.

Again, a COM or LPT conflict arises because two boards have the same COM or LPT name. If two boards both have a

COM1 on them, move a jumper or DIP switch to change one of them to COM2, or disable the COM function altogether. How do you know what switch to move? Look at the documentation. People commonly bring me a circuit board and say, "What does this do?," pointing to a jumper. I just shrug my shoulders. There's no way to know without the documentation, so remember to become a documentation packrat.

A Word About DIP Switches and POS. Since we're discussing configuration, here are few points about DIP switches.

First, not all DIP switches say ON or OFF. Some say OPEN or CLOSED. If they do, just remember that OPEN = OFF and CLOSED = ON. Sometimes they say 1 or 0—1 = ON, 0 = OFF. Sometimes (grrrr. . .) they don't say anything at all. In this case, play around with them until you've figured out their ON/OFF positions, and then write them in your notebook.

Second, if you've set the switches correctly but the PC refuses to recognize the settings, be aware that sometimes DIP switches are defective. (It has happened to me.) To test this, remove the system board and test the switches for continuity with an ohmmeter.

Finally, remember that sometimes manufacturers mislabel DIP switches or install them upside-down. It *does* happen—rarely, but it happens.

By the way, PS/2 owners will grapple with configuration also, but they'll be spared DIP switches and jumpers. PS/2 expansion boards are intended to do all that with software. Micro Channel machines have a neat feature called *POS* (Programmable Option Select) that allows a tech to reconfigure a board without removing it or setting switches. I'll discuss this more later.

Can You Have JUST the LPT2 Port? Here's a real PC configuration brainteaser. I have a PC with *only one* parallel port, which I configured as LPT2. There *is* no LPT1 in this machine. I boot it up. Once the system is running, what LPT port do I have on my system?

Answer: LPT1.

PCs have a strange feature when it comes to parallel ports. On bootup, the BIOS checks the LPTs. If there is no LPT1, it looks for an LPT2 or LPT3. If you've got an LPT2 but no LPT1, it actually converts the LPT2 to an LPT1. This is, of course, a *software* adjustment. I'll repeat: It's flat impossible to have an LPT2 without an LPT1. If you *do* install an LPT2 without LPT1, the LPT2 gets made into an LPT1 on bootup.

This is a nice feature. I just wish the documentation had *told* me about it. You see, it was late one night, and—oh, heck, I don't even want to talk about it. Now *you* know.

Next Step: I/O Addresses, DMA, IRQ, ROM Addresses. If all you do is install internal modems, you probably don't need this section. But there are more possible conflicts in your system— problems you can experience when you install things like LAN boards, scanner interface cards, 3270 boards, mouse interfaces, or basically anything that wasn't offered with the original IBM PC.

These four conflicts are:

- I/O addresses. What addresses the circuit board uses to communicate with the CPU.
- DMA channels. They're used to speed up I/O to and from the system's memory, but your system is severely limited in how many boards can be hooked up to use DMA.
- IRQ levels. Hardware must interrupt the CPU to force it to service these in some time-critical fashion.
- ROM addresses. Many boards include some of their low-level control software in ROM. The ROM requires a memory address, which cannot conflict with other ROMs or any RAM in the system.

Here's the scoop on these obscure-sounding resources.

I/O Addresses. How is information actually transferred from a peripheral like a serial port to the microprocessor? You know that CPUs have a range of memory addresses; well, there's also something similar called an *input/output address*, or *I/O address*. Much as the CPU can read and write memory addresses, it can also read and write these I/O addresses.

Each device that must communicate with the 8088 gets assigned an I/O address or, more likely, a range of addresses. This address cannot be used by

Table 7-1. Common I/O Address Uses in PCs

Hex Address Range	User
00–0F	DMA Controller 8237 #1
20–21	Programmable Interrupt Controller 8259A #1
40–43	Timer 8253
60–63	8255 Peripheral Controller (XT only)
60–64	Keyboard Controller (AT only) 8742
70–71	Setup RAM Access Address (AT only)
80–8F	DMA Page Registers
A0–A1	Programmable Interrupt Controller #2 8259 (AT only)
A0–AF	NMI Mask Register (XT only)
C0–DF	8237 DMA Controller #2 (AT only)
F0–FF	Math Coprocessor (AT only)
1F0–1F8	Hard Disk Controller (AT only)
200–20F	Joystick Controller
210–217	Expansion Chassis
238–23B	Bus Mouse
23C–23F	Alt. Bus Mouse
278–27F	LPT2
2B0–2DF	EGA
2E0–2E7	GPIB (AT only)
2E8–2EF	COM4 Serial Port
2F8–2FF	COM2 Serial Port
300–31F	Prototype Card
320–32F	Hard Disk Controller (XT only)
330–337	Bernoulli Box Controller
378–37F	LPT1 Printer Port
380–38F	SDLC Card
3A0–3AF	BSC Card
3B0–3BF	Monochrome Adapter
3BC–3BF	LPT3
3D0–3DF	Color/Graphics Adapter
3E8–3EF	COM3 Serial Port
3F0–3F7	Floppy Disk Controller
3F8–3FF	COM1 Serial Port

any other device. I'll steal an old analogy here. Think of I/O addresses as being like post office boxes. Say the keyboard has PO Box 200. When the keyboard has data for the system, it puts the data in box 200. When the CPU wants to read the keyboard, it looks in box 200. *Box 200* is, in a very real sense, a better definition of *keyboard* from the CPU's point of view than is the keyboard itself. Table 7-1, "Common I/O Address Uses in PCs," shows the probable addresses for your machines.

Now you can understand I/O address conflicts. Suppose you run a company called ABC Electronics that makes PC upgrade stuff. You come out with a device that IBM doesn't offer for the IBM PC—a clock/calendar, say. You need to assign our clock an address. IBM hasn't assigned an I/O address to the clock/calendar function for the PC (again, see the I/O addresses table), so you get to pick one. It would be monstrously stupid to create the clock to conflict with the address of a common peripheral like COM1, so you would pick one of the addresses IBM left unassigned—say, you pick address 250. You'll sell lots of clocks, and you'll be fat and happy, and so will your users.

Down the street, XYZ Electronics, a competitor, is working on a mouse interface board. IBM hasn't assigned a mouse interface address for the PC, so XYZ just picks an address out of the "unassigned" range. Through an unfortunate coincidence, they pick address 250, and sell *lots* of mice and mouse boards.

One day, a customer puts your board using address 250 into the same machine as the XYZ board, also using address 250. The customer loads software to read the clock, as well as software to interact with the mouse, not realizing what's about to happen. The first time the machine tries to read the clock, it goes to address 250 to read the date. But the mouse (unbeknownst to the computer) has just dumped some data in address 250. The clock program reads the data and tells that the date is August 2031, or something like that.

What you basically have at this point is a mouse that tells time, which isn't going to work reliably. The answer is to change the I/O address (examples coming up soon!).

This is where the jumpers and DIP switches come in. Realizing that they cannot know what addresses are currently in use on your computer, manufacturers give you a choice of possible addresses. Moving the jumpers or DIP switches allows the choice. Now, you probably won't have a clue which DIP switches do what without the documentation, so be sure to hang onto any switch-setting documentation you have.

Note: When the I/O addresses are changed, the software usually must be notified of these changes. You might not be able to resolve I/O address conflicts, as not all boards even give you the chance to change I/O addresses. It's hard to believe, but some boards are hard-wired to use only one I/O address range. I had a LIM board that conflicted with a clock/calendar, but unfortunately neither board gave me a chance to change the I/O address. One board had to be removed—the conflict couldn't be resolved any other way.

You've seen that the PC only implements 1024 addresses. The bottom 256 (hex locations 000 to 0FF) are only available to components on the system board. Plug-in expansion boards must use the 768 top locations (hex 100 to 3FF). Therefore, if they're designed properly, expansion boards will only allow you to set your I/O addresses somewhere between 100 hex and 3FF hex.

If troubleshooting is your job, it's probably a good idea to keep a roster of PCs and busy I/O addresses. Table 7-1

tells the common addresses taken up on PCs.

DMA Channels. Transferring data from a device into the computer via the CPU can be very slow, so some devices have the power to write data into the computer memory directly, without CPU intervention. This is called *DMA,* or Direct Memory Access. The PC has a single DMA controller chip, the 8237. It allows up to four DMA channels. One—channel 0—is required for dynamic memory refresh. There are two kinds of memory: *dynamic* and *static.* "Dynamic memory" sounds better than static, but it isn't. When you tell a static RAM something, it remembers it until you turn off the power or change it. Dynamic RAMs, on the other hand, forget whatever you tell them within four milliseconds. The PC is designed to drop everything and do a RAM refresh every 3.86 ms. This takes five clocks out of every 72, or about seven percent of the PC's time. Of course, if the CPU is doing a lot of INs, OUTs, internal calculations, or the like, you don't notice the slowdown, as the whole idea of DMA is to work in parallel with the CPU. Wouldn't static RAMs make a slightly faster computer? Yes, but they're more costly; Dell Computing (PCs Limited) used them in their 16 Mhz 386 machine. The floppy disk controller usually employs channel 2. The hard disk controller uses channel 1. In general, 3 is unused.

AT-type machines (those with 16-bit bus slots) have two DMA controllers, and thus eight DMA channels to the XT's four. Note that not all AT clones have this second DMA controller. *Four DMA channels is just plain not enough,* so don't even think of buying a 286/386/486 without eight DMA channels.

Notice that this implies you have only *one* free DMA channel on your average XT-type machine. AT-types have the 16-bit bus and extra DMA channels, but

Table 7-2. Common DMA Channel Uses in the PC Family

Channel	Use
0	Dynamic RAM Refresh
1	Hard Disk Controller
2	Floppy Controller
3	Unused
4–7	Available on AT & PS/2, but often not exploited

your circuit board must be a 16-bit board to use the extra DMA channels.

Some well-designed boards recognize that, while DMA makes boards fast, a given system may not have *any* DMA channels available. So these boards offer you the chance to disable DMA and just force all data to go through the CPU. It's not the greatest thing in the world, because it is slower, but at least it makes the board work.

So, in summary, if you have an expansion board that needs a DMA channel, the only one available on the eight-bit boards is generally DMA channel 3.

- If you're installing a 16-bit board, try whenever possible to use the extra 16-bit-only DMAs, channels 4 through 7, to leave room for the eight-bit boards in your system.
- If you're out of DMAs, see if the board offers the option to disable DMA. It will be slower, but it will work.

IRQ (Interrupt Request) Levels. To get the CPU's attention, Interrupt Request (IRQ) lines are used. The PC's bus implements lines 2 through 7. They're prioritized, line 2 more important than line 7. When a line is activated, the processor drops everything and loads a spe-

cial subroutine written to handle ("service") that particular interrupt.

Peripherals sometimes need to get the CPU's attention in a time-critical fashion. Here's an example: The keyboard controller is pretty dumb. It has no memory to speak of, so every time a keystroke arrives at the controller, it must hand off this keystroke to the CPU (which then puts it in the keyboard buffer) before another keystroke comes in. Essentially, once the keyboard controller gets a keystroke, it wants to say to the CPU, "HEY! STOP EVERYTHING! COME SERVICE ME **NOW** BEFORE THE USER PRESSES ANOTHER KEY!!!!," so it "rings the bell"—it activates its interrupt line (line number 1, as you can see in Table 7-3). The CPU stops and executes the program that moves the keystroke to the keyboard buffer.

If, in the above instance, the CPU was busy doing something else, or if the CPU had chosen to ignore interrupts (some programs can tell the CPU to do that), the keyboard controller might well have waited for quite some time. Then the user might have pressed a key, and the original keystroke could have been lost.

If you're installing a board and it needs an IRQ, look first to interrupt 2 on a PC or 5 on an AT. If those aren't available, try 3; if you don't have a COM2, there's no conflict. Failing that, try (believe it or not) 7. The printer port doesn't actually need its interrupt.

As with DMAs, 16-bit machines have extra interrupts. You can use them only if you're inserting a 16-bit board in a 16-bit slot. Use them if possible, so as to leave room in the lower eight IRQs for other boards. PCs and XTs only have IRQs 0-7, as Table 7-3 shows.

I've mentioned this earlier in the I/O address discussion, but let me repeat: Some boards don't have jumpers and

Table 7-3. Common IRQ Uses in the PC Family

Interrupt Line	Device	Comments
0	Timer	
1	Keyboard	
2	Unused	Used in ATs as a gateway to IRQ 8/15, also by EGA/VGA video boards
3	COM2	
4	COM1	
5	Hard Disk	PC & XT only—usually free on ATs
6	FDC	
7	LPT1	
8	Clock	Interrupts 8–15 only available on 286/386 machines (often not accessible from expansion boards)
9	PC Network	
10–12	Unused	
13	Coprocessor	
14	Hard Disk	
15	Unused	

DIP switches. This means *there's no way to get them to work with conflicting boards*. For example, a client I regularly visited had installed an IBM 5251 (System 36 terminal emulator) board and an old Quadram Quadboard in a PC. The printer port on the Quadboard and the terminal emulator wanted the same resource—which one, I'm not sure. In any case, neither had jumpers. One board was thrown away. Moral: find out if the expansion boards you buy have adjustable DMA, IRQ, and I/O addresses.

I hesitate to mention this, but sometimes device conflicts can be solved by doing surgery on the boards. Just lobotomize the chips performing the function you wish to defeat. An example I've seen a couple of times is in serial ports. A client wanted me to set up a multifunction board in a PC with clock, memory, printer, and serial ports. He already had a board installed that provided both serial ports COM1: and COM2:. The jumpers on the multifunction board allowed me to set the multifunction board's serial port to either COM1: or COM2:, but not to disable it altogether. What to do? A chip called the *8250 UART* (Universal Asynchronous Receiver/Transmitter) is the heart of most serial ports. I found the 8250 on the multifunction board and removed it. The problem was eliminated. *Please don't try this unless you understand what you're doing.*

ROM Addresses and RAM Buffers. Added to I/O addresses, DMA channels, and IRQ lines is a fourth source of conflict: ROM addresses. Some controller cards (like EGA and hard disk controllers) require some ROM on board to hold some low-level code. For example, many hard disk controller cards contain code to do a low-level format of the hard disk; just load DEBUG (a DOS command) and type G = C800:5. (Please don't even think of doing this before you read the chapter on hard disks unless you know what you're doing.) The XT controller board's ROM starts at C800:0000. As before, a possibility exists that two different boards may require some onboard software, and if the two boards *both* try to locate their ROM at the same location in the PC's memory address space, neither one will work.

Fortunately, some boards include jumpers to allow you to move the start address of the ROM. Most of the major boards that include ROM (like the EGA, VGA, XT-type hard disk controller, and the like) should *not* have their ROM addresses changed, even if it's possible. Too many pieces of software rely on their standard addresses.

Table 7-4. Common ROM and RAM Buffer Addresses

Function	Address Range (hex)	Address Length
XT Hard Disk Controller	C8000–CBFFF	16K
EGA	C0000–C3FFF	16K
VGA	C0000–C4FFF	20K
LIM boards (may vary)	D0000–DFFFF	64K
Token Ring ROM	CC000–CFFFF	16K
Token Ring RAM	D8000–D9FFF or DBFFF	8K or 16K
PC Network Card	CC000–CFFFF	16K

A few boards, like LAN boards, may have a little RAM right on board. A LAN board needs it to buffer incoming or outgoing messages. A LIM memory board needs 64K of RAM for the 16K page buffers, so most LIM boards incorporate some ROM also.

PS/2 Configuration Notes. Those of you with the "real" PS/2s (Models 25 and 30 owners excluded) may never have to deal with as much preceding pain and suffering.

The Personal System line includes the *Micro Channel Architecture (MCA) bus,* an improvement in some ways over the old PC bus. It includes a feature called *POS* (Programmable Option Select) that eliminates the need for DIP switches. Like the ISA-based 286s and later machines, PS/2 machines have 8 DMA channels and 16 IRQ lines—plenty for any application.

You may know that the AT uses battery-backed memory (called *CMOS memory*) to retain some configuration information: It recalls things like how much memory the system has, what kind of drives it has, whether or not it has a coprocessor, and the like. It does not, however, assist in installing new expansion boards.

The PS/2s have taken this idea and extended it to expansion boards. In PS/2s, CMOS memory remembers IRQ, DMA, and I/O port information for circuit boards as well. When the machine is powered up, it checks each board against CMOS configuration information. If a new unknown board is detected, the user will be requested to run a setup program.

There has been a lot of hype in the popular press about how you'll never have to worry about configuration again with the PS/2. It's not really true. You still have to worry about two boards not using the same IRQ lines, but fixing the problem is easier—you run a setup program rather than pull the board out and set DIP switches. The extra DMA and IRQ channels make the configuration job easier, too.

By the way, IBM wasn't the first manufacturer in the PC business to make this possible. Orchid Technologies has been doing it with their expansion boards since the beginning of 1986.

Support for the New Board: BIOS Upgrades. If you have one of the earliest PCs, the ones manufactured in 1981 or 1982, you must upgrade your BIOS software in order to use an EGA board, a hard disk, a LAN card, or any other expansion board that has ROM on it. BIOS, you may recall, isn't loaded from disk, but rather is stored in a ROM chip, the one farthest from the empty ROM socket.

IBM used to sell these ROM upgrades, but it doesn't anymore. Some vendors who do sell ROM upgrades are:

Mentor Electronics
7560 Tyler Blvd. #E
Mentor, OH 44060
(216) 951-1884

Self-Reliant PC Products
1750 Kalakaua Ave. #3-133
Honolulu, HI 96826
(808) 946-1808

Other machines may need a BIOS upgrade. Older ATs, for example, only supported a small number of hard disk types and cannot support $3\frac{1}{2}$-inch drives. You can remedy that with a $50 BIOS upgrade. You can find upgrades at some of these vendors.

Alltech Electronics Company
1300 E. Edinger Suite E
Santa Ana, CA 92705
(714) 543-5011

Storage Dimensions
2145 Hamilton Ave.
San Hose, CA 95125
(408) 879-0300

If you have a clone, it may have a compatible BIOS written by Phoenix Technologies. Phoenix periodically updates their BIOSes to speed them up, make them support new devices, and fix bugs. However, the person from whom you bought your clone may have gone on to selling land in Florida. You can buy upgrades for your Phoenix ROMs from Wholesale Direct:

Wholesale Direct
15251 Northeast 90th St.
Redmond, WA 98052
(206) 883-0227

Phoenix shares the market for high-quality BIOSes with Award BIOSes, which are available from Komputerwerk (I've used them and have had good results):

Komputerwerk, Inc.
851 Parkview Blvd.
Pittsburgh, PA 15215
(412) 782-0384
(800) 423-3400

Other BIOS companies I've used or heard good things about are Lolir and USA. They're available from:

Lolir
2741 Beltline Rd. #111
Carrollton, TX 75006
(214) 416-5155

USA Electronic
9090 N. Stemmons Hwy.
Dallas, TX 75247
(214) 631-1574

A Configuration Example. To underscore these concepts, let's look at installing two new real-life boards in a 286-based machine:

- A Bernoulli Box controller
- An HP ScanJet interface card

Also, to make it more interesting, we'll add a mythical LAN board:

- A 16-bit LAN Lightning card

Also, I've included (with their kind permission) excerpts from the two real manufacturers' installation manuals dealing with configuration, as examples of typical manuals. The documentation for these two companies is a bit better than the average manual. An important part of this section is to allow you to see some examples of actual documentation. The manual excerpts follow.

ScanJet Manual Excerpts. Figures 7-2 through 7-5 include excerpts courtesy of Hewlett Packard.

Bernoulli Host Adapter Manual Excerpts. The following excerpts (Figures 7-6 through 7-8) are courtesy of Iomega Corp. By the way, for those who don't know, a *Bernoulli Box* is a high-density, high-speed floppy disk that offers the same performance as a hard disk. This involves putting a Bernoulli controller (called the PC2/50 by its manufacturer) into the PC.

Lightning LAN "Manual" Highlights. Recall that our LL card is a 16-bit card. For the LL card, let's just say you need to worry about:

- **DMA Channel.** Options are:
  - 1 or 3 (when used in an 8-bit or 16-bit slot)
  - 5, 6, or 7 (when used in a 16-bit slot only)
- **Interrupt Level.** A wide range of options:
  - 3, 4, 5, 6, 7 (when used in an 8-bit or 16-bit slot)
  - 9, 10, 11, 12, 14, or 15 (when used in a 16-bit slot only)
- **I/O addresses.** It uses 16 consecutive addresses, with the following options (addresses are, of course, in hex):
  - 300-30F
  - 310-31F
  - 320-32F
  - 330-33F
  - 340-34F

And that's it. Now let's configure these things.

So now we've seen the documentation (real and, in the case of the Light-

Figure 7-2 ScanJet Installation Manual Excerpt (1 of 4)

Resetting the Switches   Remove the plastic cover from the configuration switches. Change the position of the switches to a new setting as described in the following paragraphs. See Figure A-1.

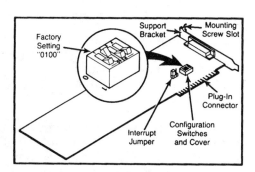

Figure A-1. HP 88290A Interface Card

NOTE   If you are a novice user, you may want to skip the shaded sections of this appendix. The shaded sections provide an advanced method for solving addressing conflicts.

Figure 7-3 ScanJet Installation Manual Excerpt (2 of 4)

Background Information

Your computer has two different types of address space: memory space and I/O space. Within the memory space is a section called Expansion ROM memory space. Most computer cards use addresses located in either I/O space or Expansion ROM space, or both. If two cards are configured to use the same address locations, a conflict occurs and your computer system does not operate correctly.

Most cards, including the HP 88290A interface card, have switches which determine the locations in the computer address space that the card will occupy. Addressing problems can be resolved by changing the switches on one of the conflicting cards to choose a new location within the computer address space.

The HP 88290A interface card uses eight bytes of computer I/O space and 16 kilobytes of Expansion ROM memory space. The exact address locations used by the card are determined by the settings of the configuration switches.

Switch 1 on the HP 88290A determines which one of two starting addresses in the computer I/O space is used by the card. Switches 2, 3, and 4 determine which of the eight possible starting addresses is used in the computer Expansion ROM memory space.

Figure A-1 shows where the configuration switches are located on the interface card. Notice that the switch positions 1 and 0 are written upside down to the left of the configuration switch module (when the card is held as illustrated in the drawing). Each configuration switch can be set by pushing one end of it--bottom for position 1 and

Figure 7-4 ScanJet Installation Manual Excerpt (3 of 4)

top for position 0. The factory setting is illustrated in Figure A-1.

Selecting I/O Switch Position. Switch 1 is used to select the I/O address for the card, with position 0 selecting addresses 278H through 27FH and position 1 selecting addresses 268H through 26FH. Change Switch 1 from the factory-set position 0 to position 1 *only if* a parallel printer port is configured as Port 2 in your computer system.

See Table A-1 to find the situation that applies to you. Then, select the correct position for Switch 1. If you decide to change Switch 1 from the factory setting to position 1, make sure no other card in your system occupies addresses 268H through 26FH.

Other Parallel Ports		HP 88290A	
Quantity	Port Assignment	Switch 1 Setting	Addresses
None	None	"0"	278H – 27FH
1	Port 1	"0"	
1	Port 2	"1"	268H – 26FH
2	Port 1 & Port 2	"1"	

Table A-1. I/O Table

Figure 7-5 ScanJet Installation Manual Excerpt (4 of 4)

Selecting ROM Switch Positions. Switches 2, 3, and 4 select the Expansion ROM location for the card. Table A-2 shows all possible settings of these switches with corresponding Expansion ROM locations and their standard uses. The factory-settings for switches 2, 3, and 4 are **1**, **0**, and **0**, respectively (addresses C4000-C7FFF).

Expansion ROM Address	Configuration Switch Setting			
(Hexadecimal)	2	3	4	Common Usage
C0000-C3FFF	0	0	0	EGA Cards
C4000-C7FFF Factory Setting HP 88290A	1	0	0	
C8000-CBFFF	0	1	0	IBM/XT Controller Card
CC000-CFFFF	1	1	0	IBM/PC Network Card
D000-D3FFF	0	0	1	
D4000-D7FFF	1	0	1	
D8000-DBFFF	0	1	1	IBM/PC Cluster Card
DC000-DFFFF	1	1	1	

Table A-2. Commonly Used Addresses

ning LAN board, imaginary). First, the Bernoulli controller (Iomega PC2/50) documentation tells us there are DIP switches to set the following items:

- I/O addresses
- Whether or not to use DMA
- If used, which DMA channel to choose (options are 1 or 3—it's an 8-bit board, so no DMA 4-7)

The Lightning LAN board is, again, a 16-bit adapter card that attaches your PC to a Local Area Network. It has jumpers to select:

- I/O addresses
- Which DMA channel to use (0 through 7)
- Which interrupt line to use (options are 2 through 15)

The ScanJet manual shows you have to worry about

- I/O addresses
- ROM addresses

The Bernoulli controller offers the option to avoid the DMA conflict by opting not to use DMA at all. That's a nice option, but the fact is that you bought these guys for *speed*, and missing out on DMA is *not* the way to do it.

Let's start with the LAN board, as it looks to be the largest pain here. I/O address is easy, as the default (300-30F hex) doesn't conflict with anything. Which DMA channel to use? Well, since it's a 16-bit board, with the ability to use DMAs 4-7, let's just go for DMA 4, so we can leave channel 3 for the Bernoulli. IBM "reserved" interrupt 9 for a LAN board, so we'll go with IRQ 9, again exploiting the 16-bit nature of the board (it'll work faster in 16-bit mode).

Now on to Bernoulli. The manual outlines several I/O port possibilities. The factory switch settings use 340-345 hex, which don't conflict with anything. DMA options are pretty scarce, only 1 (the hard disk, recall) and 3. Thankfully, nothing uses 3—if something did, we'd be forced to forgo DMA—so we set the DMA to 3.

As I've said before, a log of this information makes configuration easier. It's no good knowing that a new board needs IRQ 7 if you don't know whether some currently installed board already uses it.

The scanner board is fairly simple. It

Figure 7-6 Bernoulli Host Adapter Installation Manual Excerpt (1 of 3)

CHAPTER 4
PC2/50 and PC2B/50
Technical Information

The information contained here is not necessary for the normal operation of the PC2/50 and PC2B/50 host adapter boards with removable cartridge drives. This information is provided for help in configuring the host adapter board for special applications.

Option Switch Settings

The option switches were set at the factory for the most typical configuration used with your computer. However, you can change the switch configurations for special applications. Figure 4-1 shows the purpose and factory setting of each option switch.

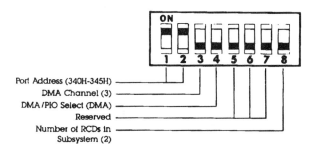

Figure 4-1. Option Switch Factory Settings.

Switches 1 and 2 — Port Addresses. These switches select one of four groups of port addresses to communicate with RCD systems. The switches were preset at the factory for port addresses 340H through 345H. (See Figure 4-2.)

NOTE: **If you select a new group of port addresses, make certain no conflicts exist with other hardware accessing the same addresses.**

needs I/O addresses (options are 278-27F and 268-26F) and a ROM address. Either I/O address is fine, as neither conflicts with anything, although if we set it to 278-27F it will conflict with a second parallel port if we ever install one.

Now the tougher question—where to address the ROMs? Hmmm. . .I'm not sure what ROMs I currently have in this system. It's an AT-type system, so there is no extra ROM for a hard disk. The only thing in the system with ROM is a VGA, but what is its ROM's address? Checking Table 7-4 (earlier in this chap-

Figure 7-7 Bernoulli Host Adapter Installation Manual Excerpt (2 of 3)

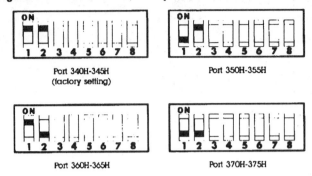

Port 340H-345H
(factory setting)

Port 350H-355H

Port 360H-365H

Port 370H-375H

Figure 4-2. Port Address Switch Settings

Switch 3 — Direct Memory Access (DMA) channel used to communicate with your computer. This switch selects DMA channel 1 or DMA channel 3. Most networking schemes use DMA channel 1 for communication; so if the computer is part of a network, you should use channel 3. (See Figure 4-3.)

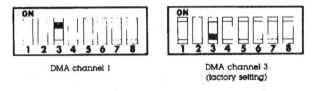

DMA channel 1

DMA channel 3
(factory setting)

Figure 4-3. DMA Channel Switch Settings

Switch 4 — DMA or Programmed Input/Output (PIO). Selecting PIO disables DMA communications and decreases transfer rates, but prevents problems with other hardware using DMA. (See Figure 4-4.)

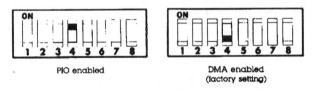

PIO enabled

DMA enabled
(factory setting)

Figure 4-4. DMA/PIO Switch Settings

ter) gives us C0000–C4FFF. The scanner interface has a factory default of C4000–C7FFF. That would be okay for an EGA, as the EGA's ROM ends at C3FFF, just short of C4000. But note that the VGA's ROM goes all the way up to C6000, which tromps all over the range C4000–C7FFF. What other ranges are available? C0000–C3FFF is also available, but that's of no value either. Next is C8000–CFFFF—perfect! Now it'll work. Notice that it works because this is an *AT*—if it

Figure 7-8   Bernoulli Host Adapter Installation Manual Excerpt (3 of 3)

Switches 5, 6, and 7. These switches are reserved. Do not change these settings.

Switch 8 — Number of drives in subsystem. This switch selects the number of 8 inch drives in an RCD external subsystem connected to the host adapter board. The switch is set at the factory for 2 drives. (See Figure 4-5.)

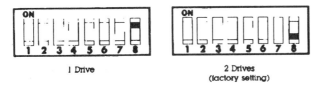

1 Drive   2 Drives
                     (factory setting)

Figure 4-5. Drive Switch Settings

were an XT, the XT hard disk controller's ROM would conflict with addresses C8000-CFFFF.

Board Installation

Once the switches have been set, it's time to insert the new board. The physical process of installing or removing circuit boards is straightforward.

Removing an expansion board:

1. The power must always be off. You won't hurt *you*, but you could damage the circuit board.
2. The back of the board has a *mounting bracket*, which is attached to the back of the PC case with a screw. Remove the screw. Put the screw in the cup with other screws. (Remember the cup? It's all right to knock it over now.)
3. If the mounting bracket has an interface connector on it, like a serial interface or a parallel interface, and something is connected to it, disconnect it.
4. Grasp the board with both hands, one on the top front edge and the other on the top rear edge.

5. Rock the board back and forth, pulling up gently.
6. The board will come out.
7. As I've said before, keep your fingers off the edge connectors.
8. When you remove a board, you should fill the empty space on the PC box's rear bracket with a bracket insert. This keeps RFI to a minimum. If you're inserting a board, save the bracket insert.

If the board you inserted/removed was a memory board, don't forget to inform the system via the DIP switches or SETUP that system memory has changed.

The insertion process is just the reverse.

Which Slot? Unusual Slots in Various Machines. People often think there's some electrical difference between slots, as if the video board must go in slot 2, the floppy controller in slot 7, and so on. In general, that's not true. In most cases, it makes *no difference* which slot boards are inserted in. The only criterion for board placement is ease of cable routing.

In the earlier "Inside the PC" chapter, we looked at the common bus slots. Here are some of the more obscure slots and slot characteristics.

- **The "bad slot" on the IBM XT.** You generally can't use the slot on the IBM XT motherboard that's closest to the power supply. Its timing lines are a mite different, and most boards won't work in this slot. IBM makes a serial card that can go in there.
- **Some accelerator boards** recommend that you install them as close to the CPU as is possible, short of using the bad XT slot.
- **Backplane slots.** Backplane systems (most Zeniths, Wyse, Telex, some Kaypros) include slots with extended connectors to accommodate the extra lines required for a split motherboard design. These designs usually divide what would be the motherboard into *two* expansion slots. Because the motherboard contains within it some electronic lines that aren't usually included in the bus, backplane manufacturers add an extra connector to a few slots to accommodate these extra control lines. If you've got one of these backplane computers, the two boards that do motherboard duty *must* go into these slots with the extra connector.
- **The 16-bit AT&T Slot.** The 8086-based AT&T systems sought to exploit the full 16-bit capabilities of the 8086, and the 6300 systems include an extra connector on several slots— kind of a poor man's 16-bit slot. Sadly, it has no relation to the 16-bit slots found on AT-bus machines, and isn't really of any value. It *can*, however, be used with no trouble as an 8-bit slot.

- As I mentioned in Chapter 4, 86 systems are hampered by the lack of a 32-bit slot for memory access. Most other boards really wouldn't benefit from 32-bit access, so the lack of a 32-bit standard isn't a real handicap. But 386 memory needs 32-bit access for full functionality. While waiting for EISA or whatever the bus of tomorrow is, vendors have taken two approaches to providing a 32-bit path for memory: motherboard memory and proprietary 32-bit slots.

    Some systems have room for up to 8MB of RAM right on the motherboard. Others, like the Zenith Z-386, have a proprietary slot that can only be used for a memory card. Other compatible vendors do this also: Compaq, Intel, and Micronics are three names that spring to mind. IBM has a proprietary slot as well; the Micro Channel can't transfer data fast enough to support the Model 70's memory.

Power Requirements. Once you've got the new board in, can you feed it?

Sure, you've heard about how PC disk drives draw a lot of power, imperiling your power supply and PC, but what about those expansion boards— any worries there? Surely not, many people say: no moving parts. Actually, memory boards draw a considerable amount of power. According to a datasheet from Mostek, a memory chip manufacturer, a 256K chip draws 0.412 watts maximum. A bank of them (nine, recall) is 3.7 watts. 64K chips draw 0.33 watts, so a bank of nine draws 3.0 watts. A full complement of 640K would require $3.7 + 3.7 + 3.0 + 3.0 = 13.4$ watts at peak—21 percent of a 63.5 watt PC power supply! By comparison, some hard disks' peak power consumption is 10 watts. This gets worse if you have an older PC or XT that only accepts 64K chips. Ten banks of 64K chips would draw 30 watts peak.

It might be difficult to get power requirement figures for some expansion boards, so use the following rough test: Run the PC for a while with the board installed. Then touch the board. A hot board is probably drawing a lot of power. That heat must be removed from the machine; again, use an improved fan in your machine to handle this.

Board Testing

It's in. Now let's figure out if it works.

Burn-In. Most *solid state components* (that is, electronic things without moving parts) tend to be very reliable if they live past the first few days ("If it works, it'll work forever."). Because of this, initial testing of circuit boards is valuable. Such testing is called *burn-in*.

When a new component like a memory board is installed, it should be tested for a 24- to 72-hour period. Some diagnostic program—generally a simple programming loop of some kind—retests the component over and over again. Some components have warranties of only 90 days, so the burn-in increases the probability that a bad component will be spotted in the warranty period.

Some manufacturers claim to do burn-in for you. You should *still* do it yourself. Why? They burned it in in the factory. Since then it has been subjected to the rigors of shipping.

Where Do You Find Diagnostic Programs? Chapter 6 mentioned the names of several generic diagnostic programs, like the Supersoft and Windsor products. You could use those to test a board like, for example, a motherboard or a memory board; they're perfectly good for that. But don't do what some folks do: I know of a group who buys a lot of PS/2s. They load up the Reference Diskette that comes with the PS/2, tell the diagnostics

to run over and over, and leave the machine. Hours later, they come back and see if there are any errors reported on the screen. If there are no errors, they ship the machine to users. But users complained that a lot of machines had malfunctioning video. It turns out that the VGA's on Model 50's had a higher-than-average failure rate; I myself saw a classroom with 30 Model 50s develop video problems in about 20 percent of the machines. (If you have this problem, it seemed most prevalent when the room was above 75–80 degrees. Maybe turning up the air conditioning could help.) The support staff was puzzled. How did this slip by them? Simple. Video diagnostics often require a user to look them over. If your reds are greens and blues are blacks, the monitor doesn't know. The video board doesn't know. You need an operator to audit the video tests.

Here's a cheap memory test. Build a *1-2-3* spreadsheet that fills memory. It just consists of a single cell A1 with the value 1, then a cell A2 with the formula A1 + 1. Then copy that cell until you run out of memory. Set Recalculation to Manual. Write a short macro that loops continuously, recalculating and recalculating again. If you really want a level of elegance, calculate the sum of this large column of numbers, and check it against the actual value (the sum of 1, 2, 3, 4,. . .N is equal to $N(N+1)/2$).

If you've got something like our previous configuration example, where we installed a Bernoulli controller and a ScanJet interface card, you've got to rely on the manufacturers. And in all three cases, they come through. Iomega supplies an RCDDIAG program that tests the controller. LAN boards are generally tested by putting a "loopback" connector of some kind on them to allow them to "hear" what they broadcast. They send out test messages, and then compare them to what they receive.

111

3Com ships a program called 3C505 with the Etherlink+ to test it. And HP provides a very thorough ScanJet test program. When you get these programs, *use them*. Remember that just running them once isn't enough; some boards don't fail until they get hot.

Installing Motherboards

The last part of this chapter focuses on a particularly important circuit board—the motherboard. Most add-in boards can generally go right into the computer at the factory default settings, but motherboards almost always require some configuration. Like some people you've probably known, computers won't do any work until you flatter them—"Tell me about myself," they say.

But this process is different between XT-type machines and AT-type machines, and Micro Channel machines vary the technique still further. Here are the details.

System boards must be informed whenever you install (at a minimum) a new drive, more memory, a coprocessor, or different video. For years, circuit boards were configured, as we've seen, with jumpers and DIP switches. But IBM

views having to ask users to open machines and flip switches as particularly undesirable. So the AT used a different approach, a more software-oriented one using a memory chip to hold the configuration information, as we'll see.

Configuring the XT and PC System Boards. The original IBM PC had two sets of eight DIP switches for configuration. The first set of DIP switches, labeled SW-1 on the motherboard, described everything but the memory size:

- Kind of display installed
- How many floppy disk drives are installed
- If a numeric coprocessor is installed

The second set of DIP switches (and two of the switches from the first set) tell how much memory is on a PC motherboard. The IBM XT doesn't have the second set of DIPs, and instead deduces with its POST memory test how much memory the system has. Most XT-type machines follow the XT's lead and have only one set of DIP switches. PCs and other machines with a second set label the second set SW-2.

Figure 7-9 XT Motherboard with DIP Switch Detail

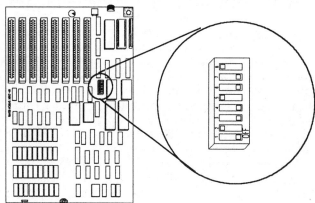

PC System Board DIP Switch Settings. Refer to Table 7-5 to set the PC's DIP switches. Use a ballpoint pen or small screwdriver to change the switch settings.

Table 7-5. PC and XT Switch Settings

IBM PC Non-Memory DIP Switch Settings			
Coprocessor			
Installed	SW-1	#2 OFF	
Not Installed	SW-1	#2 ON	
Disk Drives			
No floppies	SW-1	#1 ON	#7 ON	#8 ON
1 drive	SW-1	#1 OFF	#7 ON	#8 ON
2 drives	SW-1	#1 OFF	#7 OFF	#8 ON
3 drives	SW-1	#1 OFF	#7 ON	#8 OFF
4 drives	SW-1	#1 OFF	#7 OFF	#8 OFF

Note: always set SW-1 #1 OFF on an XT.

Monitor Type			
None	SW-1	#5 ON	#6 ON
CGA, 40 × 25 video	SW-1	#5 OFF	#6 ON
CGA, 80 × 25 video	SW-1	#5 ON	#6 OFF
Monochrome Display	SW-1	#5 OFF	#6 OFF

IBM PC Memory DIP Switch Settings

In the figures below, 1 indicates ON, and 0 indicates OFF.

Memory Size	SW-1						SW-2			
(KB)	#3	#4	#1	#2	#3	#4	#5	#6	#7	#8
16	1	1	1	1	1	1	1	0	0	0
32	0	1	1	1	1	1	1	0	0	0
48	1	0	1	1	1	1	1	0	0	0
64	0	0	1	1	1	1	1	0	0	0
96	0	0	0	1	1	1	1	0	0	0
128	0	0	1	0	1	1	1	0	0	0
160	0	0	0	0	1	1	1	0	0	0
192	0	0	1	1	0	1	1	0	0	0
224	0	0	0	1	0	1	1	0	0	0
256	0	0	1	0	0	1	1	0	0	0
288	0	0	0	0	0	1	1	0	0	0
320	0	0	1	1	1	0	1	0	0	0
352	0	0	0	1	1	0	1	0	0	0

Table 7-5. *continued*

Memory Size	SW-1						SW-2			
	3	4	1	2	3	4	5	6	7	8
384	0	0	1	0	1	0	1	0	0	0
416	0	0	0	0	1	0	1	0	0	0
448	0	0	1	1	0	0	1	0	0	0
480	0	0	0	1	0	0	1	0	0	0
512	0	0	1	0	0	0	1	0	0	0
544	0	0	0	0	0	0	1	0	0	0
576	0	0	1	1	1	1	0	0	0	0
608	0	0	0	1	1	1	0	0	0	0
640	0	0	1	0	1	1	0	0	0	0

IBM XT Memory DIP Switch Settings		
64	1	1
128	0	1
192	1	0
256+	0	0

Configuring an AT. An IBM AT has one DIP switch to set. The rest of its configuration information is retained in a battery-backed memory. So AT setup involves setting one switch and running a SETUP program. AT-type compatibles usually do *not* have this switch, but instead keep the video type in configuration memory.

Setting the AT DIP Switch. The one

Figure 7-10 AT Motherboard Detail with Video Switch, Battery Connection, and CMOS Chip

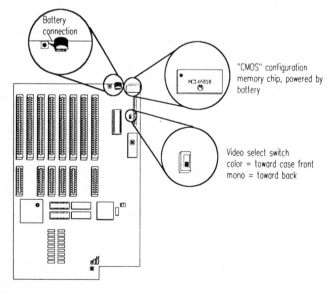

Battery connection

"CMOS" configuration memory chip, powered by battery

MC146818

Video select switch
color = toward case front
mono = toward back

DIP switch on the IBM AT motherboard tells the AT whether it has a mono-chrome display board or a color display board. The switch isn't labeled. To remember which way it goes, remember CAB: Color Away from Back, meaning the back of the case.

Configuration CMOS Memory. There are no DIP switches to set on an AT or AT compatible. Configuring a system board for most 286/386/486 machines should involve no DIP switches, but rather a memory chip that holds 64 bytes of configuration information. Commonly called the *CMOS chip,* it's often a Motorola 146818 24 pin chip. It's volatile, like all semiconductor memory, and so requires a battery to maintain the integrity of its data when the system is turned off. When the battery runs down, the computer starts acting aphasic (look it up, but it means what you'd expect it to mean). Some systems, like the AT&T 6386, use nonrechargeable lithium batteries that have lives of three to ten years. Others (the Zenith Z-248 comes to mind) use rechargeable nicad batteries. Newer systems (like the PS/2 Model 30-286) use a memory-and-battery-all-in-one chip from Dallas Semiconductor. It's distinguished by the alarm clock on its face and contains a battery that Dallas Semi claims is good for ten years.

Running the Configuration Programs. Such configuration memory chips must be loaded, and the program to do the loading is generally called SETUP. The SETUP program for Zeniths and for those with recent Award BIOSes is, conveniently, in ROM so you're not required to hunt around for a disk—quite nice. The Zeniths activate the program with Ctrl-Alt–Ins. The Award only offers the option when you boot up; if you have one, it'll note that you can press Ctrl-Alt–Esc on startup if you desire. It's extremely annoying to have to paw through your floppies looking for SETUP

when you change a battery or add an option, so be sure you know where SETUP is.

When running SETUP, it will ask you things like:

- Date and time
- Floppy drive type (360K, 1.2M, and so on)
- Hard drive type (a number from 1 to 47, generally)
- Amount of conventional memory (it might call it *base* memory)
- Amount of extended memory (it might call it *expansion* memory)
- Primary display type (monochrome, CGA, EGA/VGA)

Most of the questions are easy to answer, except *What hard disk drive type do you have?* That's a bit more intricate, so I'll save discussion of that for the hard disk chapters.

Replacing the Configuration Battery. As I said above, if your AT-type system insists on being set up every day, you probably need a new battery. New batteries can be bought in the $17–$30 range.

Egghead Discount Software sells inexpensive AT-type batteries. Alternatively, go to Radio Shack and get their "Four AA Battery Holder" (89 cents). Put four AA batteries in it and solder the wires from the holder to the AT battery contacts. This works, but it raises the question of where to put the battery holder.

When you replace the battery, you'll notice it's connected to the motherboard with two wires, a red and a white. If you didn't pay attention when you took the old battery off, you might wonder how the new battery is connected. In that case, remember RAP: Red Away from the Power supply.

Setting Up the PS/2 with the Refer-

ence Disk. Like the AT, the PS/2s (the *real* PS/2s, the Models 50 to the 80) use some nonvolatile RAM to hold configuration information. But the PS/2s take it a bit further. They have no DIP switches at all and, in fact, can configure their expansion boards in software, also.

PS/2's come with a *Reference Disk*

(RD), which contains, among other things, configuration software. The very first thing you should do with a new PS/2 is to copy the Reference Disk, as the RD is write protected and you'll want to write your configuration onto the disk.

Next, boot the PS/2 from the backup RD. If you haven't configured the ma-

Figure 7-11 Main Menu from PS/2 Reference Diskette

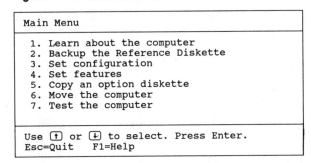

```
Main Menu

  1. Learn about the computer
  2. Backup the Reference Diskette
  3. Set configuration
  4. Set features
  5. Copy an option diskette
  6. Move the computer
  7. Test the computer


Use ⬆ or ⬇ to select. Press Enter.
Esc=Quit    F1=Help
```

Figure 7-12 Configuration Menu from PS/2 Reference Diskette

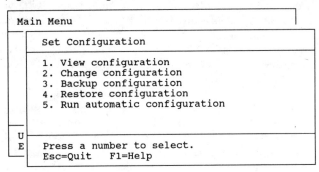

```
Main Menu

    Set Configuration

      1. View configuration
      2. Change configuration
      3. Backup configuration
      4. Restore configuration
      5. Run automatic configuration



 U
 E    Press a number to select.
      Esc=Quit    F1=Help
```

Figure 7-13 Main Menu from PS/2 Reference Diskette

```
Main Menu

  1. Learn about the computer
  2. Backup the Reference Diskette
  3. Set configuration
  4. Set features
  5. Copy an option diskette
  6. Move the computer
  7. Test the computer


Use ^ or V to select. Press Enter.
Esc=Quit    F1=Help
```

chine before, it'll squawk about not being configured and because the date and time hasn't been set. If you've booted from the RD, you'll eventually see a main menu like Figure 7-11.

Now choose 3, *Set configuration*. A submenu appears (Figure 7-12).

If you choose Automatic Configuration, the system will configure itself and reboot. At this point, everything's fine, provided you haven't added any expansion boards. If you have added a board or boards, the system will continue to squawk, because it doesn't know how to configure the expansion boards.

Every type of expansion board in the PS/2 universe has a unique five-digit identification number called its *Micro Channel ID*. A 2MB memory board might have ID 10000, an ESDI controller might be 20000, and so on. Venders are expected to ask IBM for an MCA ID when designing new boards.

Once a new board is in a machine, the system—the RD, in this case—must be informed of just *how* to configure the board. That information is summarized in a 2K file called an *Adapter Definition File*, or *ADF*. The name of the ADF file for a board with MCA ID xxxxx is xxxxx.ADF; so in my above example the file for the ESDI controller would be called 20000.ADF.

Figure 7-14   Sample Screen from PS/2 Model 50 Setup Program (1)

```
 ┌──────────────────────────────────────────────────────────────────┐
 │ Change Configuration                                               │
 │                                                                    │
 │  Total System Memory                                               │
 │     Installed Memory ..................... 1024KB (1.0MB)          │
 │     Usable Memory ........................ 1024KB (1.0MB)          │
 │                                                                    │
 │  Built In Features                                                 │
 │     Installed Memory ..................... 1024KB (1.0MB)          │
 │     Diskette Drive A Type ................ [1.44MB 3.5"  ]         │
 │     Diskette Drive B Type ................ [Not Installed      ]   │
 │     Math Coprocessor ..................... Not Installed           │
 │     Serial Port .......................... [SERIAL_1]              │
 │     Parallel Port ........................ [PARALLEL_1]            │
 │                                                                    │
 │  Slot1 - Empty                                                     │
 │                                                                    │
 │  Slot2 - The IBM 3270 Connection                                  │
 │     Resources Used ....................... [Only Choice]          │
 │                                                                    │
 │ ─────────────────────────────────────────────────────────────    │
 │  Esc=Quit   F5=Previous   F10=Save                                 │
 │  F1=Help    F6=Next              V   End    PageDown               │
 └──────────────────────────────────────────────────────────────────┘
```

Figure 7-15   Sample Screen from PS/2 Model 50 Setup Program (2)

```
 ┌──────────────────────────────────────────────────────────────────┐
 │ Change Configuration                                               │
 │                                                                    │
 │  Built In Features                                                 │
 │     Installed Memory ..................... 1024KB (1.0MB)          │
 │     Diskette Drive A Type ................ [1.44MB 3.5"  ]         │
 │     Diskette Drive B Type ................ [Not Installed      ]   │
 │     Math Coprocessor ..................... Not Installed           │
 │     Serial Port .......................... [SERIAL_2]              │
 │     Parallel Port ........................ [PARALLEL_1]            │
 │                                                                    │
 │  Slot1 - Empty                                                     │
 │                                                                    │
 │  Slot2 - The IBM 3270 Connection                                  │
 │     Resources Used ....................... [Only Choice]          │
 │                                                                    │
 │  Slot3 - Empty                                                     │
 │                                                                    │
 │  Slot4 - IBM Fixed Disk Adapter                                   │
 │     Type of drive ........................ [ 30]                   │
 │     Arbitration Level .................... [Level_3 ]             │
 │ ─────────────────────────────────────────────────────────────    │
 │  Esc=Quit   F5=Previous   F10=Save      Home   PageUp             │
 │  F1=Help    F6=Next              V   End                           │
 └──────────────────────────────────────────────────────────────────┘
```

When you buy an expansion board for a PS/2, you should get a disk containing, among other things, the ADF file to configure the board. This must be merged onto the RD with choice 5, *Copy an option diskette*.

Alternatively, you can just copy the files with the extension .ADF to the RD.

Once you've merged the option diskette onto the RD, reboot and configure again. Now the RD has the information it needs to configure everything in the computer.

The auto-configuration feature is nice, but sometimes it gets confused as to what kind of hardware you have. At that point, you'll have to directly edit your configuration. When you do, you'll see the following two screens of information (this is from a Model 50 with a 3270 adapter card in it).

Chapter 8
Repairs with Circuit Boards and Chips

If the problem isn't software, everything's plugged in, and it isn't something obvious like a burnt-out motor, a broken wire, a gummed-up printer, or an imploded display, then it's probably a circuit board. Step 1 is to identify the faulty part. I'll talk about diagnostic approaches (they don't cost anything but time) in this chapter. Step 2 is repair. There are two levels of repair here: board level and chip level.

The most important, and the more difficult, of these operations is the first, *identification*. How do you know which board is bad? There are several approaches we'll examine here. Next, should you fix or replace the bad board? You'll see the pros and cons. Further along, some repairs can involve chip replacements. Finally we'll examine diagnosing and repairing memory problems—the most likely chips you'll install and replace.

Fix or Replace Boards?

Assuming (as we'll discuss presently) you can find the bad board, do you just replace it, or do you try to fix it? Sure, it's macho to get out the soldering iron and

fix an errant board. But, in general, you won't find it cost-effective to repair a circuit board. This is basically because (1) the inexpensive boards are far cheaper to replace than to repair and (2) the more expensive boards require even more expensive equipment to repair them.

Inexpensive boards, like a PC floppy controller, can be bought for $30 to $80. You can see typical board prices in the accompanying Table 8-1, but a cursory glance shows that most boards are indeed cheap. Chips on these boards are primarily soldered, not socketed, and so can only be fixed by someone trained to solder chips without destroying them. Add the hourly cost of this person to the cost of replacement chips, and the amount soon adds up to a total in excess of the cost of a $30 board. More and more boards are four-layer boards, which are tough to solder correctly. *Four layer* means the board not only has printed circuit traces on the top and bottom, but two layers in the middle! Even if the board is a simple two-layer, don't forget that time is wasted inserting the board and powering up the computer after each chip replacement.

Table 8-1. Typical PC Board Prices

Product	Approximate Cost
Turbo XT/PC System Board	$90
Turbo AT System Board	$330
386 System Board	$1200
Floppy Disk Controller Board	$30
XT Hard Disk Controller Board	$80
Hard/Floppy Controller (AT)	$130
Display Controller Board:	
Color/Graphics Adapter (CGA)	$50
Monochrome Display Adapter (MDA)	$13
Monochrome Graphics Adapter	$60
Enhanced Graphics Adapter (EGA)	$160
Video Graphics Array (VGA)	$270
Memory Expansion Board (XT)	$49
Memory Expansion Board (AT)	$120
Asynchronous Communications Adapter (serial port)	$30
Printer Adapter (parallel port)	$49
Real Time Clock/Calendar	$49
Multifunction Board (clock, printer, serial, memory)	$60
Power Supply	$60
More "Exotic" Boards:	
3278 Emulator Board	$600
Local Area Network (LAN) Board	$600
Expanded (Paged) Memory Board	$99

Example prices are taken from two discount houses: VF Associates (301) 652-4232 (as advertised in the March 1987 Capital PC Monitor) and Jameco Electronics (advertised in March 1989 BYTE magazine.) Jameco is in California at (415) 592-8097.

More expensive boards (those in the $1000+ range) could be financially rewarding to fix, but two factors hinder such repairs. First, more and more boards are being designed as *Surface Mount Design (SMD)* boards. These require expensive tools to solder and desolder, and normal soldering skills don't directly translate to SMD. Even more ominous for the do-it-yourselfer is the greater and greater use of *ASICs*

(Application Specific Integrated Circuits). ASICs are used by companies to reduce the chip count on a board; what was once 20 chips is reduced to one chip. They introduce problems for a troubleshooter because they're *proprietary*—you can't buy replacements. You might be the best engineer in the world, but you can't fix bad ASICs. If you can't fix 'em and you can't buy 'em, you've got no choice but to replace the entire circuit board.

There are exceptions to the above, of course. Some manufacturers are far-sighted enough to take the chips that are most likely to fail and socket them. That doesn't help the proprietary chip problem, but it addresses the "it's a pain to solder" problem.

Maintenance Considerations for the PS/2 Family. As I've said previously, the PS/2s have workaholic motherboards: the video, disk, parallel, serial, mouse, and keyboard controllers all exist on proprietary chips (ASICs), mounted using surface-mount technology to the motherboard. Auggh! Worst-case scenario for troubleshooting!

Now, it's not *all* bad news. There are fewer boards to worry about, and you have to fuss with fewer DIP switches. Reducing chip count should produce a more reliable machine overall. But it limits what you can troubleshoot. Replacements for the PS/2 motherboards are quite expensive—over $1,400 for the Model 50. Again, it doesn't matter how good or bad an engineer you are, fixing a faulty PS/2 motherboard is just plain impossible.

A PS/2, then, is a risky proposition. It's not likely to fail, but if it does, it'll cost lots of money.

By the way, while I'm discussing the PS/2s, you should be aware of a few known problems.

- The early (1987) 60 and 80 ESDI hard disk controllers have a problem that will, over time, cause loss of data. If you have one, contact IBM to see if you have one of the bad ones. Don't wait to see if a problem arises; get the serial number off the board and call IBM.

- An uncertain number of motherboards (some say as many as 40 percent) will not take a configuration. They may stay configured for a while, but turn the machine off overnight and it will forget the configuration. You can replace the battery, and the problem will reappear in a few weeks or months. Engineers tell me the problem is that the design of these motherboards drains batteries too quickly, and a motherboard swap for a more recent model is necessary to solve the problem. Be sure you actually have a problem: Recall from the previous chapter that you've got to merge .ADF files onto your PS/2 Reference Disk in order to enable the RD to configure third-party add-in boards. If the PS/2 is complaining about newly added third-party boards, your problem isn't with the motherboard but with your configuration job. On the other hand, if it was configured fine yesterday and now complains of not being configured when no changes have been made, you could have a problem motherboard. Another favorite cause for a false 162 configuration error is forgetting to turn on the external floppy disk. In any case, if you have a truly troublesome motherboard, remember that the PS/2s have a one-year warranty, and *get on it before the warranty expires!* Those motherboards are expensive if you're beyond your warranty.
- The PS/2s and DOS 3.3/3.2 don't get along very well. IBM has released a patch program called

DASDDRVR.SYS that you should get a copy of (IBM offers it free of charge). DASDDRVR fixes many, but not all, DOS-PS/2 problems. DOS 4.0 doesn't require DASDDRVR.SYS.

The most striking example of the PS/2's trouble with DOS 3.x arises when formatting floppy disks. Suppose you format a floppy successfully, and DOS asks if you'd like to format another. You say *yes* and try to format a second floppy, but FORMAT tells you the diskette is bad. No matter how many diskettes you try, it says each is bad. You must reboot to format any more diskettes unless, again, you have DASDDRVR on your hard disk and it has been activated by putting DEVICE = DASDDRVR.SYS in your CONFIG.SYS file.

How Do You Find the Bad Board?

I've said as much as I need to say about "fix or repair?" Now let's hunker down to the tough part—figuring out which board is the problem child. Here's the overall roadmap.

1. Make *sure* you've checked steps 1 to 7 in the previous Troubleshooting chapter. You *know* by now that a switched outlet (or one with a tripped circuit breaker) isn't the culprit. You're not ripping the machine apart to figure out why it won't boot when the last thing you did was install a new expansion board (and the machine hasn't worked since you put the board in) without first removing the new board to see if the problem goes away.

   Again, just be lazy and follow the beaten path. Don't get original. Just make sure you've followed the seven steps.

2. Assuming the machine does boot, use the machine to help diagnose its own problems. Run the diagnostics to find if it's the keyboard, video, and so on. That'll give you an indication of what's wrong.

Suppose the problem is clearly video. What now? Again, be lazy. Before you remove the top and begin to swap, check the easy stuff. First swap the cable, not the monitor or the video board.

Even lazier, is the problem specific to something like a time of day or, more likely, a piece of software? If the video works well enough to boot the system, run DOS commands, and the like but dies when you're running, say, *PageMaker*, the problem is likely software, not hardware. Either

- You've installed *PageMaker* incorrectly (easy to do, as it's a Windows product, and not simple), or
- There's a bug in the *PageMaker/Windows* code that talks to your video board, or
- Your video card isn't 100-percent compatible with the IBM standard.

In the above situation, I'd take the exact same copy of *PageMaker* on a floppy disk and move it over to an identical system, identical right down to the version of DOS and contents of CONFIG.SYS and AUTOEXEC.BAT. If the problem shows up on the second machine, common sense tells us it's either a software problem with *PageMaker*, an installation problem, or that the brand of video board both machines have isn't 100-percent compatible. We can't fix the first or third problem (I assume you can't redesign circuit boards or debug machine code), so look more closely at the second. Is installation right? Call the vendor of the software and hardware; do they (1) know of the compatibility problem and (2) have a fix?

3. Assuming the machine boots, but the above alternatives don't fix the problem, *then* you can start swapping boards to figure out which is the problem. You very rarely get to this point.

4. If the machine doesn't boot at all, consult the next section.

Night of the Living Data: Making a Dead Machine "Undead"

Suppose it's completely unresponsive. You can't run the diagnostics, as the machine won't talk at all. Here are two approaches for bringing your machine back from the dead, and a few other possibilities and solutions.

Identifying the Problem Board, Part I: With Two Machines. First of all, assume there's only one problem. Ideally, you have two machines, one sick and one well. A simple strategy here is to swap boards, one by one. Each time you swap a board, turn on *both machines* and note which machines are currently well. Ideally, you'd like to induce the problem from the originally sick PC to the originally well PC.

By the way, did you check the old "intensity turned down on the monitor" trick? I've turned down the intensity on my monitor, left the machine, come back to the machine after a while (forgetting I had turned down the intensity), and panicked, thinking that (at best) I had a bad monitor.

Ghost in the Machine (Contagious Components). Be careful here, however. Sometimes you end up with *two* sick machines. Why? I've seen components that, being damaged, damage other components. Suppose you have a dead system, and you've stripped the system to the motherboard and power supply. You try to ascertain what's causing your problems, so you swap motherboards. Still no luck. You try swapping power supplies. *Still* no response. What's happening?

You've got a demon in the power supply: Not only is it not working, it destroys motherboards. Originally it stung motherboard number one; then you fed it another one. I've seen this in two situations: bad power supplies damaging motherboards, and bad keyboard interfaces on motherboards damaging keyboards.

Moral:

1. Swap the power supply before the motherboard.
2. Before swapping the keyboard, test the keyboard interface with a voltmeter as described in the keyboards chapter.

Identifying the Problem Board, Part II: With Just One Machine. If all you've got is one machine, here's a nice, minimalist approach. Some people call it the *min/max* technique, short for *minimum/maximum.*

Start with a machine that won't boot up at all and assume there's only one thing wrong with it. We'll break it down to the bare essentials, and then add pieces until the machine refuses to boot. Once the machine refuses to boot, we'll know that the last item that we added is the trouble board.

Start off by removing everything but the following:

- Power supply
- Motherboard
- Speaker

Turn on your computer. You should observe several things:

- The fan on the power supply should start right up. If it doesn't, either the power supply isn't getting power, or the fan's burned out. If the fan is burned out, the problem's easy—you cooked your PC the last time you used it.

  There's *one* other reason the fan wouldn't start up. The power supply's pretty smart and can sense short circuits on the motherboard. If it senses such a short, it will shut down and refuse to do anything until the short's resolved. You don't believe me? Try taking a board out while the power's on. If you do it just right, you'll create a short and the machine will shut down. (This isn't a particularly smart idea, actually, and it's not recommended. You might want to just trust me on this one.)

- The power supply should also produce a "click" on the speaker (you've probably never noticed it, but it happens each time you turn on the machine.) Another aspect of the intelligent power supply is that, once it feels it's up to the task of getting to work, it sends a signal to the motherboard that resets the system. The result is the "click." Once you hear that, you know the power supply believes itself to be functional.

- Assuming the two above things happened, you'll probably get a long beep and two shorts ones out of the speaker; this is the motherboard's way of saying, *I can't find the video card.*

If the above three things have happened, congratulations—the machine booted. (It didn't do that before, remember?) If it didn't, there are only three possible culprits: the motherboard, the power supply, or the speaker. It's child's

123

play now to figure which is the offending component: Just swap the speaker, power supply, and/or motherboard. Remember what I said before about swapping the power supply first, in case it's got a demon. Remember that, in the PC repair business, the cheapest and most effective piece of test equipment is a spare part. At this point, it's a quick swap.

Assuming that the machine booted, the next step is to add the video card. Try to boot the machine. Again, if it doesn't boot, try another video card. If it boots, you'll get error messages complaining about the lack of keyboard and drives—errors 301, 601, and 1701 on an IBM machine. (You'll not see the 1701 error on an XT-type machine, as the BIOS error is generated by the hard disk BIOS on the XT controller itself. Because the controller board isn't yet in the machine, the error can't be generated.)

Keep adding boards until the machine fails. As you reassemble the machine, you'll probably get the following results:

Table 8-2. Steps in Assembling an IBM PC

Add This	Expected Outcome
Motherboard, Power Supply	1 long, 2 short beeps
Video board & display	blinking cursor, 301, 601, 1 beep
Keyboard	blinking cursor, 601, 1 beep
Disk controller	blinking cursor, 601, 1 beep
Floppy A:	blinking cursor, 1 beep, boot
Floppy B:	same; try B:
Hard Disk Controller	boots from hard disk
other boards	they should function

Note that this isn't gospel—your machine, depending on the manufacturer, will probably do something different from the above. Try it sometime, on a functioning PC. Note the outcomes. Do it before you must work with an ailing PC.

Again, I must stress this strongly: **Do this on a healthy PC so you can see what a healthy machine looks like at various stages of reassembly.** If you don't know what healthy looks like, you can't recognize disease.

Now, you may have gotten down to the last board, the machine may have been booting fine, and you inserted that last board, thinking, "Aha! Gotcha. Now to prove it. . . ." But then the machine booted fine. Why? Either (1) it just wanted some attention; (2) it fails when boards are hot, and the disassembly and reassembly cooled it to the point that it works; or (3) you didn't do the greatest job the first time you took it apart, cleaned it, and put it back together.

Other Problems and Solutions. The remaining chapters in the book cover peripherals in depth, but here are some ideas and pointers to other sections in the book.

Hard Disk Problems. If you seem to have a hard disk problem, look at the extensive coverage of drive recovery in the hard disk chapters.

Keyboard Problems. Keyboard problems are covered in the keyboards chapter, but here are a few possibilities:

- The system board may be at fault. Test keyboard test points (see chapter on keyboards).
- Is the keyboard plugged in?
- Is it an AT keyboard on a PC? Vice versa?
- Are you leaning on the space bar accidentally?
- Is this a turbo AT? Some ATs are so fast that they get confused during a reboot (Ctrl-Alt–Del) unless you take your fingers off the keyboard *very* quickly.

Many Beeps When Booting, No Video. If you get one long beep and two short beeps, the drive A light goes on, but there's no display, the problem is most likely the display board. Type *dir b:* and press Enter. If the drive B light comes on, the system is responding—you just can't see it. Swap the display board. Take a look at the video chapter.

Drive A Light Stays On. You try to access drive A, and the floppy light comes on and stays on. Check the floppy disk chapter.

Another reason—are you loading a program from floppy? The problem could be insufficient memory to run your application. Try your backup diskette, also.

PARITY CHECK Error (Memory Error). See the next chapter on memory.

What Makes Boards Fail? If you're reading this, you might already have a dead board. I've said to just replace it, but if you're interested, here's what generally zaps boards.

Most component problems boil down to either environmental trouble, damage due to mishandling, or faulty manufacture. The most common ailments are the following:

- Socketed chips creep out of their sockets due to expansion and contraction; rock the chips.
- Bad solder joints can disconnect or cause short circuits; resolder.
- Weak components fail under heat.
- PC board traces can be scratched.
- Dirt and dust build up heat.
- Edge connectors or chip pins corrode.
- RFI/EMI become impaired.

Finding and Replacing Bad Chips

Okay, you *insist* on trying to fix some boards? Sometimes, you *can* be a real hero and actually fix a circuit board. Most maintenance shops do very little board repair, instead returning the boards to the manufacturer or, more often, just disposing of them. Board repair can be time consuming and therefore expensive, not a great idea when most boards are under $100–$200. You'll spend a minimum of an hour and a maximum of forever fixing a board.

This isn't to say it should never be attempted. The most prominent chip level installations/troubleshootings are for:

- Memory chips
- Replacement microprocessors
- Coprocessors
- ROMs (Read-Only Memories)

If you're going to handle chips, please first take a look at the section on chip handling in Chapter 9. In general, finding bad chips is done in one of the following ways:

- Manufacturer notification
- Software identification of chip malfunction
- Temperature testing
- Digital probe and pulse testing
- Use of specialized (and expensive) signature analyzers
- Exhaustive chip replacement

Chip "Recall." The most common method is the first, *manufacturer notification.* That is, the manufacturer will send you a replacement chip and a notice that "some boards built in 1986 malfunction due to a faulty 65X88 chip. Enclosed find a replacement 65X88. . . ." This is like a car recall.

Software Chip Testing. Software identification is possible when the chip isn't so vital to the system that the system can't run without it. For instance, if the 8088 or 80286 microprocessor goes on vacation, there's no way to run a diagnostic program. Many memory prob-

125

lems can be tested with software, however, as well as some problems with some major chips, like the 8284 clock chip and the 8237 DMA controller. ROMs often contain a checksum that can be used to verify that the contents of the ROM haven't been damaged. You usually get the program that checks the checksum with the board that has the ROM in question. For example, most PC system diagnostics know where the checksum for the BIOS ROM is, and they check that as part of their routine.

Temperature Chip Testing. Some faulty chips can be traced through their temperature or lack thereof. A properly functioning chip should be slightly warm to the touch—warmer, at least, than after a night of deactivation. A completely cool chip, particularly a large one (large chips tend to run warmer) is probably dead. Similarly, a very hot chip of the finger burning variety is probably dead or dying.

A worse situation is when the device works *sometimes* but fails after a while (generally just before you're going to save your work). Heat can make a marginal component stop working, and the marginal component might not seem unduly warm. In this situation, how do you locate the bad component? By controlled application of heat and cold.

First, start up the device—PC, modem, whatever—with the cover off. Then use a hair dryer to blow warm, *not hot*, air onto the circuit board (100 degrees will do nicely). The intermittent chip will fail eventually. Now get a can of component coolant (Radio Shack part number 64-2321, for example) and direct the cold blast directly onto the suspect chip. If there's no suspect chip, start at the big ones. Now try to restart the device. If it starts, there's a good chance that the cooled chip is the bad one. If it doesn't restart, try another chip. Keep notes.

Finally, there's the brute force method. Get a digital probe and pulser and test each chip, one by one. This method's sure-fire, but slow.

Identifying Chips. As long as we're trying to replace chips, let's see how to find the silly things in the first place, and what do those numbers atop the chip mean? A chip can be described by its function, its identification number, and its manufacturer.

Function: A chip can be something as simple as just four NAND gates, each with two inputs (called a quad two-input NAND chip), or as complicated as a microprocessor. Physical size is some indication of a chip's complexity, but it isn't tremendously important. Memory chips are fairly small, but they're complex.

Identification Number: When a manufacturer designs a new chip, it's given an identification number. For example, an 8088 is a particular microprocessor chip, and a 7400 is a quad two-input NAND chip. Generally, chip designs are patented, so another manufacturer must be licensed before it can offer a chip it did not design. Intel designed the 8088, but Advanced Micro Devices (AMD) probably makes more of them than Intel does, now. I don't know who developed the first 256K × 1 dynamic RAM chip, but virtually everyone in the chip business makes them now.

Prefixes and suffixes can be added to a chip's ID number. The suffixes refer to the package it's in (usually *DIP*, for Dual Inline Pin, which is indicated by the suffix AN) or the temperature range (S is military specification, N is normal). Thus, 7400AN refers to a 7400 chip in a DIP package. A two-letter prefix refers to manufacturer. Some manufacturer codes are HD for Hitachi, WD for Western Digital, DM for National Semiconductor, R for Rockwell. Another code might be present, like B8544. This means (ignore the B) the chip was made in the

44th week of 1985. Some vendors, like Intel, don't put a date code on their chips. Instead, they put a serial number on the chip. A motherboard in front of me has a chip with serial number L5450275. If you have a 80286- or 80386-based computer, it's probably a good idea to examine and write down your serial number. Periodically, bugs will pop up and certain serial numbers will be recalled. Understand that there's no one single 8088 chip; it has gone through several revisions.

Other suffixes refer to performance, as in the 8088-1 and 8088-2 microprocessors. The -2 runs up to 8 Mhz, but the -1 only runs reliably up to 5 Mhz. In the case of memory chips, there are more specific speed codes, as we'll see in the upcoming memory chapter.

Soldering and Desoldering. If you're going to change chips, a few words about soldering are in order.

It isn't hard, but it *does* take some practice. *If you have never soldered before, the place to learn isn't your PC!* Get some practice elsewhere, or just decide not to bother with soldering tasks. If you *do* want to learn, Heathkit has an excellent "Soldering Self-Instruction" kit. It's $20 and comes with a simple printed circuit project. The kit has a fair amount of information, and I like it quite a lot.

We seek to minimize the amount of soldering required—more on sockets later.

The trick with soldering is to heat up *both* components to the desired temperature, and then apply the solder. You want just enough heat to melt the solder, but not so much as to destroy whatever it is that you're soldering.

Soldering irons come in various powers or wattages. For PC work, you want a low power iron, like a pencil iron under 50 watts.

Here are a few tips to remember when soldering:

- Use a pencil iron under 50 watts.
- Use a 60/40 solder with rosin (*not* acid) core, 1/32 inch width.
- Don't apply the tip more than ten seconds—this should be more than sufficient.
- For desoldering, *do not* use solder suckers or vacuum bulbs unless they have grounded tips. They can build up static charges. Use wire braid instead.
- Remove the board first. Don't try to solder things on/off boards that are installed in the PC.
- When replacing chips or transistors, socket them first (see next section).
- Buy a solder *jig* (sometimes called a *third hand*) so you have enough hands to hold the board, the soldering iron, the chip, and the desoldering tool. Edmund Scientific (see earlier) sells one for $25.95 called the "Extra Hands Work Station."

    (By the way, my friend Scott, a co-worker, claims true techies scoff at solder jigs. To the true techies, I apologize. *I've* used the things, and I like them.)
- If replacing a diode, transistor, or capacitor, draw a picture of how the original is installed. Memory (the human kind) gets faulty when faced with the normal frustration of soldering. It doesn't matter which way you insert a resistor.
- When desoldering a chip from a circuit board, don't desolder each pin in order. This builds up too much heat in one area. Jump around. Use a heat sink. Alternatively, use a solder tip designed for DIP packages.
- As mentioned before, many system boards are now "four layer" boards. They're *very* tough to work on competently with the usual inexpensive equipment.

Chip Sockets and Chip Insertion/ Removal. Chips need not be soldered

Figure 8-1 Chip Numbering

```
        ┌─n─┐
1       │   │       16
2       │   │       15
3       │   │       14
4       │   │       13
5       │   │       12
6       │   │       11
7       │   │       10
8       │   │        9
        └───┘
```

directly to the motherboard. Chip *sockets* (like light bulb sockets) are available. As long as you're removing and replacing a chip, think about installing a socket for the replacement. Most chips are soldered directly onto the printed circuit board.

The advantages of socketed chips are that (1) they're easy to remove and replace, and (2) it's a lot easier to damage a chip while soldering it in place than

while inserting it in a socket. On the other hand, a soldered chip saves money—no socket must be bought. Also, it can't creep out of the socket.

As mentioned before, a socketed chip's problem may be no worse than that it has crept far enough out of the socket to impair electrical connection. Recall that an early step in troubleshooting is to push all socketed chips gently back into their sockets.

Whether installing a socketed or directly-mounted chip, you must be sure to install it with the correct side up. Chip pins are numbered counterclockwise, with the farthest pin on the left-hand side labeled 1, then counting down on the left side and finally up the right side (see Figure 8-1).

A chip, then, can fit into a socket in one of two ways. Install a chip backwards, and you generally destroy the chip. So pay attention when installing.

The top of the chip generally has a

Figure 8-2 Chip Notches

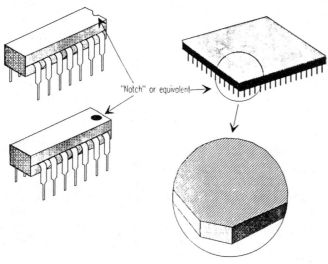

"Notch" or equivalent

notch (indicated in Figure 8-2 as *n*) to orient you when installing. To make things even easier, most circuit boards are designed so all the chips face the same way. This is essential: Insert a chip with the notch facing the wrong way, and you may damage the chip. Just make sure you place the new chip so its notch is facing in the same direction as the chips already on the board.

Chapter 9
Semiconductor Memory

I said in the last chapter that you generally won't handle troubleshooting down to the chip level. There are, as I noted, exceptions. Memory is one of them. So let's talk about the chips you *will* replace.

No discussion of circuit board and chip problems would be complete without some talk of memory chips. Memory, or RAM, chips are the chips you're most likely to mess with. Generally, you'll handle *dynamic RAM (DRAM)* chips, but some computers use *static RAM (SRAM)*.

This chapter acquaints you with memory characteristics, how to read the numbers on the top of a chip, how to read memory error messages, what kinds of things can lead to false memory errors, and some tips on handling and installing memory chips.

Reading Memory Chips: Size, Access Time, and Wait States

Chips commonly come (as of this writing) in sizes of 16K infrequently, more commonly 64K and 256K, and increasingly as 1MB chips. In general, dynamic RAMs used in PCs and ATs are 64K × 1 bit or 256K × 1 bit. This means each chip stores 64K bits or 256K bits. Thus, to store 256K bytes, eight 256K bit chips are needed—8 bits equals 1 byte. That's why each 64K or 256K group is a row of eight chips. (Actually, nine chips are used. The extra chip is for error checking with parity.) A 256K chip is the same physical size as a 64K chip.

On the PS/2s and other high-end machines, manufacturers are using more and more *SIMMs (Single Inline Memory Modules)*. These look like mini-circuit boards containing a number of tiny chips. SIMMs are an entire bank of memory on a miniboard. You can't change a single chip; you must replace an entire bank. SIMMs come in sizes of 256K and 1MB.

Another important criterion is *access time*, which is part of a chip's cycle time. *Cycle time* is how quickly the chip can respond to a request: If the CPU says, "Get me the value in location 31,824," what's the longest that the memory chip will require to respond? Access time, like cycle time, is measured in *nanoseconds (ns)*, or billionths of a second. Typical access times are:

250 (slowest)
200
150
120
100
80
70 (fastest)

Chips are classified by their access, not cycle, time. The slowest memory you'll ever see on the PC is 250 ns. Access times of 100 ns and faster are being used in speedier 286/386 AT compatibles.

How do you know what memory speed your PC needs? Either look at the documentation that came with it, or look at the memory it *currently* uses, or see the table in the next section about memory speeds.

Memory Chip Markings. The official names of memory chips reveal two things: their capacity (16K, 64K, 256K, 1024K) and their access time. Chip names look like 41XX-YY, where XX = size and YY = access time in tens of nanoseconds. Some examples:

4164-25   64K, access time = 250 ns
41256-10   256K, access time = 100 ns
4164-15   64K, access time = 150 ns

Recall that the number may be hidden in a longer ID code, like SN4164-20N. Some manufacturers don't use 64 for 64K or 256 for 256K, but some nearby number, like 65 or 257. (Perhaps they're

expressing that their chips are just a *bit* better than the competition's?) The 41 may be replaced by some other two-digit code, most likely 66, 37, or 42.

Summarizing, you may see any of the following codes atop a 64K, 200 ns memory chip:

4164-20
3764-20
6665A20
4264-20

You may also see a 4464 or 44256 chip. This is, as you'd surmise, a 64K or 256K chip respectively, but it's unusual in that it's a chip not with 64K bits, but with 64K *nybbles*—four-bit groups. That means a bank of 64K need not be nine 64K single-bit 4164s, but rather (as is seen on some motherboards) two 64K nybble 4464s and a 4164 to total nine bits. IBM used 4464s on the motherboard of the XT286: two 256K SIMMs (for a total of 512K), and four 4464s and two 4164s to add the 128K needed to bring system memory to a grand total of 640K.

Finally, when indentifying memory remember also that manufacturers can do anything they like—there are no Memory Label Police—so you could come up against a 128K chip that simply says Z1250L. You wouldn't find anything out about this chip short of getting a copy of the manufacturer's spec sheets on it.

Figure 9-1 64K, 150 ns Memory Chip

Table 9-1. Common 286/386 Clock Rates and Corresponding Clock Duration

Clock Speed (Mhz)	Duration (ns)
6	167
8	125
10	100
12	83
16	63
20	50
25	40
33	30

Background: Wait States. Although they really don't have anything to do with troubleshooting, it's common for people at this point to ask, "What's a wait state?" So, here's the answer.

On 286/386 machines, memory must be able to respond to a CPU request in two clock ticks. *Clock ticks* are just the reciprocal of the clock rate: 8 Mhz means 8 million clock ticks per second, so each clock tick is 1/8,000,000 second. Punch 1 divided by 8 million into your calculator, and you'll get 0.000000125, which is 0.125 microseconds, or 125 nanoseconds. You can do this for all the popular 286/386 clock rates (see Table 9-1).

The memory must be able to respond to a memory request in two of these clock ticks, so, for example, the memory for a 10 Mhz computer must be able to respond in 2 × 100 ns = 200 ns. Most people think the access time is the only time required by the memory when fetching data, but there's another part. The chips have a *charging time* that may equal or exceed the access time. Typical charging times (for a Mostek 64K and 256K DRAMs) are shown in Table 9-2.

So access time is important, but the total cycle time is more important:

Memory Cycle Time = Memory Access Time + Memory Charging Time

For example, suppose we're going to design a computer using a 10 Mhz clock and 256K, 120 ns chips, as cited above. We've got to keep an entire memory cycle below 2 × 100 = 200 ns. The cycle time equals the access time plus the charge time, and we know that the access time is 120 ns. Charge time for the 120 ns 256K chips is 90 ns, so total cycle time for the chips is 120 + 90 = 210 ns—the memories are just 10 ns too slow.

What to do? Obviously, we could install faster memories (for more money), or slow down the processor. There's a third alternative—add wait states. A wait state is just an extra clock tick added to each memory access. Thus, instead of requiring that each memory cycle be done in just two clock ticks (200 ns, in our case) we relax the constraint, requiring that a cycle be finished in just *three* clock ticks. Three clock ticks is 300 ns—plenty of time for our memory to complete its 210 ns cycle.

Sounds great, eh? Not really. Consider that a 10 Mhz computer is supposed to get a memory access done in two cycles. With a wait state, it takes *three* (300 ns). What speed computer would

Table 9-2. Memory Timing Statistics for 64K and 256K DRAMS

Access Time (ns)	Plus Charging Time	Equals Cycle Time
200	170	370
150	120	270
120	90	210
100	75	175
80	65	145

Table 9-3. Memory Requirements for 286/386 Computers

Clock Speed (Mhz)	Duration (ns)	Acceptable Cycle Time for 0 Wait State (2 clocks)	Acceptable Cycle Time for 1 Wait State (3 clocks)	Minimum Memory Speed for 0 Wait State	Minimum Memory Speed for 1 Wait State
6	167	334	501	150	200
8	125	250	375	120	200
10	100	200	300	100	150
12	83	166	249	80	120
16	63	126	189	N/A	100
20	50	100	150	N/A	80
25	40	80	120	N/A	N/A
33	30	60	90	N/A	N/A

complete a memory access in two clock ticks normally (with no wait states)? One with a 300/2 = 150 ns clock tick. That would be a 6.7 Mhz computer, a considerably slower one than a 10 Mhz computer. Thus, adding a wait state really means slowing the computer down by *50 percent* whenever memory accesses occur.

Put together memory cycle times and clock durations, and you can compute Table 9-3, "Memory Requirements for 286/386 Computers."

Caches: Why There's No Such Thing as a "Zero Wait State" 386. A topic that gets raised more and more is the question, "What is a memory cache?" (There's something called a *disk* cache, but that's for later in the book.) Put simply, a *memory cache* is a way to get around the fact that CPUs nowadays are faster than the memory available for a reasonable price.

As you've seen, memories come in different speeds. From 1981 to 1986, memory chips pretty much got faster at about the same rate as processors: an 8 Mhz computer could generally be out-fitted with memory of like speed without breaking the bank.

Then 16 Mhz came around.

At 16 Mhz, the usual dynamic memory chips just couldn't keep up. Nobody makes a dynamic memory chip with a 126 ns total cycle time. Manufacturers would either be forced to insert wait states, (a sleazy way, as we've seen, of making a slow machine sound fast), or they'd have to look elsewhere for faster memories.

As it turns out, there *are* faster memories, but they're *static* RAMs, and they're expensive—ten or more times the cost of dynamic RAMs of comparable size. One company did indeed go to all-static memory, but they soon discontinued the product, cost, no doubt, having something to do with it.

As has happened before, a leaf was taken from the mainframe's book, and *cache memory* was included in most 16 Mhz and faster computers. Cache memory is a small amount (generally no more than 64K) of the expensive static RAM, which is fast enough so the CPU can address it at no-wait-state speed. There's

133

also a larger amount, perhaps mega-bytes, of the relatively slower 80-or-so ns dynamic memory. The last piece of hardware is a *cache controller* to manage the whole mess.

A cache controller tries to speed up the much larger RAM using an assumption about computer use. The idea is that computer programs tend to stay within one area of code for a while, then move to another area and stay there for a while, and so on. The same phenomenon occurs with data. The cache controller gets an idea of what part of memory to work with and guesses that the CPU will soon need the data that follows in that part of memory. Then it goes to that area in the slow dynamic memory and grabs a piece of it—not the whole 64K, more commonly 4K or thereabouts—and transfers it into the cache. Now, if the cache has guessed right, the next data the CPU needs won't be in the slow memory: it'll be in the cache. The cache is fast enough to accept reads and writes at zero-wait-state speed.

That's *if* the cache has guessed right. If not, the CPU must go all the way out to the slow dynamic memory and endure *two wait states*. (Auggh!) That means the cache had better be good, or you'll have a two-wait-state machine. In practice, caches are right 80 to 99 percent of the time, so you should end up with a machine that's zero wait state 80 to 99 percent of the time and two wait state the other 1–20 percent of the time.

Most 386 machines use the Intel 80385 cache controller to handle cache management. The 486 actually includes the 385 right in it with a small amount of static RAM.

Reading Memory Error Messages

So much for the theory. Now let's look at diagnosing memory error messages. There are three ways to find memory problems: (1) run a rigorous memory test periodically, (2) get a memory error message when the PC does the POST, or (3) get a PARITY CHECK error while in the middle of an application. Let's see how to read the cryptic POST messages for memory problems.

PARITY CHECK 1 means the problem is on the motherboard. PARITY CHECK 2 is on an expansion board.

The POST, recall, runs a memory test each time you power up the PC. How does the test know how much memory the system has? You tell it by setting DIP switches on the PC system board, or by running the SETUP program on the AT. Most XT-type computers (the IBM PC excepted) deduce the amount of memory in a POST memory test.

The IBM PC and AT-type machines depend on the setup information, and they're distressed when a memory test finds a different amount of memory than the setup information lead them to expect. So, if you've just installed new memory on an IBM PC or an AT-type computer, and you get a PARITY CHECK message, the first thing to check is whether you reset the system board switches correctly or run the SETUP program. If you installed 512K on a PC and told the system that 640K exists, you'll get a parity error every time. This is, again, not true for XT-type machines. They really don't pay attention to the DIP switches to determine how much memory they have. For example, if an XT-type computer does the power-up test and finds a problem in the 384K block of memory, it won't issue an error; it will just assume that only 320K memory exists. An IBM PC or most AT-type machines would issue an error message saying in effect, "You lied to me about memory."

Recall that the POST memory error message is a code 201. A POST 201 error

XT motherboard with memory bank detail.

will be accompanied by a four-digit code such as

1020 201

followed quickly by the familiar PARITY CHECK 1 or PARITY CHECK 2 error. On an XT, the same message would look like

10000 20 201

An AT error message might look like

10000 0020 201

All three messages allow you to narrow down the memory error to a single chip. All three messages can be decoded to point to, first, the bad bank of memory, and then the bad chip within that bank.

Decoding IBM PC and XT Error Messages. First, simplify the XT error message to look like a PC error message. In general, an XT message can be converted to a PC message by ignoring the last three digits in the 10000. Thus, a **20000 04** for the XT is the same as 2004 for the PC. The four digits will help you locate the bad chip. So first collapse the XT message to a PC message.

Next, understand that the two leftmost digits point to the bad bank, and the two rightmost digits identify the bad chip in that bank.

Suppose you have an error message like 3008 201 (30000 08 201 on an XT). The first two digits identify the bank with the bad chip, the last two digits identify the bad chip within the bank. 201 just tells you that you have a memory error, and that's no surprise. So the problem is in

135

Figure 9-2   How to Read a Memory Error Message

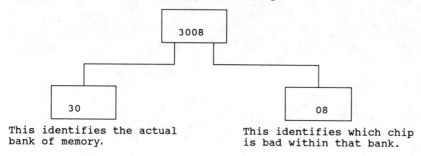

This identifies the actual bank of memory.

This identifies which chip is bad within that bank.

the bank referred to by 30, (not bank 30, there isn't one) and the bad chip is the one with ID 08 in that bank (no, it's not the eighth chip, either).

In order to use these error messages, you must first identify which kind of motherboard you have. There are three:

Figure 9-3   16K–64K Motherboard Memory Arrangement

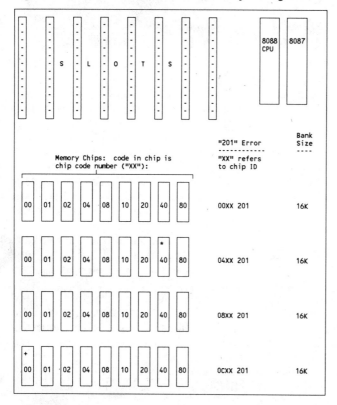

Figure 9-4 64K–256K Motherboard Memory Arrangement

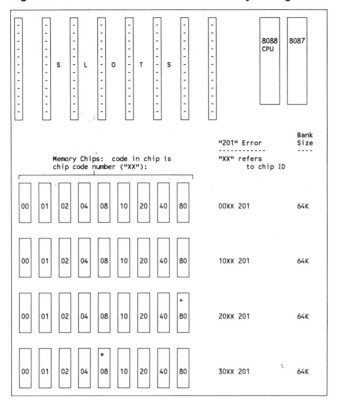

- Original PC (1981/1982)
- PC-2 and original XT (1983–1987)
- 640K XT motherboard (1986–1987)

The following pages show an outline of an IBM PC or XT motherboard. On the left is the 201 message: 30XX 201 refers to any 201 message that starts with 30. The *XX* refers to the chip ID, which is written in the chip position on the board.

PC Motherboard Type 1: Original PC 1981–Early 1983. Marking on motherboard: 16 - 64K CPU. Contained 4 16K banks on the motherboard for a total of 64K on the motherboard (See Figure 9-3).

Examples:
0C01 201 is on the bottom row, first chip

on the extreme left. There's a plus sign (+) in the chip in the diagram.

0440 201 is on the second row (counting from top), second chip over from extreme right. There's an asterisk (*) in chip in the diagram.

PC Motherboard Type 2: PC-2 (1983– 1987) and XT (1983–1987). Marking on motherboard: 64-256K CPU. Contained four 64K banks on the motherboard for a total of 256K on the motherboard (See Figure 9-4).

Examples:
3008 201 on the PC, or **30000 08 201** on the XT, indicates the last row, middle chip, as designated by an asterisk (*).

Figure 9-5 640K XT Motherboard Memory Arrangement

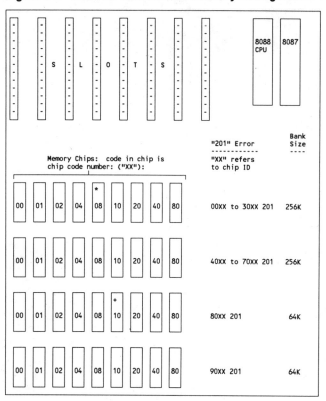

2080 201 on the PC, or **20000 80 201** on the XT, indicates the third row, rightmost chip, as designated by a plus sign (+).

640K XT Motherboard: (1986–1987). Marking on motherboard: 256K-640K CPU. Two 256K banks, two 64K banks for a motherboard total of 640K (See Figure 9-5).

Examples:
Again, looking at **300000 08 201**, it's now in the first row. Note that codes **00000 08 201**, **100000 08 201**, and **20000 08 201** would all designate the same chip, indicated with an *.

Error **80000 10 201** is in the third row, one of the 64K rows, first chip to the right of the middle chip as designated by a + (plus sign).

Special Case: "40FF 201" Error. One special case is an error message of the form 40FF 201 followed by a *Parity Check 2* message on a 256K PC. Examine the preceding motherboard memory decoding guides and you'll see that 40XX errors aren't on the motherboard—30XX is where errors stop on the 256K motherboard. That means 40FF refers to the first bank on an expansion board for this machine. The chip ID, however, is FF, so the FF indicates *all nine* chips in the bank are failing! (Add up the codes for the chips, and they sum to FF hex.) This error occurs when the memory expansion board cannot be accessed at all. You'll see this message when the dip switches indicate there's more than 256K installed but there's no expansion board, or when the memory board is defective.

An Example PC Error Message. Assume you've got the 256K PC motherboard. You turn the computer on and get a cup of coffee while it goes through the memory test. When you return, you see PARITY CHECK 1 on the screen. To diagnose the problem, you need to see the 201 error. The only way to get it back is to turn the machine off, count to 5, and then turn it back on. KEEP YOUR EYES OPEN! The 201 message will only last for a second. You would see, for example, 3008 201 and then the PARITY CHECK 1 message.

First, 30 indicates that it's in bank 3, the one nearest the front of the computer. Code 08 indicates it's chip 5, the one in the middle of the row. Simply replace the middle chip in the forward-most row and you'll be up and running again.

Understanding Error Messages in 8088 Clones. We've already seen that memory is organized into banks of nine chips. Virtually no non-IBM computers offer chip-specific diagnostic information; rather, they just tell you which bank is in error. You'll see a message like

Error at 3000:12A0

The number of interest is the leftmost one, 3. Think of memory addresses as being organized into 64K groups. If 0 is the first, 1 is the second, and so on, then 3 refers to the fourth 64K group, and that's the bank to replace. So if you've got a motherboard with four banks of 64K on it, you would replace the fourth 64K bank to resolve the above error.

But the memory might not be organized in physical 64K banks. The AT&T 6300, for example, commonly uses physical 64K banks for the first two logical banks, then two physical 256K banks for

the latter eight 64K banks. (Just to make things confusing, it also has the option to do the reverse. It can alternatively put 256K chips in the first two banks and 64Ks in the following banks.) When there are 256K physical banks, just consider one physical 256K bank as standing in for four 64K banks:

Physical Bank	Error Address
First (64K)	0XXX:XXXX
Second (64K)	1XXX:XXXX
Third (256K)	2XXX:XXXX 3XXX:XXXX, 4XXX:XXXX, 5XXX:XXXX
Fourth (256K)	6XXX:XXXX, 7XXX:XXXX, 8XXX:XXXX, 9XXX:XXXX

A typical motherboard's memory arrangement might look then like Figure 9-6.

Again, now you've got to replace the whole bank. Generally non-IBM computers give only enough information to identify the bad bank, not the bad chips. If you had a lot of time, you could change them chip by chip to find the bad one. At chip prices these days, it might not be worth it.

Understanding Error Messages In 8086-80836 Compatibles. Before I explain the IBM AT's error messages, I want to discuss AT-type clones so the AT's memory diagnostics, which are pretty Byzantine, will make some sense.

The notion of 64K banks is simple enough with the 8088-based machines. That's largely because the 8088 has an *8-bit data bus*. That's where the nine chips come from: eight for data, and one for error checking. Recall that the 8086 and 80286 are *16-bit* chips. It turns out to be a lot faster to access memory 16 bits at a time by alternating nine-chip groups when reading the memory. If the machine in the previous section was a 286

Figure 9-6   Hypothetical 8088 Motherboard Memory Arrangement

	Addresses	Bank #
`6` `4` `K` `☐` `b` `a` `n` `k` `☐`	0 --> 64K-1	0
`6` `4` `K` `☐` `b` `a` `n` `k` `☐`	64K --> 128K-1	1
`2` `5` `6` `K` `☐` `b` `a` `n` `k`	128K --> 384K-1	2 - 5
`2` `5` `6` `K` `☐` `b` `a` `n` `k`	384K --> 640K-1	6 - 9

machine, its memory organization might look like Figure 9-7.

Notice why each ''bank'' is 18 chips. You couldn't just add 9 chips to the motherboard. If you did, *you'd only get the even-numbered locations!* (You'd need pretty fancy software to run on such a machine, eh?)

Be very sure you understand this: The top two rows *together* act like a single 128K bank, not two 64K banks. Any error messages referring to the first 128K could point to a problem in either one of the top two rows. Similarly, the bottom two rows act like a single 512K bank.

In fact, we can state a general rule: *The size of a physical bank is the same as the data path to that group of memory.* The

80286 CPU in the AT has a 16-bit data path, so memory on the motherboard is in 16-bit banks. The 8086 CPU used in the Compaq Deskpro also has a 16-bit data path and, once again, chips are in 16-bit banks. For 80386 based machines, we need 32 bit groups, if we use the 32-bit bus, and there must be 36 chips in a bank. If you put an AT memory card into the 16-bit bus of a 386 machine, then you'll be dealing with 16-bit banks on that card.

The idea that the physical bank is the same as the data path is important when you add memory to a PC. For the 386 you must add either 36 chips or four SIMMs. Since chips and SIMMs come in two sizes, 256K and 1 M, you can add memo-

Figure 9-7   Hypothetical 80286 Motherboard Memory Arrangement

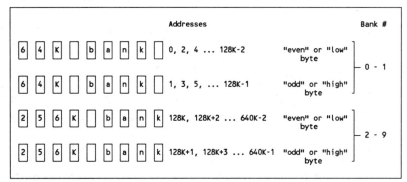

	Addresses		Bank #
`6` `4` `K` `☐` `b` `a` `n` `k` `☐`	0, 2, 4 ... 128K-2	"even" or "low" byte	0 - 1
`6` `4` `K` `☐` `b` `a` `n` `k` `☐`	1, 3, 5, ... 128K-1	"odd" or "high" byte	
`2` `5` `6` `K` `☐` `b` `a` `n` `k`	128K, 128K+2 ... 640K-2	"even" or "low" byte	2 - 9
`2` `5` `6` `K` `☐` `b` `a` `n` `k`	128K+1, 128K+3 ... 640K-1	"odd" or "high" byte	

AT motherboard with memory bank detail.

ry in groups of 4 × 256K = 1MB or 4 × 1MB = 4MB. Be careful when you choose a 386 machine if you need lots of memory now! Several popular machines are using static column SIMMs that vary greatly in price depending on size. A 256K static SIMM costs about $200, so it will cost me $800 to add a megabyte. But if I need to use 1MB SIMMs, I'll have to pay $2,000 each for a cost of $8,000 for four megabytes. Ouch!

Use the same rules as before to identify which bank is the bad one, but now do you have to change *18 chips*? Nope. Look at the picture again—you can tell which of the 9-chip groups is the bad one because one group has the even addresses (the *low* ones) and the other has the odd *(high)* addresses. Go back to the memory error address (recall that it looks something like 1234:5678). Look at the *rightmost* digit now. If it's 0, 2, 4, 6, 8,

A (no, that's not a misprint—this is hexa-decimal), C, or E, change the low 9 chips. Otherwise, change the high 9 chips.

Reading AT Memory Error Messages. Like 286 clones, the AT is a 16-bit machine and so organizes memory into 18-chip banks, not 9-chip banks.

There were two models of the AT motherboard:

- The earlier motherboard with 36 128K chips
- The model 339 with just 18 256K chips

Remember that 286s use 18-chip banks, so from the AT's point of view the old motherboard has only *two* 256K banks on it, and the 339 has only *one* 512K bank.

IBM error messages are designed as if memory still only came 64K to a chip.

This means that one *physical* bank of 256K chips is treated as four *logical* banks of 64K chips. If that's not clear, let me re-state it: a given 256K chip, if it fails, could display one of *four* error messages—one for each of its four logical 64K areas.

Recall that the PC error messages were in two parts: which 64K bank, and which chip in the bank.

Both models of the IBM AT contained a total of 512K on the mother-board. The first version used four rows of 128K chips with nine chips in a row. Two rows formed a physical bank totalling 256K, which is equivalent to four logical banks of 64K. Thus the two rows in the first physical bank contains errors with the logical bank numbers 0, 1, 2, or 3.

The second version of the AT contained two rows of 256K chips totaling 512K in bank 0. Errors in logical banks 0 through 7 all occur in the one bank of memory.

If two rows are now one logical bank, how do I find the bad chip? Four digits are used with the AT to indicate the chip error, with the first two digits indicating a chip in the high byte (bits 8 through 15) and the second two digits indicating an error in the low byte (bits 0 through 7). For example, you might get the error message 30000 0008 201, with the middle four digits indicating the bad chip. Either the first or last two digits will be zero; the error is in the byte with the non-zero digit. Here you would look to the chip indicated by 08 in the low byte, namely, bit 3. What if a parity chip is bad? Then the chip error is 0000, and you have to swap a parity chip to isolate a problem.

On clones and memory expansion boards you might see the bits labeled as

Figure 9-8 Original AT Motherboard Memory Organization

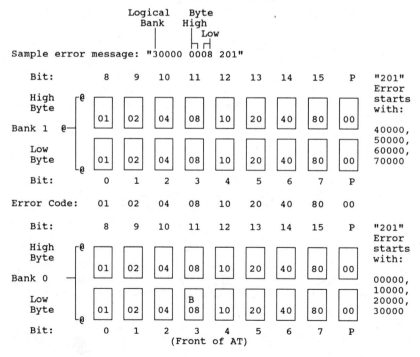

142

Figure 9-9 AT Model 339 Motherboard Memory Organization

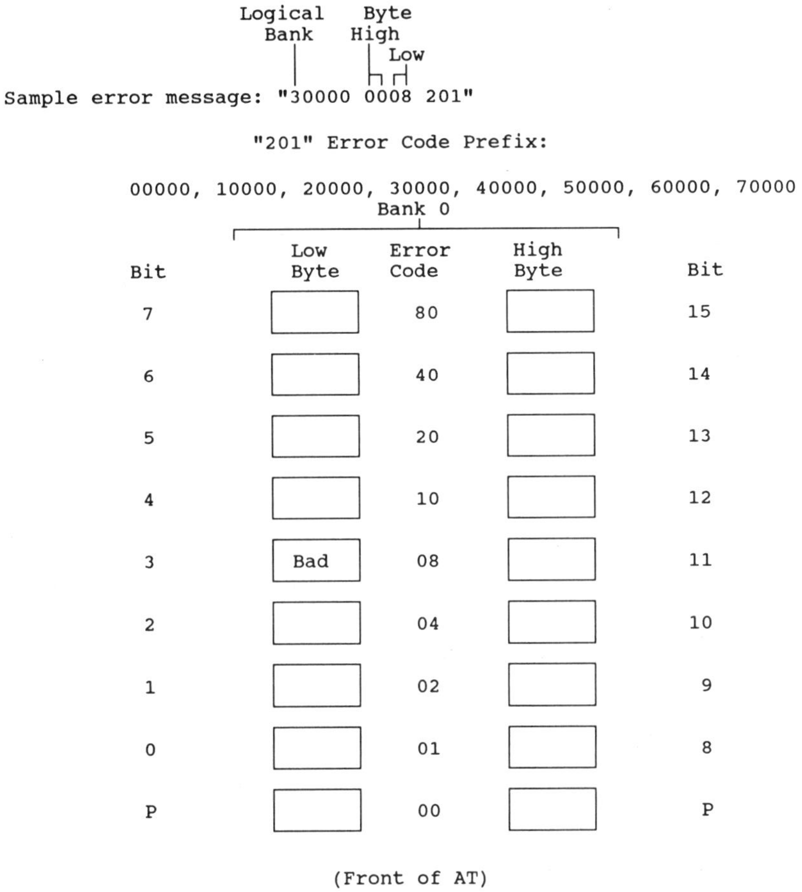

```
                    Logical    Byte
                      Bank     High
                        |       | Low
                        |       | |
                        |      ⊓ ⊓
Sample error message: "30000 0008 201"

                    "201" Error Code Prefix:

    00000, 10000, 20000, 30000, 40000, 50000, 60000, 70000
                        Bank 0
```

Bit	Low Byte	Error Code	High Byte	Bit
7		80		15
6		40		14
5		20		13
4		10		12
3	Bad	08		11
2		04		10
1		02		9
0		01		8
P		00		P

(Front of AT)

IBM does or simply with a label indicating the high and low byte. As you might expect, boards with no label whatsoever are quite common. A useful tool for this situation is simply a 256K chip with a bent address pin (pins 5 to 7 and 9 to 13), which will help you map out an unlabeled board by giving you a complete error message. Remember you can use the 256K chip in place of a 64K chip as well.

AT Motherboard type 1. Marking on motherboard: 256/512K

Two physical 16-bit banks consist-ing of 18 128K chips, for a total of 256K in each physical bank and a total of 512K on the motherboard.

AT Motherboard Type 2 (Model 339). Marking on motherboard: 256/512K

One physical 16 bit bank consisting of 18 256K chips, for a total of 512K in the bank and on the motherboard.

Other Causes of Memory Errors

If a chip seems okay but causes errors, consider the following rules:

- Never mix chip speeds in the same row. Don't install a row with some 200 ns chips and some 150 ns chips, even if 200 is the speed required. Remember that if your computer requires 200 ns chips, then a speed of 200 or faster (like 150, 120, 100, or 75 ns) will work fine. You can have one row of 75s, a row of 120s, a row of 150s, and a row of 200s for all it matters—*just don't mix chip speeds in the same row!* (Actually, if your computer only requires 200 ns chips, there's no point in spending the extra money for faster, more expensive chips.)
- Whenever possible, avoid mixing *manufacturers* in the same row. I flatly cannot explain this, but I've seen cases like the following. I've had two rows of chips—one entirely Mitsubishi, another entirely Toshiba—that worked fine. Then I mixed the rows. Errors occured. I restored the rows, and the problem disappeared.
- Remember to check chip seating: Has the chip crept out of its socket? Are all the legs in their socket holes, or is one bent under the chip, barely touching the contact?
- Is there enough power? Insufficient power can cause parity errors. This one can be a real pain, since it waits for some large disk access to trigger the parity error, like when you try to save your data to disk.

You see this one with underpowered clones and *Lotus*. Your *1-2-3* spreadsheet might work fine until you want to save the file, and then you get a parity check. The problem is you're running the power supply to the poor thing's limits, and then you want to fire up the hard disk. There's not enough power, the memory gets shortchanged, and bang! a memory error happens.

- Noisy power can cause memory errors. A surge, such as a static electricity zap, can randomize memory contents, looking like a memory failure to the system.
- Improperly shielded sources of RF noise can alter memory, causing parity errors.

Tips on Installing Memory Chips

A lot of manuals include some really scary instructions for installing memory chips. I've probably installed a gigabyte or so myself (1MB chips have made it easier to get to the 1GB level), so here's what works for me.

First, as always, be aware of static electricity. Your acrylic sweater and the soles of your shoes are powerful producers of static. If I'm worried about the static level of an area, and I'm not prepared with a ground strap, *I take my shoes and socks off.* I know it sounds a little bizarre, but I kill very few chips that way, probably fewer than a half dozen in all the time I've been installing memory.

Second, the memory chips go into sockets in a circuit board. As before, don't insert memory into boards while the power is on. Orient it so its notch is facing the same way as the notches on other chips on the board. The legs of a new chip will be spread a bit too much to fit into the socket. Just insert one row of pins into their holes, and then coax the other row into *their* holes. At this point, you've got some tension, since the legs on both sides are eager to just spring out of the socket. Double-check that the legs are all positioned to slide into their holes, and then push the chip into the socket firmly with your thumb.

If you make a mistake or must remove old chips, use a small "tweaker' screwdriver. With it gently pry up one end of the chip, and work the screwdriver completely under the chip. It will come up easily. Make sure you put the

144

screwdriver under the chip, not the socket. The socket won't come up easily, and if it does you'll have damaged the motherboard.

DO NOT use one of the "chip remover" tongs that seem to get included in every PC toolkit these days. They work okay if you've had practice with them, but they scare me because they make it a lot easier to damage a chip while taking it out. Stick with a small screwdriver, and remember that *patience* is the keyword here. Look at what you're doing, and take your time if you're new to the process.

Chapter 10

Power Supplies and Power Protection

The PC doesn't come with batteries included. You plug it into the wall socket and it works. The PC itself doesn't directly use wall current, as this is 120 volt alternating current. Like most digital devices, it needs fairly low power direct current at 5 and 12 volts.

By the way, a word to European readers: Everything I say here applies to you *except* for references to the mains. Your mains aren't 120 volts but more like 230, and the power frequency is 50 cycles per second, not 60. DO NOT try any of the tests here that refer to the actual alternating current unless you already know about working with the mains safely.

Enter the power supply. The power supply doesn't *supply* power—it *converts* it from AC to DC, so it's a *switching* power supply. A switching design means it can handle quite a range of power problems without trouble. The alternative, a *linear* power supply, isn't quite so robust, and it's found on virtually all PC peripherals. Power supply troubles can be mysterious and annoying. Just as bad are similar-looking troubles

with the supplied power itself. This chapter looks at both.

The line current isn't squeaky clean, and that can damage PCs. Safeware, a computer insurance firm, reports that 1986 saw $250 million in insurable PC damage, *$35 million of which came from PCs damaged by surges.*

Components of the Power Supply

The power supply is the black or silver box in the back of the PC with the large yellow label telling you in five languages not to open the box up, warning you that it's dangerous. Despite the fact that I can only understand a few of the multilingual messages, I'm inclined to take them at their word.

The reason is mainly due to a large (1000 microfarad) capacitor in the power supply. The capacitor is utilized to smooth out some power glitches, which is a good thing, in general. But the capacitor retains power like a battery. Thus, even though the power supply is unplugged, it can still do you some harm. Power supplies cost under $100; just replace them if they're faulty. I recommend replacing and not repairing floppies just

Figure 10-1 System Board Detail with Power Connectors

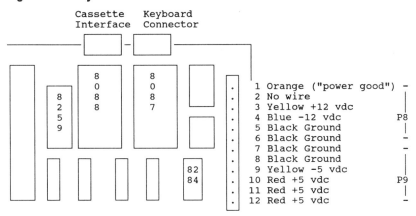

```
                Cassette   Keyboard
                Interface  Connector
─────────────────┌─────┐─┌─────┐────────────┐
                 └─────┘ └─────┘            │
┌──┐                                        │
│  │    ┌──┐  ┌─────┐  ┌─────┐  ┌──┐  ┌──┐  │
│  │    │8 │  │8    │  │8    │  │  │  │  │   · │  1 Orange ("power good")  ─
│  │    │2 │  │0    │  │0    │  │  │  │  │   · │  2 No wire                 │
│  │    │5 │  │8    │  │8    │  │  │  └──┘   · │  3 Yellow +12 vdc          │
│  │    │9 │  │8    │  │7    │  │  │         · │  4 Blue -12 vdc         P8 │
│  │    └──┘  └─────┘  └─────┘  └──┘  ┌──┐   · │  5 Black Ground            │
│  │                                  │  │   · │  6 Black Ground            ─
│  │    ┌──┐  ┌─────┐  ┌─────┐        │  │   · │  7 Black Ground            ─
│  │    │  │  │     │  │     │  ┌──┐  └──┘   · │  8 Black Ground            │
│  │    │  │  │     │  │     │  │82│         · │  9 Yellow -5 vdc           │
└──┘    └──┘  └─────┘  └─────┘  │84│         · │ 10 Red +5 vdc           P9 │
                               └──┘         · │ 11 Red +5 vdc             │
                                            · │ 12 Red +5 vdc             ─
```

because it's a pain to repair them, but I recommend not repairing power supplies because they can hurt you. (I still recall a shock from a high school power supply project.)

Power Supply Connections

On the side of the power supply is the on/off switch for the computer. Sprouting out of the other side are the power connectors. You'll recall P8 and P9 from the discussion of PC disassembly. The other connectors—two or four of them—are for floppy, tape, or hard drives.

The motherboard receives power through the power strip in the northeastern corner of the board. (This assumes you're looking at the board so that the memory chips are closest to you, and the expansion connectors, the 8088, and the keyboard connector are farthest from you.) The connector is actually two six-pin connectors lined up one atop the other. They're generally labeled P8 and P9.

P8 has only five wires and connects above P9, which has six wires (see Figure 10-1).

The power supply lines (the yellow, blue, and red wires) can be tested against a ground (any of the black wires). If you're actually testing a power supply, all of the black wires should be tested. Table 10-1 lists the specifications for these lines.

Table 10-1. Specifications For PC Power Supply Output

Wire Color	Rated Voltage (Volts)	Acceptable Range (Volts)	Current Range (Amps)
Yellow	+12	+8.5–+12.6	0.0–2.00
Blue	−12	−8.5–−12.6	0.0–0.25
Red	+5	+2.4–+5.2	2.3–7.00
Yellow	−5	−4.5–−5.4	0.0–0.30

Table 10-2. System Board Resistances

Common Lead (Black Probe)	VOM Lead (Red Probe)	Minimum Resistance (Ohms)
8	10	0.8
8	11	0.8
8	12	0.8
5	3	6.0
6	4	48.0
7	9	17.0

You can then do a resistance test of the motherboard. The tests are conducted on the power supply pins. Table 10-2 contains the *minimum* resistance for each connection. If the measured values are less than this, the motherboard is definitely faulty.

As we've seen, P8 connects to the motherboard toward the back, with P9 in front of it. As to P10 and P11, the drive power connectors, *it doesn't matter which connector goes to which drive*—they're interchangeable. You can use either connector for floppies, hard drives, or whatever.

IBM ATs have a third connector, P12. It can't be used on most hard disks, as it doesn't supply enough power, so use it for a floppy. Clone power supplies generally have four power connections that are all full-power connections. They can be used for anything from hard disks to floppies. Also, they don't need to be used; just because you have four drive power connectors doesn't mean you must have four drives (I get asked that now and then).

Maintenance

Good news here: There's no maintenance required. The fan and the power switch are the only moving parts. If you suddenly notice that the PC is very quiet

but still operating, then your fan might have died. If that happens, save everything and *shut down immediately!* The computer's own heat can quickly damage or destroy itself if the fan isn't present to dissipate it.

Don't block the vents the PC uses for cooling, and use compressed air to blow the dust out of the fan now and then. Please remove the power supply first so the dust doesn't immediately settle on the computer.

Upgrading the Power Supply

IBM PCs and some clones have wimpy 63.5-watt power supplies. This is insufficient for many applications. Memory boards, hard disks, 3278 emulators, and other plug-in enhancements can raise the total power requirements over the 63.5-watt supply's capability. But even if you're only using 50 watts, you should think about upgrading.

The standard sizes of power supplies for various computers are included in Table 10-3.

A 63.5-watt power supply works harder supplying 50 watts than a 135 watt power supply. Both a Volkswagen Beetle and a Porsche 944 can travel at 65 miles per hour, but it seems like real

Table 10-3. PC Power Supply Capacities

Computer Type	Power Supply Size (Watts)
PC	63.5
XT	130.0
AT	192.0
Model 50	94.0
Model 50Z	94.0
Model 60	225.0
Model 70	105.0
Model 80	225.0

work in the Beetle. A power supply running near its limit won't be as reliable as one with a little comfort space.

Don't confuse *watts capacity* with *watts used*. Sure, a 150-watt bulb uses more power than a 60-watt bulb—that is it's watts used. A 130-watt power supply means a power supply that can convert *up to 130 watts*. Notice the *up to;* putting a 130-watt power supply on a system that only requires 50 watts will only cause the power supply to convert 50 watts. A lot of folks misunderstand that. Even an IBM engineer in 1983 warned me that putting an XT's 130-watt power supply on an IBM PC would "burn up the motherboard." That was wrong, but I didn't know any better.

You've got worries with the desktop PS/2s, also. The Models 50 and 50Z have fairly inadequate power supplies. Their maximum power output is 92 watts, but the Model 50 requires 73 watts *with no expansion boards.* This hasn't been a problem so far, but wait until people start putting extra memory, internal modems, and the like into the systems.

So pushing a power supply too far isn't a good idea. How do you know how much power your machine is using? One simple device is a Power Meter from PARA Systems:

PARA Systems, Inc.
1455 LeMay Drive
Carrollton, TX 75007
(214) 446-7363
(800) 238-7272

The Power Meter looks like a power strip with a gauge on it. You just plug it into the wall, then plug your system unit into the Power Meter. It has a wiring tester, so it tells you if your outlets are wired correctly. (See "Protecting the PC from the AC," coming up.) Then turn the system unit on and look at the needle on the gauge. It measures amperes of current flowing. You'll get a value between 0.5 and 3. Just multiply that ampere value by 58 and you'll get the number of watts your system unit uses. If the reading is close to its rated power supply, it's time to get a bigger power supply.

Why 58? You may know that Power (watts) = Volts × Amps, and that you ordinarily get 120 volts from the wall outlet. Why not multiply amps by 120? Simple—this isn't direct current, where amps and volts are always in phase. Instead, you're dealing here with AC, or Alternating Current. In AC, current and voltage follow sine wave-like paths that can fall out of step. That means multiplying amps by 120 would overstate the total actual power requirements.

When buying upgrade power supplies, consider the fan. Recall that the power supply's fan is responsible for heat dissipation in the PC, as we've discussed in the preventive maintenance chapter. Another benefit from an upgraded power supply is availability of additional floppy connectors. The IBM XT and IBM PC power supplies only offer two connections for drives, the IBM AT only three. Many third-party supplies have four connections. You could then have two half height drives, a hard disk (half height), and a tape drive, as well as the power to drive them.

The XT and PC use the same case type for the power supply. PC and XT replacement power supplies are about 135–150 watts. The AT power supply case is a bit larger, and replacements are in the 190–200-watt range. You probably wouldn't replace your AT power supply for reasons of power except in unusual circumstances. You might, however, replace it because the fan is so noisy or to improve cooling.

Speaking of replacement power supplies, remember the discussion of the power supply lines in the chapter on circuit boards? You may have noticed the first line on P8, called *Power Good*. This is a digital signal enabled by the power supply once it views itself as warmed up and ready. A flaky Power Good leads the computer to issue either a long beep, short beeps, or generally unusual noises. Some inexpensive replacement power supplies cause computers to emit a loud or long beep, then settle down to good service. I've experienced this myself, and can only account for the beeps if the power supply doesn't wait quite long enough to first enable Power Good. A little initial up and down activity on the line would induce the clock to issue a RESET command to the PC.

Troubleshooting the Power Supply

You turn the computer on and nothing happens at all. It's plugged in, so it's not that—where next?

The Power Supply Troubleshooting Trail. First, check the outlet. The outlet should be providing between 104 and 130 volts AC current. Just set the VOM to read AC voltage and put one lead in each hole of the outlet.

Second, check the cables. The cables should be in place on the system board.

Third, is power getting to the power supply? The fan gets it first, so if it isn't turning, the power supply isn't getting power. When some power supplies are first turned on, the speaker emits a low click.

Fourth, test the power supply with another one.

Replacing a Power Supply. If you suspect the power supply, replace it. It's simple.

1. On the back of the PC, you'll see four screws bolting the power supply to the chassis. Remove these.
2. Disconnect the system board (P8 and P9) and the drives. Draw a pic-

ture and make notes of what connects to what. Note wire colors. P8 goes toward the back, P9 toward the front.
3. Slide the power supply forward just a bit—it's hooked to the chassis from below. It will now lift out.
4. Install the new power supply by reversing the procedure.
5. To be extra careful, strip the PC down to the minimum circuit boards. Then power up and do whatever diagnostics you use.

Protecting the PC from the AC

You can control a lot of things in your environment, but you have little control over one aspect of the PC environment: the power delivered by the electric company. For various reasons, it doesn't come out clean and regular like it's supposed to. Worse yet, you can't even always blame the power company; sometimes it's your or your building management's fault.

Do You Have Power Problems? Power or wiring problems can show up as:

- The computer mysteriously "freezing up"
- Random memory errors
- Lost data on the hard disk
- Damaged chips on a circuit board
- Data transmission noise and peripheral errors

Recently I was at a hotel doing a presentation that involved a demonstration PC. The PC did the strangest things:

- Once, it stopped the memory test at 128K and froze.
- Another time, it gave a memory error message around 400K.
- The hard disk wouldn't boot about 30 percent of the time, despite a fresh format.

- It stopped talking to the keyboard a few times, requiring the Big Red Switch.

What was wrong? The old "hotel power" problem. When the coffee machine was on, the machine did strange things. Additionally, the PC shared an outlet with two 600-watt overheads in continuous use and a slide projector. I moved it to another outlet, and the problem disappeared.

Having said that, what can you do about power problems? The four steps to power protection are:

- Check that your outlets are wired correctly.
- Find out what else is on the power line.
- Provide a common ground for all devices.
- Protect against noise: surges, spikes, under-and over-voltage.

Here are the facts to "empower" you to solve your line problems.

Check Outlet Wiring. AC outlets have three wires: a large prong, a small prong, and a center cylinder. The cylinder is the safety ground, the prongs are the *hot* or *phase* line (the "official" term is *phase*, but anyone who has ever accidentally touched it calls it the *hot*), and the *return*, *common*, or *neutral* line. The wires in the wall are supposed to be wired, so green is ground, white is return, and whatever's left (usually black) is phase.

It's not unheard of for the hot and the return to be reversed. This actually isn't a problem so long as everything is wired backwards. But if you plug, say, the PC into a correctly wired outlet, and a printer into a wrongly wired outlet, and if one of the devices connects the ground and the common—again, not an unusual occurrence—*and* there's a break in the neutral, then you'll get 120 volts across

the cable from the printer to the PC. Lots of destruction will follow. Worse yet, miswired outlets can hurt you; if you're touching both the PC and the printer, you're the electrical path.

You can buy circuit wiring testers from most hardware stores. I got mine at Sears for $6.

Check What Else Is on the Line. Ensure that there isn't any equipment on the same line as the PC that draws a lot of power. That includes:

- Large motors, such as in air conditioners, refrigerators, or power tools
- Heating coils, such as in small space heaters or coffee makers— "personal" coffee makers are included here
- Copiers and their cousins, laser printers.

Anything that draws a lot of current can draw down the amount of voltage being delivered to a PC on the same breaker or fuse. Worse yet, heating coil devices like coffee makers inadvertently create something called a *tank circuit* that can inject high frequency spikes into the power line; it's noise that can slip through your power supply and go straight to the chips on the circuit boards.

One simple solution is to just get a separate power circuit to the box. Another is to get an isolation transformer such as we find in a power conditioner. An RF shield between the primary and secondary coils of the transformer removes the high frequency noise.

Lasers draw 15 amps all by themselves. That implies that, like it or not, you've got to put in a 20-amp breaker for each laser printer/PC combination. PCs without lasers don't draw much power, and so don't require a separate breaker.

Ensure Common Ground Among Devices. Electrical ground is intended, among other things, to provide an electrical *reference point*, a benchmark value like *sea level*. A computer communicates 1s or 0s to a modem, for instance, by varying voltage relative to ground: Greater than +3 volts means 0, less than −3 volts means 1. A voltage near 0 means nothing is being transmitted.

The problem arises when the two communicating devices don't agree on the value of *ground*. If, in the above example, the modem's ground is a 7-volts potential below the computer's ground, the modem and the computer each think the other is sending data when neither actually is.

Generally, it's not that bad. But if the computer's ground is 3 volts different from the modem's, the occasional bit will be lost or garbled.

The answer? Simple—just ensure that all devices plugged into your PC share the same ground. A simple six-outlet power strip will do this. There's one flaw in this approach, however: What about a Local Area Network (LAN)? Basically, a LAN is one big ground problem. Some people have suggested grounding the shield of the network cables every hundred feet or so. The only true solution is to use fiber optic LANs, but they're still a wee bit expensive.

Please note: Ensuring that all equipment has a common ground has nothing to do with having a "good" ground. A proper ground is for mainly for safety, not data protection. (If someone insists that you must have a good ground for proper data transfer, ask him how airplanes and spaceships manage it, hmmm?) We'll look at proper grounding soon.

Protect Against Power Noise. We've already discussed undervoltage, overvoltage, spikes, and surges in Chapter 5 on preventive maintenance. Remember:

- *Undervoltage* is undesirable because the power supply reacts to too *little* voltage by drawing too *much* current. This heats up and can destroy components.
- *Overvoltage* can damage a chip because too much voltage destroys the circuits inside the chip.

When some outside force causes your power line to deliver more voltage than it's supposed to, this is called an *overvoltage condition*. Such conditions are, in general, dangerous to the computer.

The physics of it is this: The heart of the computer resides in its chips. The chips are especially designed crystals. Crystals are highly structured molecules; many of them would be happier in a less structured environment. Applying electronic and heat energy to the crystals allows this breakdown in organization to occur. One spike might not do it, but even small spike damage is cumulative.

Damage is proportional to energy. Energy is voltage × current × time.

Brief overvoltages under a millisecond in length are called *spikes*. Longer ones (milliseconds to seconds) are called *surges*.

- *Spikes* are temporary overvoltages that may be of high enough frequency to introduce RFI-like problems.

You (or your boss) could be skeptical about the actual level of power problems. This may all be, you suspect, a tempest in a teapot. If you don't think you have power problems, spend $130 on a simple device that can monitor the quality of your power. Called the AC Monitor, it's from Tasco Ltd:

AC Monitor $138
Tasco Ltd
2875 W. Oxford Ave. No. 5
Englewood, CO 80110
(303) 762-9952

It will continuously monitor the voltage you're receiving at the outlet and indicate power drops, surges, or spikes (no frequency variation, sadly) with a light and an audible warning.

Solutions to Power Problems. Solutions to power problems fall into three categories:

- Isolation
- Shielding
- Proper grounding

Isolation means isolating the noise (surge, spike, and so on) from the computer and draining it off harmlessly. This is done with filters, transformers, gas discharge tubes, and *MOVs (Metal Oxide Varistors)*. A MOV is an important part of a surge protector. When a surge comes in, an MOV shunts it off to ground. Unfortunately, the MOV is a kamikaze component, since it "throws itself onto the grenade." Each MOV is only good for one big surge, or a bunch of little surges. (No, there's no easy way to test to see whether an MOV is still working or not, at least not without a $2,000 tester.) Power conditioners and surge protectors provide isolation in varying quality.

Shields minimize high frequency noise. Shielding is evident in the filter capacitors in surge protectors, RF shields between the primary and secondary coils in a power conditioner, the metal case of the computer, and shielded cable.

Grounding is viewed by some people as a magic answer to noise problems. Just run a wire from the device in question to a metal stake pounded into the ground (called a *ground stake*), and all of your ground problems go away (kind of like an electronic Roto-Rooter, ". . .and away go troubles down the drain.")

Nahhh.

First, having a proper ground *is* important. It makes electronic equipment safer (it keeps you out of the circuit), but, as we've seen, a *common* ground is important to minimize communication errors between devices. So the main reason for a proper earth ground is safety.

The idea behind a ground stake is to provide a nice electrical path to earth ground. It *doesn't* eliminate noise, however: Two ground stakes a few yards apart will pass current and noise between themselves. Ground stakes are less effective when there's a drought. I once heard of a ground stake that provided a better connection to ground than others on a particular site because it was, err, "watered" by local fauna. (No, I'm not sure I believe it, but ground *is* magic, and magical stories accompany it.)

A final thought on grounding: Some companies are extra careful to ground their computer rooms, thinking this will somehow protect their data. They're not so careful about the other areas in the building, however, so you've got a computer room with a cleaner ground than the rest of the building. Step back for a moment and ask: What effect would differential grounding have on lightning protection? If lightning strikes a building, it takes the easiest path to ground. If the easiest path to ground is through your computers, so be it. Basically, if you ground your computer room well but not the rest of the building, it's like putting a big "EAT AT JOE'S" sign on the computer room, as far as lightning is concerned.

Devices to Remedy Electronic Problems. Okay, now we've seen the problems and some approaches to solutions. Now let's look at what's available on the market to solve the problems.

If you're looking here for a recommendation, please understand that I don't have good news. Electric power in the 90s in most of the Western world is getting worse and worse due to aging equipment and lack of new capacity being pitted against ever-growing energy demand.

The PC really needs cleaner power than the stuff you feed your refrigerator, cofeemaker, or desk lamp. The only absolutely reliable way to get clean power is to rectify the power, put it in a battery, and then use the DC power in the battery to reconstruct the AC power. A device that does this is a sine wave UPS; a good one will cost about $800 minimum. So choose the best compromise. Some of the people I work with use surge protectors, some use SPSs, and others use power conditioners. Me? I'm building a Faraday cage for my office (just as soon as I get some time and money. . .).

Surge Suppressors and Spike Isolators. Many of us have purchased *surge protectors*, or as they're also known, *spike isolators*.

The idea with suppression devices is that once they detect a large surge coming, they redirect it out to the electric ground, kind of like opening the flood gates. The most common redirection device is called a *Metal Oxide Varistor*, or *MOV*. It's an impassable barrier between the supply voltage and protective ground until the voltage reaches a certain level. *Gas discharge tubes* and *pellet arrestors* are slower but beefier devices.

Coaxial arrestors fit somewhere in the middle.

The best suppressors use several lines of defense: MOVs, coax arrestors, and gas discharge tubes, for example.

Of course, an overzealous surge suppressor can redirect too much power for too long, creating a worse surge of its own.

Another important question is, *what voltage level triggers the surge suppressor?* They're not waiting for 120.00001 volts to get going: some will pass 1000 volts before calling in the Marines. By then, your PC is toast.

PC magazine did tests of surge suppression devices in its May 27, 1986, issue. They created spikes and measured how much of the spike was allowed through. Some suppressors emitted smoke and flames when subjected to a real surge. Others died quietly, not informing the owner that they no longer protected the PC (they still pass electricity, so there's no way to know.) The most impressive performance was turned in by PTI Industries' Datashield 85, a six-outlet suppressor that let no more than 290 volts through. Some of the more commonly known ones, like Curtis Manufacturing's Diamond six-outlet suppressor, passed 1,440 volts.

PC was happiest with:

Figure 10-2 Surge Protector

The Datashield 85 $92
PTI Industries, Inc.
269 Mt. Herman Rd.
Scotts Valley, CA 95066
(408) 439-6600

The Bad News About Surge Protectors.
But I can't, in good conscience, recommend surge protectors to you.

The best suppressors use several lines of defense: MOVs, coax arrestors, and gas discharge tubes, for example. But the heart of surge protectors are MOVs. As we've said before, MOVs are one-time-only devices. One surge, and they're history. Worse yet, they can't be tested.

Yes, some surge protectors come with a little light that goes out when the surge protector doesn't protect any more. But those little lights can't be trusted, either. The light is in series with a fuse, and the fuse is in series with the return from the MOV—it's called a *bleeder fuse*. Given a large enough surge, the fuse will blow (along with the MOV, recall) and the light will go out. So in the case of a single large surge, the light *is* effective. But an MOV can also be destroyed by a number of smaller surges. In that case, the fuse would be unaffected, and the light would stay on.

Summarizing, there's no way to know whether or not your surge protector is still protecting. If you have a light on your surge protector, and it goes out, you definitely have a dead surge protector. But if the light's on, that's no guarantee of surge protector effectiveness.

Power Conditioners. Between a surge protector and a backup power supply is another device, also in-between in price, called a *power conditioner*. A power conditioner does all the things a surge protector does, filtering and isolating line noise, and more. Rather than relying on MOVs and such, the power conditioner uses the inductance of its transformer to filter out line noise. An isolation transformer is a far superior device for removing noise than a capacitor or an MOV. Additionally, most power conditioners will boost up undervoltage so your machine can continue to work through brownouts.

Recall that the surge protector's MOVs fail with no sign, so there's no good way to know if your surge protector is doing any good. Power conditioners don't have that problem; when a transformer fails, you know it—the power conditioner just plain doesn't provide any power.

Which power conditioner is right for you? The one I use is Tripplite's LC1800. I've seen it in mail-order ads for as little as $190.

Backup Power Supplies. In addition to protection from short power irregularities, you might need backup power. I've lived in a number of places in the northeastern U.S. where summer lightning storms will kill the power for just a second—enough to erase your memory and make the digital clocks blink. Total loss of power can only be remedied with battery-based systems. Such systems are in the range of $350 to $1200 and up.

There are two types, *Standby Power Supplies* (SPS) and *Uninterruptible Power Supplies* (UPS). SPSes charge the batteries while watching the current level. If the power drops, they activate themselves and supply power until their batteries run down. A fast power switch must occur here, and it's important to find out what the switching time is. Four ms or under is fine. Fourteen ms, in my experience, isn't fast enough.

A UPS constantly runs power from the line current to a battery, then from the battery to the PC. This is superior to an SPS because there's no switching time involved. Also, this means that any surges affect the battery charging mecha-

Figure 10-3 UPS AC Waveforms

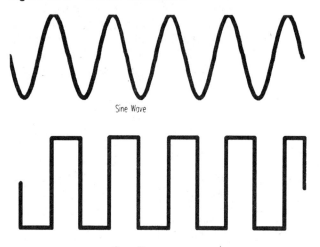

Sine Wave

Square Wave

nism, not the computer. A UPS, then, is a surge suppressor also.

A UPS or SPS must convert DC current from a battery to AC for the PC. AC is supposed to look like a sine wave. Cheaper UPS and SPS models produce square waves (see Figure 10-3). Square waves are bad because they include high-frequency harmonics that can appear as EMI or RFI to the computer. Also, some peripherals (printers in particular) can't handle square wave AC. So, when examining UPSes, ask whether they use square wave or sine wave. Some produce a pseudo-sine wave. It has the "stairstep" look of a square wave, but not as many harmonic problems.

Ordinarily, the purpose of a UPS is to allow you enough time to save whatever you're doing and shut down gracefully. If you're in an area where the power might regularly disappear for hours, you should look for the ability to attach external batteries to the UPS so you can run the PC for longer periods.

Remember that a sine-wave UPS is the only way to really eliminate most power problems. The reason *everyone* doesn't have one is cost.

A decent compromise can be found in a fast ($\leq$4 ms) square-wave SPS. I know I said square waves are bad for your peripherals, but consider: How often will the SPS actually be doing anything? Not very often—remember that it only supplies power when the line voltage drops out, not a common occurrence. The brief minute or two each month of square wave power that your peripherals end up getting won't kill them. And you'll save a pile over a UPS.

On the other hand, remember that a UPS is always on line, and so must produce sine wave output. But UPSs have the benefit that they provide surge protection by breaking down and reassembling the power; SPSs *do not* provide this protection. You must still worry about surge protection when you buy an SPS, but not if you buy a UPS. So make the choice your budget allows.

Backup power supplies:

- If it's an SPS, it must switch in less than or equal to four ms.

- If it's an SPS, square wave output is acceptable.
- If it's a UPS, it *must* have sine wave output.

The Grandaddy of Power Problems: Lightning

When Thor's hammer falls near your site, you won't need any special equipment to note its passing. Curled-up, blackened circuit boards are pretty easy to spot.

I travel around North America and Europe teaching troubleshooting classes. You know what *everyone* tells me? No matter where they are, the natives tell me they're in the "lightning capital of the world." Take a look at Figure 10-4 to find out where you rate.

- Lightning affects your system even if it doesn't strike your building.
- It's *good* to leave a machine plugged in—the lightning has an easy path to ground.
- As mentioned earlier, taking special care to ground the part of the building that the big computers are in just makes those computers more vulnerable. A better-grounded path is the one lightning will take.
- Lightning arrestors can reduce the likelihood of lightning damage.
- Newer hi-tech lightning rods are being used in some sites. They look like an umbrella built of barbed wire standing about 30 feet tall.
- A cheap lightning protection is overhand knots in the power cord. Believe it or not, some researchers discovered this one. It makes the

Figure 10-4 Mean Annual Number of Days with Thunderstorms

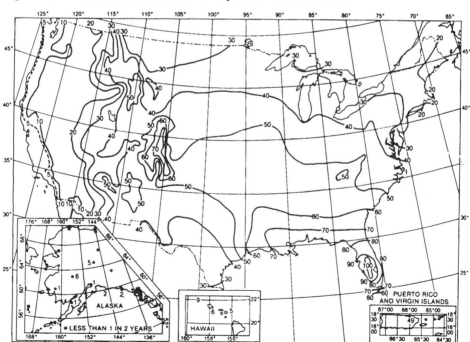

lightning surge work against itself and burn out the power cord, *not* the PC. And it works—Washington had the biggest thunderstorm it had seen in years in the summer of 1989, and my stuff with knots in the cords rode it out without a hitch. My TV didn't have knots in the cord, and now I've got to get around to buying a new TV.

- Optical isolators will, of course, protect you from lightning.

Chapter 11
Hard Disk Drive Overview and Terminology

Hard disks have become an absolute necessity. Some programs require them, and most are enhanced by them. But they're a common source of failure, and so require some maintenance attention.

As hard disks are sealed, you can't directly fix some hardware disk problems. Other hardware, however, is directly accessible and can be replaced, and there are many programs to help you monitor your disk's health, tune up its speed, and recover from disaster.

Disk Structure: Hardware and Software

First, some terminology. Disk technology has gone through a lot of changes in just a few decades. There are a lot of options for disks today, and a wide variety in price. *Sectors, seek time, clusters, and the like—what do they mean? I briefly explain them here.*

Cylinders, Heads, Platters, Tracks and Sectors. Let's start off by understanding floppy disk structure, as it's a bit simpler.

We can describe a 360K floppy as follows:

- A floppy has two sides.
- Each side contains data.
- Each side is divided into 40 concentric *tracks*. There's a related notion called *cylinders*, so a 360K floppy has 40 cylinders.
- Each track is divided, like pieces of a pie, into eight or nine wedges called *sectors*.
- Each sector stores ½K (512 bytes) of information.

2	Sides or Surfaces or Heads
40	Tracks per Side or Cylinders
9	Sectors per Track
½K	Bytes per Sector
360K	Bytes/Disk total

A hard disk drive contains rigid metal disks called *platters* that are stacked up inside an air-filtered enclosure. For example, the original XT 10MB drive had two platters. Other drives may have more. Again, a floppy is like one platter, but it's not rigid.

Like a floppy disk, the hard disk has an electromagnetic read/write *head* for each side of each platter. For example, on the original XT 10MB drive, there were four heads: two heads per platter times two platters. As the disk drive is sealed, you cannot align or clean these heads.

Each side of each platter (sometimes called a *surface*) is divided into concentric tracks, like a floppy. A floppy typically has 40 tracks, but hard disks start at 305 tracks and go up from there. The platter is commonly 5¼ inches in diameter like a floppy, so obviously the tracks are squeezed closer together in a hard disk than in a floppy.

Figure 11-1   Forty Tracks on a Floppy

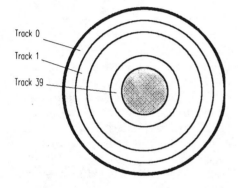

Each surface is then figuratively divided up with cuts, like a pie. A floppy, recall, divides each track into 8 or 9 sectors. Hard disks typically divide each track into 17, 26, 33, or 34 sectors. Drives with 26 or more sectors are called *RLL*, or *Run Length Limited*. Seventeen-sector disks are called *MFM, Modified Frequency Modulation*. (More on those later.)

As with a floppy, each sector contains 512 bytes of data.

The specs on the 10MB XT hard disk:

- There are four surfaces.
- There are 305 tracks on each surface.

Figure 11-2   Tracks and Sectors on a Floppy

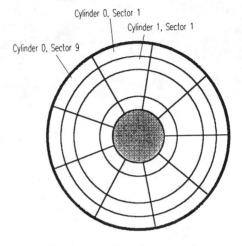

- There are 17 sectors to a track.
- There are ½K bytes on each sector.

4 * 305 * 17 * 0.5K = 10,370K bytes.

As you examine other disks, you'll find that 512 bytes/sector is pretty constant. Seventeen sectors is the rule also, although RLL drives are growing in popularity (the 26- and 34-sector drives, recall). The number of tracks and platters vary. Most manufacturers don't report the number of platters, but instead use the number of heads, which equals the number of surfaces. The XT 10MB hard disk has four heads.

All four heads are attached to a bracket called an *actuator arm*. This means when head 0 (as usual, you would count 0 to 3, not 1 to 4) is positioned over track 142 on surface 0, head 3 is also positioned over track 142 on surface 3. Disk heads cannot be independently positioned.

Hard disk with cover removed.

Closeup of hard disk actuator arm and heads.

The process of reading a sector involves two steps. First, move the read/write head over the desired track. Then wait for the disk to rotate so the desired sector is under the head, and read. In general, moving the head takes the most time. This means you'd most quickly read a file with sectors on the same track, and with tracks that lay above one another. Thus, if you need track 271, surface 1 for the first 17 sectors of your data on some file, it would be nice to be able to get track 271, surface 0, 2 and 3 for the rest of your data. Then these data (512 bytes/sector $\times$ 7 sectors/track $\times$ 4 tracks = 34,816 bytes) could be read without moving the read/write head.

The collection of a given track number on all surfaces is called a *cylinder*. Our example XT 10MB hard disk's 200th cylinder is the collection of side 0/track 200, side 1/track 200, side 2/track 200, and side 3/track 200. Most manufacturers don't report the number of tracks; instead they report the number of cylinders. Although they mean different things, a 305 cylinder disk, which has 305 tracks/surface, is sometimes called a *305 track* disk.

Let's take another example. One of my XTs uses a Rodime disk drive. It has 639 cylinders and six heads. What is its capacity?

Let's assume that, as with most of the PC drives today, it has 512 bytes per sector and 17 sectors per track.

512 bytes/sector $\times$ 17 sectors/track $\times$ 639 tracks/surface $\times$ 6 surfaces $\times$ 33,371,136 bytes. Recall that a megabyte isn't a million bytes, but 1,048,576 bytes, and you see that this is a 31.8MB drive.

Getting Information on Your Disk: CORETEST. CORE International is a company that sells some of the fastest disks around. It's no good being number 1 (or close to it) if no one knows it. So they wrote a benchmark program and put it in the public domain. It's called (appropriately) CORETEST.EXE. You can get it from:

Core International
7171 N. Federal Hwy.
Boca Raton, FL 33487
(407) 997-6055

To run it, just type *CORETEST*. Take a look at a sample run, depicted in Sample CORETEST screen. Here's how to interpret it.

Figure 11-3 Sample CORETEST Screen

```
            CORE Disk Performance Test Program Version 2.6
            Copyright CORE International, Inc.  1986
```

Seek Times	Hard Disk 0	KBytes Read
80+	Size : 33.4 MB Heads: 6	2048+
75	Cyls : 639 Sects: 17	1920
70	Data : 663 KB HD0 Time : 4.0 secs	1792
65	Data Transfer Rate: 164.3 KB/sec	1664
60	Average Seek Time : 57.6 ms (639	1536
55	Track-Track Seek : 8.6 ms cyls)	1408
50	Performance Index : 1.933	1280
45		1152
40		1024
35		896
30		768
25		640
20		512
15		384
10		256
5		128
0 HD0		HD0 0

```
              Transfer Block Size:  51KB
```

For our purposes, CORETEST offers five interesting numbers:

- Cylinders
- Heads
- Sectors
- Average Seek Time
- Data Transfer Rate

CORETEST is a quick-and-dirty way to find out how your existing hard disk is currently set up. You cannot use it to, say, plug in a mystery disk and find out its sectors/tracks/heads. I know you're wondering what *seek time* and *data transfer rate* are, but I'm going to explain them in an upcoming section about disk performance measurement, so hang on until then.

Software Structure of a Disk. DOS doesn't concern itself with tracks, cylinders, and the like. It organizes data on a sector-by-sector basis. As far as DOS is concerned:

- Disks are divided into *absolute* sectors.
- Absolute sectors map into *DOS* sectors.
- The DOS sectors are grouped into *clusters.*
- A *directory* entry refers to the first cluster number in the file, which is

our initial pointer into something called the *File Allocation Table* (FAT). The FAT keeps track of where files are located.

- Then the FAT contains information that DOS uses to locate the remaining clusters. There's a FAT entry for each cluster.
- A FAT entry can be (1) a number pointing to another cluster, (2) a 0 indicating an unused cluster, (3) a *bad sector* marking, or (4) an *End Of File* (EOF) indicator.

Absolute Sectors and DOS Sectors. Identifying an area on a disk by its cylinder/head/sector refers to what DOS folks call its *absolute sector:* cylinder *x*, head *y*, sector *z*. DOS doesn't directly use absolute sector locations. Instead, it refers to sectors with a single number called the *DOS sector number.* As DOS traverses a disk, it orders sectors by starting at cylinder 0 head 1 sector 1: This is *DOS sector number 0.* (Note that cylinder 0 head *0* doesn't have a DOS sector number designation; it's *out of bounds,* so far as DOS is concerned.) The remaining sectors on the track are DOS sectors 1 through 16. DOS then moves the next head, number 2. The 17 sectors on cylinder 0, head 2 are the next 17 DOS sectors. DOS keeps moving up the heads until the cylinder is exhausted, and then it moves to the zero head of cylinder 1. It continues in this fashion, moving further and further inward toward the center of the disk.

Why use DOS sector numbers? I don't know, really. It's probably because every four or eight sectors are grouped into a *cluster,* and it's easier to divide up a nice one-dimensional number like a DOS sector than it would be to have to constantly figure out that cluster 200 is on cylinder 40, head 2, sectors 15–17 and cylinder 40, head 3, sector 1. (I just made those numbers up, so don't try to figure out from where I got them.)

Supposing you had the XT 10MB hard disk described earlier, Table 11-1 relates the two sector notations.

Clusters. Finally, DOS sectors are grouped into *clusters.*

A cluster is the minimum space allocated by DOS when DOS gives space to a file. For example, if you create a file that is 1 byte long, you take up not just a byte on the disk, but instead the minimum allocation, a cluster. Cluster size varies with the disk type, as you can see from Table 11-2. A single-sided floppy uses clusters that are just one sector long, but

Table 11-1. Some Absolute and DOS Sectors for a Four-Head Disk

Cylinder	Head	Sector	Equivalent DOS Sector
0	0	1	N/A (outside DOS sectors)
0	0	17	N/A
0	1	1	0
0	1	17	16
0	2	1	17
0	2	17	33
0	3	1	34
0	3	17	50
1	0	1	51

Table 11-2. Cluster sizes (DOS 3.X)

Disk Type	Cluster Size (Bytes)	Sectors/Cluster
Single-sided floppy	512	1
Double-sided floppy	1024	2
3½-inch floppy	1024	2
1.2MB floppy	512	2
0–15 MB disk or disk partition	4096	8
16 + MB disk or disk partition	2048	4

a 10MB hard disk uses clusters that are eight sectors long, or 4096 bytes (4K). That means a 1-byte file on a single-sided floppy would take up 512 bytes on the disk, as would a 500-byte file. A 1-byte file would take up 4096 bytes on a 10MB disk drive.

Think of the following analogy. Suppose you're the guy running the Trump Shuttle. The Trump Shuttle promises a seat on a jet going from Washington, D.C. to New York every hour, without a reservation. Let's say the DC-9 jets they use can accommodate 100 people. How many jets must you run this hour? If you've got 1–100 people, run 1 jet. Just one person, the 101st person, forces you to go to a second jet. There are no "half" jets.

Depending on what kind of storage medium DOS uses, different size *jets* are used. First the floppies appeared, then the 10MB disk drive, then the 1.2MB floppies and the 16 + MB drives. If you're feeling brave, DOS 4.x even supports drives up to 512MB in size—it uses a 16-bit FAT (65,536 entries), clusters of size 8192, and will support up to a 512K B drive.

You've seen that cylinders and heads are counted starting at 0, and sectors start at one, so it won't be *too* strange when I tell you that clusters start

Table 11-3. Partial 10MB Disk Geography

Cylinder	Head	Sector	Equivalent DOS Sector	Cluster Number	Description
0	0	1	N/A (outside DOS sectors)	N/A	Partition Record
0	0	17	N/A	N/A	Unused
0	1	1	0	N/A	DOS boot record
0	1	1	1	N/A	FAT sector #1
0	1	17	16	N/A	FAT sector #16
0	2	1	17	N/A	Root directory sector #1
0	2	17	33	N/A	Root directory sector #17
0	3	1	34	N/A	Root directory sector #18
0	3	15	48	N/A	Last root directory sector
0	3	16	49	2	First data sector
0	3	17	50	2	Second data sector
1	0	1	51	2	Third data sector
1	0	2	52	2	Fourth data sector
1	0	6	56	2	Eighth data sector
1	0	7	57	3	Ninth data sector

at number 2. By the way, clusters only start in the data area, after the FAT and directory.

Table 11-3 relates cylinders, heads, sectors, DOS sectors, and clusters for our 10MB XT disk.

The FAT and the Directory. As has been said, the directory and the FAT are a team in locating files. The directory tells you names of your files, and the FAT tells you where the file is located.

A directory entry contains 32 bytes of information about a file:

- The file name (8 bytes)
- The file extension (3 bytes)
- Its attributes (1 byte)

Each bit of the attribute byte refers to a particular attribute. The most interesting are: the *archive* bit, which refers to whether or not a file has been backed up; the *read-only* bit, which keeps DOS from erasing or altering a file; and the *hidden* bit, which hides a file from most DOS functions. You can't see these attributes with the normal DIR command. *Archive* and *read-only* can be viewed or changed with the DOS ATTRIB command.

- Ten bytes, unused, kept for future DOS functions
- The date (two bytes) and time (2) of last update
- The starting cluster number (telling DOS where a file begins); the FAT (where the rest of the file is found)
- Finally, the last four bytes containing the file size in bytes

Figure 11-4 DOS Data Areas

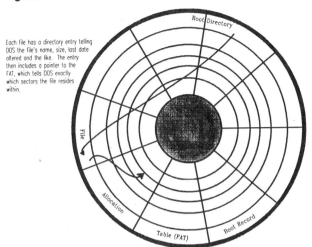

Each file has a directory entry telling DOS the file's name, size, last date altered and the like. The entry then includes a pointer to the FAT, which tells DOS exactly which sectors the file resides within.

For example, a file entry for a mythical file called ORDERS.DAT might tell us the following;

Name: ORDERS
Extension: DAT
Attributes: none
Date last modified: 28 October 1989
Time last modified: 11:23:44 AM
Starting cluster: 40
Size: 11120 bytes

You don't have enough information yet to know exactly where this file is on disk. You *do* know that it starts in cluster 40. You can even deduce in how many clusters to expect to find the file living. How? Simple. Say it's a 30MB drive. Since it's larger than 15MB, you know the clusters are 2K, 2048 bytes apiece. Since the file is 11,120 bytes long, that would imply it takes up $11120/2048 = 5.42$ clusters. But, recall, DOS won't give a file a partial sector; 5.42 clusters is no good, so DOS rounds up to 6 clusters.

But which six clusters? The FAT answers that question. The *FAT* is a table of numbers representing which clusters belong to what files. There are two kinds of FATs:

- 12-bit FATs with enough entries for 4096 clusters maximum, used on floppies and hard drives up to 15MB. A hard disk with a 12-bit FAT has clusters 4K in size.
- 16-bit FATs with enough entries for 65,636 clusters maximum, used on drives larger than 15MB. (16-bit FATs are only available under DOS 3.x and later.) Clusters are 2K on drives with 16-bit FATs up to 128MB disks.

Each cluster on the disk has a corresponding FAT entry. Given an entry for cluster X, the entry must be one of the following:

- A zero (0), indicating the cluster is unallocated
- An EOF, indicating it's the last cluster in a file
- A BAD, indicating the cluster con-

165

Figure 11-5 Directory and FAT Example

```
                  Directory Entry:

|ORDERS | DAT | no attribs | 10/28/89 | 11:23:44 | 40 | 11,120 |
       |_____|
                 |
                 |      FAT Entries:
                 |
                 |   Fat Entry #      Entry in FAT
                 |       ...               ...
                 |       39               EOF
                 |___> 40                 41
                        41                42
                        42                44
                        43                BAD
                        44                102
                        ...               ...
                       102                103
                       103                EOF
```

tains a bad sector or sectors and shouldn't be used

- A non-zero cluster number that is a pointer to the *next* cluster in the file of which X is a part

Figure 11-5 adds to the ORDERS.DAT directory example an excerpt from the FAT table with the entries relevant to ORDERS.DAT.

Reading this FAT excerpt, you see that cluster 39 is the end of some file—you don't know which one. You start looking for ORDERS.DAT in cluster 40 because the directory entry tells us to: Entry 40 contains 41, meaning that 41 follows 40 as the next cluster in ORDERS.DAT. Entry 41 contains 42, meaning that 42 is the next cluster in ORDERS.DAT. 42 contains 44, telling us to skip 43, which was skipped because it's a cluster with unusable areas in it—a *bad cluster*. 44 tells us to skip up to cluster 102 for the next cluster, and 102 points us to 103, which is the end of the file. You skipped over 45, which is the end of some file; again, you don't know which file.

Note that each cluster's FAT entry in a file links to the next cluster's FAT entry in that file. This is called a *one-way linked list*, one way because you can only follow

it in one direction. (If this is unclear, look only at entry 103, the EOF for ORDERS.DAT. Looking only at that information, what would tell you that 102 was the previous entry? Nothing. On the other hand, the FAT *will* tell you to go from 102 to 103.)

Disk Performance

Some disk/controller combinations are faster than others. You measure drive speed by looking at (1) how long it takes to find a particular piece of data, and (2) once there, how quickly it can be read off the disk. The first measurement is called the *access time* and the second is called the *data transfer rate*.

Access Times, Seek Times, and Latency Periods. The hard disk drive is somewhat like a phonograph. The platter itself is like the record, and the read/write head is like the phonograph stylus. To play a selection on a phonograph, you do two things:

1. Position the stylus arm to the beginning of the song.
2. Wait for the music on the track to come around.

Step 1 takes a lot longer than step 2.

Almost instantaneously after positioning the stylus, the music is found.

Disk reads and writes work the same way. The head must first be positioned over the track, and then it waits for the desired sector to come up.

The formula to remember is:

**ACCESS TIME =
SEEK TIME + ROTATIONAL
LATENCY PERIOD**

or, in English,

Time to find a sector = Time to move to the sector's cylinder + Time to wait for the sector to rotate.

The two components are called *seek time* and *latency period*. Seek time is the time required for the head to position over a track. Latency period is how long it takes for the desired sector to move under the head.

Disk Seek Time. Of the seek time and the latency period, the seek time is usually the longer wait. It varies according to how many tracks must be traversed. A seek from one track to the next is usually quick, 5 to 16 ms, but most seeks aren't so convenient. A common measure of an average seek is the time required to travel one-third of the way across the disk. This is the one used in most benchmark programs. You might wonder, "Why not half-way across the disk, rather than one-third?" The reason is that most accesses are short seeks—just a few tracks.

Table 11-4 shows some typical average seek times for a range of hard disks. Seek times are "built in" to a drive. There's no way for you to improve upon it, short of getting a new drive. Seek

times vary in part because there are two approaches to seeking: *band steppers* and *voice coils*. A band stepper is never quite sure over what track it's positioned, because it has no guidance mechanism. It does, however, have a *Track Zero Indicator*, so it knows when it's at track zero. To find a track, it just seeks out track zero and then steps, track by track, to wherever it's going. A voice coil, on the other hand, is much faster because it devotes an entire surface to head position information. I've got a Seagate ST4096, for example, with nine surfaces. (In actuality, it's got ten, but the tenth is used for head positioning information.)

Table 11-4. Common Drives and Seek Times

Drive Description	Seek Time (ms)
Toshiba 3100 10MB	175
XT original 10MB	94
PS/2 Model 50 original 20MB	80
Seagate ST225 (20MB)	75
Rodime 33 meg in XT	57
AT original 20MB	30
Priam HD 60MB	22
Maxtor 140MB in AT	19

Rotational Latency Period. Once a head is positioned over a track, the job's not done: Now the head has to wait for the desired sector to rotate under the head. How *much* time is a matter of luck. If you're lucky, it's already there; if you're really unlucky, you just missed the track and will have to wait an entire revolution. This waiting time, whether large or small, is called the *rotational latency period*. A common number cited is *average latency period*. This makes the simple assumption that, on an average, the disk must make a half-revolution to get to your sector. Recall that the disk rotates at 3600 rpm. One half revolution then takes 1/7200 of a minute = 60/7200 second = 8.33 milliseconds (ms). This contributes to the amount of time the system must wait for service.

The sum of the average seek time and the latency period is called the *access time,* and is oft-quoted in product advertisements.

Disk Performance II: Data Transfer Rates and Interleave Factors. Once a disk has found the desired data, how fast can it transfer it to the PC? This is called *data transfer rate.* It's the last interesting number in the CORETEST output. It all makes sense if you keep the following assumption in mind: Remember there are only 512 bytes in a sector. That means whenever an application requests, say, sector 1 of track 100 of side 2, it'll probably need sector 2 of that track and side next. In fact, most times you need one sector from a track, you'll end up needing them all. So what's the best arrangement of sectors to allow them to be read at maximum speed?

When a disk, whether hard or floppy, is low-level formatted (more on this process later), milestones are laid down on each track called *sector IDs*. These IDs separate one sector from another and are discussed in some more detail in the section on low-level or physical formatting. What I really was asking in the last paragraph, then, is this: The IDs can be laid out in any order, so in what order should the sectors arranged? The answer to this question is the optimal *interleave factor*.

On floppies, the nine sectors are laid out like numbers on the face of a clock (Figure 11-6).

That's because reading all of the

Figure 11-6 Simple Floppy Interleave Order

sectors on a floppy in one pass doesn't tax the controller, speed-wise. They have nine sectors on a track, and the disk only rotates five times per second. At maximum, the most burden a floppy could put on its controller would be to throw it ½K bytes/sector times 9 sectors/rotations times 5 rotations/second or 22.5K bytes per second. Heck, the serial port on most PCs can run at almost that rate; consecutive sectors on a floppy is no big deal.

Hard disks usually don't work that way. The problem is that hard disks rotate a lot faster than floppies. Hard disks spin at 60 rotations per second, and floppies rotate at 5 revolutions per second. In addition, hard disks pack more sectors on a track, you'll recall. To see the problem, suppose you had a hard disk with the sectors in numerical order (called a *1:1 interleave*), as pictured in Figure 11-7.

As the hard disk rotates 60 times per second, the maximum this disk could throw at the controller per second would be ½K bytes/sector times 17 sectors/rotation times 60 rotations/second = 510K bytes/second! Most hard disk controllers (and some computers) can't handle a half megabyte per second.

So let's look in detail at what happens when two sectors are read in succession on a 1:1 interleaved disk:

1. DOS and BIOS request the hard disk controller to read a sector.
2. The controller instructs the disk

Figure 11-7   1:1 Interleaved Hard Disk

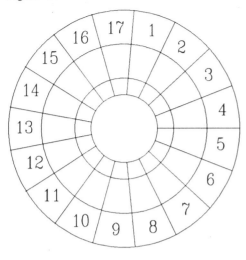

Figure 11-8   How Interleaving Affects Disk Speed (Part 1)

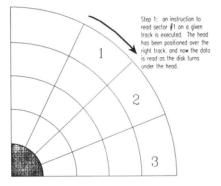

Step 1: an instruction to read sector #1 on a given track is executed. The head has been positioned over the right track, and now the data is read as the disk turns under the head.

head to move to the track and read the sector.

3. The head reads the data and transmits it to the controller.

4. As hard disks are fragile devices, the controller always includes *extra* data when it writes information to the disk. This information, when read back, enables the controller to detect whether or not errors have arisen in the data. This extra information is called the *ECC (Error Correcting Code)*. It involves a mathematical function and takes a little while to compute. (The microprocessors on hard disk controllers aren't the fastest things in the world. I mean, you don't find too many 386s on disk controllers.) Meanwhile, the disk continues to spin.

Figure 11-9   How Interleaving Affects Disk Speed (Part 2)

Step 2: the data has been passed from the disk head to the controller. The controller checks that the data was not corrupted while on disk. It does that check using a mathematical computation called an ECC (Error Correcting Code) test. Meanwhile, the disk keeps turning.

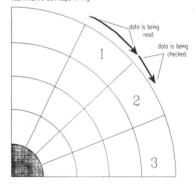

data is being read:

data is being checked:

5. Once the controller has checked the data, it passes it to BIOS and DOS, which are also paranoid about hard disk data loss. BIOS and DOS have their own small amount of overhead—proportionately less than the controller's, but relevant nonetheless. Meanwhile, the disk continues to spin.

169

Figure 11-10 How Interleaving Affects Disk Speed (Part 3)

Step 3. After the controller pronounces the data "okay," DOS and BIOS do a very short check of their own. Finally they're ready to request sector 2 -- but sector 2 has just passed by! We ARE in perfect location, however, for sector 3. Why not, then, put sector 2 where sector 3 is now?

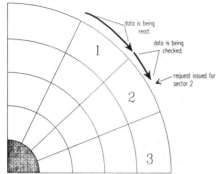

Figure 11-11 1:6 Disk Interleave

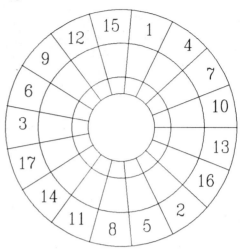

6. Now that everyone is happy with the data, DOS wants the next sector. But since the controller, DOS, and BIOS were taking so long with the last sector's data, the disk continued spinning. If you had put sector 2 right after sector 1, you would *always miss the subsequent sector*. That implies you would have to wait a whole rotation to get the next sector. This process would *always* occur.

Thus, on a disk with the sectors laid out clock-fashion in numerical order, you'd always end up getting only one sector read per rotation. As the disk rotates 60 times per second, it's only read 60 sectors/second. Each sector holds, as you'll recall, ½K; so the maximum data transfer rate from this disk would be 30K bytes/second, a rather poor transfer rate. (A 1.2MB floppy could outperform this disk, since it transfers data at 45K per second!)

But suppose you staggered the sectors, to give the controller time to get ready for the next sector. IBM did that on the XT, as pictured in Figure 11-11.

This is called a *1:6 interleave*. Start at 1 and then count clockwise six sectors. You're now at 2. Count six more. You're now at 3, and so on. This gives the XT time to do computations and still catch the next sector. Inspection will show that the XT can read *three* sectors on the first rotation, or about 180 sectors/second. That means we can get three times the throughput from an XT by changing from a noninterleaved disk layout to a 1:6 interleave.

As controllers get faster, they can compute error correcting codes faster. The AT controller is fast enough that you can move your disk's sectors closer together than the XT controller allowed. IBM interleaved the AT disk at 1:3, as illustrated in Figure 11-12.

This is a *1:3 interleave factor*. Six sectors can be read on a single rotation—twice the XT's throughput, or 360 sectors per rotation. Remember why we can't make the IBM XT a 1:3 disk—the sectors would be too close, and we'd always miss the next sector. The net effect would be, again, getting only one sector per rotation.

This might seem like a somewhat

Figure 11-12 1:3 Disk Interleave

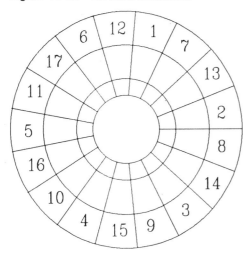

academic discussion, but you'd be surprised how many computers are interleaved wrong. For example, IBM formatted XT drives at 1:6 although 1:5 is the best interleave, and they formatted AT drives at 1:3 although 1:2 is the best interleave for that machine. How important is this? Take a look at Table 11-5.

You can see that on an IBM XT, re-

Table 11-5. Theoretical Disk Data Transfer Rates

Drive Type	Max Data Transfer (K Bytes/Second)	Sectors Read/ Rotation
360K floppy, XT	22.5	
360K floppy, AT	27	
1.2MB floppy, AT	45	
Hard disk 1:6	85	2.8
1:5	102	3.4
1:4	128	4.3
1:3	170	5.7
1:2	255	8.5
1:1	510	17.0

formatting from IBM's default 1:6 interleave to a 1:5 interleave would improve disk throughput by 20 percent. Changing the interleave on an IBM AT from 1:3 to 1:2 would increase disk throughput by 50 percent. Other companies are guilty of the same thing. The AT&T 6386, for example, is formatted at 1:3, although it should be 1:2. The right interleave factor means that your controller, your computer, and your disk are right in step, pulling data off the disk as quickly as is possible.

So it's up to you to ensure that your machine disk is formatted to its optimal interleave factor. The optimal interleave factor is determined, again, by the kind of controller you have.

One way to breathe new life into a tired old machine is to replace the disk controller with one that allows a smaller interleave. You can speed up an XT-type machine with either the XT-type controllers from Data Technology Corporation (DTC5150CX) or Western Digital (WD1002-WX1 or XT-GEN), dropping the interleave factor on your XT to 1:3. Adaptec even makes an XT-type controller that'll handle 1:2 on an XT. You can replace the standard-issue Western Digital WD1003 1:2 interleave controller on AT-type machines with WD's WD1006 or Data Technology's DTC7280, both of which actually support 1:1 interleave factors.

Recall that interleave factor is set when you low-level format a hard disk. Recently, some software writers have started offering *interleave fixer programs*. These both measure your disk's optimal interleave, and then allow you to reset your disk's interleave factor without backing up, reformatting, and reloading. Their approach is really a simple one: just read a track, store it in memory, reformat the track to the proper interleave factor, and rewrite the original information.

There are several such programs on the market; Steve Gibson's *SpinRite* is probably the best known. I use and recommend HOPTIMUM from Kolod Research. HOPTIMUM is packaged in the hTEST/hFORMAT program set, a set of utilities I feel everyone must have if they're to do major data surgery on a hard disk.

You can get the hTEST/hFORMAT collection from Kolod Research:

hTEST/hFORMAT $89.95
1898 Techny Court
Northbrook, IL 60062
(708) 291-1586

At $90 for the whole collection, it's a steal. Some sample HOPTIMUM output is shown in Figure 11-13.

Cautions About Using Interleave Fixers. HOPTIMUM and company are nice to have around (and the rest of the hTEST/hFORMAT collection is indispensable as well), but here are a couple of cautions.

- It's perfectly fine to test your XT-type controller's optimal interleave

with an interleave adjuster program, but don't actually allow the program to do a *nondestructive reformat.*

The problem is that the nondestructive format consists of a lot of separate *format track* commands, rather than the more normal destructive format's single *format multiple tracks* commands. At the beginning of each format command, the controller *recalibrates* by moving back to track 0. In the case of a format multiple tracks command, one recalibration is required for the entire destructive format. But, again, the nondestructive formats work by reading a track, formatting the track, restoring the track, and then repeating the process on the next track until the disk is done. XT controllers insist on recalibrating, then, for *each track!* That's a lot of head movement; in fact, it's not unusual to see HOPTIMUM or *SpinRite* require eight or more hours to run

Figure 11-13   Sample HOPTIMUM Program Output

```
C:\MACE>hoptimum
HOPTIMUM - Hard disk interleave OPTIMIZER Program -      Version 1.0.3
Copyright (C) 1986 Kolod Research, Inc.
                Box 68 * Glenview, Il. 60025 * 312-291-1586
Licensed Program Materials
Drive - C - will be formatted and tested as:
        read/write heads:   6
              cylinders: 639
                sectors:  17
Formatting parameters will be:
          beginning surface:   0 (surfaces start internally at 0)
            ending surface:   5
        beginning cylinder: 628 (cylinders start internally at 0)
          ending cylinder: 638
        sector interleaves   1 through   7
              machine type: PC/XT (or compatible)
Do you wish to change
any of the above formatting parameters ? (Y/N): n
      ... more output ....
Summary is as follows...
   Interleave          Total access time        Total clock ticks
                      (rounded to nearest sec.)  (normally 18.2 / sec)
   ----------         -------------------------  ---------------------
        1                     20                 364
        2                     20                 365
        3                      4                  65
        4                      5                  86
        5                      6                 106
        6                      7                 126
        7                      8                 146
Program has terminated normally
```

on an XT-type machine. That's a real torture test of what is probably a low-end drive anyway. It would be nice if it worked, but it really isn't a good idea. Instead, do it the hard way: Back up, reformat, and restore.

- It's likely that, if CORETEST reports that you have more than 17 sectors on a track (likely values are 25, 26, 33, or 34), these low-level format or interleave adjustment programs won't work *and will destroy all data on your hard disk.* So back up before you use them for the first time. (Don't say I didn't warn you.) CORETEST, on the other hand, is nondestructive; I've seen a couple of controllers it won't run on, but it never destroys data.
- Western Digital XT-type controllers write important information on the first sector of the disk. This information often doesn't get rewritten on reformat, rendering the drive useless. Avoid this if possible by telling the reformatter not to touch cylinder zero. HOPTIMUM lets you do this; *SpinRite* does not.

1:1 Hard Disk Controllers. Controllers waste a lot of time checking data and rereading data they've read just recently. Full-track and caching controllers seek to eliminate that waste and speed up disk access.

Some controllers, like the Western Digital WD1006 for ATs, and the hard disk controllers shipped with the PS/2 Models 50 through 80, take another approach to interleaving. They assume (reasonably) that most of the time when you want *one* sector on a track, you'll end up wanting *most* sectors on a track. Think about it: Why look at a track as 17 sectors, each requiring separate read operations, when another approach is to read the whole track in one operation? In this

case, you don't really have to worry about plucking out a single sector and checking it before you go on the next. This is called *full track buffering.* In this approach, you read the whole track, then do the error checking on the entire track.

For instance, if you have an AT-type 286 or 386 clone, you almost certainly use the Western Digital WD1003 hard disk controller. For under $200 (when last I checked), you could buy the WD1006, a 100-percent compatible replacement that reads entire tracks at a time. Reading an entire track in one shot means the disk can support a 1:1 interleave, allowing a 510 kilobyte/second data transfer rate from your hard disk—quite nice indeed, and highly recommended.

If you use such a controller, DOS, of course, knows nothing of this and continues to request only single sectors. The net effect is that the first sector requested of each track takes a little longer to retrieve than normal. Subsequent sectors are instantaneous, requiring no disk work at all.

Will this approach always work better than sector-by-sector reads? Not if for some reason the program only wanted one or two sectors per track. This is, however, unlikely.

Caching controllers are another story. The idea here is to put a microprocessor and some memory on the controller, and allow the controller to cache requests for data. The problem is that it often confuses DOS or an application, and may render you unable to run OS/2 or UNIX. This is a nice option, but only if you're certain it will cause you no regret.

Encoding Schemes: FM, MFM, RLL. . . As time goes on, everyone finds that hard disk space is like All Good Things In Life: there just isn't enough of it. The same microcomputer market that grinned from ear to ear just six years ago when IBM offered the voluminous 10MB disk (most manufacturers were only offering five megs at the time) is now saying, "Just *how* do I get a third 300MB drive on my Novell server?"

Then there's the second question, "And can I get those 300MB disks to read data *faster?*"

Well, mass storage manufacturers are eager to meet those needs, so they're constantly working to put more space on a hard disk and to figure out how to pull it off the disk faster. This section tells you how they're doing it.

The method to increase storage space that most quickly comes to mind is to add platters to a hard disk, or perhaps to squeeze more cylinders onto the disk. But there are limits to that, both space and cost constraints. To go further, manufacturers have looked to putting more sectors on a track.

To an extent, all one needs do to put more sectors on a track is just to write some software: Most disks could accommodate an extra few sectors without too much trouble, so all the 17-sector disks out there could become 20-sector disks, and become 3/17ths larger. But manufacturers are looking for a quantum leap to allow them to build drives that reach to near-gigabyte levels. They do this by changing the *encoding scheme. MFM (Modified Frequency Modulation)* is the encoding scheme that has been used for years on disks. A newer one, *RLL (Run Length Limited),* puts 50 percent more data on a given disk (although, as you'd expect, at a cost of reliability). Here's some more details.

Basically, data is stored on a magnetic medium by encoding what are called *flux reversals* onto the magnetic medium. A reversal means either negative to positive or positive to negative. The reversal shows up as a "pulse" when reading the data, so I'll refer to reversals as *pulses.* Disks use pulses and the lack of

pulses to represent data on a disk drive.

The easiest approach, it seems, would be to encode something like

0 = **no pulse**
1 = **pulse**

But there's a practical obstacle to this simple method. You see, if there's a long string of zeros, then there would be a long period of no pulses. Too much silence and the controller gets lost. Pulses not only send data, they keep the controller's internal clock in synch with the data on the disk. Think of if this way: If you set your watch to the same time as some time service, both your watch and the time service's will match each other for a while. But as a few months go by, you'll find that your watch is getting a little ahead or behind the time service, so you reset your watch periodically. Data comes off the disk in a time-dependent fashion, so the timing that was used to *write* the data must match the timing that's used when *reading* the data. It sounds simple to do, but it's not. The clock circuit on the hard disk controller is less precise than, for instance, the clock circuit on your digital watch. It may run a bit slower or faster from day to day and second to second. Pulses help resynchronize the data and the controller. (There's more to it, but that's as technical as I want to get, since I assume you're not going to design hard disk controllers for a living.)

So if we used the simple *pulse = 1, no pulse = 0* approach, and got a long string of 0s, the resulting silence could cause the controller to get out of synch with the data. Therefore we need an encoding scheme that ensures that we must never go too long without a pulse.

One way to handle the synchronization problem is to include clocking bits with the data. A simple approach called

Frequency Modulation, or *FM,* encodes a 1 as two pulses, and a 0 as a pulse followed by no pulse:

1 0 0 0 1 1 becomes
PPPNPNPNPPPP (P = pulse, N = no pulse)

This seems fairly effective, eh? Yes, but it's wasteful—I only told you half the story before. To see why it's wasteful, you need one more piece of the puzzle: You can fit more *pulses* and *no pulses* on a disk if the number of *pulses* is relatively small. (Yes, that conflicts with our desire to ensure that we never go too long without a pulse.) The scheme pictured above, as you can see, includes a lot of pulses. It does eliminate the "long run of 0s" problem, however. The minimum length run of 0s is 0; that is, sometimes two pulses occur next to each other. The maximum length is 1, so you never have more than one 0 in a run. We can say that this is a (0,1) run length limited scheme. FM is an old encoding scheme that's not used much any more.

So our criteria for a good encoding scheme are:

- It should minimize the number of pulses necessary to store a given piece of data so the maximum amount of data can fit on the disk, BUT
- It should be careful not to allow too long a run of "no pulses" to occur, as the clock on the disk controller

board can lose track if it doesn't re-calibrate with a pulse now and then.

FM led to *MFM,* or *Modified FM.* MFM is a bit more daring, creating minimum zero runs of one 0 and maximum runs of 3, for a (1,3) run length limited scheme. IBM uses this for floppy and most hard disk encoding.

MFM is encoded so:

- 1 is always no pulse, then a pulse (NP)
- 0 as in 00 is coded pulse, then no pulse (PN)
- 0 as in 10 is coded as two no pulse's (NN)

So 101100 looks like
1 0 1 1 0 0
NPNNNPNPNNPN = 4 pulses

Compare FM:
PPPNPPPPPNPN = 9 pulses

Recently, a new kind of controller has arrived called *2,7 Run Length Limited,* or, as it's usually referred to, *2,7 RLL* (or just *RLL*). It pushes the density of data on a hard disk a little further—50 percent further. RLL first appeared on mainframes in the early 80s, and it will be an important technology in the PC field in the years to come.

RLL uses a more complex encoding scheme:

Table 11-6. RLL Encoding Patterns Compared to MFM

Pattern To Encode	RLL Encoding (N = No Pulse, P = Pulse)	# Pulses	MFM Encoding	# Pulses
00	PNNN	1	PNPN	2
01	NPNN	1	PNNP	2
100	NNPNNN	1	NPNNPN	2
101	PNNPNN	2	NPNNNP	2
1100	NNNNPNNN	1	NPNPNNPN	3
1101	NNPNNPNN	2	NPNPNNNP	3
111	NNNPNN	1	NPNPNP	3

So 101100 encodes as 101 100 or
PNNPNNNNPNNN = 3 pulses

One common RLL configuration combines the Seagate ST238R (a 21MB drive, actually the ST225 with a different label) and an RLL controller to yield a 30MB system. (Seagate also makes real 30MB disks, like the ST238—31.5MB). *Be careful with these.* Experts say they're a proven technology, but I've seen a higher proportion of disk problems with RLL controllers. As the RLL technology pushes the disk a bit closer to its limits, many disks will work fine on MFM but not RLL. A drive designed for RLL is fine, but don't try just any disk (my XT's Rodime, for example, can't use RLL).

A final benefit from RLL is that, since the data is stored in a denser fashion, it's transferred off the disk faster. When RLL works, it makes your disk *faster* and *bigger*.

Types of Interfaces Between Controllers and Drives. How does the controller talk to the drive? Obviously, an interface like RS232 isn't fast enough.

Originally, Shugart Technologies used something they called the ST 506/

412 interface or, as it's more commonly called, *ST506*. This interface is installed on both the controller side and the disk side: you need an ST506 controller to talk to an ST506 drive. Most drives are ST506. An ST506 interface is five million pulses per second, which can translate to about 7.5 million bits per second if using 2,7 RLL encoding. But it's also an *analog interface*; the magnetic pulse strengths are transmitted over a ribbon cable from the drive head to the controller for interpretation. That's kind of scary, as propagating analog signals for any distance at all over ribbon cables at high speed isn't a real prescription for data integrity. Most hard disk cables are fairly short to address this problem.

Real "muscle" drives are using a replacement interface called *ESDI, Enhanced Small Device Interface*. ESDI-ready drives are harder to find and more expensive, but that's changing with time. You can often spot ESDIs because they pack 34 sectors to a track. (Actually, they put 35 on a track, but then they use the thirty-fifth as a spare.) ESDI uses a digital interface between controller and drive, and so will allow greater speed expansion as time goes on. ESDI should be able to support a maximum data transfer rate of 24 million bits per second.

Another interface not used much in the PC world now but on the horizon is *SCSI* (pronounced—I kid you not—"scuzzy"), *Small Computer Systems Interface*. Probably the best selling SCSI computers are the Macintoshes. This interface transfers data at up to 20 megabits per second. The Bernoulli Box uses SCSI also, on the PC. Eventually SCSI will support over 100 megabits per second, but for now it's in the ESDI range of speed. One final item about SCSI devices is that they actually puts the controller on the drive; the board in the computer really doesn't have much to do, and is, strictly speaking, not a controller but a *host adapter*. (That's why Iomega calls the Bernoulli interface cards host adapters, not controllers.)

Write Precompensation and Reduced Write Current. Here are two intimidating-sounding terms that you ordinarily wouldn't have even have heard of, except for when you have to low-level format a drive. Everybody's curious about what they mean, however, so here they are.

Write precompensation corrects a problem that occurs when the hard disk uses the higher numbered cylinders, the ones closer to the center of the platter. There's less space there to store data, yet recall that the same amount of data gets stored on each track. That means the linear density of, say, cylinder 500 is considerably higher than that for cylinder 0. Recall that data is stored on the hard disk by magnetizing the disk to create pulses that the head detects as the platter whizzes by underneath it. These magnetic areas are like small magnets, with *north poles* and *south poles*. Remember north and south poles from science class? Put two souths or norths together, and they repel. Put a north and a south together, and they attract.

Sometimes the data on a disk works out so the magnetic areas for two adjacent bits end up with their north poles facing each other (souths would do the same thing). The bits actually move *away* from each other, and the data on the disk actually changes due to magnetic repulsion.

Write precompensation, well, "precompensates" for this by writing the data closer together than it should be, so when the magnetic areas repel each other, they end up exactly where the controller wanted them in the first place. The *write precompensation value* is the cylinder at which to start the write precomp. If a drive has 600 cylinders and the write precomp cylinder is 600, that means the drive doesn't require write precomp. The manufacturer determines when designing the drive at which cylinder to start write precompensation.

Figure 11-14 What Write Precompensation Does

Recall from Science class that magnets each have a "north" and "south" pole, and that opposite poles attract:

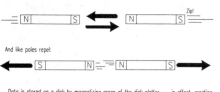

And like poles repel:

Data is stored on a disk by magnetizing areas of the disk platter -- in effect, creating magnets on the disk. They've got north and south poles, too:

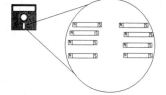

Now, data is represented not only by magnetism at any one spot, but also by the *lack* of magnetism in some spots. So the spaces between the magnets are important, also.

The inner cylinders of most hard disks are sufficiently small that the data ends up getting crammed pretty close together. Attraction and repulsion take effect immediately, affecting the spaces between the magnets (and therefore the stored data).

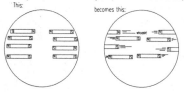

Write precompensation just writes the magnets a little further apart or closer together so that once they're finished repelling and attracting they end up where they're supposed to be.

Reduced write current cylinder refers to a similar problem. Think of writing data on a magnetic medium as being like writing on paper with ink. The "ink" here is the electric current used to create the magnetic field. The more ink, the "larger" the letters. Large letters are easier to read later, and a little smear or smudge (some kind of data corruption) won't make the data unreadable. So disk drive designers prefer to turn up the juice as far as possible to make the data as safe as possible.

But if you write too big, the letters run over each other. That happens on those troublesome inner cylinders as well. Too much electric current makes magnetic domains that are physically too large, and they overrun each other. So the drive turns down the current starting from the reduced write current cylinder to the center of the drive.

Again, you'll see these numbers when formatting a drive. Some disk controllers insist on knowing when to start precompensating or turning down the write power.

Hardware: The Controller and the Drive

The hard disk subsystem consists of the sealed drive itself and a controller board, which plugs into a slot in the PC expansion bus. Controllers are available that act as both floppy and hard disk controller, saving you a slot. Some firms have developed *hardcards,* which mount a narrow drive on a short controller board to yield a plug-in hard disk and controller all in one. We'll consider the two components separately.

The Controller. The controller is a printed circuit board that generally contains some *VLSI (Very Large Scale Integration) chips* on it and, commonly, a simple microprocessor. More than 10,000 transistors on a chip makes it VLSI. More than a thousand transistors per chip is *LSI (Large Scale Integration);* more than one hundred is *MSI* (you guessed it, *Medium Scale Integration);* and more than ten is *SSI,* which is left as an exercise to the reader. The controller acts as the "go-between" for the hard disk and the system board. Controllers are identified by:

- XT-type or AT-type

    Unlike most expansion boards, the controllers in the XT and the AT are designed differently and are largely incompatible. Some controllers talk with the computer via DMA (XT types), and others use an odd IRQ approach.

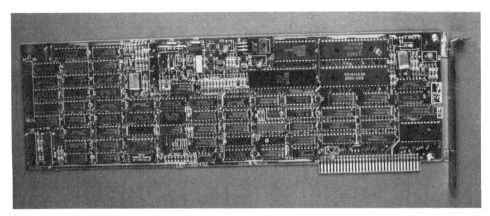

IBM XT hard disk controller.

IBM AT hard disk controller.

In the IRQ approach (used in the AT), the controller first fills a 512 byte buffer on the controller board itself. Then a hardware interrupt type 14 is issued, and the 80286 CPU reads the data from the buffer and stores it in memory. This sounds counter-intuitive, as the whole idea of DMA is to be able to transfer data into memory without the CPU slowing you down. The reason it works is due to the design of the interface between the controller's buffer and the 80286. Most controller designs spoon out data in 8-bit bytes. The AT controller hands data to the CPU in 16-bit chunks. A second reason for the success is two 80286 commands that the earlier chips don't have, which allow fast block transfers from an I/O port. The raw transfer rate for these transfers can be as fast as 16 million bits/second.

- What interleave the controller can handle

Controller manufacturers are turning out faster and faster controllers. 1:1 controllers are becoming a common sight in AT-type machines, and 1:3 is now the most common in XT-type machines.

- The controller's encoding scheme (MFM, RLL, ARLL)

Again, there's no such thing as an RLL drive—the controller determines the encoding scheme. But there is the fact that some drives are of higher quality than others, and to squeeze 26 sectors on a track we can't usually get away with a run-of-the-mill drive.

- Their interface (ST506, ESDI, SCSI)

There *is* such a thing as an ST506 or ESDI drive. Ensure when you buy a drive that it uses the same interface as your controller.

- Cabling on the interface:
  - normal two-cable
  - single-cable expensive oddballs, like Compaq and Zenith (for LP286)
  - very oddball edge connector types, like the PS/2 desktop models (25, 30, 50, 50Z, 70)

I'll talk more about this in the drive installation chapter, but for now let me just say that *most* microcomputer drives use a fairly standard set of hard disk cables, a 34-wire and a 20-wire cable. Those cables are used for both ST506 and ESDI drives. And that's great; it means you can buy a drive from Dastardly Dan's Double Discount House of Clones, and then buy a drive from someone else, and they'll work together. Or it means you can get a new 80MB drive and put it in your vintage 1985 XT.

Usually.

Some vendors have apparently decided that all this compatibility wasn't doing a thing for their profit margin, so

they've retained the ST506 (or ESDI) signals but rearranged the cable! So the underlying electronics are exactly the same, but the cable's different. That means you must buy a drive with the same unusual cable connections as the controller.

Who does this? Compaq was the first I can remember. The Deskpros of various stripes use a strange cable (one cable, not the usual two) to connect to the regular ST506 drive, which also had the strange one-cable connector. Because the demand for drives that have the strange one-cable connector is much lower than demand for the usual drives, fewer vendors offer them, and those who do charge about a $600 premium over the equivalent two-cable drive. Your choices are either to dump your already-bought Compaq drive and controller and replace them with a normal two-cable drive and controller, or to pay through the nose for a second Compaq-ready drive. Zenith did the same thing with their small footprint LP286. Ditto IBM's PS/2s, all of them. Buy clones, I say.

The Winchester Sealed Drive. Most microcomputer hard disks are *sealed* units: the heads and platter are in a sealed, air-filtered compartment. It wasn't always like that for hard disks.

On some mainframe disk drives, the disk is in a separate *disk pack* that mounts atop the drive motor and control circuitry. The drive motor and circuitry contain the heads. The disk packs, which look like Tupperware cake carriers, just contain disk platters. They're not sealed, since they must be "mounted" atop the drive motor and control circuitry. It's convenient to be able to have a whole shelf of disk packs, each storing megabytes and megabytes of data. But they're less reliable because dust can more easily get on the platters; the heads can pick up the dust and scratch it across the platters, sometimes damaging them irreparably.

10MB Winchester-type hard disk.

IBM changed this years ago with the *fixed drive:* a drive sealed in an air filtered compartment that couldn't be mounted or dismounted. (That's why IBM calls the hard disk the fixed disk drive. And all this time, I thought *fixed* meant it wasn't broken. . .)

How did it get to be called a *Winchester* drive? I've heard two stories. The first one: The model number was the 3030 drive. The model number reminded technicians of the Winchester .3030 rifle, and the drive became known as a Winchester drive. The name has stuck through model numbers. The second one: The drive was invented at the Hursley Research Center in Winchester, England. Either way, the name stuck. Any sealed drive is called a Winchester drive.

Until recently Winchesters for microcomputers have been based on 5¼-inch platters. It's interesting that, whether the drive is 5MB or 180MB, it's contained in the same size housing. You can't look at a drive and detect its capacity by its physical size.

We're seeing the appearance of more and more 3½-inch hard disks.

They're nice in that they have lower power requirements, but of course it'll take some time to shake the bugs out of them. At this writing (fall 1989), I've heard mixed reviews. I've used the 3½-inch drives in the portable Toshiba 3100 and found them reliable but slow. The 3½-inch drives used on the PS/2 desktops are also fairly lackluster in performance, but they've come a long way since early 1987. I hear nothing but bad news about the Seagate 157 SCSI drive, but the 125/138 drives (20 and 30MB) seem to perform about as well as their 5¼-inch counterparts.

So the jury is still out about 3½-inch drives. If the drives progress like most storage technology, they'll have the bugs shaken out by the early 90s. But when buying a 3½-inch drive, look at the usual criteria: speed and capacity. Don't be too impressed by their lower power consumption unless you're running a battery-powered computer. Remember the low power 10MB drives that eventually have trouble starting up?

Hardcards. A *hardcard* is just a printed circuit board with the controller and drive mounted on the same board.

To work this minor miracle, two fairly new technologies are mated: RLL controllers and 3½-inch Winchester drives. Some hardcards go further beyond the pale and put variable numbers of sectors on a track, with more on the outer tracks. Actually, this isn't that odd among minicomputer and mainframe drives. It's called *ZBR, Zero Bit Reduction*. You'll also find it in some of the super-large CDC Wren drives for the PC.

A hardcard's design goal seems to be, *Minimize drive power consumption and space taken up in the computer*. I can't disagree more. Larger power supplies are cheap and easy to install, and I'm certainly not willing to give up reliability just to save some space. Remember that *normal* hard disks are probably the least

reliable things in your system. You cannot afford to give up even more reliability in the disk department.

I've already expressed misgivings about both 3½-inch drives and RLL on low cost drives, so I'll say no more except *be very careful when buying hardcards*. Are you only buying the drive because it's low power? See my comments on that in the previous section on 3½-inch drives.

On the other hand, Plus Technology makes the original Hardcard, and they still make the best. They've matched an RLL controller with a high-quality drive to produce a good quality product, given (again) the design goals.

I'll echo Paul Mace's advice at this point: "If you've got a hardcard, fine. Just be sure to back it up regularly."

Chapter 12
Hard Disk Drive Installation

Okay, you went out and bought a new 16000MB, 1 ms access disk, and you want to put it in your Belchfire 8800 clone. What do you do? You've got to first handle the hardware end of the installation, then the software end.

Hard Disk Hardware Installation

To get the hardware installation done, you've got to:

1. Find the *drive select jumper* and set it properly to tell the system if the drive is the first drive in the system or the second.
2. Find the *terminator chip* and remove it if it's on the second drive in the system. (If you're only installing one drive, you needn't worry about this.)
3. Cable the drive properly and install it in the chassis.
4. Inform the controller with what kind of drive it will be dealing.
5. Tell the controller what kind of drive you have.

Drive Select Jumpers on The Drive. As I've hinted, drive controllers can usu-

ally service more than one drive; two is the most common. (The desktop PS/2s are an exception, as they only allow one drive.) You don't buy a *C:* drive or *D:* drive from a manufacturer—any drive can act as drive #1 or drive #2 in a system. How, then, does the controller know which is which?

On the drive's circuit board, near the data connections, you may find a number of places to put a jumper. The places are generally labeled *DS0, DS1, DS2,* and *DS3.* There should be a jumper on one, *and only one,* of these positions. Alternatively, there may be only a *jumper pack,* a chip-shaped piece of black plastic with metal bands across it. You might recall that I mentioned them in the chapter on installing new circuit boards. You'll notice that most of the bands are broken, but at least one is intact; it's serving as the drive select jumper. I've even seen a few drives with DIP switches to select their drive address.

Finding these things could take some study, and even when you've found them they're often not labeled. My experience is that you'll see at least four jumper positions, one for each drive

Figure 12-1   Hard Disk Drive Select Jumper and Terminator

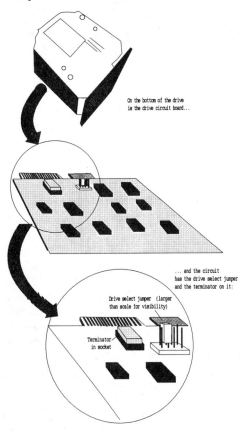

On the bottom of the drive is the drive circuit board...

... and the circuit has the drive select jumper and the terminator on it:

Drive select jumper (larger than scale for visibility)

Terminator in socket

location of the drive select jumpers and terminators.

The Terminator "Chip." Once you've found the drive select jumper, look around on the circuit board. Near it may be a chip-like object in a socket—the socket is the giveaway here. It's called the *terminator*, and you only need worry about it if you're installing a second hard drive.

Putting more than one drive on a single cable requires some special considerations. How do we have multiple devices talking on a single line without having them (1) interfere with each other and (2) blow up the poor chips that are listening to them? The same problem exists on the motherboard, which, you might recall, must talk to a variable number of expansion boards. The generic answer is a *bus*.

There are different kinds of buses, but the drives (floppy and hard) use a method called an *open collector bus*. In order for the bus to work, it must have a resistor called a *pullup resistor* at the physical end of the bus. This resistor "terminates" the bus, so it's called a *terminator*. It's not in a typical resistor package, however. It's in a chip-like package, so it often gets called the *terminator chip,* although it isn't a chip. This bus circuit is designed to work best with a particular resistance value.

So one drive—the one on the physical end of the cable—must have a terminator chip. Drives come with terminators standard, so you'll need to find it on the drive attached to the middle connector and remove it. If you leave both terminators on the drives, you'll have two of these resistors in parallel, which looks to the controller like a single resistor with *half* the resistance of either of the terminators. Less resistance means more current runs through the chips, which can cook the chips on the controller. Leave both terminators off, and the bus

address. Only one is jumpered. If it's one on the end, I assume that's location DS0. If it's one in from the end, I assume that's DS1. This works most of the time. So, assuming that *O* means a jumper point that's open (no jumper) and *J* means a jumpered jumper point, you might see this arrangement:

OOOJ or JOOO means DS0, and
OOJO or OJOO means DS1

Don't take that information to the bank, it's just a guideline. If you ask, the vendor will often send documentation on is "open"—near-infinite resistance. That makes signals "float" and introduces noise into the bus. So, either way, tend to your terminators; you want just *one* between the two drives, and that one must be on the drive that's on the physical end of the cable.

Hard Drive Cabling. A controller board is commonly connected to a drive with two ribbon cables. The larger cable has 34 lines, the smaller one 20. Many controllers have one 34-pin connector and two 20s. The second 20-pin connector is for connecting a second drive.

In about half of the cases, there's a twist in lines 25–29 in the middle of the 34-pin cable. In the rest of the cases, there's no twist. There could be one or two 34-pin connectors on the cable. So check to see if your cable has a twist.

With the no-twist cable, just set the first drive to DS0 and the second to DS1. The twist, however, throws the controller a curve: The drive connected to the twist gets its DS0/DS1 reversed. Set the jumper for DS0 on the drive connected to the twist, and it behaves like DS1. Set the jumper for DS1, and it behaves like DS0. That means you set *both* drives to either DS1 or DS0. Set both to DS0, and the drive with the twist becomes the second drive. Set both to DS1, and the drive with the twist becomes the *first* drive. I hope that's clear. If it isn't, look at Figure 12-2. It covers all four twist/no twist cases.

Telling the Controller What Kind of Drive You Have. Controllers and disks aren't manufactured together. Controller manufacturers like OMTI, Data Technology Corporation (DTC), and Western Digital build controllers to be generic. For example, when I first received my 33MB Rodime drive (from a company called PCs Limited, since renamed Dell Computers), it was supplied with a Xebec controller. I formatted the drive and used it for a while, finding it a bit slow. A CORETEST showed an access

Figure 12-2 Hard Disk Configuration and Cabling

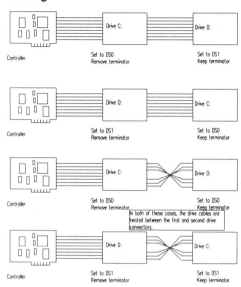

time of 639 ms that was substandard or, as the tech support person said, "substandard." I got a DTC 5150X controller and connected it—again, standard cables and connectors. It was built to handle a variety of disks. Disk type 4 was 639 cylinders, 6 heads—the Rodime. I selected disk type 4 with a set of jumpers. (On an AT controller, recall, you do it with the SETUP program.) The drive formatted without trouble and yielded a seek time of 57.5 ms.

That's just one example. Every disk/ controller combination must be, in essence, "properly introduced." There are three ways, by my reckoning:

- The Western Digital WD1002 XT-type controller keeps the "what kind of drive is this?" information on the partition record of the drive. The drive comes with software that allows you to put that information on the partition.
- Most other kinds of XT-type control-

lers require you to move a jumper, so the controller knows what kind of drive it's using, and some really old ones aren't configurable at all.

- AT-type and PS/2 computers use software, storing a "drive type number" in CMOS configuration memory. You use SETUP to tell the system what kind of drive it has.

Configuring Older XT-Type Controllers. On most XT-type controllers, either the controller will only talk to one kind of drive (IBM XT types) or you must move a jumper to tell the controller what kind of drive you have. Many older controllers, like the IBM XT controllers, will only communicate with a 10MB or 20MB drive. That's unfortunate, but then a replacement from DTC, Western Digital, or OMTI won't cost much.

There's not much to say about controllers that use jumpers. You just find the drive type that fits your hard disk, move the jumper, and you're off! This *does* assume, by the way, that you have the documentation. If you don't, you could be out of luck.

Configuring Western Digital XT-Type Controllers. More and more XT clones use a different, more flexible (but also troublesome) controller, one made by Western Digital. WD has an entire family of XT-type controllers, all with similar (but not identical) characteristics. They're called *auto-configure* controllers. (There are, by the way, other auto-configure controllers, particularly most ESDI controllers, but the WDs are the most common and so we'll focus on the WD 1002s in this section.)

On these controllers you have to run a program in the controller's ROM to tell the controller what kind of drive you have. That's nice, because the controller can then accommodate an infinite number of drive types.

On an auto-configure controller, this infinite flexibility is possible because the controller doesn't mess with jumpers; drive information is encoded onto a sector on the drive. **So be very careful with these drives!** If you run most utilities that can low-level format a drive, such as *SpinRite*, IAU, or HOPTIMUM, they might destroy this configuration information. The information is stored in the first few bytes of the partition record (also known as the *Master Boot Record,* or *MBR*). These controllers tend to confuse people, so I've summarized the high points of WD configuration in the next couple of pages.

When you run one of the WD controllers and activate the low level formatter with DEBUG (a program supplied with DOS), you'll be prompted for the following things:

- Drive number (0 for first drive, 1 for second)
- Interleave factor (probably 3 for the MFM controllers, 4 for the RLL controllers)

  Then it may (depending on the BIOS version) ask, "Do you want to dynamically format this drive (y/n)?" Respond *y*. Then it wants to know
  - # cylinders
  - # heads
  - lowest cylinder that uses reduced write current (RWC)
  - lowest cylinder that uses write precompensation (WPC)
  - maximum correctable error burst (legal values 5 or 11)
  - ccb option byte

You can find the number of cylinders, number of heads, RWC cylinder, and WPC cylinder in Appendix F of this book.

Maximum correctable error burst refers

to the *Error Correction Code (ECC)* used by the controller to ensure that data read off the hard disk wasn't corrupted in storage. An ECC is much like a checksum, or the parity bit in memory. It goes beyond simple error *detection,* however; it can actually correct a short string of bad bits. Depending on how complex the controller's ECC method is, it can correct from 5 to 11 bad bits in a row. That's what the controller wants to know—how far should it go in writing error-correction stuff on the disk. Go for the security and pick 11 bits.

The *ccb option byte* prompt refers to the *step rate* of your drive. Step rate refers to how quickly multiple seek commands can be sent to a disk head. The numbers vary considerably, and WD has chosen an odd bunch of values, as you can see in Table 12-1.

Table 12-1. WD1002 ccb Option Byte Codes

ccb	Step Rate
0	3 microsec/step
1	24 microsec/step
2	24 microsec/step
3	24 microsec/step
4	8 microsec/step
5	24 microsec/step
6	24 microsec/step
7	8 microsec/step

The step numbers can be hard to find, so I just usually go with the majority and use the value 5, the default. No, I don't know why there are so many *24 microsecond/step* options.

As mentioned above, these drive characteristics are written to the first half of the sector that contains your MBR. I cannot stress this enough—*back this up!* The only program I know that will do this

is XFDISK, another part of the set of extremely useful hTEST/hFORMAT collection I've mentioned before.

Installation Details on Some WD 1002 Controllers. Nearly every XT compatible you'll come across has one of the WD 1002 controllers in it. Western Digital, in its quest to retain its amazing control of the XT controller market, offers a version of the WD 1002 for every occasion. That means there are quite a number of controllers available in this line, but I'll restrict my discussion to the six most common ones.

To tackle setting up a WD controller, you need to

1. Make sure you've got an MFM controller for an MFM drive or an RLL controller for a RLL drive.
2. Check the date of the BIOS chip on the controllers that have a separate BIOS chip (some incorporate the BIOS into other chips). The latest BIOS is dated 62-0000094-XXX, where *XXX* is three digits that are irrelevant. If you have a controller with a lower BIOS ID number (such as the 62-000043-010 I have in my hand at the moment), upgrade the BIOS. Call WD at 1-800-777-4787 to order the upgrade.
3. Set the jumpers, if there are any on the board.
4. Configure and low-level format the drive, as described in the previous section.

Table 12-2 summarizes which controllers have BIOS chips and jumpers and whether they support dynamic configuration, as well as showing their encoding scheme.

In general, you'll see from zero to ten jumpers on a WD 1002. They're labeled from W1 to W9, and there's often

Table 12-2. Western Digital WD1002 XT Controller Features

Controller Name	Encoding	BIOS Chip?	Which Jumpers?	Supports Dynamic Configuration?
WD 1002A-WX1	MFM	Y	W1-W8, SW1	Y
WD 1002-27X	RLL	N	W1-W9, SW1	Y
WD 1002A-27X	RLL	N	W1-W2	Y
WD 1002S-WX2	MFM	Y	W1-W7, SW1	Y
WD 1002S-WX2A	MFM	Y	W6 only	Y
WD XT-GEN	MFM	N	None	N (except model F300)

a larger jumper set called SW1 with nine positions. *Not every board has all ten jumpers,* and indeed most don't have more than seven. The jumpers are set as follows (* indicates factory defaults):

W1 and W2
On most WD drives, these are hardwired—and WD ain't tellin' what they do anyway.

W1/W2 RLL Translation (1002-27X Only)
On one RLL controller, the WD 1002A-27X, you have the option to "fool" the system into thinking it has an MFM controller and drive. So long as your drive has 663 or fewer cylinders, the 1002A-27X will translate instructions to read or write 1024 cylinder, 17 sector disks into instructions to read or write 663 cylinder, 26 sector disks. The translation mode is enabled by jumpering *both* W1 and W2. Disable translation by removing both jumpers. Recommendation: Don't do it. It confuses disk utilities, and an otherwise innocuous program could trash your data because of it.

W3 BIOS Enable
1–2 to enable the BIOS *
No jumper; disable BIOS

W4 I/O Address
1–2 selects address 324 hex; 2–3 selects address 320 hex *

Note: This must agree with Controller Select *jumper if W8 is present.*

W5 ROM Size
1–2 is hardwired, allows use of 2732 and 2764 ROMs. *
Break 1–2 trace and solder 2–3 to allow use of 2716s

W6 Reduced Write Enable
1–2 drive can have up to 16 heads, but no RWC.
2–3 drive can have up to 8 heads, *and* RWC enabled.*

W7 Interrupt Select
1–2 hardwired controller uses IRQ5. *
Cut 1–2, jumper 2–3, and jumper position 7 on SW1 to enable IRQ2 instead.

W8 Controller Select
1–2 controller is first controller in PC. *
2–3 controller is second controller in PC.
Note: Controller Select jumper position must match I/O Address jumper position.

W9 (unused)
If you have W9, as in a Wd1002-27X, just leave it open—no jumper.

SW1
This is actually a set of jumper positions labeled from 1 to 8. In most cases, don't put jumpers across any of the positions.

That's your quick & dirty guide to configuring WD 1002 controllers. It's not the whole story, but it'll cover 99 percent of the cases. WD has a semi-automated tech support service at (800) 777-4787. If you're out of the U.S., direct dial (714) 747-2033 extension 34700.

Specifying AT Hard Drive Type. How do you tell a 286/386/486 type machine what kind of hard disk you have? Not with jumpers—the SETUP program does the job here. The information is, you might recall from our discussion of motherboard configuration, saved into a battery-powered memory chip generally called the CMOS chip.

Supplying hard disk information to the CMOS chip is, sadly, the most troublesome part about running an AT's SETUP program. The program asks, "What type is your hard disk?" If you answer *Seagate ST225*, or the like, it just beeps at you. Unfortunately, the drive type number isn't particularly descriptive. Table 12-3 shows the drive types offered for IBM machines. Your clone may well vary in its drive table, although the first 14 drive types are almost invariably the original IBM drive types.

This drive type information is in your computer's BIOS ROM, not on the hard disk controller.

Some clones will tell you what hard disk table they have if you respond with a question mark (?) when their SETUP program asks, "What drive type is your hard disk?"

Now, there might not be a prestored drive type that exactly matches your hard disk, so you could have to find the closest one. Here's how. Suppose you've got a machine with the drive type table from the next page, and you want to install a drive with 1024 cylinders, seven heads, and no write precompensation? (You might be wondering, "Where would I get that information about the drive anyway? Simple—call the manufacturer, or look it up in the table at the end of this book.) You quickly see there are no exact matches. Now what? Find the best match. There are four steps:

1. **Eliminate all drives with write precompensation different from your drive's.** If it's just a few cylinders different, you can get away with it, but the write precomp *is* important. Notice in the drive type table that IBM thought it sufficiently important to include *two* 21MB drive types in the original 14—types 2 and 6 only vary by their write precompensation values. Since your drive doesn't need write precomp, you eliminate the drive types that *do*, so what remain are types 6, 8–12, 14–16, 18, 26–28, 37, 41–42, and 44–46.

2. **You can't exaggerate about cylinders.** It's all right to use a drive type that doesn't exploit all your drive's cylinders, but if you pick one with *more* cylinders than your drive has, the computer will try to format nonexistent cylinders. Trying to format, say, cylinder 900 on a 700-cylinder machine could destroy the drive. No drive types exist that have more than 1024 cylinders, so you're still looking at the same possibilities as before.

3. **Eliminate all drive types with more heads than your drive.** You also can't exaggerate about heads. Remove the drive types with more than seven heads, and you are left with types 6, 8, 10–12, 14–16, 18, 26–27, and 44.

4. **Now choose the greatest capacity.** Any of the remaining drive types are fine to use, but you want the largest amount of drive space possible, so examine the capacities, and

Table 12-3. Built-In AT Drive Types

Drive #	# of Cylinders	Heads	Write Precompensation	Capacity	Examples
1	306	4	128	10.6	Seagate ST412, ST212, ST112
2	615	4	300	21.4	Seagate ST225
3	615	6	300	32.1	Tulin TL240, Rodime RO206
4	940	8	512	65.4	Atasi 3080
5	940	6	512	49.0	
6	615	4	no	21.4	The Dread CMI 20 MB
7	462	8	256	32.1	Quantum Q540
8	733	5	no	31.9	Seagate ST4038
9	900	15	no	117.5	Maxtor XT-1140
10	820	3	no	21.4	Micropolis 1302, Vertex V130
11	855	5	no	37.2	Vertex V150
12	855	7	no	52.0	Vertex V170
13	306	8	128	21.3	Seagate ST425, Rodime RO204
14	733	7	no	44.6	
16	612	4	no	20.3	
17	977	5	300	40.5	
18	977	7	no	56.7	Priam HD60
19	1024	7	512	59.5	
20	733	5	300	30.4	
21	733	7	300	42.5	
22	733	5	300	30.4	
23	306	4	0	10.1	
25	615	4	0	20.4	
26	1024	4	no	34.0	
27	1024	5	no	42.5	
28	1024	8	no	68.0	
29	512	8	256	34.0	
30	615	2	615	10.2	
35	1024	9	1024	76.5	Seagate ST4096
36	1024	5	512	42.5	
37	830	10	no	68.8	
38	823	10	256	68.3	
39	615	4	128	20.4	
40	615	8	128	40.8	
41	917	15	no	114.1	
42	1023	15	no	127.3	
43	823	10	512	68.3	
44	820	6	no	40.8	
45	1024	8	no	68.0	
46	925	9	no	69.1	
47	699	7	256	40.6	

(Note: Your AT might not have all 47 types. IBM added them over time.)

you'll come up with type 18. Now, note that the actual drive is a 60MB drive, and type 18 describes a 56.7MB drive, so we're wasting 3.3MB. But it's as close as this ROM allows.

Expanding Your AT's Drive Types. If you have a drive that won't match any AT drive type within a reasonable number of megabytes, think about buying an add-on ROM to enlarge the AT drive table. Alternatively, there are software answers, such as products called Speed-Stor or DiskManager, but I don't recommend using a device driver to communicate with your hard disk. One reason is that it's another piece of software that must be functioning properly for your programs to use the hard disk, and thus it can complicate your troubleshooting hassles. Another is that a ROM is usable for any operating system, so you'll have no trouble going to OS/2, Novell, or UNIX systems in the future. One such ROM is sold by OnTrack Systems:

SuperPROM $150
OnTrack Computer Systems
6321 Bury Drive
Eden Prairie, MN 55346
(612) 937-1107
(800) 752-1333

Hard Disk Software Installation

There's more to hard disk preparation than FORMAT C:/S. There are three steps to drive preparation:

- Physical (low-level) format
- Partition creation
- DOS (high-level) format

Physical Formatting. Physical, or *low-level, formatting* is a process whereby 17 sectors are "drawn" on each track, using magnetism as the "ink." Each sector is then filled with ASCII 229 (the

sigma character). It's at this level that the interleave factor is set. This formatting is generally done by the manufacturer.

The low-level format process not only tests the disk medium itself, it also writes out the *sector IDs* that will be used by DOS to locate data on the disk. The physical format process matches up a drive and a controller. Since every controller and drive has its own quirks, this means a controller might not be able to read a disk formatted by a different controller, even if the new controller is the same model as the old one.

You'll do a physical format for one of four reasons:

1. You've purchased a new controller or drive.
2. You experience a large number of disk problems. Try backing up the hard disk, do a new physical format, create a partition, and directory format, then reload your files. They'll come back. Recall that sector IDs are laid down at physical format time. These IDs, like all magnetic images, fade over time. (Ever seen a *sector not found* error from DOS? That's what causes it.) You could have a perfectly good disk with old, faint IDs that ends up looking like it's bad. A new physical format will make it good as new. As I've said before, it's a good idea to reformat the drive every year or so.
3. You wish to experiment with the interleave factor to increase your data transfer rate from your hard disk. We covered interleave factors previously.
4. You suspect a faulty format, as in a case where a disk is accidentally formatted as a 20MB drive when it's actually a 10MB drive.

Once I tried to use a rental XT under

191

DOS 3.1. The XT was delivered to me with the disk formatted under 2.1, so I tried to reformat it. The drive ground a lot and finally told me that it had formatted a 20MB disk and had found 10MB of bad sectors. It was, of course, a 10MB disk, which in reality had gotten an odd formatting. I ran a physical format, then created the partition, and did the DOS format; there was no further trouble.

How you physically format is a controller-specific question. If you have:

- **Any XT-type MFM controller other than a Western Digital WD1002, WD XT-GEN, or RLL controller:** Use HFORMAT from the Kolod collection. Alternatively, your dealer may have included a low-level format program with your disk.
- **A WD1002 or XT-GEN, or an RLL (XT or AT) controller:** Each requires its own format program. It's sitting in the ROM on the hard disk controller, so you need only use DEBUG to activate it. The built-in program is generally at address C800:5 or C800:6. Adaptec RLL controllers put the program at C800:CCC.

  Warning: The procedure I'm about to describe will irrevocably destroy any data on your hard disk drive. Don't do it unless you've backed up the drive in entirety!
  Load DEBUG:

```
C>debug
-G = C800:5
```

I've discussed formatting the WD controllers in the earlier section on setting up and using WD XT-type controllers.

You'll get some kind of prompt, like *What interleave factor would you like to use?* The prompts will depend on the manufacturer. See the documentation that came with the controller. If you don't have documentation, call the manufacturer's tech support line.

- **An MFM AT-type controller:** Again, use HFORMAT. Alternatively, the IBM AT Advanced Diagnostics disk includes a low-level format program.
- **PS/2 Model 25, 30, or 30/286:** You've *got* to use HFORMAT. It's the only program I know of that seems to reliably format these drives.
- **PS/2 Model 50 to 80:** If you have a PS/2, there's a low-level format program on the Reference Disk; boot from the Reference Disk. Once you're at the Main Menu, press Ctrl-A and an *Advanced* menu will pop up. One option is low-level format of the PS/2 disk.

Make sure you know how to do physical formats. If you're responsible for several or many machines, get the instructions and try it out once. The reason for this: You want to see all diagnostic procedures on a properly functioning system. Then you'll know how to spot troubles.

Partitioning. In order to accommodate multiple operating systems, DOS allows you to create multiple *partitions* with the program FDISK. Suppose you have a 30MB drive and want to run both DOS and XENIX. Using FDISK, you can create a (say) 20MB partition for DOS, and a 10MB partition for XENIX. Even if you're going to give it all to DOS, you still must run FDISK.

Until recently, using FDISK has been a two-minute operation: Tell it to give DOS the entire disk; then it reboots the system, and you're ready to format. But nowadays, you could find yourself spending a little more time in the partition process.

You see, as of DOS 3.3, FDISK has another value. DOS 3.x can't handle a disk larger than 32MB. Previously, this meant that an 80MB drive either wasted 48MB or required a device driver to access the latter 48MB.

Under FDISK 3.3, you can divide the disk into a drive C with 32MB, a 32MB D drive, and an E drive 16MB in size. Here's how.

The disk gets divided into two partitions, a *primary DOS partition,* and an *extended DOS partition.* The primary DOS partition can't be larger than 32MB, but the extended can be as large as you like. So Step 1 is to divide the example 80MB drive into a primary DOS partition of 32MB, and an extended DOS partition of 48MB.

Next, the extended DOS partition gets divided up into "logical" drives. You can have as many as you like, each of any size up to 32MB. If you wanted, you could create drives D:, E:, F:, G:, H:, I:, and so on, each 1MB in size. (You should probably consider professional counseling if you'd really like to create piles of tiny logical drives, however.) All this is pictured in Figure 12-3.

Here are the steps to go through to set up an 80MB disk under DOS 3.3.

1. Invoke FDISK and create the pri-
   mary DOS partition. You'll see an opening screen with four options:

   1. Create DOS Partition
   2. Change Active Partition
   3. Delete DOS Partition
   4. View Partition Information

If you have two hard disks, there will be a fifth option to allow you to choose on which disk to work. Right now, select option 1, Create DOS Partition. You'll then see another menu offering:

1. Create Primary DOS Partition
2. Create Extended DOS Partition

First we make the primary partition, so select 1 again. FDISK will then offer to automatically create the maximum size DOS partition and make it bootable. Don't take this option, as it immediately reboots the system. Answer *no.* It will then say something like:

Enter number of cylinders for partition . . . . . . [450]?

It has already computed the number of cylinders that will allow a 32MB primary DOS partition. Press Enter and it'll display the information on the new partition. Press Esc and you'll return to the FDISK main menu. By the way, it will beep at you—that's normal.

2. **Create the extended partition and logical drives.** Enter 1 to go to the Create Partition menu again, but this time choose 2, Create Extended

Figure 12-3 DOS 3.3 Partitioning of Example 80MB Drive

80 MB Physical Drive	=	Extended DOS partition 48 MB	=	16 MB logical drive E:
				32 MB logical drive D:
		Primary DOS partition 32 MB		32 MB logical drive C:

Partition. It will, by default, suggest that you devote the rest of the disk to the extended partition. Like the primary, it'll display a message somewhat like this:

Enter number of cylinders for partition . . . . [550]

Take its suggestion. It will beep again and remind you that no logical drives have been created. The extended partition must be further divided into logical drives. Press Esc and it will suggest a number of cylinders to allocate to logical drive D (the amount needed to bring it up to 32MB). Again, take its suggestion. It will then suggest the remainder for drive E. Accept its suggestion. You'll see the information on the new partitions and logical drives on the screen. Press Esc, and you're back to the main menu.

3. **Make the DOS partition bootable.** Oops, that's "active." The PC has to know to which partition it should go in order to boot. That partition should be called the bootable partition, (in my opinion, anyway), but FDISK calls it the *active partition*. Choose option 2, Change Active Partition. It will ask which partition to make active. The primary DOS partition should be partition number 1, so choose number 1. Then press Esc to get to the main menu, and another time to get out of FDISK. The system will reboot, and you're partitioned.

Under FDISK 3.3, you can create as many volumes as you like, all smaller than 32MB. Perhaps even better, Compaq DOS 3.31 and PC DOS 4.0 allow you to create disks up to 512MB in size. It's a

nice innovation, but be careful: Some hard disk utilities, like older versions of Norton, Mace, or *PC Tools* were written before such DOSes existed and might not know how to talk to your disk. Worse, some can actually damage your data when you run them.

Having gone through all that work to create the DOS partition, you might wonder, "What happens if the partition information is destroyed?" This is a real problem; in this situation, the PC will refuse to even recognize that a disk exists. Kolod Research, mentioned earlier, offers some utilities to help. XFDISK, one of the programs that comes with hTEST/ hFORMAT, can back up your partition record. In fact, it's the only one of the major utilities that can back up the partition record—Norton, Mace, and *PC Tools* cannot.

The latest editions of the popular disk utilities—The Norton Utilities version 4.5, The Mace Utilities version 5.0, and *PC Tools*—all support the latest disk formats.

DOS Formatting. Finally, you run the DOS FORMAT program. It doesn't actually overwrite sectors and physically format hard disks. Disks have five areas, some of which we've heard about earlier in this chapter:

- The partition record or Master Boot Record (MBR)
  This contains the disk partition information to divide the physical drive into logical drives. On auto-configure controllers, it also contains a few bytes that describe the disk. This resides (under DOS 3.x) on cylinder 0, head 0, sector 1. The remaining 16 sectors on the first cylinder/head are unused.
- The DOS boot record
  Originally, this only contained a snippet of code used to start boot-

ing up the system. In later versions of DOS, other disk ID information was added. Among other things, the DOS boot record contains a pointer to the FAT, so if the boot record is damaged, the FAT will look strange to DOS. The boot record resides on *DOS sector 0,* which is cylinder 0, head 1, sector 1.

DOS numbers sectors sequentially starting at cylinder 0, head 1, sector 1. Sectors 2 to 17 of that cylinder/head are the next 16 "DOS sectors." The next group is the 17 sectors on cylinder 0, head 2. Next is head 3, and so on. To traverse the DOS sectors in order, first increment sectors until you're out of them; next increment the head numbers until they're exhausted; then increment the cylinder numbers.

- The FAT (File Allocation Table)

The FAT is a map of what clusters are associated with what files. DOS keeps two copies of the FAT, the primary and the secondary. There are two kinds of FATs: a 12-bit FAT, with 4096 12-bit entries, requiring 6K total on the disk for each copy, and a 16-bit FAT, with 64K 16-bit entries, requiring 128K for each copy. Under DOS 3.x and 4.x, floppies and 10MB hard disks use the 12-bit FAT, and 20+MB hard disks use the 16-bit FAT. DOS 2.x uses the 12-bit FAT for all disk types.

- The Root Directory

The root directory is the basis of the tree-structured file system. There are 128 entries for a disk with a 12-bit FAT and 512 entries for a disk with a 16-bit FAT. *Entries* means room for directory information for a file. Twelve-bit FAT disks can only have 128 files in their root directories. Try to create a 129th, and you get an *unable to create directory entry* error message.

The root directory immediately follows the second copy of the FAT on the disk.

- The Data Area

Actual user data goes here. It follows the root directory.

  - IBMBIO.COM or IO.SYS

If the disk is bootable, the first directory entry, and the first cluster, refer to the first *hidden file,* IBMBIO.COM (for PC-DOS) or IO.SYS (for MS-DOS).

  - IBMDOS.COM or MSDOS.SYS

If the disk is bootable, the second directory entry will refer to the second hidden file, IBMDOS.COM (for PC-DOS) or MSDOS.SYS (for MS-DOS).

The FORMAT command creates the DOS boot record, FATs, and root directory—it doesn't touch the MBR or the user data area. Since the FORMAT program doesn't destroy or overwrite data in the data area, this implies that *formatted hard disks can be recovered.* See Chapter 14 on failure recovery for more information.

There are, incidentally, a few exceptions to this rule. Earlier versions of AT&T, Compaq, and Unisys MS-DOS actually torpedo the whole disk. There's no recovery from this.

A Note About Bad Areas. One of DOS's most important jobs is to ensure that unreliable, or "bad," areas on a disk aren't used. The FAT helps DOS avoid these bad areas.

Bad areas have either *hard errors* or *soft errors.* Hard errors are problems in the disk surface itself, so that it cannot record data at all. This is caused by manufacturing defects or later abuse. Soft errors occur when some data has faded on the disk to the point where it cannot be read. The idea is, "If it faded once, it could again, so we'll cordon off the area and not use it again (kind of like a hazardous waste dump for your system)." Programs like Norton *DiskTest* or Mace *Remedy* detect these things.

Hard errors are designated by the system at low-level format time. Low-level format programs can format an area with a specific code that will upset the DOS FORMAT program when FORMAT does its quick sector scan. When FORMAT can't read the sector, it marks it as bad in the FAT.

Soft errors, on the other hand, can allow FORMAT to read the sector just fine, so a cluster previously marked bad might not be remarked on a subsequent format. Soft errors, you'll recall, don't always show up when tested. The fact that FORMAT hasn't remarked all of the bad areas as bad leads some people to think that they can get rid of bad sectors by just reformatting the drive. All that does is erase DOS's information about where bad areas exist, which is not a great idea. Low-level formatting, on the other hand, might help a failing drive, for reasons I've already mentioned.

Chapter 13
Hard Disk Preventive Maintenance

Hard disk preventive maintenance mainly refers to protecting the data and the drive. The drive is fairly fragile, so some careful handling and simple procedures can minimize chances of harm. The disk's data is also important, more so in fact than the drive itself. Backups are the key here, although you probably never even thought of making the kinds of backups we'll discuss here.

Hard Disk Mechanical Protection

- Leave the machine on all the time.
  I think I've beaten this one to death, so I'll say no more on the subject.
- Get good surge protection.
  Surges go through the whole system, including the drive head. And if the drive head happens to be near the FAT or partition. . .
- Don't smoke around drives.
  More on this below.
- Park the head.
  More on this below.
- Be careful what length screws you use to secure a drive, particularly Seagate ST2XX drives.

I've mentioned it before, but it's a common mistake, so I'll mention it again. DO NOT use the standard $\frac{3}{8}$-inch screws to secure Seagate ST225, ST238, or ST251 drives. They're too long and can actually push in the drive housing. Back off the screw, and the problem is often solved.

- Don't secure Seagate ST2XX drives on all four sides.
  Some of the ST2XX drives seem to have their mounting holes drilled out of line with one another. That means when you tighten four screws to secure the drive, two on each side, you warp the drive and it stops working. Panic ensues. The answer is simple. Just loosen one of the screws, and the problem disappears.
- Format a drive in the position and at the temperature it'll be used.
  The small effects of gravity are important. If you're going to use the machine on its side, low-level format the drive on its side. Don't format a drive when it's cold. Don't run test programs on it when it's cold, either.

197

- There's some merit to the idea that using a disk cache program lengthens the life of your drive, as it reduces wear on the drive. See below for more information.
- Attend to squeaky drives. Not only are they annoying, they might be trying to tell you something.

You Can't Fix It, So You Must Protect It. There's not much to be done in the way of regular maintenance on the sealed Winchester drive. You can't clean the heads, and you can't align them. If the drive itself is fried, about all you can do with it is cut it open and leave it on your bookshelf as a conversation piece.

What kills hard disks?

- Smoke (the filters aren't perfect)
- Vibration

I've mentioned the effects of smoke before. When a smoke particle sits on the disk, the head whips around and crashes right into it. Then it drags it around the platter, leaving scratches in its wake. On a 5¼-inch platter rotating at 3600 rpm, a particle on the outermost track would travel at 56 miles per hour. The outermost track is, by the way, the most important track, as it contains the directory information for the rest of the disk.

Vibration is a problem because of the way in which the head travels above the disk platter on a cushion of air. The distance between the platter and the head (called the *head gap*) is fairly small. Any bouncing around, then, can cause the head to literally crash onto the platter below. This plows a small furrow in the platter and grinds down the head. Do this enough, and you'll lose the data in the furrow and possibly the head.

A similar thing happens whenever you turn off power from the hard disk. Deprived of its cushion of air, it crash-

lands onto the platter below. If you always have the head positioned over the same spot when you power down, you'll eventually create a new bad sector there.

Another way you can protect your data is to buy quality drives. How is the magnetic material put on the platters in the first place? The cheaper and less effective approach is to simply *coat* the platters—in effect, to glue rust onto the platters. A better and more expensive approach is to *plate* the magnetic oxide onto the platters. Plated media are superior and more expensive.

Disk Protection: Parking the Heads I. One of the best ways to reduce the damage from the head hitting the platter is to move the head outside the data area, and then power down. This is possible because the actual number of tracks the disk has is greater than the number you use, by a few. For example, on the 305 cylinder XT hard disk, you can position the head over cylinder 306, then power down. This is called *parking the heads*. Do it when you're going to be away from your machine, at lunchtime or for the evening.

Parking the Heads II: The Deadly SHIP-DISK. Most of us have heard of disk parking, and many know that IBM includes a head parking program on the IBM Diagnostics disk called SHIPDISK. The notion is that when you're going to subject the disk to some jarring, such as when you're moving the XT, you should first boot the Diagnostics disk and use SHIPDISK to position the head, then turn the system off.

In general, SHIPDISK works fine *when you use it this way:* Boot off the Diagnostics disk and then run the program. But a lot of people decided to just copy SHIPDISK off the diagnostics disk onto their hard disk, and run SHIPDISK before powering down for the night. This is a bad move, as SHIPDISK presumes the presence of some software routines that only exist on the special version of DOS included on the Diagnostics disk. Run under regular DOS, SHIPDISK can destroy data.

Here's another SHIPDISK item to watch: If you use XT SHIPDISK on an AT hard disk, the disk is zapped. (In the words of Bill Cosby, "'Zap' means 'dead'.")

Parking the Heads III: Safe Remedies. What, then, should you do? Two possibilities: First, you could leave your PC on all of the time, as has been discussed earlier. Second, use a safe park program. If you work in an environment with a lot of vibration, don't hesitate to park the heads whenever you're not using the PC, even if it's still turned on.

Disk Caching Programs. The most demanding mechanical activities for a drive are starting up in the morning and moving the head throughout the day. You can avoid the first stress by leaving your machine on all the time. You can avoid the second with a cache program, as a cache minimizes the number of head movements the disk must do. In the process, it also makes the system work more quickly. Here's how.

A disk cache works on the principle that a sector used on disk tends to be reused soon. It watches each disk "read" operation, and copies the information read into a section of memory set aside for disk caching. Subsequent DOS requests to read anything from disk that the cache already has in memory are intercepted by the cache, which delivers the data to DOS by transferring it from the cache memory. Reading memory is, again, lots faster than reading disks, so the system speeds up considerably.

If bug-free, disk caches are truly neat. They make the disk do less work, and they can use some memory that you haven't been doing anything with any-

way. Remember that extended memory that's only good to heat up the room under DOS? There are disk cache programs that change all that and use the extended memory as cache space. (You don't really want to have to give up some of your 640K, do you?)

There are lots of cache programs out there, but let me recommend the best: Multisoft's *PC-Kwik Cache*. (No, they can't spell, but they can sure write code.) You can find them at

Multisoft Corporation
15100 SW Koll Pkwy.
Beaverton, OR 97006
(503) 644-5644

Here are some cache tips. You can load a file into the cache by copying it to NUL:. Copying to NUL:, DOS's "bit bucket," doesn't really do anything except force DOS to look at the file. Cache programs watch what DOS is watching, and so a side effect of copying to NUL: is to load a file into a cache. For example, if I had a file called BANANA.WK1 that I wanted in the cache, I'd just type *COPY BANANA.WK1 NUL:*. Caches don't know which sectors are most likely to be read, so they take a while to "learn" which sectors are most profitably cached. And, of course, if you have an application that jumps all over the disk (unlikely, but possible), the cache will actually slow you down. What if cached data is sitting in memory and the computer is powered down? Won't that lose data? No, any *writes* requested are done directly to disk. It's really disk *reads* that benefit from caching, although a smart cache observes when a sector that the system wants to write doesn't vary from the current disk value.

Squeaky Drives. Many hard disks make high pitched squeals and squeaks.

How to handle this? There are three reasons for squeaky drives.

First, ensure that the disk is fully secured, and either lying flat or on its side. A slightly askew disk will whine. By the way, it's perfectly acceptable to store a hard disk on its side, but you'll get better results if you also low-level format the drive in this position.

Second, check how well supported the drive is. The XT- and PC-type machines ordinarily only support the drive on one side. This makes the drive bend just a little and sets up vibration. The vibration is then picked up by the case, and the whole computer starts squealing. The answer is simple: Damp the vibration between the drive and the case. This can be done by using a small piece of cardboard or folded construction paper as a shim between the drive and the chassis.

The third approach involves something on the drive called the *static wiper*. Remove the drive. On its bottom there's generally a circuit board. The board may have a cutout in the middle: if not, remove the board. You'll see a flat piece of spring metal lying on a small bearing.

This piece of metal is a *static wiper*. It drains off static charges from the drive. Over time, the charges and the friction of sitting against the bearing cause the wiper to become pitted. The pitted surface against the rotating bearing is the source of the squeak. One answer is to remove the circuit board (you can remove the circuit board without unsealing the disk), and use a fine emery cloth to shine the static wiper. An easier answer is to use some GE silicone putty. Just a drop on top of the wiper (*not between it and the bearing!*) changes the mass of the wiper just enough to damp the squeak. The small blob of silicone will fall off after six months; when it does, just replace it.

At my company we once tried lubricating the bearing to stop the noise. We used WD40 (a common silicone-based lubricant) to quiet a drive. It quieted the drive somewhat, and in a few months it quieted it completely: the WD40 attracted gunk, and the gunk dirtied the whole works so badly that the drive stopped working. I'm told (although I've not tried it yet) that you *can* lubricate the bearing, but that you should instead use Tri-Flow, a teflon-based lubricant. You

View of static wiper on underside of hard disk.

can find it in hardware stores. Supposedly, the gunk doesn't stick. My partner Rob observes that the "teflon doesn't stick" part is right, but notes that Tri-Flow uses some kind of oily stuff to suspend the teflon particles, and *that* oily stuff might attract and hold gunk. Sorry I can't give you a definite *yea* or *nay* on this, but if you've got a marginal drive that's noisy and is probably going to be replaced soon anyway, give it a try. But be sure, of course, to back up regularly.

There's actually a fourth reason for squeak, but there's really nothing you can do about it. Sometimes the bearings fail and start to grind against each other. You can tell for sure by using a stethoscope (any long narrow piece of metal will do, actually) and listening to the bearings while the disk is running. If the bearings are grinding, you'll hear it. The answer is to back up the disk, throw it away before it fails, and replace it.

Hard Disk Data Protection

- Back up user data periodically (see below).
- Back up, low-level format again, and reload your data on the drive once or twice per year.

  Recall that each track is divided with sector IDs recorded by the head at format time. Those IDs can fade and/or the mechanical head positioning equipment can move, causing a host of problems. Reformat periodically to keep the mechanicals in line with the data, and to refresh the IDs on the disk. A nondestructive low-level format program like *Spinrite* or *HOPTIMUM* can greatly simplify this task, as you needn't reload your data after each

reformat. Remember that nondestructive low-level formats probably aren't a good idea for a machine with an XT-type controller. Better to just do it the hard way with such a machine and back up, format, and reload.

- Back up the first track (actually, the first *sector*—head 0, track 0, sector 1). This protects the partition record and possibly the autoconfigure record. Use a program like XFDISK from hTEST/hFORMAT.
- Back up the FAT and root directory automatically with a program like FR (Norton), RXBAK (Mace) or Mirror *(PC Tools)*. *Be sure you have the most recent version of the software!* (An old Mirror once trashed the FAT on our LAN server.) Put the program in your AUTOEXEC.BAT.

  FAT backup programs make unerasing or unformatting data easier. As we'll discuss in the next chapter, the major effect of erasing data or formatting disks is seen mostly in the FAT, not the user data areas. So it makes sense to back up the FAT to make things easier for a program like Norton when you're trying to undo some user-inspired damage.

- Unfragment your files monthly or semimonthly with an unfragmenter like Norton SpeedDisk, Mace Unfrag, or *PC Tools'* Compress.

  These programs basically tidy up your disk so DOS can read the files faster. Most people use them for speed, but truthfully I run them because putting all my files in nice neat consecutive order makes data recovery easier: If a file isn't scattered all over the disk, it's easier to find when the directory and FAT have gone south. See below for more details.

- Run a disk tester program like *DiskTest* to provide early warning of hard disk problems.

There are a lot of problems with disks DOS doesn't tell us about:

- If DOS detects a read error, it performs several retries without informing the user. If the retries succeed, the user never knows there's a problem.
- In responding to DOS, BIOS might execute retries of its own. DOS knows nothing about this.
- When following BIOS orders to read a sector, the controller's firmware can not only detect but actually *correct* a few bad bits in each sector. BIOS knows nothing of this.

Between all this, it'd be nice to have a program around to monitor all the things DOS and the gang aren't telling you. *Spinrite* and *Disk Technician* both try to do this while they're doing disk testing. Norton *DiskTest* and Mace Remedy are in this class also. They do sequential disk read tests, and try to move data from flaky areas on disk to more reliable places.

File Unfragmenters. As mentioned before, files can be *fragmented*. This means that a given file may be divided into sectors 30–40 (one contiguous group) and 101–122 (another contiguous group). Noncontiguous files are bad for two reasons.

First, noncontiguous files take longer to read. The fact that the disk head must go chasing all over the disk to read them slows down disk access. Putting the whole file together makes read operations quicker.

Second, you have a higher probability of recovering an erased file if it isn't fragmented. Keeping disks unfragmented just pushes the odds a little further in your favor.

How do files become fragmented? Well, when DOS needs a sector, it basically grabs the first one available. When the disk is new, only a few sectors have been taken, and the rest of the disk is one large free area. New files are all contiguous. But as files are deleted, they create "holes" in the disk space. As DOS is requested for new sectors, it responds by taking the first sector available. This can easily lead to a new file being spread out over several separate areas.

You can test this with CHKDSK *.*. Here is a sample output from CHKDSK:

Volume IC-DISK
    created March 17, 1987 9:00a
  730112 bytes total disk space
   23552 bytes in 3 hidden files
    1024 bytes in 1 directories
 207872 bytes in 40 user files
 497664 bytes available on disk
 655360 bytes total memory
 363152 bytes free
C:SETUP10.EXE
Contains 2 noncontiguous blocks.

Like most DOS utilities, CHKDSK only operates on a subdirectory at a time. To get fragmentation information about the whole disk, you'd need to run CHDKSK on each subdirectory (no, there's no /S option). Microsoft attempted to solve this problem with DOS 3.x. DOS 3.x reduces the fragmentation problem, but it doesn't solve it entirely.

Programs exist that will rearrange the disk so all files are contiguous and no holes exist. The best known is *Disk Optimizer* from SoftLogic Solutions. The latest version even allows you to specify most-used files so they can be moved to

Figure 13-1 A Fragmented and Unfragmented File

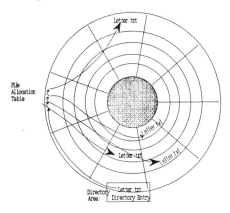

A Fragmented File

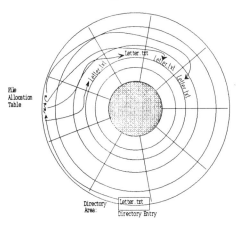

The same file, unfragmented

the front of the directory, speeding access by a bit. Mace will also do this with its UnFragment option. Norton's *Speed Disk* program (offered as part of Norton Utilities) is another program in this genre.

If you use copy-protected software, like *Lotus 1-2-3*, talk to the vendor before trying this. *Lotus*'s annoying copy protection scheme will cause *1-2-3* to be destroyed if you optimize a disk with

Lotus installed. If you run copy-protected software, uninstall it before optimizing; then reinstall it.

Better yet, *remove* the copy protection. Lotus sells a Value Pack that includes two neat utilities and removes the protection from your copy of *1-2-3*. Version 2.2 and 3.0 never had copy protection to begin with. I'm *not* advocating piracy. But I *am* advocating protecting your investment.

The Best Insurance: Good Backups. There are two kinds of hard disk users: the ones who have had a disk failure and lost data that wasn't backed up, and the one's who are *going* to. (Actually, I first heard this as "there are two kinds of pilots: the ones who have landed and forgot to lower their landing gear, and. . . .") You seek to stay in the latter category as long as it possible.

I can't stress this strongly enough: **At the first sign of unusual behavior, back up the entire disk.** Backup approaches fall into three categories:

- SBB—Software-Based Backup (only uses floppies)
- HBB—Hardware-Based Backup (tape drives and the like)
- PBB—Prayer-Based Backup (hope it'll never happen)

Informal surveys indicate that about 20 percent of the corporate users employ special hardware and the other 80 percent claim to use software-based schemes. Many of the 80 percent use a hybrid software/PBB system.

By the way, those of you who are smiling smugly because you use a tape or something to back up, have you ever tried to *restore* that data you've been saving? What's that you say—you trust that the people who sold you the tape drive wouldn't sell you buggy software? Heh, heh. . .

Software Based Backup. These programs assist the user in transferring data onto floppies. Their main features are:

● Speed
● Maintaining indices of backed up data
● Use of the DOS archive bit
● Splitting large files over several floppies
● File compression
● Error correcting data formats

Despite its difficulty and bugs, the DOS BACKUP program is probably the most used software alternative. It isn't particularly fast, and it stores data in a nonstandard format, but it comes free with DOS. It will break up files that are too large to fit on a floppy to several floppies, and it manipulates the DOS archive bit. No compression or error-correcting is used.

Fifth Generation Systems' *Fastback* product is well known and widely used. It's much faster than BACKUP and formats disks on the fly. It uses error correction but no compression, and stores data in a nonstandard fashion.

Similar programs are offered by other vendors, but here's another approach. Under DOS 3.2, a new command, XCOPY, appeared.

XCOPY has several features that recommend it for disk backup:

● It's faster than COPY.
● You can tell it to prompt you for filenames.
● It operates on the archive bit.
● The resulting files are in DOS format.

The main drawback is that XCOPY isn't smart enough to break up large files over several disks. XCOPY is smart enough to only copy the files that have changed since the last backup, and to search subdirectories (with COPY, you must specify each subdirectory). It will also create subdirectories on the target disk. From the root directory, just issue the command

XCOPY C: A: /V/M/E/S

/E/S says look at all subdirectories, not just the current one, and create an identical subdirectory structure on the target disk. /M is the important one: It says, *Only copy the files that haven't been backed up and, once copied, mark the files as backed up.* (It uses the file's archive bit.) /V verifies each copy.

XCOPY will then fill up a floppy (it must be formatted first). Insert a new floppy and issue the command again. It won't try to recopy files it has already copied, as their archive bits are cleared. Continue until there's nothing left to copy. Then use BACKUP for the files too large to fit on one floppy.

No matter what system you use, inserting and removing floppies is a large pain. If backups are difficult, they won't get done. That's why hardware backup solutions are superior and worth the money.

Backup Hardware. There are several backup hardware options:

● Tape drives with special controllers
● Tapes based on the floppy controller
● Removable hard disks, like the Bernoulli Box
● LANs
● A second Winchester

Tape drives cost from $450 up. For an office of XTs, a good solution would be to get a portable tape drive that can plug into the back of the floppy disk controller (you wondered what that 37-pin port was good for, eh?). Then one

$700 tape drive can be shared among many computers. Irwin Magnetics makes a 20MB drive that plugs into the floppy controller. It is available for $540 from:

Alphanumeric International
13360 E. Firestone Blvd. Suite F
Santa Fe Springs, CA 90670
(213) 921-8689

Bernoullis are reliable, fast devices

that double as an extra hard drive (they are just as fast) and backup device. Because there are two drives, backing up a Bernoulli cartridge is simple. To use a Bernoulli to back up a hard disk, Iomega includes backup software, or you can use the XCOPY approach outlined above.

One writer has suggested that, as hard disk drives have become so inexpensive, it could be cheaper to just install a second hard disk and use it to back up the first.

Chapter 14
Hard Disk Failure Recovery

Now that you're a hard disk expert and you've started covering your backside (magnetically speaking) with various automatic backup programs, you're beginning to feel virtuous.

But then disaster strikes. . . .

Resurrecting a Dead Drive

What do you do, exactly, when you turn on your computer and the drive doesn't respond? In this section, I'll describe the steps your computer goes through to boot from the hard disk, suggesting where failures happen and what to do to try to resolve the problem.

I'll assume we're talking about a drive that worked yesterday in the very same machine and the very same controller, and you didn't drop it from the back of a truck, and you didn't add any new boards between then and now. If you're having installation problems, look back at the section on installation.

Before we get started, prepare what I call a "toolkit" floppy (on both 5¼-inch and 3½-inch media, of course) to assist in troubleshooting. Remember, you're try-

ing to fix a nonbooting drive, so the floppy should be bootable with whatever device drivers you need to get to your hard disk. It should also contain:

1. FDISK
2. FORMAT
3. Some low level formatter, like Kolod's hFORMAT
4. XFDISK from hTEST/hFORMAT,
5. DEBUG (in case it's needed to activate a low level formatter)
6. A head parking program, preferably one that you can exit from without rebooting
7. Mace *Remedy* or Norton *DiskTest*
8. SETUP, if your computer's an AT or 386
9. NU from the Norton Utilities
10. NDD (Norton Disk Doctor) from the Norton Utilities.

By the way, that will all take up about 600K, so you'll obviously have to break it up over a couple of 360K disks, but 1.2MB, 720K, and 1.44MB disks can handle it with no problem.

The Hard Disk Boot Procedure (Overview)

Here's what the disk does on a normal day to get started.

1. The hardware must function and be configured properly.
2. The partition record is read.
3. The boot record is read.
4. The hidden files are loaded.
5. IBMBIO.COM or IO.SYS executes and reads CONFIG.SYS.
6. IBMDOS.COM or MSDOS.SYS executes.
7. The user shell (COMMAND.COM) loads.
8. The shell loads and executes AUTOEXEC.BAT.

The Hard Disk Boot Procedure (Details and Suggested Fixes)

Now we'll look at the eight steps in detail. On each step, I'll outline:

- **What it's trying to do:** details on the eight steps.
- **Recognizing errors at this step:** it's not an exact science, but I'll list common symptoms of problems *at this step*.
- **Fixing problems at this step:** once you know you have a problem, what you can do to fix it.

1. Hardware problems. The hardware and cables must be functioning.
   Possible Symptoms of Problems:

   - Disk Boot Failure
   - Not even attempting to boot from the hard disk
   - 1701 or 1780 or 1781 or 1790 or 1791, followed by an *F1 to continue*, and finally BASIC popping up on your screen

What to Do: Let's start from here, before the system even tries to boot. The drive won't talk to you if:

- The drive is too cold, or, less likely, too hot.

  Is it Monday morning? Did you just bring the drive in from the outside, if the computer is a laptop? Make sure the drive is warmed up to room temperature before you try to use it (this goes double if you're about to format it).

- Its cables have come loose, or have been reconnected incorrectly, or might just be bad.

  Do you have another set of cables? Give them a try.

- An AT, PS/2, or 386 has lost its SETUP info.

  If the battery's run down on your 286/386/486 computer, it may have forgotten that it has a hard disk or, worse, it may *misremember* what kind of hard disk it has. Run the SETUP program to check to see that the computer remembers correctly what kind of hard disk it has.

- The drive has been physically damaged.

  This is a toughie. Scratches out on cylinder 0 (location of the vital partition record, or Master Boot Record) can be fatal. Some drives fail only because the circuit board on the drive has failed; swap that and the problem could go away.

  I've heard of a situation (although I haven't tried it yet) where a head stepper motor burned out on a Miniscribe drive. Now, the stepper motor is inside the sealed area of most Winchester drives, so replacing it exposes the drive to dust—not a good idea. The repair person did not have the requisite "clean room" (such a room must be cleaner than a hospital operating room!) in which to open the drive, so he used a clear plastic bag. He put his tools in the bag before starting, put the drive and the stepper in the bag, opened it, and swapped steppers without taking the drive from the bag until the operation was over. It allowed him to get the data off the drive. I can think of several reasons why it might not have worked, such as the plastic bag creating static that would damage the drive, some dust in the bag, and so on—but it worked. Hey, what did he have to lose?

2. **Read the partition record.**
Assuming SETUP, the cables, and so on are okay, the drive light will come on for a very brief time, just a "flash" during a normal boot when the computer is turned on. The controller is reading (at BIOS's insistence) the partition record or Master Boot Record (MBR). The MBR resides on head 0, cylinder 0, sector 1. (The rest of the sectors on that track are unused, by the way.) If this fails, the drive is ignored.

Possible Symptoms of Problems: some kind of message indicating that the drive doesn't exist, like *invalid drive specification* when you boot from the floppy and try to read C:, or a message like *0 drives found* or *0 drives ready*. It might act like there's no hard disk there at all. If the hardware is okay but there's no partition record, you won't see any error messages on bootup—it just won't recognize the hard disk at all.

What to Do: Find out what's going on with the partition record. Here are some alternatives.

a) Run FDISK. If it fails altogether with a message like *There is no drive there*, recheck the hardware items in the previous step.

b) If FDISK loads okay, select the *display partition status* option. If it says you have a partition, check that the message makes sense: Are they DOS partitions? Do the cylinders range to a silly value, like up to cylinder 900 on a 500-cylinder drive? (You can check this by running FDISK on a machine with an identical drive.) If the partition is okay, move to the next step, checking the DOS boot record.

If you see a *Non-DOS partition*, don't get trigger-happy with your tools. Since DOS is a pain about talking to disks bigger than 32MB, a number of vendors have offered various software workarounds to allow large drives to work in a DOS environment. Some common ones are OnTrack Disk Manager, SpeedStor, Golden Bow VFeature, Priam EDISK, and a host of others. You can spot these easily: They have (1) a small DOS partition to allow your system to boot, (2) a large non-DOS partition of their own design, and (3) a device driver to allow the system to use the alien non-DOS partition. I'll have more to say about this later, but for now, don't start repartitioning if you see a small DOS partition up front and a larger non-DOS partition following it.

c) If FDISK tells you *no partitions defined*, then something trashed the partition record. DO NOT use FDISK to create a new partition record, as FDISK unfortunately also gets a bit gung-ho and zaps the DOS boot record and some of the FAT when asked to create a new partition record. The game plan here is to get an MBR from a working machine, copy it to floppy, and then move the good MBR to the drive. The tools: GETSEC and PUTSEC, two programs that come with hTEST/hFORMAT (the Kolod Utilities, you'll recall). They allow you to grab a particular sector and move it to/from a floppy. Try it. Alternatively, Kolod's XFDISK does FDISK-like duty without the excess data destruction, confining itself exclusively to the MBR.

d) Did it work? It might not, *if the low-level format information has been destroyed*. Sometimes a power surge can cause the disk head to torpedo the sector IDs on a track, effectively deformatting it to a pristeen state. Kolod XFDISK and FDISK can't read or write tracks with garbled sector IDs. Try low-level formatting *just cylinder 0, head 0* with HFORMAT from hTEST/ hFORMAT. Then the partition record ought to go on just fine.

Autoconfigure Pitfall. If cylinder 0, head 0 has been deformatted on an autoconfigure controller (like the common XT-class WD1002 discussed earlier), you've got extra trouble. Recall that the autoconfigure controllers store a few very important drive identification bytes in an otherwise unused part of the MBR. If they can't find those bytes, they can't talk to the drive at all, just

as if your AT-class machine had lost SETUP. Some of these controllers have a jumper that converts them from *autoconfigure* to *extremely dumb*, that is, they think they're talking to a Seagate 225. Enable the Seagate 225 mode. You don't want to do it forever—just long enough to convince the controller to write out a new cylinder 0, head 0, sector 1. Recall that the autoconfigure information is placed at the start of the MBR, so you'll be fine (as far as the autoconfigure controller is concerned) once you've snatched an MBR off a working machine with a similar controller. Two birds, autoconfigure and the MBR, are killed with the single stone of restoring cylinder 0, track 0, sector 1.

There's a similar story for the RLL controllers that report there are only 17 sectors on a track. They're lying—there are really 26 sectors on a track, but they don't want to confuse application software. So they translate *on the fly* requests for 17-sector data to requests for 26-sector data. For example, RLL controllers won't report that a Seagate ST238R is what it truly is, a 615 cylinder, 4 head, 26 sector/track disk. Instead, they insist that it's a 910 cylinder, 4 head, 17 sector/track disk. These controllers confuse low-level formatter programs. Again, there's usually a jumper to disable this translation feature. Deactivate the feature, and try to just work on the first cylinder/head.

e) If you're still having no luck, you might be unable to reformat the first cylinder. This happens sometimes, if the platter is scratched on that position. Now, you're in some trouble, since you can't move the MBR somewhere else; everything else is movable but that.

Here's a powerful trick that might help. **Warning: it may destroy a perfectly good drive.** This requires an already-working, formatted, identical drive, and your bad drive. We'll assume, hope, and pray that the only problem is in the boot section of your disk. The trick here is to get DOS to boot from the disk and recognize it.

You're going to connect the good drive, boot from it, and then, with the power still on, park the good drive and disconnect it, using a park program you can get out of without rebooting. Then we'll connect the bad drive and see if DOS can talk to it. If it does, we'll back everything up and throw the drive away.

Simple, I hear you cry, but does it work? You bet—I once tried it when all else failed, and I saved the data.

3. **Read the DOS boot record (DBR).** Assuming that the MBR problems are out of the way, the system next tries to load and execute a sector's worth of information called the DOS Boot Record, which I'll call the DBR. (MBR isn't my acronym, it's Paul Mace's.)

Possible Symptoms of Problems: *Disk Boot Failure*, or *Non System Disk Or Disk Error*. (At this point, some systems even have a bug in their system software that asks you to *Insert a new disk in drive C and press any key to continue*. Nice to know computer designers have senses of humor.)

What to Do: Reconstruct the DBR. It's a similar problem to reconstructing the MBR, with two differences, a minor one and a major one. The location of the DBR is cylinder 0, head 1, sector 1. (That's the minor difference.) If the track has lost its sector ID information, however, you can't just zap the track and start over—the FAT uses sectors 2–17 of that track. (That's the major difference.)

If you end up having to reformat the entire cylinder 0/head 1 track, you're basically in the same position as someone who has had their hard disk formatted and is trying to unformat it. So turn to the section on unformatting hard disks.

An excellent first tool to try for reconstructing DBRs is Norton's *Disk Doctor* version 4.5.1 or after. Among other things, it rebuilds the DBR if it finds it corrupt.

4. **Load the hidden files.** Next, two files that are the heart of the operating system are loaded into memory. The two files might have become corrupt (either from a software or hardware problem), or DOS just might not be able to find them because the FAT has been damaged.

Possible Symptoms of Problems: either a boot failure type message, or the system locking up partway through booting.

What to Do: Your best bet is just to reload the hidden files, just to be safe. Ordinarily, you should be able to just boot from a floppy and type *SYS C:* to retransfer the system files to the hard disk. (SYS, for those who don't sleep with their DOS manuals, is a DOS command that attempts to install the operating system's two hidden files to the hard disk.) If that does the trick, terrific. If not, read on.

Background on Hidden Files.
The two "hidden" files are the heart of the PC-DOS or MS-DOS operating system. PC-DOS and Compaq DOS name the files IBMBIO.COM and IBMDOS.COM, even though they're not really .COM files. MS-DOS generally names the files IO.SYS and MSDOS.SYS. These files *must* be in a particular place in order for the system to find them and boot. SYS requires that several conditions be met, or it will refuse to run, claiming there's *insufficient space on destination disk.* The three basic rules under DOS 3.x and 4.x for SYS to work are as follows:

- IBMBIO.COM or IO.SYS must be the *first* file in the root directory of the boot disk.
- IBMBIO.COM or IO.SYS must have its starting cluster as cluster number 2. (By the way, the file need not be contiguous afterward.)
- IBMDOS.COM or MSDOS.SYS must be in the second directory entry in the root directory of the boot disk.

So you try the SYS command, but it fails. What to do? Here's a sure-fire method to bend SYS to your will.

Convincing the SYS Command to Work to Restore Your Hidden Files. Here are some more specifics on SYS's three rules. Again, you must force these conditions to be true on your disk:

- The first two directory entries must be empty—not merely available, as when a file is erased; these entries must be clean as a whistle. (You see, when a file is erased, its directory entry isn't zapped completely. In fact, only the first byte

is changed. That's a good thing, as we'll see later, because it helps us recover erased files.)

a) If there are files currently in the first two entries, copy them elsewhere and erase the files. Remember there are also oddball things that are classified as files: subdirectories and the volume label.

b) Then clean out the first two directory entries by using the Norton Utilities' NU program. Recall from the disk introduction section that each directory entry has 32 bytes that describe file's name, size, starting cluster, and the like. *Clean* means there's nothing but binary 0s there. Now, NU will only let you directly punch 0s into the directory in a second editing mode, the hex (hexadecimal) edit mode. Type *NU c:\,* and choose *E* for *Explore* for *Explore Disk* and then *E* for *Edit/Display.* You'll see the root directory. Press F2 to switch the display to a hex format. Then enter 128 0s—you're filling two 32-byte directory entries with hex 0s.

- Of course, there must be sufficient disk space for the hidden files.
- Cluster 2 must be available for IBMBIO.COM/IO.SYS. If that's currently taken by file *X,* you can free it up by copying file *X* to another file and then erasing file *X.*

Example: Let's force my drive E (a Bernoulli cartridge) to take a SYS. First, I start off trying a *SYS E:* and am rebuffed. So I take a look with Norton at the E drive. Displaying the root directory, I see the problem.

The first two directory entries

Figure 14-1   Norton Utilities Display of the Root Directory of E: Before SYS Fix

```
┌ Root dir ─────────────────────────── Directory format ┐
│ Sector 83 in root directory                 Offset 0, hex 0   │
│                                             Attributes        │
│ Filename Ext    Size     Date      Time    Cluster  Arc R/O Sys Hid Dir Vol │
│   .                                                                          │
│ PUBLISHI NG              11-19-88   1:27 pm          Arc              Vol │
│ WORD                     11-19-88   1:27 pm     2                Dir │
│ MS                       11-19-88   1:57 pm   1882              Dir │
│ σPRINT                   12-10-88  10:15 am    602              Dir │
│ PE                        1-21-89   1:46 pm   3699              Dir │
│ σEPORT           2016     3-19-89   8:21 am   7303   Arc │
│ WIN286                   12-28-88   9:44 am    717              Dir │
│ DESIGNER                 12-28-88  12:03 pm   6504              Dir │
│ CADD                     12-29-88  10:41 am   5349              Dir │
│ WIN386                    8-11-89   1:53 pm   9637              Dir │
│ σASRULER DRW     1507     8-10-89  10:35 am   9446   Arc │
│          unused directory entry │
│          unused directory entry │
│          unused directory entry │
│          unused directory entry │
│          unused directory entry │
│   .                                                                          │
│       Filenames beginning with 'σ' indicate erased entries │
│                   Press Enter to continue │
│ 1Help   2Hex   3Text  4Dir   5FAT   6Partn  7      8Choose 9Undo   10QuitNU │
└──────────────────────────────────────────────────────────────┘
```

are taken. The first entry is the volume label PUBLISHING. (I know that because it has the *Vol* attribute on the right-hand edge of the screen.) That's easy enough to get rid of with the DOS Label command. The second is a subdirectory, WORD. Note that the WORD subdirectory is also using the all-important cluster number 2. WORD can be eliminated easily by creating a subdirectory called WORD2, moving everything over to WORD2, and then just removing WORD.

So, you would remove the label with the label command, then create WORD2, and copy every-

Figure 14-2   Figure Norton Utilities Displays After Erasing First Two Entries

```
┌ Root dir ─────────────────────────── Directory format ┐
│ Sector 83 in root directory                 Offset 0, hex 0   │
│                                             Attributes        │
│ Filename Ext    Size     Date      Time    Cluster  Arc R/O Sys Hid Dir Vol │
│   .                                                                          │
│ σUBLISHI NG              11-19-88   1:27 pm          Arc              Vol │
│ σORD                     11-19-88   1:27 pm     2                Dir │
│ MS                       11-19-88   1:57 pm   1882              Dir │
│ WORD2                     8-19-89  12:00 pm   3816              Dir │
│ PE                        1-21-89   1:46 pm   3699              Dir │
│ σEPORT           2016     3-19-89   8:21 am   7303   Arc │
│ WIN286                   12-28-88   9:44 am    717              Dir │
│ DESIGNER                 12-28-88  12:03 pm   6504              Dir │
│ CADD                     12-29-88  10:41 am   5349              Dir │
│ WIN386                    8-11-89   1:53 pm   9637              Dir │
│ σASRULER DRW     1507     8-10-89  10:35 am   9446   Arc │
│          unused directory entry │
│          unused directory entry │
│          unused directory entry │
│          unused directory entry │
│          unused directory entry │
│   .                                                                          │
│       Filenames beginning with 'σ' indicate erased entries │
│                   Press Enter to continue │
│ 1Help   2Hex   3Text  4Dir   5FAT   6Partn  7      8Choose 9Undo   10QuitNU │
└──────────────────────────────────────────────────────────────┘
```

thing from WORD over to the sub-directory. Erase everything in WORD and finally enter RD WORD. Now reinvoke Norton (see Figure 14-2).

Flip over to the hex display with F2 and you'll see a screen similar to Figure 14-3.

Figure 14-3 Norton Hex Display Before Cleaning Directory Entries

```
┌ Root dir ──────────────────────────────────────── Hex format ┐
│  Sector 83 in root directory                    Offset 0, hex 0 │
│ E555424C 49534849 4E472028 00000000 00000000 0000646B σUBLISHING (.........dk │
│ 73110000 00000000 E54F5244 20202020 20202010 20202010 s .....σORD    .....│
│ 00000000 0007796B 73110200 00000000 4D532020 20202020 ......yks  .....MS │
│ 20202010 00000000 00000000 0000206F 73115A07 00000000 .......... os Z.....│
│ 574F5244 32202020 20202010 00000000 00000000 00000560 WORD2     ..........│
│ 1313E80E 00000000 50452020 20202020 20202010 00000000 ....PE        .....│
│ 00000000 0000D560 3512730E 00000000 E545504F 52542020 ......m̄5 s ....σEPORT │
│ 20202020 00000000 00000000 0000AA42 7312871C E0070000 ...........¬Bs ç-α ..│
│ 57494E32 38362020 20202010 00000000 00000000 0000894D WIN286    ..........ëM │
│ 9C11CD02 00000000 44455349 474E4552 20202020 20202020 £ - ....DESIGNER   ....│
│ 00000000 00006F60 9C116819 00000000 43414444 20202020 ......o`£ h ...CADD │
│ 20202010 00000000 00000000 00002355 9D11E514 00000000 ..........#U¥ σ ....│
│ 57494E33 38362020 20202010 00000000 00000000 0000BA6E WIN386    .........|n │
│ 0B13A525 00000000 E5415352 554C4552 44525720 00000000 Ñ%....σASRULERDRW ....│
│ 00000000 00006454 0A13E624 E3050000 00000000 00000000 ......dT  µ$π .........│
│ 00000000 00000000 00000000 00000000 00000000 00000000 ...................│
│ 00000000 00000000 00000000 00000000 00000000 00000000 ...................│
│ 00000000 00000000 00000000 00000000 00000000 00000000 ...................│
│ 00000000 00000000 00000000 00000000 00000000 00000000 ...................│
│ 00000000 00000000 00000000 00000000 00000000 00000000 ...................│
│ 00000000 00000000          Press Enter to continue       ........│
│ 1Help  2Hex  3Text  4Dir  5FAT  6Partn 7        8Choose 9Undo  10QuitNU │
└─────────────────────────────────────────────────────────────┘
```

Notice that we're looking at the same information as before (the root directory), we're just looking at it in a different way. Ensuring that the cursor is at the start of the E5 in the upper left-hand corner, just lean on the 0 key until the first 64 bytes are 0 (each byte is represented by two hex digits, so you must enter 128 0s). The screen then looks like Figure 14-4.

Figure 14-4 Norton Hex Display After Cleaning Directory Entries

```
┌ Root dir ──────────────────────────────────────── Hex format ┐
│  Sector 83 in root directory                    Offset 0, hex 0 │
│ 00000000 00000000 00000000 00000000 00000000 00000000 ...................│
│ 00000000 00000000 00000000 00000000 00000000 00000000 ...................│
│ 00000000 00000000 00000000 00000000 4D532020 20202020 ...............MS │
│ 20202010 00000000 00000000 0000206F 73115A07 00000000 .......... os Z.....│
│ 574F5244 32202020 20202010 00000000 00000000 00000560 WORD2     ..........│
│ 1313E80E 00000000 50452020 20202020 20202010 00000000 ....PE        .....│
│ 00000000 0000D560 3512730E 00000000 E545504F 52542020 ......m̄5 s ....σEPORT │
│ 20202020 00000000 00000000 0000AA42 7312871C E0070000 ...........¬Bs ç-α ..│
│ 57494E32 38362020 20202010 00000000 00000000 0000894D WIN286    ..........ëM │
│ 9C11CD02 00000000 44455349 474E4552 20202020 20202020 £ - ....DESIGNER   ....│
│ 00000000 00006F60 9C116819 00000000 43414444 20202020 ......o`£ h ...CADD │
│ 20202010 00000000 00000000 00002355 9D11E514 00000000 ..........#U¥ σ ....│
│ 57494E33 38362020 20202010 00000000 00000000 0000BA6E WIN386    .........|n │
│ 0B13A525 00000000 E5415352 554C4552 44525720 00000000 Ñ%....σASRULERDRW ....│
│ 00000000 00006454 0A13E624 E3050000 00000000 00000000 ......dT  µ$π .........│
│ 00000000 00000000 00000000 00000000 00000000 00000000 ...................│
│ 00000000 00000000 00000000 00000000 00000000 00000000 ...................│
│ 00000000 00000000 00000000 00000000 00000000 00000000 ...................│
│ 00000000 00000000 00000000 00000000 00000000 00000000 ...................│
│ 00000000 00000000 00000000 00000000 00000000 00000000 ...................│
│ 00000000 00000000          Press Enter to continue       ........│
│ 1Help  2Hex  3Text  4Dir  5FAT  6Partn 7        8Choose 9Undo  10QuitNU │
└─────────────────────────────────────────────────────────────┘
```

Figure 14-5 Norton Directory Display After Cleaning Directory Entries

```
┌─ Root dir ────────────────────────── Directory format ─┐
│  Sector 83 in root directory                Offset 0, hex 0   │
│                                               Attributes      │
│ Filename Ext    Size      Date      Time    Cluster Arc R/O Sys Hid Dir Vol │
│         .                                                     │
│              unused directory entry                          │
│              unused directory entry                          │
│ MS                      11-19-88   1:57 pm   1882              Dir │
│ WORD2                    8-19-89  12:00 pm   3816              Dir │
│ PE                       1-21-89   1:46 pm   3699              Dir │
│ σEPORT           2016    3-19-89   8:21 am   7303   Arc            │
│ WIN286                  12-28-88   9:44 am    717              Dir │
│ DESIGNER                12-28-88  12:03 pm   6504              Dir │
│ CADD                    12-29-88  10:41 am   5349              Dir │
│ WIN386                   8-11-89   1:53 pm   9637              Dir │
│ σASRULER DRW     1507    8-10-89  10:35 am   9446   Arc            │
│              unused directory entry                          │
│              unused directory entry                          │
│              unused directory entry                          │
│              unused directory entry                          │
│              unused directory entry                          │
│         .                                                     │
│          Filenames beginning with 'σ' indicate erased entries │
│                     Press Enter to continue                  │
│ 1Help   2Hex   3Text  4Dir   5FAT   6Partn  7      8Choose 9Undo  10QuitNU │
└──────────────────────────────────────────────────────────────┘
```

Then flip back to the *Directory* format with the F4 key, and you'll have good news—the two entries (Figure 14-5) show up as never-used.

SYS E: now works like a charm.

5. **Commence the boot process by loading and executing the first hidden file, which in turn loads and executes CONFIG.SYS commands.**

Possible Symptoms of Problems: CONFIG.SYS error messages or inability to talk to nonstandard devices like OnTrack Disk Manager partitions, Bernoulli Boxes, tape drives, and so on.

What to Do: Basically, this part screws up if (1) your CONFIG.SYS has gotten trashed or (2) one of the programs called by CONFIG.SYS has gotten trashed.

It's fairly easy to check out the first problem. Just boot from a floppy, then examine the CONFIG.SYS file of the boot drive. If it looks strange, just rewrite it.

Strange doesn't only mean that it looks hieroglyphic; strange can also mean that your device drivers are missing. Take, for instance, my CONFIG.SYS file:

```
shell = c:\command.com /P /E:512 c:\
buffers = 20
files = 32
device = d:\dos\ansi.sys
device = d:\bernoulli\rcd.sys
device = d:\dos\driver.sys /d:1
DEVICE = D:\XDOS\386MAX.SYS
INCLUDE = 1000-A000
FRAME = E000
```

The first four lines are pretty basic CONFIG.SYS, but the latter three look a bit bizarre. Why are they there? RCD.SYS makes my Bernoulli Boxes work. If my CONFIG.SYS somehow loses the line that says to use RCD.SYS, my Bernoullis are useless. The next line, loading DRIVER.SYS, makes my 3¼-inch drive work like a real 720K drive. Without it, it reads and writes 720s okay, *but formats 720K disks as only 360K!* This could be a very subtle bug. Imagine: Your 720K disk drive stops formatting properly, but reads and writes okay. Would you think of CONFIG.SYS first? The last line invokes a program called *386 To The Max,* a program that does a few tricks to squeeze the most out of my 386-based computer. For one thing, it allows me to load my TSR programs out of the 640K DOS workspace. If I forget this device driver, strange things happen later when I try to load programs into the area outside of the 640K.

But my CONFIG.SYS is tame compared to some of my clients'. Several, for example, use a device driver that I hate called *OnTrack Disk Manager.* The file name of this device driver is DMDRVR.BIN.

OnTrack Disk Manager is a device driver intended to allow DOS 3.x users to get around the 32MB disk size barrier. Under PC-DOS 3.2 and earlier, you could only use a 32MB or smaller disk. Put an 80MB disk on a PC-DOS 3.2 machine and you'd get a 32MB disk with 48MB of wasted space. OnTrack's idea, then, was to write a device driver that would allow DOS to talk to a new kind of device—a disk that could be hundreds of megabytes in size. So you create two partitions on your 80MB drive: a small (1MB or so) bootable DOS partition (drive C) that's mainly used to store the boot programs, and a second, non-DOS partition (drive D, 79MB or whatever's left) that's only accessible once the DMDRVR.BIN has been loaded. Let me repeat: That second partition is an alien partition. Norton, Mace, *PC Tools,* and the gang have no idea how to handle this partition

unless the device driver has been loaded.

Summarizing, the new potential problems that arise from using a non-DOS partition and a device driver to access your disk are:

- If the DEVICE = DMDRVR.BIN statement is lost from the CONFIG.SYS, your users won't be able to figure out why their D drive has disappeared.
- If something goes wrong in the partition, you won't have the panoply of recovery tools available that you'd have in a DOS partition.
- The device driver is another piece of software between your disk and DOS, just one more thing to go wrong on your disk. I'm not saying OnTrack is buggy, but why would anyone want to introduce a new potential source of bugs?

OnTrack isn't the only company that does this. My 60MB Priam, for example, shipped with a device driver called EDISK.SYS already on it, again to allow me to get around the DOS 32MB barrier. (I immediately reformatted the drive and got rid of the driver.) A program called SPEEDSTOR was pretty popular for a while in the same genre. *Disk Manager* is the program you tend to run into more often because, Seagate has been giving it away free with their drives. Let me say it again: If you have the choice, avoid device drivers that change the way DOS talks to your hard disk.

Don't get me wrong. OnTrack makes some great stuff, it's just that I hate using device drivers to talk to a hard disk. Hard disks have enough potential problems without creating opportunities for new ones.

What's the alternative to these device drivers, by the way? PC-DOS 3.3 or Compaq DOS 3.2. FDISK under DOS 3.3 gets around the 32MB problem by allowing you to divide the disk into two partitions, a *DOS partition* and an *Extended DOS partition*. The DOS partition can't be larger than 32MB, but the Extended DOS partition can be any size. You create the DOS partition, and FDISK calls it drive C and makes it bootable. Then you allocate the remainder of the disk to the Extended DOS partition, even if it's larger than 32MB. FDISK then breaks this Extended DOS partition up into logical drives, which can then be FORMATted. For example, my 80MB drive divides into a C drive of 32MB (the DOS partition), a D drive of 32MB (part of the Extended DOS partition), and an E drive of 16MB (the remainder of the Extended DOS partition).

Some of you are out there asking, "Doesn't he know about DOS 4.0, which can format drives up to 512MB?" Sure I know. At this writing (fall 1989), they haven't worked the bugs out of it yet, so I'm willing to wait, and I'm not the only one. Corporate Software reports that DOS 4.0 displaced about half of their DOS 3.3 sales in fall of 1988, but that as of April, 1989, the DOS 4.0 sales had dropped to less than one-quarter of the DOS 3.3 sales.

Another potential device driver problem is the simple one of file corruption. You might have a perfectly bug-free device driver, but if for some reason the file that contains the device driver is corrupted, the system can crash when loading the driver. Try reloading your device drivers from floppy disk.

6. **The user shell COMMAND.COM loads.** A corrupted or out-of-date copy of COMMAND.COM can keep the system from booting. One way to avoid users accidentally overwriting COMMAND.COM is to make COMMAND.COM read-only with the DOS ATTRIB command (only in 3.3 and later):

ATTRIB +R
C:\ COMMAND COM

Possible Symptom of Problems: system crash or, more likely, *Bad or Missing Command Interpreter* followed by a system freeze.

What to Do: Boot from a floppy and COMP (a DOS file comparison command) the COMMAND.COM on the floppy to the one on the hard disk. You might find that a user has copied a pile of files to the hard disk, not realizing a COMMAND.COM from an old version of DOS was also copied over the COMMAND.COM on the hard disk's root directory.

A less likely alternative (but one that has happened to me) is that a spontaneous bad sector has arisen in the middle of COMMAND.COM. Just use Norton's *DiskTest* or DOS's RECOVER COMMAND.COM to locate and lock out the new bad sectors. Then recopy COMMAND.COM from the floppy drive.

7. **COMMAND.COM executes the commands in AUTOEXEC.BAT.**

Any bugs in the programs called by AUTOEXEC.BAT will, of course, hang the system.

Probable Symptoms: application specific. The big question is, did the system do okay *until* AUTOEXEC.BAT started executing?

What to Do: Rename AUTO-EXEC.BAT to AUTOEXEC.BUG or something like that so it isn't found by COMMAND.COM, and reboot. If the system boots okay, you've got a problem in one of the commands in AUTOEXEC.BAT. It's probably a TSR that's conflicting with another program. As usual, try rearranging the order of the TSRs. Remove one command at a time until the problem goes away, then zero in on the program that caused the crash. Does it run all right by itself? Does it only not run on a particular XYZ Turbo 8800 clone?

This is the procedure I use to bring a dead drive back to life. It can't solve every problem, but this will resolve 99 percent of your hard disk problems. But if you're *still* stuck . . .

Send Your Drive to the Mayo Clinic: Data Recovery Services

Still can't get it to talk to you? Hey, look, even Dr. Kildare lost a few patients. If you *really* need that data, there's a last hope. It ain't cheap—from $1,000 to $20,000—but you can send it to a service. They disassemble the disk, remove the data, and then send it to you on floppies. OnTrack, the same people who wrote Disk Manager and other utilities, offer the service. They charge $200 to diagnose the problem, and then you negoti-

ate over the recovery cost. It's expensive, yes, but cheaper than going out of business.

OnTrack Computer Systems, Inc.
6321 Bury Drive
Eden Prairie, MN 55346
(612) 937-1107
(800) 752-1333

Miscellaneous Drive Problems

Track 0 Bad or Unusable **Error.** Sometimes a disk won't accept a DOS format, and FORMAT complains that track 0 is bad, rendering the whole disk unusable. If this happens, you probably cannot save your data.

To save the disk, try one of the following remedies.

1. Try a low-level format. That solves many of these problems.
2. There's a "trapdoor" in DOS. Prepare a diskette with the system on it, and ensure that the CONFIG.SYS file on the diskette contains this line:

FILES = 99

If there's another line with FILES = and some number, delete it. Then reboot and try DOS FORMAT again. DOS is now a lot less picky about what it will and won't format. I don't know why the trapdoor is there, but it is. It only exists in DOS 3.1, 3.2, and 3.3, as far as I know.

Once the drive is formatted,

you can return to the old FILES = value.

Damaged Boot Record. To boot from a floppy disk, early versions of DOS put some computer code onto the first sector of the disk. The ROM in the PC knew just enough on powerup to load that sector and execute the code found within. This sector was called the *boot record*. This sector is, you'll recall, 512 bytes long, like all sectors.

IBM uses the boot record (previously only for bootstrap code) to contain DOS version and disk-type info. The twenty-first byte is important, as it's the *Media Descriptor*. The accompanying table by that name (Table 14-1) lists these descriptors. Another boot record item is *number of sectors on disk*. Two bytes are allocated for this. The biggest number you can represent with two bytes is $2^{16}-1$ or 65,535. As sector sizes are 512 bytes, this leads to the current maximum volume size under PC DOS 3.X of 65,535 sectors $\times$ 512 bytes/sector = 32,767K, or 32MB.

Table 14-1. FAT Media Descriptor Byte Values

Code	Description
FF	8 sector DS floppy (320K)
FE	8 sector SS floppy (160K)
FD	9 sector DS floppy (360K)
FC	9 sector SS floppy (180K)
F9	1.2MB floppy and 3½-inch floppies
F8	Hard Disk

If your boot record is damaged, you'll be completely unable to read the disk, even if you don't need to boot from it. You can reconstruct and repair a boot sector with the help of a special utility like Mace. *Restore Boot Sector* in Mace will either use a backup boot sector (which

you must allow Mace to create before the problem exists) or copy a boot sector from an identical disk.

Norton Disk Doctor can rebuild a boot record, but sometimes NDD gets a little rambunctious and fixes a little *more* of the disk than you intended. You can, however, construct a boot record in DEBUG and write over the damaged boot record. One simple way is to:

1. Read a good boot sector from a similar drive into memory with DE-BUG, and then
2. Write the boot sector in the memory to the troubled disk.

How to Fix a Damaged Floppy Boot Record. Simplicity itself. Find a formatted disk so you can steal a good boot sector from it.

1. Insert the good disk of the same size, density, and so on, in drive A.
2. Load DEBUG. It's on the DOS Supplemental Programs diskette, and should be in your DOS subdirectory.
3. Instruct DEBUG to load the boot record off the good disk: Type *L 0 0 0 1*.
4. Remove the good disk from A and insert the disk with the bad boot record.
5. Tell DEBUG to overwrite the bad boot record with the good one: Type *W 0 0 0 1*.
6. Quit DEBUG.

Warning: Don't mix boot sectors! Don't try to patch a boot sector on a hard disk with one from a floppy. It won't work.

Recovering a Boot Sector on a Hard Disk. Floppies aren't the only disks that can be saved. You can also use the boot sector from one hard disk to save another. It's a similar procedure to the one above. The idea is to read the boot sector off the good hard disk, write it to a floppy, transport the floppy to the computer with the bad hard disk, read the boot sector off the floppy, and write it back out to the hard disk.

1. On the computer with the good hard disk, insert a blank formatted floppy in drive A.
2. Load DEBUG.
3. Tell DEBUG to read the hard disk's boot sector and store it on the floppy:

   L 0 2 0 1

   W 0 0 0 1

4. Take the floppy to the computer with a bad boot record on the hard disk. Load DEBUG off a floppy. Insert the floppy with the boot record from the good computer.
5. Instruct DEBUG to read the floppy data and put it on the hard disk:

   L 0 0 0 1

   W 0 2 0 1

Sometimes this will work. Sometimes it won't, if other data (like the partition record on the hard disk) is damaged.

PC DOS 3.2 Tip:

Final point on the boot record: The fourth through the eleventh bytes contain a string with the manufacturer ID (called the *OEM name and version*), like *IBM 3.2* on a PC-DOS 3.2 formatted diskette. This was fairly irrelevant until PC-DOS 3.2. As of 3.2, however, the boot record information became absolutely essential. One of the things in the boot record is the location of the FAT. If you have a disk written under a version of DOS that doesn't bother with the location of the FAT, DOS 3.2 could become confused and try to read a FAT where one doesn't exist. You'll get a *sector not found error*-type message. This only occurs under PC DOS 3.2 and later as far as I know. This can be remedied fairly easily. Just format a blank floppy under DOS 3.2, and then do the above procedure. Use DEBUG to copy the 3.2 boot record off the blank disk to the other disk.

This problem doesn't always occur, but if it does, try this. Better yet, try it on a *copy* of the disk.

Recovering from a Damaged FAT and Understanding CHKDSK Errors. The next area is the FAT, the File Allocation Table. As you've seen, it causes its own share of problems.

You've seen that it's a linked list of clusters, one FAT entry for each cluster. There are two kinds of FATs: 12-bit and 16-bit. A 12-bit FAT can keep track of $2^{12}-1$, or 4095 clusters. It's used for floppy disks and 10MB hard disks. A 16-bit FAT can keep track of $2^{16}-1$, or 65,535 clusters.

Most disk formats keep a second copy of the FAT. I guess it was originally included for fault tolerance or redundancy, but earlier versions of DOS before 3.2 don't use it. If your FAT is damaged, you can copy the secondary FAT back to the primary position with DEBUG or, more simply, Mace will do it. Unerasing programs manipulate the FAT.

The FAT causes all of those cryptic CHKDSK woes. You see, CHKDSK doesn't check the disk, it checks the FAT.

Recall how space allocation is managed under DOS with the directory and FAT. A normal file could, for example, have a first cluster of 100; the FAT entry for 100 could be 101, 101 could point to

102, and 102 could contain EOF. That would mean that the file resides in 100, 101, and 102. Potential problems in FAT chains, then, are

- A chain ending with a 0 (invalid cluster, file truncated)
- A chain ending with a bad sector (invalid cluster)
- A chain being extended inadvertently (allocation error)
- A chain without a beginning directory link (lost clusters)
- A chain that cannot match its directory size information, either much too small or much too large (allocation error)
- Two or more intersecting chains (cross-linked clusters)
- Damaged subdirectory file (invalid subdirectory)

Another consideration is file size. When a file is created, the creating program tells DOS how big the file is, or rather gives DOS some clues. Text editors commonly suffix their files with a Ctrl-Z. DOS sees this and then computes file size, which goes in the directory. Even though DOS retains file size in the directory, recall that it actually must allocate space in terms of clusters. Taking hard disks as an example, a cluster on a 20MB hard disk is 2048 bytes long. If I create a file of a single byte, it still takes up 2048 bytes.

It's important that I stress here: *CHKDSK errors usually don't point to hardware errors.* They either indicate bad software or operators. Let's examine a few of the most popular messages briefly.

Lost Clusters. Sometimes CHKDSK reports *lost clusters*. This basically means loss of the pointer from the directory to the FAT. This pointer is often the *last thing written when the file is created*. This means a program that died in the middle

of manipulating the FAT could have created some FAT chains but not yet written the pointer from the directory to the FAT. Another cause of this is operators who realize they've made a mistake, and so turn off the machine in the hopes of saving themselves. If they do this while a file is being written, there will definitely be lost clusters. The problem is often caused by mixing DOS 3.x and 2.x, or application program bugs such as are found in *dBase* and *MultiMate*.

Remedy: Do a DIR, and print it out. Run CHKDSK/F. New pointers will be created and the lost chains will be given filenames FILEnnnn.CHK, where *nnnn* is a four-digit number. Data *might* be recoverable; *dBase* or *1-2-3* files may not be recoverable.

Cross Linked Clusters. Another CHKDSK complaint is *cross linked clusters*. It refers to multiple pointers into the same cluster. It means that more than one file thinks it owns a disk area: Cluster 14 (for example) reportedly might be owned by more than one file.

Remedy: (1) Copy all affected files. (2) Erase the affected files. The copied files will have as much data as can be recovered. In all probability, some data has been lost.

Invalid Subdirectory. A subdirectory's information is contained in a file. If this file is damaged, DOS doesn't know how to get to the files in the subdirectory. CHKDSK reports an *invalid subdirectory* error. **Don't execute CHKDSK /F until you first print out the directory listing of the subdirectory! The reason: CHKDSK just eliminates the subdirectory information—it isn't too smart about recovering subdirectory information.**

Now CHKDSK sees a whole lot of FAT chains without directory entries, as their directory is gone. It then converts these to FILEnnnn.CHK files. Your problem is to match up the .CHK files with the former subdirectory contents.

Your hints are the order and size of the files. The sizes might not match exactly, as CHKDSK just reports entire cluster size. The directory, with more specific file size information, is gone, so the best CHKDSK can do is just to add up the number of bytes in the clusters and report that as the file size.

For example, imagine you have the following files in an invalid subdirectory:

ORDERS.TXT 2010 bytes
NAMES.DBF 3000 bytes

Let's say this is a hard disk, with 2048 byte sectors. After CHKDSK mauls the subdirectory, you find you have two new .CHK files:

FILE0000.CHK 2048
FILE0001.CHK 4096

Notice that the file sizes have been rounded up to the nearest 2048 multiple. To finish the recovery job: First, rename the files. Second, use Norton Utilities to revise the directory file size. *This is important*, as Lotus will refuse to read a file that has been completely recovered but has the wrong directory file size.

Recovering From and Avoiding *Sector Not Found.* Found during any DOS operation, fading or loss of a sector ID causes a *Sector Not Found* error.

Remedy: Keep it from happening by doing low-level formats regularly. As you've seen, programs exist that will do this *without disturbing the data.* If it occurs anyway, see the next section.

Recovering Lost Data Due to Disk Media Failure. As you know if you've ever formatted a floppy disk, not all sectors are created equal. Sectors that started out reliable can suddenly go south for the winter, taking important data with them. There are some things that can be done in this case, however. You're not helpless.

The initial formatting process tests for bad sectors and ensures that DOS doesn't try to use them. The FAT is where DOS keeps track of bad sectors. If the initial FORMAT locates bad sectors, it will inform the FAT. The FAT entry for the cluster where that sector resides would then indicate that this is a "don't use" cluster.

What about newly created bad sectors, like ones that appear when the disk "crash lands" on your surface too many times? These spontaneous bad sectors must be reported to the FAT.

There are two parts to this problem. The first one is that the sector probably contained data you need; you'd like to recover this data. The second is that the sector must be reported to the FAT.

First, recovering the file: You can use a utility to do this, but I prefer to do it by hand, as some of it's just luck. First, COPY the file. In the process, you'll probably get a message like one of the following:

Sector Not Found Reading Drive X
Data Error Reading Drive X
General Failure Reading Drive X

That's followed by the question *Abort, Retry, Ignore?*

The data is probably not *dead*, but rather the magnetic field is weakened. (As Monty Python would say, "It's not dead—it's just *resting*.") Retry it to see if the problem can be resolved. Retry several times. When it's obvious that you're not getting anywhere, use Ignore. Here's what Ignore does: The sector is probably not completely garbaged. Only one byte out of the 512 may be damaged. Ignore tells it to copy it, warts and all. In some cases, this may mean an innocuous error. In other cases, it may mean that the data is irretrievably lost.

Now you've recovered as much of the data as is possible. If it has errors and you want to sew the data back together,

221

and you're stout of heart and long of patience, you can load up DEBUG and try patching the data. For example, one bad byte in the wrong place can render a *dBase* or *Lotus* file useless. You can get a book that describes file formats for the big programs, and use it to try to repair data. The name of the book is *File Formats for Popular PC Software,* by Jeff Walden, published by Wiley. I stress that this book doesn't tell you how to fix files, but just what undamaged ones look like. It's no simple task to rebuild files, but it can be done sometimes with patience and time.

Now update the FAT. There are several programs that do this. The DOS program RECOVER is one. RECOVER doesn't do the above-mentioned retries and ignores; it just assembles whatever doesn't give it trouble, collects it into a file with a name like FILE0001.REC, and marks the bad sectors on the FAT. The .REC file is of no use to you, just erase it (it's in the root directory, by the way).

Another approach is to use the Norton Utilities' *DiskTest* program or the Mace Utilities *Remedy* program. These are better programs, as they'll scan an entire disk for you, but they don't do the retry/ignore work—you've still got to do that yourself. Mace has a command, DI-AGNOSE, that will alert you to bad sectors without trying to update the FAT and kill the sectors. Norton will do the same with DiskScan. *DiskTest* can also be invoked for a single file with bad sectors, as in *dt banana.exe.*

This bears repeating: As soon as your hard disk starts showing spontaneous new bad sectors, back up the whole disk *now* and run a reformatter program.

Recovering Accidentally Erased Files. Sometimes, carelessness and haste bring a painful cost: accidental erasure of files. There are lots of ways to do this, and I need not dwell on them. Let's see how to recover from the problem.

First, how can unerasure be done?

Recall that disk has clusters for data, a FAT, and a directory. The directory points to the FAT, which then maintains a list of clusters connected to the file.

Erasure is done not by blanking out clusters, but instead by changing the first letter of the name of the file, as the name is kept in the directory. DOS doesn't go to the trouble of erasing the clusters, so they just sit there, available for use the next time a new file is created (or an old file is expanded). *As long as you unerase before a new file is created, the file can be saved.*

The process could be done by hand with a lot of patience and DEBUG, but fortunately there are products to do this. The best known one is, of course, the Norton Utilities. The original product included UnErase, and versions since 3.1 have included Quick UnErase (QU). Mace Utilities also include a program like that called UnDelete.

Simple unerasures can be done with QU or UnDelete fairly easily. I prefer Mace's UnDelete, as Mace will unerase nondestructively to another disk. If a number of files have been erased or new files have been created, the unerase programs can be fooled. With a program like Mace, you can try the process a few times under different assumptions. With Norton, you cannot do this.

Recovering Accidentally Formatted Hard Disks. This is a more painful problem. It's more likely under DOS 2.0, 2.1, and 3.0 than in 3.1 or 3.2, but it still happens. As mentioned before, the DOS FORMAT command doesn't actually erase sector data, but only erases and creates the boot record, the FAT, and the root directory.

So the sectors are all there, but how do you sew them back together? (A 32MB hard disk has 65,536 sectors.) There are two approaches, which I call Class I and Class II unformatters. Class I can recover an entire disk but requires some preparation before the format occurs. Class II, on the other hand, can't recover the entire disk but will work even if you've not prepared the disk prior to the format.

The Class I approach is to keep a compressed copy of the FAT, the directory, and the boot record in a specific physical location. (I've already discussed this in Chapter 13, "Hard Disk Preventive Maintenance.") As long as you keep it up-to-date, the disk can be restored. Mace uses this approach when it creates a file called BACKUP.M_U. Norton uses the FR/S command in the Norton Advanced Utilities, creating a file called FRECOVER.DAT in the root directory. In Mace, a program called RXBAK.EXE is run periodically and the information is kept up-to-date. Then, rather than unformatting, just restore BACKUP.M_U and your data is restored entirely. *PC Tools* uses a program called MIRROR to do a similar thing. Great, but you must do the FAT/directory backup first. Many users put either FR, RXBAK, or MIRROR in their AUTOEXEC.BAT files, so the FAT image is backed up daily.

Of course,if you've modified the FAT since the backup (created new files, or made existing files larger), FR and its ilk can't help you out. You can't recover what you haven't backed up.

The alternative Class II approach can only recover information in subdirectories, and even then there are no guarantees. Subdirectory information is maintained in files, and those files are recognizable by their format. Unformatting programs first locate these files, then use the information in them to reassemble data files. The subdirectory files contain a link to the first FAT entry. Since the FAT is a blank FAT, it's only of use to tell us what the first sector was. Unformatters then read sectors until they come to another file. This means that fragmented files cannot be saved in entirety, and garbage sectors may be tacked on the end of data files. But it's better than nothing, and your chances of suc-

cess can be improved by running an unfragmenting program now and then (also discussed in Chapter 13). It also means that any files kept in the root directory cannot be restored. The only programs I know of that attempt this more difficult unformatting are Mace Unformat and Norton 4.5's FR.

Keeping Users from Accidentally Formatting Disks. Some support people protect user's hard disks by just removing FORMAT from the disk altogether. I'd recommend against this, as they'll need to format diskettes. Besides, treating users like children often comes back to bite you.

Under DOS 3.3 and later, a user must enter the hard disk's volume label in order to format the disk. It might not be a bad idea to put volume labels on all user's hard disks. That way, they have to *really* want to format the disk in order to get it to work. Any user who actually types in the volume label, responds *yes* to the message explaining that the data on the disk will be destroyed, and then finally explains that he didn't know he would lose all his data when formatting probably can't be helped.

Another approach is to rename FORMAT to TAMROF and create a batch

FORMAT.BAT:

```
echo off
if a == %1a goto formata
if %1 == A: goto formata
if %1 == a: goto formata
if %1 == b: goto formatb
if %1 == B: goto formatb
if %1 == c: goto formatc
if %1 == C: goto formatc
rem otherwise, we don't know what they want.
echo I'm sorry, your FORMAT command didn't make sense.
echo Call the Help Desk at 234-9999 for help.
goto end
:formata
tamrof a:
goto end
:formatb
tamrof b:
goto end
:formatc
echo ^G    <-- this is "CTRL-g", not shift-6 and G
echo YOU HAVE ATTEMPTED TO FORMAT YOUR HARD DISK!
echo THIS WOULD DESTROY ALL INFORMATION ON YOUR DISK.
echo You can't do this.  If you have a question, call
the echo Help Desk at 234-9999
:end
```

file. Note the effect: Whenever you type *FORMAT*, you're forced to format only in the A or B drive. This could be moderately effective, but it leaves the TAMROF.COM program on the user's disk. I don't know about you, but I'm a curious person. If I notice a program I've never seen before, I'll try it out.

We can put the icing on the cake with a DOS 3.x trick. Most people don't know this, but you can hide a program under 3.x (2.x won't do this) and DOS can still run it. So, just use the Norton Utilities or something similar to hide TAMROF.

Chapter 15
Floppy Disk Drives

Virtually 100 percent of the PCs or PC clones today have floppy drives. (That's *virtually* 100 percent because a few secure locations have "diskless" workstations that use a LAN for mass storage so employees can't take data off of the job site.) IBM's inclusion of a cassette interface was never taken seriously. When was the last time you saw a program that could be bought on cassette? (I think the Diagnostics was the only one I ever saw.)

Floppies and the PC

Floppies are responsible for some of what little downtime a PC experiences. They're less troublesome than they were several years ago, not because they're manufactured any better, but because we use them less. Hard disks are the medium of choice for many home users and most corporate users. The floppy's role nowadays is mainly (1) a program distribution medium and (2) an archival device. As most hard disks can't travel, most computers still rely on floppies to get information from the outside world.

A floppy disk system is a fairly ingenious device in some ways. Part turntable, part cassette recorder/player, it un-

fortunately relies on a fair amount of moving parts. This makes floppies a weak point in your computer's reliability armor. Fortunately, they're inexpensive enough ($100 or less) that a fast, relatively cheap repair can be effected by someone with no troubleshooting ability at all by just replacing the bad drive.

In this chapter, you'll look at the components of a floppy system and learn how to test, replace, and adjust these components.

Pieces of the Picture

The floppy disk subsystem is, like the rest of the PC, modular. As before, we'll use this modularity to allow us to "divide and conquer." The subsystem consists of the drive, a controller board, the cable connecting the drive to the controller, and the floppy diskettes themselves.

The Floppy Diskette. I said above that the floppy drive is part turntable, part cassette. The floppy diskette is, then, the record/cassette. It comes with a built-in feature that audio records lack, however. You might recall in your past (or present) audio buff days getting out the Discwasher and cleaning the record

225

Figure 15-1 Floppy Diskettes

prior to playing it. For some people, ritual like this is comforting. For them, I must sadly report that no such thing occurs with floppies.

Floppies are stored inside their own "Discwasher": a semirigid case lined with fleecy material. The case has a hole cut in it so the disk can be read/written without having to remove it from the case. In general, there's no need to clean a floppy diskette.

A reasonable life expectancy for a floppy diskette is said to be about three to four years by diskette manufacturers. There are, of course, better and worse diskettes. All diskettes are created in the same location and then tested. The question of single vs. double density and single vs double sidedness is determined by the results of the tests. Most diskettes these days are at least double density. Some double-density diskettes can format quad density—it's a matter of luck. Similarly, some single-sided diskettes can format double sided. Are the manufacturers ripping you off when they charge extra for double sides or higher density? It would seem so at first glance. If FORMAT likes a diskette, it should be all right, regardless of whether the manufacturer says it's double or single sided, double or quad density, right? Actually, this isn't true. We're not only interested in how well the diskette stores data now, but how well it stores data in the future.

FORMAT only tests how well a diskette retains information for a few seconds. That's not a good enough test; put important information on the wrong kind of floppy, and it won't be reliable in the long term.

Take my advice: If the manufacturer says it's single sided, use it single sided. Manufacturers have equipment that can test signal strength of data written to a diskette vs. what's read from the diskette, and thus can distinguish more than just "data is there" vs. "data isn't there." You only save pennies per diskette like this, and remember that you're using these diskettes to save data that cost you a lot of money to generate. There's a fundamental physical difference between 360K and 1.2MB floppies, also, that makes mixing them up not a good idea; the floppies actually have a different coating on them.

In order to hold the floppy so it can be spun, the drive "clamps" onto the edge of the hole in the middle of the floppy. Tandon drives ensured good speed control by clamping rather hard, and so with the advent of the PC (the first major computer to use Tandon drives) we slowly saw the growth of floppy drives with hub rings. (Back in the early 80s, companies sold retrofit hub ring kits: hub rings and glue with an applicator.) Nowadays, virtually all double-density floppies have them. They're actually unnecessary today, as most drives are half-height drives that don't need to exert as much pressure.

The Floppy Drive. The drive itself varies in several ways:

- Half height vs. full height
- Size (8-, 5¼-, 3½-inch)
- Density (double vs. quad density)

Half height or full height? Height has no effect on data storage; disks read or written with a full-height drive can be read or written with a half height. There are even ⅓-height drives (Okidata makes them). Your major concern maintenance-wise is that the half heights are a bit more troublesome to work on, but at $65 for a drive, you won't do much work on them anyway. Occasionally you'll have trouble putting in two half heights where previously there was one full height. If you're installing two half heights on a PC or XT (IBM only—the clones have no problem), be sure you have a mounting bracket to allow you to do this.

Most of the PC world uses 5¼-inch drives, but increasingly machines are using the 3½-inch 720K and 1.44MB drives. More and more machines, like portables, PS/2s, and many "small footprint" computers, lack 5¼-inch drives altogether, so it's worth examining how to put a 3½-inch drive in an existing XT- or AT-type machine. The 3½-inch drives can be outfitted with mounting cases so they fit where a half-height 5¼-inch would be. The connection is the same, the controller is the same; you'll need to get software support, as I'll discuss later in the chapter.

Density varies somewhat. Density is measured in *Tracks Per Inch (TPI)*. Regular double-density drives are 48 TPI drives—the 40 tracks fit in 5/6 of an inch. The 1.2MB megabyte floppies used in the AT are quad density drives, 96 tracks per inch, 80 tracks on a disk. 3½-inch drives are even more finely packed at 135 TPI.

The quality of the drive also determines how many sectors can be placed on the disk. Table 15-1 below summarizes these data.

Many things can go wrong with disk drives. You can learn to fix them (we'll talk about repairs in this chapter), but they're sufficiently cheap that you could reasonably consider them disposable. In any case, be sure to have a few on hand for spares. Fixing drives takes time, and you might not have that time when a drive dies.

The Disk Controller Board. As with other devices, the floppy drive needs a controller board. AT-type machines generally put both the floppy controller and hard disk controller functions on a single board. On XT-type machines, you can buy combination hard/floppy disk controllers for about $150. A floppy-only

Table 15-1. Floppy Disk Formats

Disk Type	Capacity	Tracks	Sectors/Track	Bytes/Sector
360K DSDD Floppy	360/320K	40	8 or 9	512
1.2MB Floppy	1.2M	80	15	512
3½-inch	720K	80	9	512
Zenith 2-inch	720K	80	9	512
HD 3½-inch	1440K	80	18	512

controller for the XT-type machines is about $30. Again, controllers can be fixed if you have time and are patient (most chips on controllers are *not* socketed), but it can't hurt to have a spare one or two around for quick diagnosis.

Figure 15-2 XT-Type Floppy Controller Board

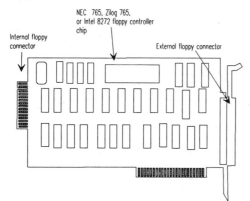

You can swap the controller board in just a few minutes. There are generally no DIP switches to set. You'll see a ribbon cable extending from the edge of the controller card. This ribbon connects to the disk drives; disconnect it from the controller card. The card *should* be keyed so you cannot connect it upside-down, but check at this point. Don't forget the Pin 1 Rule! If there's any ambiguity, draw a picture. Use a magic marker to write *up* and an arrow on the connector. Do whatever makes reassembly easy. Then unscrew the mounting screw and remove the disk controller board (you have, of course, turned the power off before doing any of this). Install the spare in the reverse manner and try to reboot. If the problem goes away, fix the controller or throw it away and buy another one. This is an effective diagnostic procedure that literally only takes minutes.

The main chip on a floppy controller board is the big one labeled either NEC 765 or INTEL 8272. It's probably not worth replacing on an XT-type controller, but if you have a "does it all" motherboard like an AT&T 6300 or 6386 with the floppy controller function right on the motherboard, this could save you some money. The controller chip costs about $4, but unfortunately it isn't socketed.

The Cable. The drive is connected to the controller by a 34-wire ribbon cable. The cable is usually "keyed" between lines 4/5 and 6/7 so that it's inserted correctly. Most of the cables have three edge connectors: one for the drive controller, one for drive A, and one for drive B.

The connector from the drive controller to B is a *parallel* cable: pin 1 on the drive controller side is connected to pin 1 on the floppy side, 2 is connected to 2, and so on. The connector to A has a twist in it, however. It's this twist that identifies A from B. The ribbon cable has three connectors: one on one end and two on the other end. The lone end goes on the controller. The one in the middle goes on drive B. The one on the end goes on drive A. If you're likely to forget (as I am), get a magic marker and write *controller*, *B*, and *A* on the appropriate connectors.

Figure 15-3 Floppy Cable with Twist for A Drive

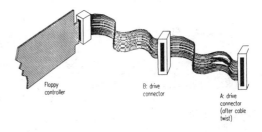

It never hurts to have a couple of extra cables around. The cables are about

$20–$30 from any mail order house or computer discounter. Keep an extra one around. Swapping the cable is easy. Testing continuity is a pain.

Maintenance

For all of their moving parts, disk drives behave rather well. I still have the same A drive on my original PC as when I bought it in August 1981. A few simple procedures will greatly extend the life of your drives and diskettes.

How Often Should You Clean the Heads? Like audio cassette drives and videotape recorders, floppies have a magnetic read/write head that collects magnetic oxide. The similarity has lead some people to conclude that it's a good idea to remove this buildup now and then. This has lead to floppy head cleaning kits.

Like all good PC owners, you've probably purchased a floppy head cleaner to ward off floppy evil spirits. Once procured, however, the first question is: How often should I clean the floppy heads?

The head cleaner people say to do it weekly. Some people cynically claim that this is because they want you to use it up and buy some more. Other people claim that cleaning this often would be disastrous, as the procedure wears away a little of the head each time—you'll always have a clean head, but it lives a shorter time as a result of the cleaning process. The books are split on the question.

Personally, I clean my heads only when the drive fails. I have some computers I've *never* cleaned the heads on, and they work fine. My recommendation: Clean the heads only when you start experiencing read/write errors.

And *be careful* in choosing a floppy head cleaner! Some cleaners don't use a cleaning fluid and a cotton cleaning floppy but just a *sandpaper* floppy! (I

know, it's not sandpaper, but it might as well be. It's abrasive, and it's not a good idea to use it on your floppies.)

Remember another head-saving tip: On full-height drives, keep the doors open when you're not using the drive. Otherwise, the two heads grate against each other. Some people think it's smart to leave the drive doors closed, as an antidust measure. The doors aren't dustproof by a mile, so it's a silly idea. Leave them open and save your disk heads.

Environmental Factors that Affect Disks and Diskettes. We've all seen the "do not" cartoons on the back of the diskette jackets. They lead you to believe that floppies are very fragile items. As those of us in the real world know, this isn't really true. Yes, you must take care of them, but you needn't get crazy about it. Don't put them on the radiator or leave them on a shelf that gets three hours of direct sunlight every day. Don't store them under the roof leak. Given the choice, store them upright stacked left to right rather than on top of each other.

Remember thermal shock. If your portable computer has been sitting in the back of the car in freezing temperatures overnight, bring it in and let it warm up before using it. Just a little heat expansion/contraction can temporarily realign your drives. More extreme temperatures can damage the diskettes. Vendors claim that diskettes should never be stored below 50 degrees nor above 125 degrees. (The *50 degrees* part is probably paranoia: I order software through the mail regularly, and when it's delivered in January it often sits outside in freezing temperatures for the entire day. I've never had a problem. When it sits out in the rain or in the hot sun, or when the postal carrier bends it, that's another story.)

Dust, smoke, and dirt can cause damage to the head and/or to a diskette.

As before, don't smoke around the machines. It's nice to work with the windows open on a sunny Spring day, but there's a lot of pollen and road dust in the air. To see this, clean your windowsill thoroughly, and then leave the window open for a day. Check it the next day. On a normal Spring day when the weather has been dry, you should see a noticeable film after just one day. You sure don't want that on your heads.

A Disk Drive Tester. Part of maintenance is monitoring. Several disk drive test programs are on the market today. For the price, I like a product called *TestDrive* from Microsystems Development. The program itself is very inexpensive ($25), but you need an alignment diskette or diskettes to go with it. You can order them from MSD at:

Microsystems Development
4100 Moorpark Ave. #104
San Jose, CA 95117
(408) 296-4000

You'll want three alignment test floppies: one for 360K drives, one for 1.2MB drives, and a single diskette that serves both 720K and 1.44MB drives.

MSD even gives away a free version of the program that will only work on 360K floppies. For $25 they'll send you the full-blown version that works on anything. See the "Floppy Testing" section later for details on what drive test programs do and how to understand their output.

Removing, Configuring, and Installing Floppy Drives

You generally won't repair drives; rather, you'll replace them. That means it's most important to be able to take them out and put them back in.

Removing Floppy Drives. Floppy drives are removed in three steps:

1. Remove screws from mounting brackets.
2. Remove power connection.
3. Remove data connection.

The floppy drive is secured to the computer case with two mounting screws on an XT. These can be a pain to remove, as the two screws on the left side (the A drive) are usually close to expansion boards. To loosen these screws you sometimes need to remove all of the expansion boards. A useful tool here is an *offset screwdriver*. This is a screwdriver with a bent handle. Get an offset screwdriver, and you won't have to remove all of the expansion boards. As we've seen before, AT-type machines secure the drives in front with metal tabs. Remove the tabs, and the drive slides out like a drawer from a desk.

On the back of the floppy is a connection from the power supply. It has four wires attached to a connector: a yellow, two blacks, and a red. The connector is keyed so you cannot connect it backwards. There are two of these (four on some power supplies), one for each floppy drive. Many power supplies label them P10 and P11, with P10 on the A drive and P11 on the B drive. Actually, it doesn't matter which is connected to which. It's the twist in the drive ribbon cable that decides which is the A drive. The connector may be under the back of the printed circuit board. Disconnect it with a gentle pull, or rock it side to side. Be gentle—I've seen circuit boards on floppies broken when Macho Man disconnects the power connectors on a drive. You might find it easier to pull the floppy out just a bit so you have room to reach around back and disconnect cables.

A blue or gray edge connector on the data cable connects to the back of the drive. Remove it, being sure as always to

Figure 15-4 Common Floppy Cables and Configuration

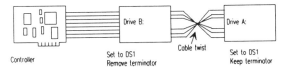

Controller — Drive B: — Cable twist — Drive A:

Set to DS1
Remove terminator

Set to DS1
Keep terminator

The typical PC floppy cable

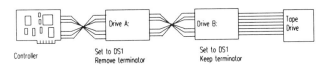

Controller — Drive A: — Drive B: — Tape Drive

Set to DS1
Remove terminator

Set to DS1
Keep terminator

Compaq Deskpro Cable

diagram it. As before, don't be afraid to get a marker and write right on the cable.

Now the drive will come out fine. As you remove the drive, be careful of parts on the drive that stick up. Don't break them off as you remove the drive.

Installing Floppy Drives. Installing a floppy is just the reverse of removing one, except the drive must be configured. To configure a new floppy, you must:

- Terminate the drive properly.
- Set the drive select jumper.
- Connect the drive using the twisted or nontwisted connector, as appropriate.
- Attach a power connector (P10, P11, and so on).

First, the last drive on the drive cable—A, in the case of the PC—must be terminated. *Termination* just means that a resistance must be present across two electronic lines or the drive controller will think there's nobody home. As with hard disks (see Chapter 12 on hard disk installation), the drives will probably work with both terminators in place; but that shoves twice as much current

through the controller, cooking the chips over the long run. Termination is done with a terminating resistor or *terminator*. It looks like a chip—in fact, it's a resistor

Figure 15-5 Typical Floppy with View of Drive Select Jumper and Terminator

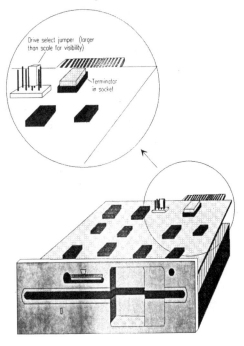

Drive select jumper (larger than scale for visibility)

Terminator in socket

in IC's clothing—and comes on a drive's circuit board socketed. To unterminate, just remove the chip. Remember: drive A must be terminated, regardless of whether or not drive B is present.

Note that some half-height drives have the terminators soldered in place. There's then a jumper labeled *TM*. To remove the terminator, remove the TM jumper.

Second, the drive must be selected. This means certain jumpers must be added or removed. On Tandon full-height drives (the most popular ones), there's an area that looks like a socket for a chip. With the jumper installed, it looks like Figure 15-6.

Put a jumper across the holes shown above, third from the right. A regular staple works fine and is probably the

Figure 15-6 Tandon Drive Select Jumper

Back of Drive

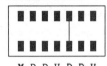

```
M  D  D  H  D  D  H
X  S  S  M  S  S  S
   3  2     1  0
Front of Drive
```

jumper of choice for 90 percent of the Tandon floppies installed in PCs today. For other drives, look for *DS0* (Drive Select 0) or a marking like that. Some drives show DS0 through DS3, others show DS1 through DS4. *Take the second value:* if the drive jumpers are labeled from DS0, pick DS1; if the drive jumpers are labeled from DS1, pick DS2.

Terminator and drive select jumper on Tandon drive.

Terminator and drive select jumper on TEAC drive.

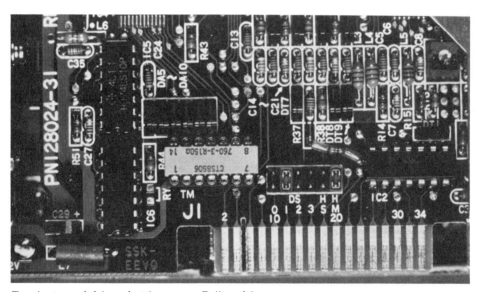

Terminator and drive select jumper on Fujitsu drive.

Sometimes you'll see two jumper positions, *RDY* and *CD*. In general, a jumper should be on one or the other, but not both. RDY is used on a PC or XT. CD is used on an AT for *change line* sup-port. See the "Drive Shows Phantom Di-rectories" section later for a discussion of this.

Remember that the A drive goes on the connector that has a twist between it

233

and the controller board—except for a few strange machines, that is.

And Compaq.

Compaq wanted the A drive to be first in line after the controller (see Figure 15-4). So they put a twist in between the first connector and the controller. That's fine, but it kind of leaves B out in the cold, since it wants *no* twists between it and the controller. What to do?

Simple—Compaq just put another twist in the cable *after* the A connection, sort of to "untwist" the twist. That means that when you put a second floppy on a Compaq machine, you must take the terminator off the A drive and leave it on the B drive.

Reviewing:

Floppy Drive Configuration Summary

Drive A
  Should be connected to the twist in the floppy cable
  Should retain the terminator chip
  Should be selected as the second drive

Drive B
  Should be connected to the non-twisted cable connector
  Shouldn't have the terminator
  Should also be selected as the second drive

And remember to inform the computer via DIP switches or the SETUP program when drives are added or deleted.

What the Other Jumpers Do. Here's a partial list of the other jumpers you'll see atop a floppy drive board:

- HM: Head/Motor. "Load" the head when the motor is turned on with the Motor On or Motor Enable (see the section "More on Drive Select: What Does the Twist Do?" for more information). In a multidrive system, there's just one Motor On signal. That would mean that all drives would be turned on and their heads could read and write. This isn't supported by IBM's software, however, so don't try to get faster floppy copies this way. IBM wrote all floppy disk software so only one drive would be on at a time, as the original machine (the PC) had a fairly low-output power supply.
- HS: Head Solenoid. The opposite of HM—you may not select both. (In the PC world, you will, in fact, usually select neither.) It says only to load the head when the drive is selected. Note that this whole discussion is a bit moot in the PC world, since the heads load as soon as the drive door is closed.
- MX: Multiplex. If activated, the drive is always active. Again, don't take this option in the PC world.
- HI, HO, LHI, LHO, OP: Applies to 1.44M drives. Manufacturers include a *media sensor*. This tells the drive when a 720K diskette has been loaded in the drive. An attempt to format it as 1.44M will fail because of the media sensor. You can shut off the media sensor with these jumpers. Exactly how you enable or disable it varies with the drive, but TEAC or Mitsubishi do it as shown following:
  - Mitsubishi: There are some jumper points looking something like the following,

  HO HI SW
  . . . .

where the periods are jumper points. To enable the sensor, jumper the two points closest to SW. To disable, move the jumper to the two points closest to HI.

- TEAC: Here there are separate pairs of jumper points for each option:

HHO . .
OP   . .
LHI   . .
HHI   . .
D1   . .
D0   . .

To enable the sensor, jumper OP. To disable, jumper HHI. (Those tips are courtesy of Maureen Lancaster, the very helpful person you'll talk to if you call MicroSense.)

Installing 3½-inch Drives. The 3½-inch, or microfloppy, drives are here to stay. They're a bit slower to seek than the bigger 5¼-inch minifloppies, but they're rugged and store a lot of data. The biggest problem with machines mixing micro- and mini-floppies is data transfer. How do you get data from your mini to your micro?

The best answer (and the reason for this section) is to put a microfloppy on the machine you use as your "main" machine, the one on your desk on which you do the most work. Install it as the B drive; then transferring from minifloppy to microfloppy is as easy as COPY A:*.* B:. Microfloppy installation is really pretty simple. It's relatively easy to install a 720K drive on an XT or AT-type machine, or a 1.44MB on an AT, but an XT-type floppy controller will *not* support a 1.44MB floppy. Only DOS 3.2 or greater will support 720K floppies.

Installing a microfloppy drive is like installing a floppy drive, but you must

ensure that you have software support. You get software support for a 720K floppy with DOS 3.2 in the form of a program called DRIVER.SYS, but it doesn't work very well for 1.44MB drives. I strongly suggest that you get BIOS support if you intend to put a 1.44MB drive on your AT-type machine.

If you're installing the drive in a system with a SETUP program, such as a 286/386/486 system, check to see if your system supports 720K and/or 1.44MB drives. Just run your SETUP program and look at the floppy drive options it offers. If your BIOS doesn't support the microfloppies, think about upgrading. BIOSes for IBM ATs to expand the drive table and support 3½-inch floppy drives come from the same place as motherboard upgrades, as discussed in Chapter 7.

Now let's install the microfloppy drive:

1. Remove the B drive, if you have one, from your current system. Keep it as a spare drive.
2. Install the microfloppy in a 5¼-inch mounting kit so it fits where the old B drive used to be. Most microfloppy vendors sell these "universal" mounting kits. I've used Toshiba's and TEAC's with good results.
3. Install the microfloppy in the computer, just as you would a normal drive. Ensure that the drive select jumper is in the second position and remove the terminator, if any, from the drive. Again, don't install a 1.44MB drive on an XT-type machine unless it has a special controller that can support that drive.
4. If you have a computer with BIOS support for the microfloppy, use SETUP to inform it that you've changed the B drive. If it's an older

computer that only recognizes either 360K or 1.2MB floppies, tell it the microfloppy is a 360K drive or try to get a BIOS upgrade.

5. If you don't have BIOS support, change your CONFIG.SYS file to include the following line:

DEVICE = DRIVER.SYS /D:1

This instructs DOS to support a 720K floppy. Now, it can't redefine what *B* means to it, so it creates a new drive letter, such as D, E, or whatever. You'll see a brief message something like *driver loaded for drive E* at boot time. Use that drive letter when referring to the $3\frac{1}{2}$-inch drive.

Again, DRIVER.SYS doesn't work very well for 1.44MB drives, but if you want to try it, the line would be

DEVICE = DRIVER.SYS /D:1 /S:18 / F:2

In DRIVER.SYS you inform the system which physical drive is to be affected with the /D:d parameter. If d equals 0, it refers to the first drive, the A drive; d = 1 refers to the second drive, the B drive; d = 2 would refer to a third, external disk drive. /S:18 says there are 18 sectors per track. /F:2 tells DOS that it's a 1.44MB disk drive.

Now just use the COPY or XCOPY commands to transfer data between mini- and microfloppies—just refer to the B drive. One quirk arises when you FORMAT a new disk, however, if you're using DRIVER.SYS. As I said a few paragraphs back, DRIVER.SYS can't redefine what B: means, so it creates another

drive letter. If you enter *FORMAT B:*, you'll end up with a 360K microfloppy. You must FORMAT to the new drive letter in order to get a 720K formatted microfloppy.

To put a 1.44MB drive in on an XT-class machine, you need a new controller. A firm called MicroSense sells an alternate controller they call a Compaticard ($125 for the two-drive model, $150 for the four-drive model) that will do the trick. They even claim you needn't remove your old floppy controller (a real benefit for computers that have the function on the motherboard, where it can't be removed), and it seems to work for the one machine on which I tried it.

MicroSense is at

MicroSense
370 Andrew Ave.
Leucadia, CA 92024
(800) 544-4252
(619) 632-8621

Summarizing:

- Check to see if you've got BIOS support.
- 720K disks don't need BIOS support, but it's preferable.
- If the machine is a 286/386/486, consider upgrading the BIOS.
- Unless you have BIOS support, you cannot install as an A drive, so use B if possible.
- If necessary, use DRIVER.SYS (supplied with DOS 3.2 +):

DEVICE = DRIVER.SYS /D:1 for 720K
DEVICE = DRIVER.SYS /D:1 /S:18 for 1.44M

DRIVER.SYS will create a new logical drive. Use that drive's letter for formatting.

More on Drive Select: What Does the Twist Do? Only read this if you're curious about the twist in the cable, and why DS1 or DS2 is selected.

As I've said, the drive is connected to the controller by a 34-wire ribbon cable. The cable is usually "keyed" between lines 4/5 and 6/7 so it will be inserted correctly. Most of the cables have three edge connectors: one for the drive controller, one for drive A, and one for drive B.

The connector from the drive controller to B is a *parallel* cable—pin 1 on the drive controller is connected to pin 1 on the floppy, 2 connected to 2, and so on. The connector to A has a twist in it, however. It's this twist that identifies A from B. The unusual connections on the A side are in Table 15-2.

Table 15-2. Standard Floppy Cable Configuration

Pin on Controller, B	Pin on A
10	16
11	15
12	14
13	13
14	12
15	11
16	10

Why the twist?

Back in the old days, daisy-chained drives spoke, one at a time, over a shared cable. They knew what address they had by their Drive Select jumper. The first drive was DS0, then DS1, and so on.

IBM decided (perhaps rightly) that actually requiring users to select DS0 for drive A and DS1 for drive B was a bit taxing. Was there an easier way? As it turns out, by putting a twist in lines 10 to

16, *both drives can be DS1, but the one with the twist looks like DS0 to the controller*. The twist, then, makes life easier for the PC installer.

Here are the ugly details. The floppy has an edge connector with 34 lines on it. The controller has an edge connector with 34 lines on it. Just before the connector at the end, the cable is twisted from lines 10 to 16. Thus, there's one connector (the one used by the A drive) with a twist upstream of it, and one with no twists upstream (the B connector). In order for a drive to work, it must receive power on a *drive select* line and a *motor enable* line. The controller only has one generic motor enable line, but separate drive select lines. Twisting the cable, as we'll see, moves around the select and motor enable lines to activate either the B drive or the A drive.

First, consider the situation with a nontwisted cable (this is the normal situation for the B drive).

Table 15-3. Interface Functions for Floppy Controller and Drive (No-Twist Cable)

Controller pin and function		Drive pin and function	
10	Motor enable for A	10	Select drive 0
12	**Select B**	**12**	**Select drive 1**
14	Select A	14	Select drive 2
16	**Motor enable for B**	**16**	**Drive motor enable**

Why wouldn't this work for drive A? Suppose we had a *straight-through* cable—one that connected 10 on the floppy to 10 on the controller, 12 on the floppy to 12 on the controller, and so on. Well, when the controller began to activate drive A, it would put power on both line 14 to select drive A and 10 to turn on A's drive motor. (Why are there *two* Motor Enables on the controller, rather than

237

sharing one between the drives? So a future, yet nonexistent version of the PC could run multiple drives simultaneously.)

What would drive A see? A *needs* to see lines 10 (to select the drive) and 16 (to start the drive motor). But recall that the controller has powered up lines 10 and 14. Well, powering up lines 10 and 14 would activate *Select 0*—good so far—and *Select 2*. No good.

The B drive, on the other hand, would work okay, as the controller would enable 12 (select B) and 16 (motor enable), which would appear to B as Select 1 (correct, as it's jumpered to be drive 1) and Drive Motor On. That's why the nontwisted cable connector works fine for drive B. In Table 15-3 above, lines 12 and 16 are boldface because they're the ones relevant to operating the B drive.

Now consider what the twist does. When we twist from 10 to 16 *on just the A connector*, the connections work as seen in Table 15-4.

Table 15-4. Interface Functions for Floppy Controller and Drive (Twisted Cable)

Controller Pin and Function		Drive Pin and Function (What Drive A Sees)	
10	Motor enable A:	16	Drive motor on
12	Select B:	14	Select drive 2
14	Select A:	12	Select drive 1
16	Motor enable B:	10	Select drive 0

Now A is on this twisted connector. As before, the controller powers lines 10 and 14 to enable A's motor and to select the drive. But now 10 on the controller side goes to 16 (Drive Motor On) on the A side, so we're halfway there. Line 14 on the controller side goes to line 12, Select

Drive 1. Recall that A, like B, is jumpered to respond as Drive 1. The A drive thinks that it's drive 1 and its motor is enabled, so *voilà!*—the drive responds. Drive B also works because, you'll recall, it was set up fine before we twisted the cable, and the B connector isn't twisted.

Floppy Testing

Anyone can run Norton *DiskTest* on a drive, but perhaps you've never heard of disk alignment tests, hub centering, azimuth, and hysteresis—impressive, aren't they. Here's how to understand what the tests are telling you (and, of course, be the envy of your floppy-using friends). For this discussion, I'll use Microsystems Development's *TestDrive*, a fairly inexpensive ($25) test program that I've mentioned previously in this chapter.

A complete floppy check involves tests of:

- Sensitivity. How wide a range of space on the disk can a head read from a fixed point?
- Radial Alignment. Is the floppy head centered on a track?
- Hysteresis. Can the floppy find a particular track equally well no matter from which direction it approaches?
- Hub Centering. Can the hub clamp hold the floppy well enough to make it turn in a perfect circle, with no wobbling?
- Azimuth Skew. Is the head at a tangent to the tracks or skewed a bit?
- Rotational Speed. Does the motor drive the floppy at the proper speed?

Since *TestDrive* is fairly good (and cheap), I'll include sample screens from it's tests in the following sections.

Figure 15-7 Aligned and Misaligned Floppy Disk Heads

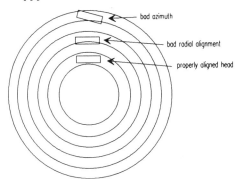

Floppy Head Sensitivity. In the perfect world, data is exactly centered on a perfectly thin track on a diskette. But the world hasn't been perfect since at *least* when the Dodgers left Brooklyn, so you can hardly expect better of floppies. Consider the width of a track. There are three track densities popular at the moment: 48 tracks per inch (TPI) for 360K floppies, 96 TPI for 1.2MB floppies, and 135 TPI for 720K and 1.44MB floppies. That works out to track widths of 20.8 milli-inches (mi), 10.8 mi, and 9.4 mi respectively. Since data doesn't generally reside ex-

actly in the center of a track, a floppy head needs the power to read a range of distance further out and further in from track center. That range is called the *sensitivity.*

Ideally, a head should be able to sit in the center of a track and be able to read almost all the way to the next track in each direction. (If it could read more than that, it would be confused by information on the adjacent tracks.) Thus, it would be nice if a 360K drive had a sensitivity just under 20.8 mi. We'll settle for about 80 percent of that. In the particular case of 360K floppies, we'll be happy with 16 mi. A 1.2MB drive can get along with 8 mi sensitivity, and 3½-inch drives are fine with 5 mi. (By the way, there's a table summarizing criteria for 360K, 1.2M, and 3½-inch floppies at the end of this section. I'm not just pulling these numbers out of the air.)

Test programs measure sensitivity with a special test disk that has data written at various previously known distances off center. They ask the user to put the special test disk (generally known as a *digital diagnostic disk,* or *DDD*) into the drive and run the test program. The program, knowing what to expect, com-

Figure 15-8 Sample Alignment Test Output

```
 ┌─────────────────────────────────────────────────────────────────────────┐
 │ Drive B:                    TEST DRIVE  Alignment Test          8/20/89   │
 │ 720 KB                                                                    │
 │             <---------------------- Track ---------------------->         │
 │             79  67  40  32  6   0      0   6   32  40  67  79             │
 │                                                                           │
 │       -4.5 er02 er02 er02 er02 er10 ••••  •••• •••• er02 er02 er02 er02    │
 │       -4.0 er02 er02 er02 er02 •••• ••••   •••• •••• •••• •••• •••• er02    │
 │       -3.5 •••• •••• •••• •••• •••• ••••    •••• •••• •••• •••• •••• ••••    │
 │       -3.0 •••• •••• •••• •••• •••• ••••    •••• •••• •••• •••• •••• ••••    │
 │       -2.5 •••• •••• •••• •••• •••• ••••    •••• •••• •••• •••• •••• ••••    │
 │       -2.0 •••• •••• •••• •••• •••• ••••    •••• •••• •••• •••• •••• ••••    │
 │       -1.5 •••• •••• •••• •••• •••• ••••    •••• •••• •••• •••• •••• ••••    │
 │ Milli- -1.0 •••• •••• •••• •••• •••• ••••   •••• •••• •••• •••• •••• ••••    │
 │ Inches             Head  0                       Head  1                  │
 │       +1.0 •••• •••• •••• •••• •••• ••••    •••• •••• •••• •••• •••• ••••    │
 │       +1.5 •••• •••• •••• •••• •••• ••••    •••• •••• •••• •••• •••• ••••    │
 │       +2.0 •••• •••• •••• •••• •••• ••••    •••• •••• •••• •••• •••• ••••    │
 │       +2.5 •••• •••• •••• •••• •••• ••••    •••• •••• •••• •••• •••• ••••    │
 │       +3.0 •••• •••• •••• •••• •••• ••••    •••• •••• •••• •••• •••• ••••    │
 │       +3.5 •••• •••• •••• •••• •••• ••••    •••• •••• •••• •••• •••• ••••    │
 │       +4.0 •••• •••• •••• •••• •••• ••••    •••• •••• •••• •••• •••• ••••    │
 │       +4.5 •••• •••• •••• •••• •••• ••••    •••• •••• •••• •••• •••• ••••    │
 │                                                                           │
 │          ─┤ Test complete, press any key to continue ├─                   │
 └─────────────────────────────────────────────────────────────────────────┘
```

pares what the head could read with what it did read. Then it can report sensitivity. Take a look at Figure 15-8. Here, the test program is showing results for tests of tracks 0, 6, 32, 40, 67, and 79 (this is a $3\frac{1}{2}$-inch disk being tested). The left-hand side of the page is showing results for the bottom head, 0, and the right-hand side of the page shows results for the top head, 1. The units are in milli-inches both positive and negative because the test examines information both toward and away from the drive center. Any cell with four dots is a perfect read; anything starting with *er*, like *er10*, is an unsuccessful read.

Take a look at head 0, track 40. It cannot read −4.5 or −4.0, but −3.5 to +4.5 presents no problem. Since 4.5 to −3.5 is a distance of 8 mi, the sensitivity of this drive is said to be 8 mi, quite adequate for a $3\frac{1}{2}$-inch drive.

If a head is insufficiently sensitive, it might only be dirty. Clean the head and try again.

Radial Alignment. Not only must a head be sensitive; it must be placed properly. The ideal head rests over the center of a track. This is its *radial alignment*. Radial alignment is deduced by ex-

amining the center of sensitivity. Basically, look at the sensitivity criterion, 6 mi in the case of our $3\frac{1}{2}$-inch floppy. (Again, Table 15-5 at the end of the section has these criteria.) That means a properly aligned $3\frac{1}{2}$-inch drive could read ±3 mi. Our drive can indeed cover that entire range, but note that (at least over track 40) it isn't perfectly centered. The pattern isn't symmetrical. If its sensitivity was only 6 mi, it could only read from perhaps +3.5 to −2.5. It would then fall short of being able to read to −3 mi and would therefore be misaligned.

So sensitivity and radial alignment go hand in hand. A somewhat misaligned head can be compensated by greater sensitivity.

Older drives have an adjustment screw that can move a head farther from or closer to the center of the drive. Test software like *TestDrive* and *Readiscope* generally offer a *continuous alignment test* option so you can try to fix a misaligned head by yourself. It's not easy; you'll need patience and steady hands. Again, you might be able to improve sensitivity by cleaning the head, thereby nullifying an alignment problem.

Hysteresis. The method for posi-

Figure 15-9   Sample Hysteresis Test Output

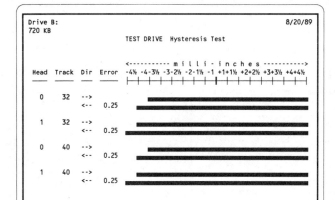

tioning a head over a track is imperfect and, in fact, results will generally vary depending on whether the head is moving farther out from or closer to the center. Basically, where a head ends up depends on where it's coming from: a head told to go to track 20 from a current location of track 30 will end up in a slightly different position from one that's told to go to track 20 from track 10. That's the thesis of the hysteresis (say it out loud) test.

A hysteresis test measures the distance between head position on selected tracks when positioned further out from and closer in towards the center. The difference between the locations in milli-inches is the result. Acceptable values are 1.5 mi for 360, 1.0 for 1.2MB drives, and 1.0 for 3½-inch drives. You can see a sample output of a hysteresis test in Figure 15-9.

The sample test ran on a 3½-inch drive; 3½-inch drives must show a hysteresis value of 1.0 mi or less. *TestDrive* ran tests on tracks 32 and 40 for both heads 0 and 1. In all cases, the difference between head position when moving in towards the center of the disk and when moving out towards the edge was 0.25

mi. This figure is well below 1.0, so the drive is working just fine. You can't do much about a drive with bad hysteresis, so replace it.

Hub Clamping. The center hub clamp holds the disk in its exact center so it spins in a perfect circle. If it doesn't, that shows up as bad alignment. *TestDrive* checks this with three test tracks on your DDD that can detect varying amounts of wobble. The smallest value in milli-inches is the loosest test, the largest value is the most stringent one. A sample output follows, again for a 3½-inch drive (see Figure 15-10).

Here, the disk tests at 2.5, 3.0, and 3.5 mi. Of these, 2.5 is the easiest test; 3.5 is the toughest. We'd be perfectly happy if the disk only passed the 2.5 and 3.0 mi tests, but this disk really (as our President says) "kicks a little tail" and passes the 3.5 mi test as well. (This is clearly a drive you'd be proud to take home to meet your motherboard.)

A serious hub clamp problem can't be resolved. But sometimes all you have to do to fix the problem is to just remove the floppy and reinsert it in the drive.

Disk Rotation Speed. Most floppies rotate at 300 rpm, except the 1.2MB

Figure 15-10 Hub Centering Test Output

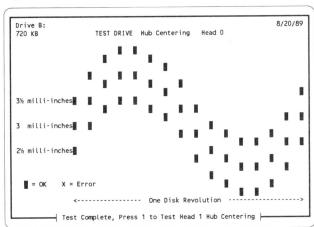

floppy drives, which rotate at 360 rpm. Small variations in this speed (plus or minus one percent) are okay, but greater differences can make the floppy malfunction.

Now, understand that you'll probably never have this problem if you buy half-height drives. They're direct drive rather than belt driven. Some of the newest ones don't even have an adjustment switch; logic on the drive automatically adjusts the speed, so there's no maintenance.

Speed tester programs exist for $5\frac{1}{4}$-inch floppies. For example, you might come across Verbatim's *Disk Drive Analyzer* or Dysan's *Readiscope; TestDrive* also tests rotational speed. These programs indicate either graphically or numerically whether the drive is too slow or too fast. You would remove the drive from its bracket and then put it on its side on the top of the power supply, a convenient flat surface where it's easy to get to the speed adjustment screw. Reconnect the cables and run the program, adjust the speed, and run it again. Keep doing

this until you get the speed just as you like it. *TestDrive*'s rotational speed test is the "spindle speed test." There's a sample output in Figure 15-11.

The disk under test again performs stunningly, clocking in at exactly 300 rpm. We'll see how to adjust a drive with a bad drive speed in the "Floppy Troubleshooting and Adjustment" section.

Head Azimuth. The drive head is built along a straight line, but it must read a track that's in a circle. In order to best read the data, the head must sit at a tangent to the circle. If it's not exactly tangent, it's said to have *azimuth skew.* The skew generally isn't much, less than a degree off, so skew is measured in minutes (1/60 of a degree, and of course a degree is 1/360 of circle). As with alignment, a good drive must be able to handle data that's a mite out of spec, so a drive's head azimuth is considered okay as long as it can read from -39 minutes skew to $+39$ minutes skew. *TestDrive* can test this with the DDD. Figure 15-12 shows such a test.

The test represents successful reads

Figure 15-11 Sample *TestDrive* Rotational Speed Test Output

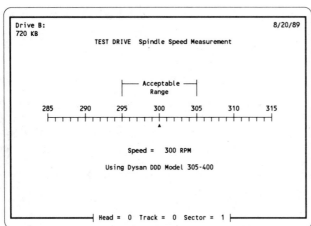

Figure 15-12 Sample Head Azimuth Test Output

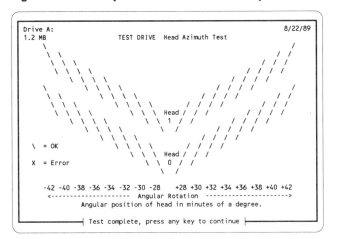

as four slashes, unsuccessful reads as four Xs. Reading from left to right, each set of slashes or Xs represents the range from −42 to −21 minutes of skew, three minutes at a time, and from +21 to +42 minutes of skew. Your drive should (as does this drive) read with no problem from −39 to +39. If it fails the ±42 minute test, it's still okay.

Floppy Drive Test Summary. So you test a drive by examining its sensitivity/alignment to ensure that the drive can write data reliably and read data that

has been written by other drives, even if they're a bit out of alignment themselves. Then you're concerned with how consistently the drive locates a track when traveling inward vs. outward on the disk: the hysteresis tests that. If the hub clamp can't hold the disk properly, it will wobble, so the hub clamping test checks that.

There are different critical values for different drives, but Table 15-5 summarizes good guesses for sensitivity, hysteresis, and the others.

Table 15-5. Typical Critical Values for Floppy Tests

Test	Value Should Be	48 TPI (360K)	96 TPI (1.2M)	3½-inch
Alignment (milli-inches)	≥	±8	±4	±2.5
Hysteresis (milli-inches)	≤	1.5	1.0	1.0
Head Azimuth	Should be readable up to ±39 minutes of arc			
Hub Centering	Must pass tests ≤	8	4	3
Rotational Speed (RPM)	±1%	300	360	300

Floppy Troubleshooting and Adjustment

In a minute, I'll talk about repairing components of the floppy system. But first—how do you know what's wrong? Let's look at some common symptoms and possible causes.

Suppose the drive is malfunctioning, and one of the following things are occurring:

- The drive refuses to read.
- The drive refuses to write.
- The drive reads, but it grinds a lot and displays *retry?* messages.
- You see a 601 message, and then the computer goes to Cassette BASIC.

Possibilities fall into two categories: software and hardware.

Software Possibilities. The problem could be caused by:

- A bad applications program
- A file destroyed by a software bug or incorrect power-down
- FAT damage
- Directory damage
- Boot record damage
- Accidental file erasure

These software problems are discussed in Chapter 14, "Hard Disk Failure Recovery." The same software that will help on hard disks will generally work on floppy drives also.

Getting the Floppy Drive Running Again. Given that a floppy drive isn't working, and it appears not to be software, what do you do?

At this point, I'd do the following things:

1. Reboot. The disk parameter table could be bad.
2. Check the diskette. Try another floppy.
3. Clean the heads on the disk.
4. Swap the drives. Check that connections are solid.
5. Try a new A drive.
6. Swap the controller.

You don't want to spend forever figuring out which one is the reason. You just want (at this stage) to determine if it's *something* on the drive that is causing the problem.

The simplest approach to this is to simply swap the drive. For details, see the previous configuration section.

If after swapping A and B you can now boot from drive A, and read/write data, then the former A is at fault. Replace or repair it.

Common Repair Points

Supposing you want to fix a drive, what common fixes can you do? Here are a few ideas. Once you have a notion of what part of the floppy subsystem has failed, how do you replace or repair it? This section addresses that.

Is It Worth Repairing Floppy Drives? As before in this text, I want to open this section by saying that if you only learn how to replace the controller board, cable, and drives, and nothing about repairing the components themselves, you're doing fine. Floppy drives are very cheap—about $100—and can be replaced without repair. Even if you want to repair the drives, there are firms that will fix floppy drives for a flat fee of $35–$45. This might be more cost effective than spending your time trying to repair a drive.

But if you want to fix a floppy problem, here's a potpourri of things that go wrong, and what you can do for them.

The floppy drive itself can malfunction for a variety of reasons:

- The head is dirty.
- The head is misaligned.
- The *index timing light* is dirty. A light-and-sensor combination detects when the index hole on the floppy (the small hole next to the large central hole) lines up with the corresponding hole in the floppy jacket.
- The rotation speed is wrong.
- The drive belt is slipping (full heights only).
- The drive door is broken or cracked.
- On-drive electronics have failed.
- Track zero adjustment is wrong.
- The *servo board* has failed. It's a small circuit board on the back of Tandon drives, and must be replaced if the Tandon drive can't maintain a constant rotational speed.
- Floppy head rails are sticky. Does the head move smoothly with the power off? Try a little lube on the head rails. I use WD40, but some techs tell me that my drive will live longer if I use a teflon-based lube like the Tri-Flow that I mentioned in the hard disk chapters.

The rest of the chapter looks at some of these problems.

Mixing 1.2MB and 360K Floppies. Both 1.2MB floppy drives (the kind found as drive A on most AT-type machines) and 360K floppy drives (the more common kind) use diskettes that are physically 5¼-inch in size. How much can they be mixed?

- Any diskette created on a 360K drive can be read by a normal 1.2 drive.

- Some folks take cheap 360K diskettes and format them as 1.2MB floppies. You end up with a 1.2MB floppy with 400K of bad sectors. Is this a good idea? Emphatically, *no*.

  There is, you see, a fundamentally different kind of surface on a 1.2MB than a 360K. It's a much finer grain, which explains why it allows 80 tracks and 15 sectors per track in the same area that only accommodates 40 tracks and 9 sectors on a 360K diskette. The data will go on the disk, but it won't stay there. The surface, by the way, isn't only a finer grain, it also requires more power to record on it. The 1.2MB drive uses greater electric current than a 360K. That's why it's physically impossible to write information on a 1.2MB diskette with a 360K drive—the 360K's recording strength is insufficient to get the 1.2's attention. (That also means, by the way, that stray magnetism will affect a 1.2MB less than a 360K; the magnetism would have to be higher strength to erase data.)

- If you create a diskette with a 360K drive and write new information to it on a 1.2MB drive, the new information is still in 360K format, but it might be unreadable by a 360K drive. Half-height 360K drives seem to have less trouble reading these diskettes than full height drives.

- If you format a new 360K diskette with 1.2MB drive, you'll probably (again) have trouble reading this diskette with a 360K drive. In fact, it's much more likely that you'll have trouble with this than if you simply write new data to a previously formatted diskette. Recall that to format a 360K diskette in a 1.2MB drive you would use the command FORMAT A:/4.

All of these problems stem from the following: The 1.2MB drive is an 80 track drive. It writes 80 narrow tracks on a diskette. The 360K drive is a 40 track drive. It writes 40 wide tracks on a diskette. When the 1.2MB drive is asked to write a 40 track diskette, it writes 40 tracks, all right—40 of its skinny tracks, not 40 fat tracks! That means that if the head trying to read this skinny track is a 360K, it might not happen to be centered the same place as the original 1.2MB head was when it wrote the track.

Worse yet, imagine that the 1.2MB head is *overwriting* old 360K data. The 360K data is written about 16 milli-inches wide. But the 1.2MB head only writes tracks about 8 mi wide. So the 1.2 writes an 8 mi swath through the middle of what used to be a 16 mi image of data. The 360K head then tries to read this and, if it's of normal 360K sensitivity, will see a *very* confusing track indeed! Data written by the 1.2MB drive, therefore, might not be readable by a 360K drive—the 360K drive isn't built to read skinny tracks.

Why not eliminate the problem by telling the 1.2MB drive to write pairs of skinny tracks? One company has done that. The utility CPYAT2PC tells the 1.2MB drive to write pairs of skinny tracks. It's $83 from:

Microbridge Computers International, Inc.
655 Sky Way Suite 220
San Carlos, CA 94070
(800) 523-8777
(415) 593-8777

A Turbo Clone Randomly Writes Bad Data To Floppy. I discovered this one when my 386 clone started writing out unreliable data on floppies all of a sudden. I asked, what have I done differently? Simple—I'd upgraded my BIOS.

Some clones mimic the Compaq in that they slow the machine down to 8 Mhz when doing floppy reads or writes. This is ostensibly done to accommodate the occasional copy protected program. Turns out this *isn't* always a good thing: I'd DISKCOPY, then DISKCOMP, and find errors. Then I'd do it again and get errors, but in different places, randomly. I put the old BIOS in, and everything was okay. I'm waiting for the version of the BIOS that doesn't do the floppy switching. If you've got an AWARD BIOS, you can test this: If you can do Ctrl-Alt-– (minus sign) and slow down your computer, then you've probably got the floppy slowdown enabled. This might not be a bad thing for your computer, by the way—it just turned out to be the wrong thing for mine.

Please note that I'm not saying that Compaqs have this problem. Compaqs seem to be able to do speed switching when reading/writing floppies without trouble.

Drive Shows Phantom Directories. The symptom here occurs when you do something, like a DIR command, on a floppy. Then you remove the diskette, put a different diskette in the drive, do a DIR, and you see the *directory of the previous floppy, not the one in the drive now!*

If you see this on a computer, this is a RED ALERT! Don't use the thing until you get the problem fixed. Reason: Let's say you put a floppy in the drive and do a DIR on it. Then you put a different floppy in the drive, and write some data to the floppy. *The PC writes data to the new floppy using the old floppy's directory!* That means the newly-written file is probably okay, but everything else on the floppy is trashed. (Let me tell you about how I lost four pages out of Chapter 3 on an old XT-type laptop that I forgot had this problem. . . .)

Where does this problem come

from? It's something called the *change line signal*. Time for a little history.

Back in the old days, when floppies were the major storage medium for micros, software designers wanted to squeeze the most performance from those floppy drives, mainly because they were pretty low-performance. One way to do that was to avoid, wherever possible, rereading information on a floppy. What information gets read the most? The directory and FAT. Way back before DOS even existed, there was an operating system called *CP/M (Control Program for Microcomputers)*. To get better speed, some CP/M applications only read the directory when a disk was first inserted in a drive. That meant if you were going to swap a floppy while in *WordStar*, you had to tell the program or it would trash your floppy. It was a real pain.

The original PC guys remembered the CP/M experience and (I'm guessing) decided they'd sacrifice a little speed for reliability. So the PC and XT (not all XT clones) BIOSes always read the disk directory and FAT prior to doing anything dangerous—they don't assume that the floppy stays in the same place. And all was well with the world.

But some compatibles makers looking to outdo IBM performance-wise sold computers with slightly different floppy drives. These floppy drives had something called *change line support*. It was no big revolution; in fact, it had been around since the CP/M days. One of the signals from the drive to the controller was a *change line signal*—it signaled that the floppy door had been opened since DOS had last looked at the drive. If the change line was activated, DOS would reread the floppy; if not, it wouldn't bother. That meant that writes needn't be preceded by directory reads, as in the IBM XT case.

The IBM AT design team, looking to show the competition who was boss, added the *change line* feature to the AT. That means there's a minor difference between XT floppy drives and AT floppy drives. The XT drives don't really use line 34 on the floppy edge connector, but the AT drives use 34 as the change line line. To complicate matters, this question of whether or not change line support is really needed is determined by what BIOS your computer has. Some XT clones need it, some don't. Some AT clones need it, others don't. The IBM AT needs it. You really can't go wrong with a floppy with change line support, as a computer that doesn't need it will just ignore it.

If you have a computer that needs change line support, and you install a floppy drive that lacks it, the computer will display the phantom directory (and possibly trash a floppy someday).

Now you know what change line support is, and that some computers need it. Suppose you find yourself with a change line problem—phantom directories. What do you do?

- **Check the floppy cable.** The aforementioned old XT (a clone) has a scratched cable. I haven't gotten around to replacing it yet, but that's the answer.
- **Check to see if the floppy has change line support.** Exactly *how* to activate change line support is tough to know for sure unless you've got the documentation, but look for a *DC* jumper point. You may alternatively see a *RDY* line. Move the jumper from RDY to DC.
- **Use DRIVER.SYS.** This won't solve all woes, but it's a stopgap. The DRIVER.SYS device driver that ships with DOS 3.3 has a /C, *change line* option. You use DRIVER.SYS to

tell DOS things about a drive. For our purposes, let's just look at the /C option.

Assuming that your problem drive is drive B (the second physical drive), and assuming that it's a 360K drive, you'd say

DEVICE = DRIVER.SYS /D:1 /C / T:40 /F:0

Don't worry about most of the parameters, but the /D:1 says we're describing drive 1, or the B drive. Drive A would, of course, be drive 0. When the system boots, you'll see a message something like *driver installed for drive E*. Use that drive letter henceforth when referring to drive B!.

- Another possibility is to fool the controller into thinking there have been lots of change line signals. One approach to this is to simply construct a cable that disconnects line 34 on the drive side but cross-connects lines 34 and 20 on the controller side. As line 20 is activated with each head step, the controller will believe it's seeing many change line signals.
- The last approach is just to remember to do a Ctrl-C keystroke when you're in DOS and have changed the floppy. It forces DOS to reread the disk directories. This isn't great, but it's a good emergency measure.

Drive Head Is Dirty. Try cleaning the drive head. Again, it's easy and might solve your problem.

Diskette Is Bad. It's fairly common for diskettes, particularly heavily used diskettes, to develop bad spots. If you always use the same diskette as your work diskette, try another one. If the problem goes away, use a disk tester like Norton's *DiskTest* or the Mace Utilities DIAGNOSE program on the original disk. Re-

cover what data remains and discard the diskette. (You do keep backups, don't you?)

Cable Is Loose. This sounds silly, but is it plugged in? Expansion/contraction and vibration can loosen the power and data cables on floppies. Maybe they weren't installed snugly in the beginning.

Cable Is Bad. The cables can get nicked when installing boards, replacing drives, or just removing the cover. How bad that is depends on which line gets nicked. A line nick on my XT-compatible laptop I mentioned before keeps the change line from working. My partner Pete had an AT that just plain wouldn't format the A drive. We always have lots of drives around, so we didn't worry much about it. One day he noticed a nick on the cable. He replaced the cable and the problem went away, never to return. It only takes a two-minute swap with another cable to find out for sure.

Controller Is Bad. Generally, you'll see a 601 error on powerup if the controller is malfunctioning. You could run the IBM diagnostics to test the controller, but, as was mentioned earlier, in some cases just swapping the controller is a quicker way.

Power Supply to Floppy Malfunctioning. At the back of the floppy where the line from the power supply connects you'll see four solder points. They'll probably be labeled, left to right, +12V GND GND +5V. These are the power lines the floppy needs to operate. You can test these while the floppy is operating with a multimeter. Put the black probe on GND and the red probe on either +12V or +5V. You should see power in the range (4.8, 5.2) for the 5-volt pin, and (11.5,12.6) for the 12-volt pin. If the values are outside of this range, the power supply is faulty.

While we're on the subject, I should mention that some "disk failures" are actually the fault of power spikes. Power protection is a good move here, as always.

Replacing the Drive Door (Full Height). When the PC first came out, people soon learned that the plastic doors on full height drives tend to break easily. The spring-loaded doors snap open, sometimes destroying themselves in the process. If the door can't be closed, the drive won't even try to read. Sometimes the door will only crack, leading to the mysterious case where the drive door is closed but DOS says the drive isn't ready.

Replacing the drive door is fairly easy. Finding a replacement is difficult. You can get replacements from:

Workman Associates
1925 E. Mountain St.
Pasadena, CA 91104
(818) 791-7979

First remove the screws that hold the drive to the computer case. Then pull the drive out a bit.

The drive is held to the spindle by a metal bar, which is held to the door by two screws right behind the drive face bezel. The bar is spring loaded, so hold it down with one finger while removing the old door. Then put the new door in, and fasten it to the bar with the two screws.

Saving a Dirty Floppy. Earlier I said, that in general, there's no need to clean a floppy diskette. That's *in general.*

I *have* seen some occasions when cleaning a floppy is appropriate—after flood damage, or when the odd glob of chocolate Haagen-Daaz ice cream gets onto the floppy. The instances when you clean a floppy are extremely rare.

Here's how to do it: You're going to remove the floppy diskette from its jacket, clean it, and replace it in a clean new jacket. Make sure you can tell which is the top of the floppy when you return the floppy to its jacket. I scratch the floppy near the center, well away from the data area, to mark it; 360K disks don't need this, as they generally have hub rings on top. Cut across the top of the floppy jacket. Carefully remove the floppy and place it on a clean, soft surface—a paper towel will do, but cheesecloth is preferable. The floppy can be wiped clean with a damp soft rag with warm-to-hot soapy water, then *gently* wiped dry with a soft clean cloth, and left to dry on a flat surface. I once saw an article claiming that floppies could be dried by stringing them up through the center hole, but I doubt that this would work well: the floppy could dry in a bent shape.

Wait until the floppy is dry. When I say *dry*, I mean it. A damp floppy could flake wet oxide bits onto your drive head and destroy or seriously incapacitate it. Then remove a blank floppy (this is the "sacrificial" floppy) from its case and throw it away. Use its case for the cleaned floppy. If you make a clean cut with a razor across the top of the disk jacket, the jacket can be reused.

This, by the way, is also useful sometimes when a floppy is mailed and the mailer is bent. (Some postal employees interpret *do not bend* written on the outside of a diskette mailer in the same way that kids understand *do not touch*.) If you can't unbend the case by running it along the table edge, take the floppy apart and steal another case.

If you've been successful here, *copy the floppy immediately*. If it's a distribution disk, send away for a replacement just in case. This is only a disaster recovery procedure, not a maintenance procedure.

The Floppy Drive Electronics. On each floppy drive, of whatever make, there's at least one printed circuit board. As always, these can be defective, but they tend to live fairly long if they survive the first few weeks. Unfortunately, there's no way to "burn in" these boards without burning out the drive stepper motor.

They aren't difficult to change, but I don't recommend it. I've never seen a floppy drive with a bad PC board. Further, it's very difficult to get replacements. Some floppy drive manufacturers won't sell you replacement doors, boards, and so on unless you're a repair facility licensed by them. Licensing usually requires some franchise money and attendance at their repair seminars. As I said before, for $100 throw away the floppy drive, or replace it and keep the bad one for parts.

Disk Rotation Speed. As we've seen, most floppies rotate at 300 rpm. The 1.2MB floppy drives on the AT rotate at 360 rpm. Small variations in this speed (plus or minus one percent) are okay, but greater differences can make the floppy nonfunctional or dangerous.

Dangerous? Yes. A few years ago, I was asked to install a copy of *dBase III* version 1.0 on an XT. It was a perfectly legal copy. When I went to install the program, it informed me that it was an illegal copy and refused to load. I tried installing it on other machines. It didn't work. Ashton-Tate first told me I was lying or mistaken, and finally (after threats of violence) sent me another master disk. Thankfully, Ashton-Tate has now commendably removed copy protection from their products. It took a while to reconstruct the problem.

What had happened was this: The floppy on the XT had a drive that was slightly incorrect in speed—not so different as to render it unusable for normal uses, but enough to upset the finicky copy protection system. Worse, the particular system being used at the time (Prolok, by Vault Corporation) would permanently alter a disk that it once saw as an illegal copy. Once Prolok thought a disk was bad, it would alter the disk so it would always seem bad. That was why

the disk wouldn't run on other XTs. (How did I eventually prove this? I have some friends at a software house who use Prolok. They Prolok-ed some disks, and we tried to load them on the XT. Same problem.) Copy protection is almost a quaint remembrance, but not yet. It pays to be able to test and adjust disk speed.

Big jumps up and down in speed can be due to slippage of the belt that drives the disk. These are only found on the bottoms of full-height drives or Qume half heights.

Testing and Adjusting Disk Speed. Recall that you'll probably never have this problem if you buy half-height drives (hint, hint), because they're direct drive rather than belt driven. Some of the newest ones don't even have a speed adjustment switch; logic on the drive automatically adjusts the speed, so there's no maintenance.

There are two basic ways to test disk speed: with a speed tester program and stroboscopically. We discussed using *TestDrive* earlier; it's an example of a software speed test.

What if you have a floppy with a incorrect rotational speed? Again, if it's a half-height, you're basically going to replace its circuit board. You can't really adjust a half-height's speed, as the speed is constantly adjusted by electronics on the circuit board atop the drive.

If you've got a full-height Tandon or CDC (also called MPI) drive, its speed can be adjusted by a *variable resistor* on the floppy. It's the tweaker screw with the red epoxy on it. The variable resistor is on a small printed circuit board sitting upright on the back of a Tandon floppy drive. It's a tall (about one inch) blue rectangular component, and there's a small screw atop it. The screw is probably partially covered with epoxy. The CDC drive has the variable resister on the circuit board on top. A Shugart half-height has it on the top circuit board on the right towards the front.

The speed adjustment variable resistor is usually easy to find, as it's often the only one on the floppy. Just break off the epoxy, adjust the variable resister with a screwdriver, and then put a dab of nail polish on it to hold the setting.

The other speed checking approach doesn't involve software. The bottoms of *some* (not all) disk drives have a design that looks like a test pattern. It's two concentric sets of spokes, one inside the other. These are used for a stroboscopic speed test. Here's how it works.

First, remove the drive. Then get the motor running: Issue DOS commands. Put a stroboscope flashing at 60 cycles per second (hz) on the spokes. The outer set of spokes will look like they're standing still when the speed is correct. (The inner set is for 50 cycles per second, European mains frequency). The easiest and cheapest 60 hz strobe is a common fluorescent bulb.

Remember to secure the variable resistor when you finish adjusting it. Either use electrician's epoxy or just regular nail polish. (Electrician's epoxy also comes in a variety of colors, unlike boring red-only epoxy.)

Chapter 16
Printer Software Troubleshooting

Generally a screwdriver isn't all you need to resolve printer problems. Many times, the problem is in the applications software, whether it's a commercial package like *WordPerfect* or some home-grown application. Printers have a powerful but complicated command language that allows programmers to tell the printer what to produce on a page. Just as a good PC troubleshooter must know some DOS in order to do a good job, so the printer repair or support person must be familiar with printer command languages. Here, I'll discuss writing batch files to test printer features and how to understand *your* printer's command language. In the process, I'll focus on the problems of soft fonts and font selection in laser printers.

Why should you learn your printer's programming codes, rather than letting the word processor do it? Here are five example batch files I've written for my laser printers that I find really useful:

- **EJECT** forces the printer to do a form feed and print whatever information is in its page buffer.

- **HP66** tells the HP to print 66-line pages. By default, the HP prints only 60 lines to a page. That confuses some software, which demands that all pages have 66 lines. The software sends 66 lines for what it thinks will be a page, and the HP prints out a full page and then a short page with just 6 lines on it. Argghh. If I run HP66 beforehand, there's no problem.
- **RESET** saves me the trouble of reaching over, pressing the *off line* button, and then holding down the *continue/reset* key to reset the printer.
- **SMALLPRT** shifts the printer into lineprinter mode.
- **LANDPRT** shifts the printer into lineprinter landscape mode, so I can print out really wide text.

I'll use a lot of examples from the HP Series II laser printers, but the general principles apply to all printers.

Most printers have sadly un-exploited features. I worked for several years with a Canon A2 laser printer (now

252

remaindered in some catalogs for $1,800, I note). It could not only do the usual underline, boldface, and the like, but it could expand any font horizontally and vertically, shade text, and support an amazing vector graphics language that produced really spectacular output. The problem was that it wasn't supported by most printer utilities. That meant I had to write a few printer drivers.

Many printers are treasure chests of features. This chapter discusses how to use those features.

The First Confusion: ASCII and Control Codes

Computers communicate among themselves and to their peripherals via a numeric code. This code represents characters—numbers, letters, punctuation, and the like. Fortunately, computer vendors have pretty much agreed on the use of a code called *ASCII*, the *American Standard Code for Information Interchange*. (For a business noted for incompatibility, it's pretty incredible that virtually all vendors support this.)

ASCII, in its most basic form, is just a set of correspondences between numeric codes and the letters they repre-

sent. You can see the printable ASCII codes in Table 16-1.

For example, to tell a printer to print *Hello*, a program would send five numeric codes: 72, 101, 108, 108, 111. It's kind of like a cryptogram.

Simple Programs to Send ASCII codes. There are a number of ways to get these codes to the printer. The simplest way:

1. Create a file with the desired printer codes called, let's say, X.
2. Then create a batch file that uses the COPY command to send the codes to the printer. Using file X as an example, the batch file would look like

@echo off
copy *x* prn

Users with a DOS previous to 3.3 should omit the @ sign from the echo off command. The file X should be a one-line set of printer codes terminated with a Ctrl-Z, NOT the usual Enter! For example, suppose you want to create a batch file that just tells the printer to print the

Table 16-1. The Printable ASCII Codes

32		42	*	52	4	62	>	72	H	82	R	92	\	102	f	112	p	122	z
33	!	43	+	53	5	63	?	73	I	83	S	93	]	103	g	113	q	123	{
34	"	44	,	54	6	64	@	74	J	84	T	94	^	104	h	114	r	124	|
35	#	45	-	55	7	65	A	75	K	85	U	95	—	105	i	115	s	125	}
36	$	46	.	56	8	66	B	76	L	86	V	96	'	106	j	116	t	126	~
37	%	47	/	57	9	67	C	77	M	87	W	97	a	107	k	117	u	127	DEL
38	&	48	0	58	:	68	D	78	N	88	X	98	b	108	l	118	v		
39	'	49	1	59	;	69	E	79	O	89	Y	99	c	109	m	119	w		
40	(	50	2	60	<	70	F	80	P	90	Z	100	d	110	n	120	x		
41	)	51	3	61	=	71	G	81	Q	91	[	101	e	111	o	121	y		

example, GREET.TXT, with only one line in it:

hello Ctrl-Z

Then invoke it with a batch file you can call GREET.BAT:

@echo off
copy greet.txt prn

The *echo off*, by the way, tells DOS not to clutter up the screen with a lot of batch messages.

Using DOS's Editor to Enter Batch Files. For my examples, I'll suggest that you enter batch files with the editor supplied free with DOS, EDLIN. Now, wait. Before you turn your nose up, consider: All expert types should know EDLIN. When you're at another person's machine, you can't count on them having your favorite text editor. There's nothing more unprofessional than hearing an expert whine, "Why don't you have a *real* editor. . . ." So here's a handy guide to EDLIN. When you see *n1* or *n2*, that means *substitute a number here.* The commands you need most are:

n1	Moves EDLIN to the line numbered n1 and allows you to edit that line
n1I	Allows you to type in lines which will be inserted starting at line n1
n1,n2D	Deletes lines n1 through n2
E	Saves the file and exits
Q	Exits without saving

When EDLIN allows you to edit a line, the DOS editing keys come in handy, also. The most useful ones are:

F3	Copies the current line to the end from edit buffer
Ins	Allows you to insert characters
Del	Removes characters from the edit buffer
Right arrow	Copies one character from edit buffer; F1 also does this.
Left arrow	Backs up one character

Trust me. One day, you'll thank me.

The Nonprinting ASCII Codes: Control Codes. You may have wondered why the codes started at 32. What about codes 0 to 31? Well, they're there, but they don't tell the printer to print a character. They tell the printer to *do something*.

When a printer gets to the end of a line, it knows to start a new line. How does it know that the line has ended? Simple: The program has not only sent the text to be printed, it also ends each line with two codes you can't see. The first one, called *Carriage Return*, says to send the print head back to the extreme left position. The second, called *Line Feed*, says to scroll the paper down one line. (Otherwise, we'd just overprint the same line again and again. Your document would just be one very black line.) Such an ASCII code that gives a command rather than just a character is called a *control code*. Carriage Return's control code is 13; Line Feed's is 10. Control codes used by printers follow in Table 16-2.

Table 16-2. Selected Control Codes

Name	Abbreviation	Decimal Code	Hex Code
Tab	HT	9	09
Line Feed	LF	10	0A
Form Feed	FF	12	0C
Carriage Return	CR	13	0D
Escape	ESC	27	1B

Since you now know control code 12 (Line Feed), you can now see how to write EJECT.BAT. Use two files, EJECT.TXT and EJECT.BAT.

Entering ASCII codes. By the way, how do you enter a code 12? There are keys on the keyboard for A, B, C, and so on, but not too much for the nonprinting codes. You enter them with a PC feature.

1. Hold down the Alt key.
2. With your other hand, type the ASCII code *using the numeric keypad*—it won't work with the numbers on the top key row.
3. Release the Alt key.

The character will pop up on the screen. Try it with 65, the code for capital *A*.

EJECT.TXT is created with EDLIN in the following way (what DOS types is in bold, what you type is in normal face):

C>edlin EJECT.TXT
new file
*i   ←tells EDLIN you want to
               enter lines
   1:^L^z ←is the code for a form feed.
*e   ←tells EDLIN to save it
C>

EJECT.BAT then is straightforward:

C>edlin eject.bat
new file
*i   ←tells EDLIN you want to
               enter lines
   1:copy eject.txt prn
   2:^z   ←tells EDLIN that's all
*e   ←tells EDLIN to save it
C>

By the way, where the batch file refers to *eject.txt*, it's helpful to include the entire path name, like *c:\pcodes*

eject.bat, so the batch file can be invoked from any subdirectory.

Most of these codes are pretty straightforward. *Form Feed* forces a new page. *Tab* moves the print head to the next tab stop. But what about Escape?

Escape (Esc) is a *prefix*. It's an easy way for printer manufacturers to build a huge library of possible control codes. Esc generally doesn't do anything by itself—it tells the printer the next character is a command, not a character to print. Here's an example.

An Okidata 92 (a kind of dot matrix printer) receives an Esc and then a *C*. Ordinarily, the Okidata would just print a *C*. But the Esc prefix means the *C* is a command, not a character. The Okidata then looks up what Esc-C means, and sees that it's now supposed to start underlining. It keeps underlining until it sees an Esc followed by a *D*. (How did I know that? I read the manual. Stay tuned.)

Putting Control Codes in Batch Files. Can you write a batch file to induce a printer to print underlined text? Sure, but there *is* one fly in the ointment.

The problem is in entering the Esc character. For DOS, EDLIN, and most text editors, Esc *means* something—it's not just a character to be entered. Some editors can be told, *the next keystroke I enter is just a keystroke—not a command*. It's just so with DOS's editor, EDLIN. I'd like to enter a line something like the following (<Esc> refers to the Esc key):

ECHO It's a <Esc>Cwonderful <Esc>D day.>PRN

But I don't really want to type *E, S,* and *C*. I want to just enter an Esc character. So there's a special sequence for entering Esc: type Ctrl-V followed by a [(square bracket). Again, we'll create a

Figure 16-1 Excerpt from HP Manual (1 of 4)

Table A-4. Printer Command Table*

FUNCTION	PARAMETER	PRINTER COMMAND	DECIMAL VALUE	HEXADECIMAL VALUE
JOB CONTROL COMMANDS				
RESET				
RESET		^{E}cE	027 069	1B 45
NUMBER OF COPIES	# of Copies (1-99)	^{E}c&l#X	027 038 108 #...# 088	1B 26 6C #...# 58
PAPER INPUT CONTROL				
	Eject Page	^{E}c&l∅H	027 038 108 048 072	1B 26 6C 30 48
	Feed from Tray	^{E}c&l1H	027 038 108 049 072	1B 26 6C 31 48
	Manual Feed	^{E}c&l2H	027 038 108 050 072	1D 26 6C 32 48
	Manual Env. Feed	^{E}c&l3H	027 038 108 051 072	1B 26 6C 33 48
PAGE LENGTH and SIZE				
PAGE SIZE	Executive	^{E}c&l1A	027 038 108 049 065	1B 26 6C 31 41
	Letter	^{E}c&l2A	027 038 108 050 065	1B 26 6C 32 41
	Legal	^{E}c&l3A	027 038 108 051 065	1B 26 6C 33 41
	A4	^{E}c&l26A	027 038 108 050 054 065	1B 26 6C 32 36 41
	Monarch	^{E}c&l80A	027 038 108 056 048 065	1B 26 6C 38 30 41
	Commercial 10	^{E}c&l81A	027 038 108 056 049 065	1B 26 6C 38 31 41
	International DL	^{E}c&l90A	027 038 108 057 048 065	1B 26 6C 39 30 41
	International C5	^{E}c&l91A	027 038 108 057 049 065	1B 26 6C 39 31 41
PAGE LENGTH	# of Lines	^{E}c&l#P	027 038 108 #...# 080	1B 26 6C #...# 50
ORIENTATION	Portrait	^{E}c&l∅O	027 038 108 048 079	1B 26 6C 30 4F
	Landscape	^{E}c&l1O	027 038 108 049 079	1B 26 6C 31 4F
MARGINS and TEXT LENGTH				
TOP MARGIN	# of Lines	^{E}c&l#E	027 038 108 #...# 069	1B 26 6C #...# 45
TEXT LENGTH	# of Lines	^{E}c&l#F	027 038 108 #...# 070	1B 26 6C #...# 46
LEFT MARGIN	Left (col #)	^{E}c&a#L	027 038 097 #...# 076	1B 26 61 #...# 4C
RIGHT MARGIN	Right (col #)	^{E}c&a#M	027 038 097 #...# 077	1B 26 61 #...# 4D
CLEAR HORIZONTAL MARGINS		^{E}c9	027 057	1B 39
PERFORATION SKIP MODE				
PERF SKIP	Disable	^{E}c&l∅L	027 038 108 048 076	1B 26 6C 30 4C
	Enable	^{E}c&l1L	027 038 108 049 076	1B 26 6C 31 4C
HORIZONTAL COLUMN SPACING				
HORIZONTAL MOTION INDEX	# of 1/20" Increments	^{E}c&k#H	027 038 107 #...# 072	1B 26 6B #...# 48
VERTICAL LINE SPACING				
VERTICAL MOTION INDEX	# of 1/48" Increments	^{E}c&l#C	027 038 108 #...# 067	1B 26 6C #...# 43
LINES/INCH	1 line/inch	^{E}c&l1D	027 038 108 049 068	1B 26 6C 31 44
	2 lines/inch	^{E}c&l2D	027 038 108 050 068	1B 26 6C 32 44
	3 lines/inch	^{E}c&l3D	027 038 108 051 068	1B 26 6C 33 44
	4 lines/inch	^{E}c&l4D	027 038 108 052 068	1B 26 6C 34 44
	6 lines/inch	^{E}c&l6D	027 038 108 054 068	1B 26 6C 36 44
	8 lines/inch	^{E}c&l8D	027 038 108 056 068	1B 26 6C 38 44
	12 lines/inch	^{E}c&l12D	027 038 108 049 050 068	1B 26 6C 31 32 44
	16 lines/inch	^{E}c&l16D	027 038 108 049 054 068	1B 26 6C 31 36 44
	24 lines/inch	^{E}c&l24D	027 038 108 050 052 068	1B 26 6C 32 34 44
	48 lines/inch	^{E}c&l48D	027 038 108 052 056 068	1B 26 6C 34 38 44

text file and a batch file. So, the EDLIN session looks something like

Making WONDER.TXT:

C>edlin wonder.txt
new file
*i   ←tells EDLIN I want to enter
             lines
   1:It's a Ctrl-V[CwonderfulCtrl-V[D
day.
   2:Ctrl-Z
*e   ←tells EDLIN to save it
C>
C>edlin wonder.bat
new file
*i   ←tells EDLIN you want to en-
             ter lines
   1:copy wonder.txt prn
   2:^z ←tells EDLIN that's all
*e   ←tells EDLIN to save it
C>

The computer's output is bold, my typing is in normal face.

Please note that the Ctrl-V trick probably doesn't work on your text editor or word processor. There's probably some other way to enter Esc. Consult your word processor or editor's manual.

Again, control codes other than Esc can be easily generated with the Alt key. It's just Esc that will give you trouble.

Finding Out the Details on Your Printer

How did I know <Esc> C starts underlining on the Okidata, and that <Esc> D stops underlining? I looked it up in the Okidata manual. Since Okidatas aren't the most common printers in the world (as you can see, I buy printers more for their features than their popularity),

Figure 16-2   Excerpt from HP Manual (2 of 4)

	FF=CR+FF	Ec&k3G	027 038 107 051 071	1B 26 6B 33 47
PUSH/POP POSITION				
PUSH/POP POSITION	Push	Ec&f0S	027 038 102 048 083	1B 26 66 30 53
	Pop	Ec&f1S	027 038 102 049 083	1B 26 66 31 53
FONT SELECTION				
ORIENTATION				
ORIENTATION	Portrait	Ec&l0O	027 038 108 048 079	1B 26 6C 30 4F
	Landscape	Ec&l1O	027 038 108 049 079	1B 26 6C 31 4F
SYMBOL SET SELECTION				
PRIMARY SYMBOL SET	HP Math7	Ec(0A	027 040 048 065	1B 28 30 41
	HP Line Draw	Ec(0B	027 040 048 066	1B 28 30 42
	ISO 60: Norwegian 1	Ec(0D	027 040 048 068	1B 28 30 44
	ISO 61: Norwegian 2	Ec(1D	027 040 049 068	1B 28 31 44
	HP Roman Extension	Ec(0E	027 040 048 089	1B 28 30 45
	ISO 4: United Kingdom	Ec(1E	027 040 049 069	1B 28 31 45
	ISO 25: French	Ec(0F	027 040 048 070	1B 28 30 46
	ISO 69: French	Ec(1F	027 040 049 070	1B 28 31 46
	HP German	Ec(0G	027 040 048 071	1B 28 30 47
	ISO 21: German	Ec(1G	027 040 049 071	1B 28 31 47
	HP Greek8	Ec(8G	027 040 056 71	1B 28 38 47
	ISO 15: Italian	Ec(0I	027 040 048 073	1B 28 30 49
	ISO 14: JIS ASCII	Ec(0K	027 040 048 075	1B 28 30 4B
	HP Katakana	Ec(1K	027 040 049 075	1B 28 31 4B
	ISO 57: Chinese	Ec(2K	027 040 050 075	1B 28 32 4B
	HP Math7	Ec(0M	027 040 048 077	1B 28 30 4D
	Technical	Ec(1M	027 040 049 077	1B 28 31 4D
	HP Math8	Ec(8M	027 040 056 77	1B 28 38 4D

Figure 16-3 Excerpt from HP Manual (3 of 4)

FUNCTION	PARAMETER	PRINTER COMMAND	DECIMAL VALUE	HEXADECIMAL VALUE
	ISO 100: ECMA-94 (Latin 1)	Ec(ØN	027 040 048 78	1B 28 30 4E
	OCR A	Ec(ØO	027 040 048 079	1B 28 30 4F
	OCR B	Ec(1O	027 040 049 079	1B 28 31 4F
	ISO 11: Swedish	Ec(ØS	027 040 048 083	1B 28 30 53
	HP Spanish	Ec(1S	027 040 049 083	1D 28 31 53
	ISO 17: Spanish	Ec(2S	027 040 050 083	1B 28 32 53
	ISO 10: Swedish	Ec(3S	027 040 051 083	1B 28 33 53
	ISO 16: Portuguese	Ec(4S	027 040 052 083	1B 28 34 53
	ISO 84: Portuguese	Ec(5S	027 040 053 083	1B 28 35 53
	ISO 85: Spanish	Ec(6S	027 040 054 083	1B 28 36 53
	ISO 6: ASCII	Ec(ØU	027 040 048 085	1B 28 30 55
	HP Legal	Ec(1U	027 040 049 085	1B 28 31 55
	ISO 2: IRV	Ec(2U	027 040 050 085	1B 28 32 55
	OEM-1	Ec(7U	027 040 055 85	1B 28 37 55
	HP Roman8	Ec(8U	027 040 056 85	1B 28 38 55
	PC-8	Ec(1ØU	027 040 049 048 085	1B 28 31 30 55
	PC-8 (D/N)	Ec(11U	027 040 049 049 085	1B 28 31 31 55
	HP Pi Font	Ec(15U	027 040 049 053 085	1B 28 31 35 55
SPACING				
PRIMARY SPACING	Proportional	Ec(s1P	027 040 115 049 080	1B 28 73 31 50
	Fixed	Ec(sØP	027 040 115 048 080	1B 28 73 30 50
PITCH				
PRIMARY PITCH	# CPI	Ec(s#H	027 040 115 #...# 072	1B 28 73 #...# 48
POINT SIZE				
PRIMARY POINT SIZE	# Pt.	Ec(s#V	027 040 115 #...# 086	1B 28 73 #...# 56
STYLE				
PRIMARY STYLE	Upright	Ec(sØS	027 040 115 048 083	1B 28 73 30 53
	Italic	Ec(s1S	027 040 115 049 083	1B 28 73 31 53
STROKE WEIGHT				
PRIMARY STROKE WEIGHT	Medium (0)	Ec(sØB	027 040 115 048 066	1B 28 73 30 42
	Bold (3)	Ec(s3B	027 040 115 051 066	1B 28 73 33 42
TYPEFACE				
PRIMARY TYPEFACE	Line Printer	Ec(sØT	027 040 115 048 084	1B 28 73 30 54
	Courier	Ec(s3T	027 040 115 051 084	1B 28 73 33 54
	Helv	Ec(s4T	027 040 115 052 084	1B 28 73 34 54
	Tms Rmn	Ec(s5T	027 040 115 053 084	1B 28 73 35 54
	Letter Gothic	Ec(s6T	027 040 115 054 084	1B 28 73 36 54
	Prestige	Ec(s8T	027 040 115 056 084	1B 28 73 38 54
	Presentations	Ec(s11T	027 040 115 049 049 084	1B 28 73 31 31 54
	Optima	Ec(s17T	027 040 115 049 055 084	1B 28 73 31 37 54
	ITC Garamond	Ec(s18T	027 040 115 049 056 084	1B 28 73 31 38 54
	Cooper Black	Ec(s19T	027 040 115 049 057 084	1B 28 73 31 39 54
	Coronet Bold	Ec(s20T	027 040 115 050 048 084	1B 28 73 32 40 54
	Broadway	Ec(s21T	027 040 115 050 049 084	1B 28 73 32 41 54

Figure 16-4   Excerpt from HP Manual (4 of 4)

FUNCTION	PARAMETER	PRINTER COMMAND	DECIMAL VALUE	HEXADECIMAL VALUE
	Bauer Bodoni Black Condensed	Ec(s22T	027 040 115 050 050 084	1B 28 73 32 42 54
	Century Schoolbook	Ec(s23T	027 040 115 050 051 084	1B 28 73 32 43 54
	University Roman	Ec(s24T	027 040 115 050 052 084	1B 28 73 32 44 54
FONT PITCH				
PRIMARY & SECONDARY FONT PITCH (Alternate Method)	10.00 Pitch	Ec&kØS	027 038 107 048 083	1B 26 6B 30 53
	16.66 Pitch	Ec&k2S	027 038 107 050 083	1B 26 6B 32 53
DEFAULT FONT	Primary Font	Ec(3@	027 040 051 064	1B 28 33 40
	Secondary Font	Ec)3@	027 041 051 064	1B 29 33 40
UNDERLINE				
UNDERLINE	Enable Fixed	Ec&dØD	027 038 100 048 068	1B 26 64 30 44
	Enable Floating	Ec&d3D	027 038 100 051 068	1B 26 64 33 44
	Disable	Ec&d@	027 038 100 064	1B 26 64 40

we'll take the rest of the examples in this section from the Hewlett-Packard series of LaserJet laser printers.

Examples

Here are some examples of batch files that make your printer perform functions from DOS. I'll only show the text files here. Remember that you must also write an accompanying batch file to copy the text file to the printer.

Compressed Print. Most printers have a way to move to a 15 or 16 Character-Per-Inch (CPI) mode. Having a batch file called SMALLPRT to shift the printer into this mode could be quite handy.

SMALLPRT.TXT:

<Esc>&l0O <Esc>(10U
        <Esc>(sp16.6h8.5vsbT

Of course, don't enter the letters *E*, *S*, and *C*: enter the Escape code. The initial string *l0O* is *lowercase L, zero,* and *uppercase letter O*. This is the command to select a 16.6 CPI font. For more explanation, see the next section on selecting laser fonts. Here's the file for landscape lineprinter fonts:

LANDPRT.TXT:

<Esc>&l1O <Esc>(10U
        <Esc>(sp16.6h8.5vsbT

The only difference is the initial part starts with *l1O* rather than *l0O*.

Reset. Sometimes you'd like to restore the printer to its power-on settings. One application in particular that can use this is *DisplayWrite*. Run *DisplayWrite*, and it sets up the printer for its own use and prints your document. The annoying thing is that *DisplayWrite* doesn't clean up after itself, perhaps leaving your printer in a strange mode of some kind. You can, of course, take the printer offline and reset it, or turn it off and then turn it back on. But a batch file is simpler, and besides, you can add it to the *DisplayWrite* batch file so the reset is automatic every time you use the program.

RESET.TXT:

<Esc>E

Sixty-six Lines Per Page on a Laser-Jet. One really annoying feature of laser printers is that they don't print 66 lines on a page. Instead, they force a margin of a few lines at top and bottom, and generally won't print more than 60 lines per page. There are a few programs that just plain assume there are 66 lines on a page, and so using them on a laser is a real pain—each page shows up as 60 lines on one page, 6 lines on the next, and a form feed.

When the LaserJet powers up, it wants a top margin of 0.5 inches and a bottom margin of 0.5 inches for a printing space of 10 inches. You *can* tell it to minimize the top margin (you can't tell it to eliminate it altogether), but can't tell it to get rid of the bottom margin. The laser engine is absolutely bent on only printing within 10.5 inches of 11-inch paper, so you can't do much to change that. But you can subtly change the height of each line so 66 lines fit in the 10.5 inches. Making the lines a bit shorter gives the printer the space to fit 66 lines, but that's not all. Finish by telling the printer that not only *can* it print 66 lines on a page, it *should* print 66 lines to a page.

So the whole code string looks like:

<Esc>E<Esc>&l14c1e7.64c66F

Selecting Fonts on an HP LaserJet

If you're working with a desktop publishing or word processing program and you want to use the many typefaces available on a laser printer, you generally have a fairly simple task; a couple of keystrokes and you've changed fonts. But suppose you want to convince *dBase* (or *Lotus)* to print a report in something other than the default font?

If you've ever looked at control codes for simpler printers, like an Epson dot matrix printer, you've seen that font selection is a fairly simple matter. But the LaserJet (and its later cousins) have many more fonts available, and so require a more complex font selection approach. Getting a handle on fonts for a LaserJet involves

- Understanding font terminology (yeah, there's jargon for that too)
- Understanding the font selection codes
- Knowing the printer's limitations in terms of memory and number of fonts

So here goes.

Font Attributes: Courier Isn't a Font. My friend Jane Mitchell, the LaserJet expert, says "You can always tell LaserJet novices. They call Courier a 'font.'" Courier isn't a font. (Jane *is* a printer snob.) It's a *typeface,* at least in HP terminology. Suppose you've printed a document using Courier, err, *typeface—* that's all just one font, right? Wrong. You change the font if you use boldface, italics, different sizes, or go to landscape mode, to name just a few possibilities.

Fonts are described by *eight* attributes:

- Orientation (portrait or landscape)
- Symbol Set (don't worry about this for the moment)
- Spacing (fixed vs. proportional)
- Pitch (width of characters)
- Points (height of characters)
- Style (upright vs. italic)
- Stroke Weight (light, normal, boldface)
- Typeface (Courier, Times Roman, and so on)

For example, you may be reading a document printed with the following characteristics:

- Portrait orientation
- IBM-US symbol set
- Proportionally spaced
- 10-point height
- Upright
- Normal weight
- Palatino typeface

Most of these characteristics are self-explanatory, but here are the details.

Orientation. This just refers to whether the text prints across the width of the page (as does the text that you're reading now), which is called *portrait mode*, or up the length of the page, in *landscape mode*. Landscape mode is mainly used to present wide data, such as a time line or a spreadsheet. Orientation is selected with the <Esc>&l#O code sequence, where # equals 0 for portrait or 1 for landscape. (Note that's an ampersand followed by a lowercase *L*, not the numeral 1. The ending character is the letter *O*, not a zero.) So standard paper for portrait mode is aligned 8.5 inches wide × 11 inches long; landscape is 11 inches wide × 8.5 inches long.

Symbol Set. Recall the discussion of the ASCII codes? Someone, at some point, decided to declare that the ASCII code for *A* is 65, and 65 it has remained. There *are* alternative code sets. The ASCII table earlier in the book did not include all codes, but rather the most-used ones. In actuality, there are 256 different codes that can refer to characters. Some are familiar, such as letters, digits, punctuation, and the like. Others may exist to support foreign language characters such as the cedilla ( ), or mathematical symbols like the greater than or equal to ($\geq$), or characters used to draw boxes.

There isn't just *one* ASCII code set. Variations are fairly common. Suppose you have an old Ohio Scientific computer. If you print the code 65 on your screen, you'll get the familiar old *A*, just as you would on an IBM compatible. But try printing code 254. On the Ohio Scientific, you'll see a little picture of an army tank. On the PC, you'll see a superscripted 2. Those are different *symbol sets.* Basically a symbol set relates code *X* with character *Y*.

As I've indicated, pretty much all symbol sets have 65 equaling *A*, 48 equaling 0, and the like. It's the codes from 0 to 31 and above 127 that tend to become

strange. A symbol set might vary from the PC symbol set because:

- The symbol set follows some international standard (ISO or ECMA).
- A computer manufacturer decided to be creative. For example, HP's microcomputers are supposed to be PC compatible, but the symbol set they show on their screens is a bit different from the IBM symbol set.
- The symbol set represents nonstandard items. Another example could be a symbol set with mathematical or legal symbols.
- The symbol set represents a non-Roman character set. Greek, Hebrew, Kanji, and Korean could be (and are) available as laser-loadable fonts.

HP has defined a number of symbol sets, but the ones you'll see most commonly are Roman-8 (the symbol set that's built into HP computers) and IBM-US (the symbol set found in most IBM compatibles). Recall that both symbol sets are very similar, in fact identical for the codes from 32 to 127. That means if all you're doing is printing simple English text, it really doesn't matter which of the two symbol sets you use. But the box drawing characters most IBM compatibles have aren't available to you if you use a Roman-8 symbol set. That's why, when you have a screen that looks like:

```
┌─────────────────────┐
│  Hello              │
└─────────────────────┘
```

the HP gives you a printout that looks like

Öáááááááááááááá¢
°   Hello   °
âáááááááááááááái

By the way, if you have a LaserJet Series II, the answer is to tell the HP to use the IBM-US symbol set. Just take the LJII offline, and then press and hold

Figure 16-5 LaserJet Series II Printer with Detail Showing Control Panel

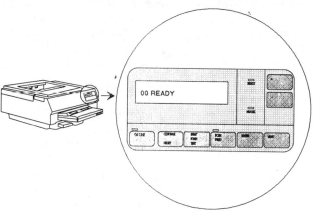

down the MENU key for about 8 seconds. (If you don't know where the control is, look at Figure 16-5.) *SYM SET = ROMAN-8* will appear on the LCD panel. Press the + key twice, and *SYM SET = IBM-US* will appear. Press the ENTER/RESET MENU key once. Then press the MENU key until READY appears. Reset the printer, and you're in business from that point on.

Symbol set is selected in software with the sequence <Esc>(###, where ### is the symbol set ID. The IDs for Roman-8 and IBM-US are 8U and 10U, respectively. Check your font documentation for the symbol sets of the fonts you've purchased. You can also find out symbol sets on an LJII by taking the printer offline and pressing PRINT

FONTS/TEST. You get output something like Figure 16-6. Note that the first Courier font shown has the 10U (IBM-US) symbol set. Note there's also an 8U, the Roman-8, and an 11U, the IBM-Danish/Norwegian symbol set.

Spacing. This either refers to *fixed* spacing as in a typewriter or *proportional* spacing as in this text, where smaller characters take up less space than larger characters. In fixed spacing, all characters take up the same amount of space, which must obviously be the amount required by the largest character in the character set (the capital *M*, for those who are interested). The escape sequence is <Esc>(s#P, where # = 0 for fixed and 1 for proportional.

Pitch. Pitch is the width of a charac-

Figure 16-6 Excerpt from LaserJet Series II Font Printout

```
-------- PORTRAIT FONTS --------
```

FONT ID	NAME	PITCH	POINT SIZE	SYMBOL SET	PRINT SAMPLE
INTERNAL FONTS					
I00	COURIER	10	12	10U	ABCDEfghij#$@[\]`` (|) ̄123 ¹6|┤┨╖╗ᵁ┴┸╚┌─╥┬╙╫┨■|απ¢
I01	COURIER	10	12	8U	ABCDEfghij#$@[\]^`(|)~123 ÀÁ˙ÇÑ¡¿£§êéàèëöÅØåæÄÜßÅDÒ
I02	COURIER	10	12	11U	ABCDEfghij#$@[\]`` (|) ̄123 ¹6|┤┨╖╗ᵁ┴┸╚┌─╥┬╙╫┨■|απ¢

ter. Note that pitch is only used for fixed spaced fonts—you'd never specify pitch when selecting a proportionally spaced font. Pitch is measured in characters per inch. Courier typefaces are typically 10 or 12 pitch, line printer faces are usually 15 or 16.6 pitch. For the truly brave, you can buy 20+ pitch faces for use in printing superwide spreadsheets. Note that pitch and spacing are reported on the series II Font Printout under the *pitch* column: If the font is fixed, the pitch is reported. Otherwise, the letters PS under the font indicate that the font is proportionally spaced. Pitch is selected with the <Esc>(s##.##H sequence, where ##.## is the pitch. To select a 16.6 pitch font, use Esc(s16.6H. The common 10-pitch Courier could be selected with <Esc>(s10H. When specifying decimal values, don't use more than two decimal places.

Height. Height is sometimes called the font's *points* because that's the unit used to measure height. A point is 1/72 inch. Height is reported in the Font Printout as *Point Size*. It's selected with the <Esc>(s##.##V sequence. For example, 12-point type could be selected with the Esc(s12V sequence.

Style. This tells if the font is upright (roman) or if it's italic. The code sequence <Esc>(s#S sets this, where # is 0 for roman, 1 for italic. Note that this doesn't direct the printer to italicize an existing upright font—the printer isn't capable of that. I make that point because people get confused that these commands can't *change* existing fonts, they only *select* fonts that are already in the printer. If no fonts match the criteria, tough. Beginners often think the LaserJet series II will make a font with an upright style into a font with an italic style; they don't realize that you must create (or buy) a font that has an italic style. Only then, once it's been downloaded to the printer, can you successfully issue a font select command that includes a request for italic style.

Stroke Weight. Specifies whether to select a font that's lightly drawn, normal, or boldface. This is activated with the <Esc>(s#B sequence, where # is an integer from −7 to 7. The setting 0 is normal, and 3 is normal bold.

Typeface. This describes how the typeface is drawn. Below, you can see how four different designers went about creating capital and lowercase A's.

Figure 16-7 Courier, Times Roman, Helvetica, and Lineprinter *A*

A A Aᴬ a a a ₐ

The different typefaces are supposed to convey different moods and messages. Typefaces are selected with the <Esc>(s#T command, where # refers to typeface number. Typeface numbers are shown in Table 16-3.

Table 16-3. HP Typeface Numbers

Value (#)	Typeface
0	Line Printer
3	Courier
4	Helvetica (Helv)
5	Times Roman (Tms Rmn)
6	Letter Gothic
8	Prestige
11	Presentations
17	Optima
18	Garamond
19	Cooper Black
20	Coronet Bold
21	Broadway
22	Bauer Bodoni Black Condensed
23	Century Schoolbook
24	University Roman
136	Bitstream Charter

Using Font Attributes to Select a Font. Now you understand the eight attributes (seven if you're talking proportional, as you recall). You understand that any given font is a unique combination of these eight attributes. How do you select a particular font?

Selecting Fonts with Complete Information and Using Shortcuts. Let's start with a simple example. Suppose the imaginary document you were reading earlier had the following attributes:

- Portrait orientation
- IBM-US symbol set
- Proportionally spaced
- 10-point height
- Upright
- Normal weight
- Palatino

Now let's match up commands with attributes:

Portrait orientation	<Esc>&l0O
IBM-US symbol set	<Esc>(10U
Proportionally spaced	<Esc>(s1P
12-point height	<Esc>(s12V
Upright	<Esc>(s0S
Normal weight	<Esc>(s0B
Charter typeface	<Esc>(s136T

String them all together, and you get

<Esc>& l0O<Esc>(10U
  <Esc>(s1P<Esc>(s10V<Esc>(s0S
      <Esc>(s0B<Esc>(s136T

Now, this will work, but there's no reason to type all that if it's not necessary. That's where LaserJet Shortcut #1 comes in handy.

LaserJet Shortcut #1:

When issuing several escape commands, *all of which begin with the same two-character string,* you can omit the Escape and the two characters on commands after the first. However, you must indicate that the shortened command is part of a series of commands by ending it with a *lowercase* letter rather than the uppercase letter used in the manual. The last command in the string should *retain* the uppercase letter. For example, rather than <Esc>(s0X<Esc>(s0B<Esc>(s5T, use <Esc>(s0x0b5T.

Apply LaserJet Shortcut #1 to the string, and it becomes

<Esc>& l0O<Esc>(10U
    <Esc>(s1p10v0s0b136T

You then can apply LaserJet Shortcut #2:

LaserJet Shortcut#2:

When the LaserJet expects a numeric value and you don't supply one, it assumes a value of 0.

That'll let us remove the zeros from 0s0b:

<Esc>& l0O<Esc>(10U
    <Esc>(s1p10vsb136T

And the font is selected. By the way, you can't remove the 0 from the first part of the command, for some reason.

Understanding How Fonts Are Selected in Depth. Suppose you give incorrect information, like requesting an 11-point font when only a 10 or a 12 is available? Suppose you request a font that's Portrait with typeface Courier, when the only fonts available are a Portrait Lineprinter and a Landscape Courier—would you get the Lineprinter or the Courier? The HP uses the following algorithm to match a request to a font.

1. First, look at the Orientation request, if included. If only one font matches the Orientation request, take it *and ignore the rest of the request.*

   Thus, if you requested a Portrait Courier and all the laser has is Portrait Lineprinter and Landscape Courier, you would get Portrait Lineprinter.
2. If there are *several* fonts that could meet the Orientation criterion (there probably are), look next to the Symbol Set request, if one was included. Is there something that matches both Orientation and Symbol Set? If there's only one font that matches the two exactly, take it and, again, ignore the rest of the request.

   Alternatively, if an invalid Symbol Set is requested, the current Symbol Set is taken *as if specified by the user.*
3. If, given the Orientation *and* the Symbol Set, there are several eligible fonts, look next to Spacing. As before, if this narrows things down to just one font, stop examining the font selection command. If proportional spacing is requested, but there are no proportional fonts in the eligible pool, just treat the request as if the user requested fixed spacing.
4. Still have more than one eligible font? Look to Pitch if Spacing is fixed. If you can match the pitch request (a 10-pitch is requested *and* a 10-pitch is in the pool of eligibles), use that to narrow the field of eligible fonts. If there's no match (for example, you requested an 11-pitch but only have 10 and 12 in the eligible pool), take the *next higher* pitch. If none are higher, take the closest lower.
5. If, given Orientation/Symbol Set/Spacing/Pitch, you still have more than one possible font, choose the font(s) in the pool with the closest Height to the requested Height. As before, stop if this narrows the field to one.
6. Look next to Style. If you can *match* the request to a font or fonts in the pool, do so. If not, just ignore the request. The vast majority of the fonts are 0 (upright) anyway, so it tends not to thin the pack very much.
7. If you're still trying to narrow down font possibilities, use Stroke Weight next. Recall that stroke weight varies from -7 (very light) to 7 (dark bold). If the printer can match the request, it will. If not, it will look for a more extreme weight. For example, if 3 isn't available, it will look first to 4, 5, 6, and 7; if -5 isn't available, it will look first to -6 and -7. Failing that, it will use the closest weight. This doesn't help narrowing things down very well, as most fonts are either 0 (normal) or 3 (bold).
8. Only *now* does the printer look at the Typeface. If there isn't an exact match, the request gets ignored.
9. Finally, if there are *still* more than

265

one possible font that meet all eight criteria, choose first from soft (downloaded) fonts, then cartridge fonts, and finally from built-in fonts. If there are multiple soft fonts that match, pick the one with the lowest font number.

To summarize, font characteristics are ranked in terms of importance. Here, they're arranged in descending order of importance:

1. Orientation
2. Symbol Set
3. Spacing
4. Pitch
5. Points
6. Style
7. Stroke Weight
8. Typeface

A Note on Using the IID and IIP Printers. The series IID and IIP printers have an extra feature the series II does not: They can rotate fonts. You needn't worry about whether a font is landscape or portrait. Just specify whether you want portrait or landscape.

Understand the difference. The series II uses orientation as a means to narrow down which printer font to use. The IIP and IID use this information as a command about whether or not to rotate an already-selected font. That means that IID and IIP font selection strings look like the II commands with one difference: the orientation string part goes at the end.

That means the previous font selection example would look like the following one on the IID or IIP:

<Esc>(10U<Esc>(s1p12vsb136T
<Esc> & l0O

Examples of Font Selection. Suppose your laser has the fonts in Table 16-4 loaded in it at the moment.

1. You request a Landscape 10U Proportional font, 12 point Courier. What do you get? The printer looks first at Orientation. There's only one Landscape font, so you get the line printer font with 8.5 point height.
2. You request a Portrait 10U Fixed 10-pitch 12-point Courier font. Which do you get? There's a soft font Courier and a built-in Courier. Both meet the criteria given: orientation, symbol set, spacing, pitch and height. It's a tie, and ties go to the soft font.
3. You request a Portrait 10U Propor-

Table 16-4. Loaded Fonts

Orient.	Sym. Set	Spacing	Pitch	Points	Style	Weight	Face	Source
Land.	0N	F	16.6	8.5	Uprt	Normal	Lineptr	B
Port.	10U	F	10	12	Uprt	Normal	Courier	S01
Port.	10U	F	10	12	Uprt	Normal	Courier	B
Port.	10U	PS	-	12	Uprt	Normal	Charter	S02
Port.	10U	PS	-	12	Uprt	Normal	Tms Rm	S03
Port.	10U	PS	-	10	Uprt	Normal	Tms Rm	S04

B—built in fonts.
Sxx—downloaded "soft" font # xx

tional 12 point Upright Normal font, as you want the 12-point Times Roman and can't remember the typeface code for Times Roman. Which do you get? Both the Charter and the 12-point Times Roman meet all criteria given. Now it's a tie. Charter happened to be loaded first, and so it got soft font ID S02. The Times Roman got ID S03, so it's ignored in favor of Charter.

4. You look up the Times Roman code, and request Portrait 10U Proportional 10.8 point Upright Normal Times Roman. What do you get? Since 10.8 is closer to 10 than to 12, you get the 10-point Times Roman. Had you asked for 11-point, there would have been a tie, since 10-point is as far from your request as is 12-point. The tie would have gone, again, to the soft font with the lower soft font ID number, and you'd end up with 12-point Times Roman.

Chapter 17
Printers and Printer Interfaces

Printers can be a real maintenance headache. As they produce tangible results (pieces of paper), malfunctions with printers can be more upsetting than their wholly-electronic brethren. For example, try telling *Lotus* you've got an Okidata printer when you have an Epson, and then print a graph. The printer will start spewing out pages, as if angry for being misrepresented.

Most of my printer problems—the vast majority—are software-related issues. The hardware problems seem more often to be cable or printer interface problems. I use mainly dot matrix and laser printers. Daisy wheel printers *are* prone to hardware failure, and I frankly recommend you don't buy them. Hewlett-Packard even offers a printer (the LaserJet IIP) that can be found for just a little over $900. At that price, it's cheaper than a daisy wheel that's one-fifth its speed, with a sheet feeder and peace and quiet thrown in for free.

Components

As always, components usually include a controller (the parallel or serial interface board), a cable, and a printer. The parallel port is simple enough that it's commonly included on other expansion boards.

Remember that the essence of peripheral troubleshooting is *isolate and test*.

Maintenance

A few things can be done to maintain printers of all types. Vacuum out the paper chaff periodically from the inside of the printer. Determine if there's a belt tightening mechanism for the printer; usually a motor moves the print head via a belt. Find the correct tension values. Keep a replacement belt on hand. In fact, find any small replaceable things and have them around beforehand. (Believe me, they're no picnic to find in a hurry.)

With a dry, soft cloth, clean both the paper path and the ribbon path. Most manufacturers suggest cleaning every six months. The ribbon path can build up a film of inky glop that causes the ribbon to jam. To clean this, go to a drug store and buy a dispenser box of 100 clear plastic gloves. Use them when working on the printer (but not chips and boards—that plastic can build up some mean static) so you don't have to wash your hands for hours to remove the ink. **Cleanup tip:** Hairspray seems to be good for removing ink from fabric. Cheap hairspray works a lot better than the expensive stuff. Spray it on the fabric, and rinse with cold water. A little soap will pick up the rest.

Most printers don't need to be lubricated in everyday use. In fact, oil can do considerable damage if applied to the wrong places. If you thoroughly disassemble the printer, you'll probably have to lubricate various points as you reassemble. If you intend to do this, I strongly recommend that you get a maintenance manual from the manufacturer. On dot matrix and daisy wheel printers, you can pretty safely lube the head transport rails: two long metal rods where the print head moves back and forth. As in the case of hard disks, it'd be a good idea to use a teflon-type lubricant.

Dot Matrix Printers. Here are a few things you can do to lengthen your dot matrix printer's life.

- **Be nice to the print head**. Dot matrix printers are, in general, very reliable. But keeping the print head cool is vital. Don't stack up things on or around the printer.

  Here's a tip that will both extend the life of your ribbon and your head: Put some WD40 lubricant on a used ink ribbon. Let it soak overnight. It'll produce good output the next day, and you won't damage the print head—in fact, putting the WD40 in the ink lubes the print heads. Let me stress, however, that this only applies to ink ribbons. If you have a thermal transfer printer, like an IBM Quietwriter or an Okimate 20, this won't work.

  Don't re-ink your ink cartridges

for the same reason that you shouldn't buy cheap cartridges: There's an acid in cheap inks that corrodes print heads, and a necessary lubricant in the inks of the more expensive cartridges. This isn't to say that kindly Mr. Jones with his discount office supplies store down the street is selling you dangerous cartridges, but it doesn't hurt to find out if the ink is the low-acid, lubricious type.

- **Teach your users not to turn the print platen rollers when the power is on**. The platen roller is turned by a stepper motor. The motor is doing its best to keep the platen right where it is. You frustrate the poor thing if you turn the platen against its will, and so it gets dangerously schizophrenic and commits suicide. Only turn the platen rollers when the power is off.

- **Don't engage both the friction feed and tractor feeds at the same time**. If you enable both the tractor feed and the friction feed, a tug-of-war between the two feeds results.

  The paper loses.

- **Teach users not to be parsimonious with paper**. Ever have a dot matrix printer that used fanfold paper that ended up curling around so the paper exiting out the back ended up running back in the front? The problem is that when people tear a sheet off the printer, they leave just a partial sheet sticking out the output end. That gets longer as the output grows, but it doesn't know quite where to go and so sometimes curls back into the box feeding the blank sheets. The answer is to "train" the paper: Shoot out three sheets from the back and start the paper folding up away from the input box.

269

Many times, a piece of cardboard taped between the *in* and *out* reduces the possibility of this happening. Better yet, when you initially feed paper to a printer, feed *several* sheets. Don't be stingy—it's just paper. If this makes you ecologically uncomfortable, don't you recycle all the wasted paper in your office anyway?

Laser Printers. The laser printer is very similar to a copy machine. Having said that, it's amazing that they're as reliable as they are.

The most common laser engines are made by Canon. The HP LaserJets, the AppleWriter, the Canon A1/A2, the QMS Kiss, and others are all built around the Canon engines. These need no maintenance except for a new cartridge every 3,500 copies or so. The cartridges, discounted, cost in the neighborhood of $70 and contain all that's needed for a routine maintenance:

- Toner
- Print drum
- Main corona wire

So, you're performing a routine maintenance every time you change your cartridge.

Lasers require proper ventilation and a fair amount of power; they draw about a kilowatt of electricity. Other than that, don't pour any Cokes in them and they'll last a long time. Here are a few PM tips:

- **Lasers need ventilation**. They'll generate a lot of heat. Plan to get rid of that heat somehow.
- **Don't use recharged cartridges unless you know the recharger isn't recharging more than once, and that it's recharging correctly**. Should

you use recharged cartridges? Here are the pros and cons.

- Pro:

    They're cheaper. Laser cartridges, especially those using the Canon engine, consist of a number of disparate items that ordinarily wear out: roller brushes, toner, and print drums, for example. These components wear out at different rates, and the recharge services claim that it's a shame to waste a good print drum just because the toner has run out.

- Con:

    The recharge people are right, up to a point. A print drum can probably stand one extra toner recharge—just one. If you buy recharged stuff, how do you know how many times it's been recharged?

    Further, some services are better than others. I've seen faultily recharged cartridges that spray toner all over the inside of the printer. It's quite distinctive. HP recognizes it and immediately voids your warranty, as they say expressly not to use recharged cartridges.

    Finally, some sources claim Canon is discouraging people from recharging by putting pieces of abrasive silicon in the toner. This chews up the print drum slowly, rendering it incapable of printing after 8,000 copies. The number you ordinarily see for a toner cartridge is 5,000.

- **Never ship a laser with a toner cartridge in place**. It can open up and cover the inside of the laser with toner.

So be careful of the "drill and fill" operators. Ensure that rechargers don't do more than one recharge; they should label their cartridges as "do not recharge" or the like. You should get a refill for the fuser wiper brush, and a cotton swab for your transfer corona.

- **When you change the cartridge, follow the instructions completely**. Don't just shake the cartridge, pull out the cellophane, and insert the cartridge. Replace the fuser roller brush and clean the transfer corona.

Troubleshooting Approaches

Isolate the Problem. As always, we'll try to isolate the problem: Is it something in the computer or its software? The printer interface? The cable? The printer? Is the printer plugged in, cabled, and *online?*

The steps I use are:

1. I'm assuming that this computer/ printer combination has worked before, and that you haven't done anything different from the last time it worked.
2. Check if it's online, plugged in, has paper, and is turned on.

   Does the printer have paper? One of my favorite tricks is to check that the main paper tray is full, and then accidentally and unwittingly select the empty alternate paper tray.
3. Cycle power switch on printer, reboot, and retry.

   The first thing I'd try would be to cycle the power switch and restart the software. One time I was experimenting with graphics on a daisy wheel printer, setting the vertical and horizontal motion increment to a very small value and then using periods (.) for graphic points. (I got some impressive results for a daisy wheel.) Anyway, I forgot to reset the motion increments. A secretary came by about an hour later, saying, "Mark, were you messing with the printer?" She

held out a letter which the printer had typed in a space of about one by two inches.

4. No luck? Do a self-test on the printer. Most printers have a built-in self test mode. Disconnect the printer from the computer and activate the self test (for more info on the HP laser printers, keep reading). Does it work okay? If not, swap the printer until you can examine it further. If it works now, *reconnect it immediately* or you'll embarrass yourself later.
5. If the printer self-tested okay, do a PrintScreen. DO NOT test a printer using *WordPerfect* or some other application; you don't know that it doesn't have a software problem.
6. Still no luck? Time to swap the cable (it's the easiest part to swap).
7. If necessary, replace the printer interface board and/or printer (not likely).

Cable Troubles. The role of cable lengths in noise and interference has been discussed before in this text, but another problem is overly long cables. Serial and parallel cables aren't supposed to be made up longer than 50 feet, and it's probably not a good idea to make up a parallel cable longer than 6 feet. If you're using long cables and getting mysterious errors, the cables could be the culprits. The cable won't refuse to work—you'll get odd transient errors.

How to solve this? One solution is offered by Intellicom. Called the Long Link Parallel Interface, it extends parallel cables by up to 7,000 feet. It's $199 from Priority 1 in southern California.

Remember to use the screws on the connector to secure your cable. I saw a situation wherein an Okidata printer printed consistently incorrect characters. I tried to understand the problem by comparing the ASCII codes of the desired characters to the codes actually

271

printed. I found in each case that bit 6 was *always 1*. It turned out that the wire for line 6 wasn't fully seated. Securing the connector did the job.

I found a similar problem with a broken wire in a cable. Here's an example. Suppose I tried to print *Hello* but got *Iekko*. Compare the codes of the desired and actual characters in Table 17-1.

Table 17-1. An Example Printer Cable Problem

Desired Character	Code	Actual Character	Code
H	01001000	I	01001001
e	01100101	e	01100101
l	01101100	k	01101101
l	01101100	k	01101101
o	01101111	o	01101111

The *e* and *o* aren't affected, but *H* and *l* are. Notice that in all cases the low bit is 1.

Port Problems. As you know, printers can have either a serial or parallel interface. On the PC, serial and parallel interfaces differ only by male connectors for serial interfaces and female connectors for parallel interfaces.

They're radically different, however. The parallel interface uses different voltages and handshakes than the serial interface. Printers can be bought with either serial or parallel interfaces. Given the choice, take parallel. It's a cleaner and faster interface. As laser printers get faster and, more particularly, support higher resolution, more high-speed interfaces will appear. For example, Apple uses an AppleTalk 230,000 bps interface to an Apple LaserWriter.

If you're using a serial interface, are the communications parameters set correctly? There are four:

- Speed (1200, 2400, 4800, 9600)
- Parity (Even, Odd, or None)
- Number of data bits (7 or 8)
- Number of stop bits (usually 1 or 2)

You'll find the parameters in the technical manual of the printer. Then construct the DOS commands:

MODE COM1: speed,parity,data bits,stop bits,p
MODE LPT1:=COM1:

In the first case, an example would be

MODE COM1:9600,N,8,1,P
MODE LPT1:=COM1:

meaning *9600 bits per second, no parity, 8 data bits, 1 stop bit*. The *P.* means it's a printer.

If you're having port problems, did you install something recently? Could something be conflicting with the printer port? Recall the story of the 5251 emulation board. You'd never imagine it, but the terminal emulation board was killing the port. Is there another printer port? Are they both set for LPT1: ?

Look at the Software. Here are some points to consider:

- **Internal printer software**. Generally, printers must be configured. The most common configuration problem is the AUTO LF, or *automatic line feed*. This says, *Every time you get a carriage return, assume there's a line feed with it*. If your computer sends line feeds anyway, everything comes out double spaced. This is generally adjustable with a DIP switch on the printer.

  Another configuration option—a more and more common one—is *printer emulation mode*. Many printers nowadays will emulate a Diablo 630 printer, or an Epson MX80, or an IBM Graphics Printer. If you've got your Hewlett Packard ThinkJet printer set up for IBM Graphics Printer emulation, don't tell your software you've got a ThinkJet, tell it you've got an IBM. This sounds simple, but you'd be surprised at the number of people who get tripped up on that one.

This final one is an indication of how international the electronics business is. Many printers speak foreign languages. If you set up your printer for British, you might get the Pounds Sterling sign rather than a dollar sign.

If you have a LaserJet series II, IID, or IIP, they don't have DIP switches but rather configuration memory. Take a look at the values there. Did the user get adventurous and convert the interface from parallel to serial on the laser printer?

- **Is the program configured for the printer?** If you just replaced your old Qume daisy wheel with a HP LaserJet, the software won't work unless you tell it you have a Laser-Jet.

Know your printer. If you're the local PC guru, get to know the bizarre escape sequences that put the printer through its paces.

On the DOS disk, there's a program called GRAPHICS.COM. It allows you to use the PrtSc key even when a graphic image is on the screen. (The original PC, without GRAPHICS, will simply ignore graphic data.) Don't install GRAPH-ICS unless you have an Epson or IBM printer. Otherwise, it won't work. This is because graphic printing commands vary widely among printer types. If you own a HP La-

serJet, an Okidata, or some other non-IBM printer, you'll need replacement software. Contact the manufacturer, or learn some assembler language and write such a routine yourself. I've had to do it for two printers, and it's not impossible. It does take some time the first time around, however.

- **The Mysterious Timeout**
  Sometimes the computer will sense that the printer is ignoring it: The printer will *time out*. When the computer says, *Abort, Retry, Ignore?* you say *Retry*, and it works fine. How can you address this problem? Simply add the following DOS command to your AUTOEXEC.BAT:

MODE LPT1:,,P

This instructs the computer to retry forever. This means, of course, that you must be sure to have a printer connected, or the first attempt to print will lock up the computer.

Beware, however. Remember the Compaq/PrtSc problem in an earlier chapter? If you don't have a printer attached and use MODE LPT1:,,P, the computer will wait forever to print. The three-finger salute (soft reboot) or the Big Red Switch are your only alternatives.

Has the Environment Changed? Everyone talks about it, but. . . .

A printer repairman told me about a day he'd had the previous October. He said that all over town a particular model of printer was failing left and right. He couldn't figure it out. We thought about it. Around the middle of October, we turn on the heat in Washington. That dries out the air and, in turn, the items in the work area. Chips don't mind being dried, but what about capacitors? Could a paper-type capacitor be malfunctioning because it was drying beyond a certain point?

A repair memo came around from the manufacturer a couple of months later. Sure enough, a particular capacitor didn't like it too dry. The answer: Either put a humidifier near the printer, or change the capacitor to a similar, less dryness-sensitive replacement. Moral: Be suspicious when the seasons change.

Power goes in this category, also. When you see the copier guys rolling in a new Xerox monster copier, ask gently what circuit breaker it'll be on.

Troubleshooting Dot Matrix Printers

Dot matrix printers are the cheap, noisy workhorse of the computer printer business. Is it worth trying to fix them? Give it a try; a lot of the tinkering won't take much time and, as the printer generally has a self-test mode, you can do a lot of testing fairly quickly. In this section, you'll see what can be done (by humans, that is) to adjust and fix printer problems. I must caution you, however. I've got to stress an important point (that's why I'll put it in a box):

WARNING:

If you're going to be working inside printers, be aware that printers, unlike PCs, don't generally have separate shielded power supplies. When you take the top off of a printer, you generally expose 110 volt AC lines. If the printer is plugged in (accidentally) when you disassemble it and you touch the wrong thing, **you could die**. Period. End of sentence. Make *sure* you unplug the printer before taking the top off of it.

I'm not kidding. Here's a good tip a printer repair tech gave me: Don't open the printer until you have the printer's plug *in your hand*. Don't let someone else do the unplugging. Someone else might inadvertently unplug the wrong thing, leaving the printer plugged in. Yeah, it's paranoid, but just because you're paranoid doesn't mean they're not out to get you.

Failure Points: Dot Matrix Printers

Here's a look at the things that fail most commonly and what to do about them. The weak points on the printer itself:

- The print head
- The print head data ribbon
- The stepper motor
- The circuit board

The last item, the circuit board, is often the price of the printer itself, so you might not want to bother with circuit boards.

The Print Head and Data Ribbon. The print head contains 9 to 24 stiff wires that are forced with solenoids to strike the ink ribbon and participate in forming characters on the paper. It can't hurt to lubricate the head with a little of the teflon lube mentioned before—just a little!

The print head is sensitive to too much heat. Print for too long a time, and the head just burns up. This isn't as much of a problem for the newer printers as it was for the old Epsons and Okidatas. The models out today have a *thermistor*, which shuts down the printer temporarily if the print head overheats. If the thermistor becomes ill, the printer shuts down regularly. Generally thermistors are pretty robust, but if such a thing happens, try changing the thermistor first; it's a lot cheaper than a print head.

Replacement print heads can be quite reasonably priced. Some companies are selling rebuilt Okidata heads for as little as $25.

How do you replace a print head? You have to do two things:

- Release the print head.
- Disconnect the print head from its ribbon cable.

The print head is held down with just two screws or, more often, just a pair of clips. Once freed, *be careful*—it's probably still connected to a ribbon cable that lets it communicate with the main circuit board. Removing the print head's cable is usually just a matter of gently pulling it out of a slot at the bottom of the print head. By the way, print heads are HOT, so be careful when removing one.

Once it's out, take a look at the ribbon. Is it kinked? That can cause problems. I once knew a woman who would *iron* Okidata cables to make them work. It worked. Clean its edges so it makes a nice contact with the print head.

I should mention also that if you get a continuous black line or white line through characters, it might not be the print head but the connections to the print head.

Replacing print heads on older Epson printers isn't really a reasonable fix, as the print heads and the main circuit board have a suicide pact. When the print head dies, it takes the circuit boards with it when it burns up.

A variation on the typical dot matrix printer is the *ink jet printer*. Rather than hammering at a ribbon, the ink jet squirts a narrow jet of ink at the paper. This is very quiet, but the jets tend to clog, leaving partial letters on the page. The answer here is simple: Remove the cartridge and push on the ink sack with a long, thin tool, like a straightened-out paper clip. The ink will push out the

small holes, unclogging them. With the HP ThinkJet, it's a pretty regular procedure. The Seiko color ink jet has the same problem.

Stepper Motors. The stepper motor drives the platen. As you've seen before, stepper motor failure can be caused by using the friction feed and tractor feed together or by users turning the platen knob by hand when the power is on. When you need one of these stepper motors, the printer companies will sell them to you for big bucks. But remove the stepper and it generally turns out to be a standard stepper that you can get at your local techie electronics supply place.

Stepper problems are sometimes manifested as slipped lines: the printer doesn't do a complete linefeed.

Miscellaneous Problems and Symptoms. Here are some things to look for:

- White bands in printout.

    Particularly showing up in graphics printout, this is a software problem. There's a software command that controls the distance between lines. Ordinarily, this distance is a bit wider than the height of a character. However, in graphics we wish our lines to just touch, so we can blanket the whole page with dots.

- Vertical lines wobble.

    The printer is attempting to print a column of vertical bars in order to form a vertical line. Each bar should be the exact same number of inches from the left margin, but the head is moving *bidirectionally*. This means, for example, that if the carriage is eight inches wide and the printer is trying to print a line three inches from the left margin, the print head must alternately move three inches from the left, then five inches from the right. This might sound trivial, but it only needs to be 1/70 inch off, and the wobble will be pronounced.

The answer is simple: Most printers have a command that tells them to print in one direction only. Set the printer for unidirectional printing, and the registration problem will go away.

Check the ribbon on the printer. Is it worn out in one spot, near the head? Does the ribbon move? Check the ribbon transport mechanism; it can become jammed.

- Transport motors can fail.

Is the ribbon moving? If not, check the ribbon transport motor. Will it turn? Is the connection to the motor intact?

What about gears—are they properly aligned?

- Jerky response.

This can be due to a bad connection between one of the motors and the drive board, or a bad drive board. Remove connections, clean, and see if the problem goes away. If not, examine the motor—does it turn easily? (Do this test with the power off.) Finally, try replacing the drive board.

- Printer doesn't print screen accurately.

This one is generally a software problem. If box-drawing characters on a screen appear as boldface *P, J,* or *M* characters, you've either got a printer that can't print the box drawing characters or that hasn't been enabled it to draw them. (Recall the discussion about this in the previous section about the LaserJet series II.) As the LJII comes out of the box, it uses something called the Roman-8 character set. Activate the menu on the LJII and choose PC-10. Now it'll print screens just fine. For

more information, see Chapter 16 on selecting fonts with the LaserJet series II.

Laser Printer Troubleshooting

Some parts of laser printers are very hot and work at quite high voltage. Please observe basic precautions when working inside lasers.

Testing Laser Printers (Including the Secret Service Test). There are three tests you can perform on the LaserJet series II:

1. System self test. This is basically what happens when you turn the printer on. You'll see a 05 or 05 SELF TEST code on the printer status panel. To start this, take the printer offline, and press and hold the PRINT FONTS/TEST key. It tests
   - Program ROM
   - Internal font ROM
   - RAM
   - Printer/Formatter interface
   - All LEDs
2. **Engine Test.** You can isolate problems simply to the printer engine with this test. There's a pen-sized hole on the right side of the printer, looking at it from the front. Figure 17-1 shows where to find it. Insert a pen or pencil in this hole and 15 ENGINE TEST will appear on the status panel. The test output should look like parallel thin lines running from the bottom to the top of the page.
3. **The Secret Service Test.** You probably already knew about the test button in the side of the laser printer, and of course one of the operator buttons on the front of the laser says TEST. But there's yet another test mode: the *service test mode*. You get to it by turning on

Figure 17-1 Engine Test Button Location

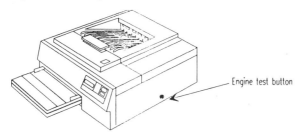

Engine test button

Figure 17-2 Close-up of LaserJet Service Test Output

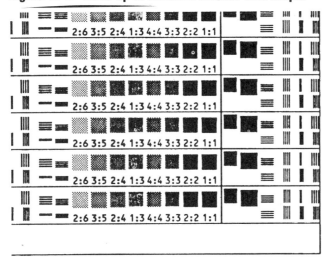

the system while holding down ONLINE, CONTINUE, and EN-TER. The display will power up blank. Now press CONTINUE followed by ENTER, and the display will show SERVICE MODE. It will do a short 05 TEST. Then press TEST and a more complex test output will appear, as you can see in Figure 17-2. This printout demonstrates registration and grayscales.

Why is it "secret?" I dunno. My strong recommendation is to run one of the tests when you first get the printer, and store it some-place. Use it at regular maintenance times as a measure of how the printer is doing as the years go on.

Resolving Laser Printing Problems. The two most common laser printing problems are:

- **Cloudy, faded output.** The whites aren't white and the blacks aren't black. Probable cause is either low toner or a corona wire that's dirty or damaged.
- **Regular horizontal lines or blotches across output**. Probable damage to a transport roller or print drum.

277

The laser works like a copier machine, by applying a large (6 kilovolt) charge to a print drum. The image is "etched" on the drum, then, in electricity. Toner is attracted to this electric charge, and so an image forms on the drum. Then the paper is fed, charged up to 6 KV in the opposite direction, and pressed against the print drum. This charge is transferred with a *corona wire*, a hair-thin wire. There are two coronas, the main corona (located in the print cartridge) and the transfer corona (located in the printer itself). The toner, being fickle, goes to the opposite charge on the paper, deserting the drum. Now we've got the toner on the paper, but toner is basically just yecchy black dust. How do we keep it from smearing on the paper? The paper runs against a hot *fusing roller* that melts the toner right into the paper. (Laser printers give new meaning to the phrase, *hot off the presses*.)

Corona Cleaning. The coronas attract toner, which can eventually get caked all over the wire and render it less useful. If the corona can't adequately charge or discharge the paper or print drum, toner doesn't go where it's supposed to, and so some toner stays in the "white" areas and not enough stays in the "black" areas. So clean your coronas. By the way, that's what the *intensity* dial does on your laser—it controls the amount of voltage put on the corona.

How do you keep the corona clean? The main corona is in the cartridge, so you could just be lazy and replace the cartridge. But don't do that; use the brush right inside the series II. Open the series II, and you won't be able to miss the green plastic brush. Note that it has one gray side with a suede-like feel. That's for cleaning the main corona. Now remove the cartridge. Note the slot atop the cartridge. You'll see that the suede end of the brush fits nicely into the

slot. Just run it across the slot once, and the corona's clean.

The *transfer corona* is a permanent fixture in the laser, so it *must* be cleaned. Near the brush for the main corona, the transfer corona is a hair-thin wire set in a shallow trough below the paper path. You can't directly get at the transfer corona because there's a web of monofilament crisscrossing above it. The monofilament keeps the paper from accidentally feeding into the trough and getting crunched up and snapping the delicate corona. You can clean it a little bit at a time with a cotton swab, some alcohol, and some patience. Dip the swab into the alcohol, then reach it between the monofilament and wipe the corona. Don't get too forceful, or you can break the corona, and then we're talking tears and sadness. Again, do this each time you change the cartridge or in the event of cloudy output.

Regular Blotches on Output. There are rubber paper transport rollers, metal fusing rollers, and a print drum in the system. Any of them can get out of round, get scratched, or just develop irregularities of some kind. These show up as regular blotches or lines in the output.

There are seven rollers and drums, so diagnosing sounds pretty rough. But HP and Canon helped us out again. All the rollers and drums have different diameters, and, again, two of the problem children are in the cartridge.

Diagnosing: As I've said, rollers and the print drums have different circumferences. Measure the distances between regular blotches to get a clue about which component has failed; then consult Figure 17-3.

Another reason for smudges in printout can be that the feed rollers or fuser rollers are dirty. Clean with a damp cloth and then dry. DO NOT try to clean the fuser rollers until the laser has been

Figure 17-3 Actual Distances Between Regular Laser Blotches and Causes

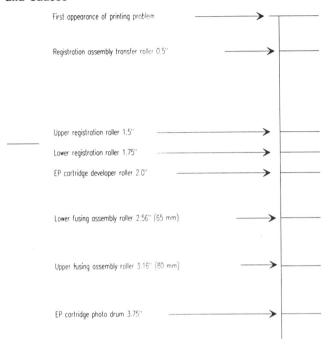

off for a couple of hours—they run very hot. (Go ahead and try. Believe me, you'll never try it again.)

Another thing that causes blurriness is if the image gets on the paper okay but isn't fused right. Electrical ground to the fuser might be faulty. This causes static buildup on the fuser, which shows up as smudges. Damp paper or paper with an unusual coating can inhibit the fusing or corona processes—try different paper. The controller circuit board could be defective, but I've never seen that.

It seems that everyone knows this, but I'll say it anyway: When a LJII says *toner low*, just remove the cartridge and shake it. The problem will go away for a while.

Images Are Stretched or Squashed. More than likely, this is caused by the drive motor not pulling the paper

through at the proper speed. Replacing it isn't fun, but it can be done.

LaserJet Potpourri. Here are some common LaserJet printer problems and solutions.

LJ Gives 20 Error. The number 20 means you asked the LJ to do something it doesn't have enough memory to do. One common reason for this is that you bought a LaserJet + or an LJ II without a memory expansion. I don't know why they do it, but HP sells both of these printers with only 512K of memory, when they need about 1MB to do full page graphics. Send a full page and you'll get a 20 error. Just press the CONTINUE key on the printer and you'll get a sheet with a half page of graphics on it, followed by another sheet with the remaining part.

The answer is generally to get more

279

memory. But another possibility is that you've filled the printer's memory with *fonts*. When I set up my printer to do desktop publishing, I end up loading about 650K of fonts into it. Even with the 1.5MB option I chose when I got my LJ II, I get into trouble with some really complicated graphics. The 850K left after loading the fonts is enough for *most* graphics, but complex pages can sometimes trigger a 20 error.

55 Error On Startup. Sometimes you'll get a 55 error when you turn the system on. It's pretty scary, particularly when you get out the shop manual and look it up. There are two main circuit boards in the bottom of the LaserJet series II: the *DC controller PCA* and the *interface PCA.* (By the way, when you read the HP manuals, they constantly refer to PCAs of various kinds. Look though you may in the manuals, they never define PCA. PCA is *Printed Circuit Assembly*—just another term for a circuit board.)

There are two circuit boards—oops, PCAs: the *DC controller board* handles charging and discharging the coronas, and the *interface board* controls the parallel and serial interfaces. If you smoke your interface with a switchbox, just replace the interface PCA. (In case you've never heard, HP says you can damage your LaserJet interface PCA with a parallel port switchbox. If they catch you at it, they'll void your warranty. I don't know if it really zaps parallel ports. I've used one for some time without trouble, and I've never met anyone who had actually experienced the problem.

Anyway, when powering up, the two boards do a communications test to ensure that they're talking all right. If there's noise in their communication, the 55 error pops up. The HP shop manual says you must replace the cards if you see this error, but don't sweat it too much. This error can just crop up due to the

normal inrush surge you get when you turn the machine on. I have a series II that was giving me 55 errors about every other day on power-up. I thought I'd have to do some surgery on the printer, but then I happened to move it to another outlet. Bingo! The error never returned. It seems that power noise of any kind on power-up shows up as a 55 error.

Fonts Do Not Appear on Page. Once you became a desktop publishing maven, you dazzled others with your documents, replete with fonts galore. But one day you found that a *really* font-intensive page wouldn't print. What's going on?

You've come up against a printer shortcoming, I'm afraid. HP lasers can only print a page with 16 fonts per page. Remember, Courier isn't a font. *Font* refers to a combination of typeface, size, stroke weight, and so on.

Actually, 16 fonts shouldn't be a great hindrance. The strangest page in this book has no more than 10 fonts on it.

Printer Picks Up Multiple Sheets. Believe it or not, this usually isn't the printer's fault. It's usually the paper. You need dry paper in order to get proper feed. Is the paper sitting in the tray for weeks at a time? Not good. When paper is removed from its ream wrapper, it's supposed to be dry. So how do you keep paper dry afterwards? If it gets used in a day or two, there's no problem. But if it sits in the tray for longer, it could pick up some humidity. Here are two thoughts: First, keep the paper in a large Tupperware lasagna carrier. It'll keep it dry as long as you burp it when you put the paper in the Tupperware. Another approach if the paper is already damp is to dry it out with a microwave oven. Also, make sure you've got the correct side of the paper up (look at the package for the arrow).

Laser Hiccups Periodically when Not in Use. Ever had your laser make a noise kind of like it was going to start printing a page, even when you didn't tell it to do anything? Don't worry. It's normal. There's a roller called the fuser roller that lives longer if it's rotated periodically. The series II rotates it every 30 minutes or so of inactivity.

Laser Printer Rumors and Truth. Here are a few laser rumors I've heard and the truth, where possible.

- **Font cartridges in the left cartridge have priority over those in the right**. Nope. The software fonts, you'll recall, establish priority on the basis of the order in which they were loaded, but the cartridges do not.
- **Toner is made of powdered chicken bones**. When I heard this one, I thought I'd make a million bucks organizing a chicken bone recycling center. No go, though. (I *did* mention it to some execs at a well-known fried chicken chain, however, so if you end up seeing separate trash cans for the bones, you'll know who's fault it is.)

- **If you press a certain set of keys on the laser panel, a full-page graphic of Elvis prints out with the caption, "The King Lives."** HP swears it ain't so, and I believe them. Here's why: There aren't enough ROMs on the laser circuit boards to store a bit-map of Elvis, even *before* he gained weight. I swear I heard this from someone in class, and others had heard of the rumor also. My guess is that HP brought it on themselves with the Secret Service Test Mode. (Why not tell everybody about it, anyway?)
- **There are pieces of glass in the toner of Canon-type cartridges that slowly chew up the print drum so it's completely unusable by about 8000 copies**. This supposedly is done to discourage rechargers.

  I just don't know. HP denies it, but Canon's patent application for the toner includes *silica particles*, conceivably another name for pieces of glass. That's for the next book, I suppose.

Chapter 18
Modems and Serial Interfaces

When computers first appeared on the scene, each was an island. Computer-to-computer communication mainly came in the form of moving tapes or card decks from one machine to another. We now jocularly refer to this method as *sneaker net* or *AdidasLAN*. Today, dozens of communications devices exist, from a simple null modem cable to a 100 Mbps FDDI fiber network adapter.

Communications troubleshooting is a separate book all in itself, so I won't try to cover the entire topic. Instead, I'll look at asynchronous communications in this chapter, and even then the discussion must for reasons of space be brief. A PC troubleshooter dealing with serial communications must understand:

- What is a RS-232.
- How it's supposed to be used.
- How it's actually used.
- How to test its components.

Components

The Asynchronous Port. On the computer end, the computer must be able to speak the language of asynchronous communications. A device to allow this to happen is variously called an asynchronous port, asynchronous adapter, communications port, or RS-232C port. RS-232 and RS-232C are the same thing, in fact, the "official" name nowadays is EIA 232D.

The connector type used is generally the standard 25-pin DB25-type connector, such as you'd find on the back of most modems. Ever since the advent of the AT, some adapters use a 9-pin connector. You won't miss the other 16 pins; asynchronous communication doesn't use them anyway. The signals are the same. You might have a cabling problem, however. We'll discuss cables later.

Most folks don't buy an asynchronous adapter on a board by itself. Instead, it usually appears on a multifunction board like the Q-Cor Quadboard or the AST SixPakPlus.

The Cable. Communications cables are the bane of a PC expert's existence. The problem is that no manufacturer follows the RS-232 standard exactly. Many manufacturers use a different connector or they rearrange the order of the pins. Neither is a fatal problem, just a pain in the neck.

Figure 18-1   A DB25 Connector

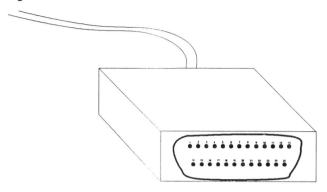

A very good introduction to the art of RS-232 cabling is the book *Computer Connection Mysteries Solved*, by Gerard Wideman and published by Sams. It's well written, funny, and about $14.

Cables can get broken wires and loose pins, or they can be wired incorrectly. The end of this chapter includes wiring diagrams for common PC cables.

The Modem. The most common use for a serial port is as a modem interface. Modems allow computers to communicate via regular phone lines. They've been around for decades. In the PC world, Hayes Microcomputer Products introduced the Smartmodem (now called the Smartmodem 300) in the early 80s, starting a whole new generation of communications devices. Now 2400 bps is fairly ubiquitous, and various kinds of 9600 bps modems are becoming more common. I use the US Robotics Courier HST, a $600 modem that transmits 17,600 bps over regular dial phone lines. (Unfortunately, it talks at 17,600 bps only to *other* Courier HSTs.)

Smart modems are *programmable* modems. What does programmable mean? Well, back in the old days, you had to flip switches to do things like:

● Turn echo on/off.

● Adjust speed, parity, data bits, stop bits.

● Turn a monitor speaker on/off.

Additionally, you had to dial your calls by hand. You can send a programmable modem commands via software in the computer. Thus, you can write a program to set some communications parameters, dial a number until it answers, log onto the computer at that number, download a file, and log off all without the operator having to be present. This is truly useful, but it also means you must learn the modem's rather terse command language in order to get the full benefits of your modem. Or you must trust that the person who wrote your communications software really knew modem programming.

The Communications Software. The best-known examples of asynchronous communications software are:

● Crosstalk by Microstuf/DCA

● Smartcom III by Hayes

● ProComm, a shareware program

If you have a programmable smart modem, as most of us do these days, be sure your communications software understands the modem's language. Most smart modems claim to use the same language as the market leader, Hayes, but if you're using a clone modem of some kind, it can't hurt to check with the software vendor. Most software has been checked out on the more popular clones, like the U.S. Robotics modems.

Maintenance

These systems are mainly solid state, and so have no moving parts. Modems tend to run hot, as many are designed around one or two fairly dense chips, so don't pile books atop the modem. Make sure the modem's ventilated. I know the ads all show a phone perched on top of a modem, but I'm not sure it's such a good idea. I know for a fact that it's *not* a good idea to stack up Smartmodems. I've had a fair amount of heat-related modem trouble. Be sure you know where to find the modem's warranty information. Most modems have two-year warranties, so don't throw that information out.

The usual stuff applies: Because they're large connectors with tiny pins, screw in the cables. Don't make the cables longer than they need to be. This increases the noise level in the cable, and if a loop of cable dangles down behind a table, it might get caught in something or be idly kicked. I know of a case where an analyst routinely braced his feet against the cable —just a nervous habit. The cable was even more nervous.

I mentioned power problems in the chapter on power supplies. *The same surge problems can appear on phone lines.* If the line from the phone company switching station to your computer is above-ground at any point, think seriously about a *phone line isolator* (sometimes called a *modem isolator*). This sits between the modem and the phone. Another measure of prevention is an RS-232 isolator. It sits between the modem and the

PC. I'd rather smoke a modem by itself than a modem and the rest of my system.

Examples of such products are offered by the Black Box Catalog:

AC/Modem Wall Protector (contains 2 AC outlets and phone protection) Stock # GB-SP136A $149.95

RS-232 In Line Surge Protector Stock # GB-SP140A $48.00

The Black Box Corporation PO Box 12800 Pittsburgh, PA 15241 (412) 746-5530

You might be wondering why I beat up on surge protectors before in the power section but am suggesting them now. It's mainly cost. Surges really don't occur that often over the phone line, save in the event of lightning. When that unlikely lightning strike occurs, you want something that'll take the brunt of the impulse and hopefully burn out in the process, cutting off the connection between your expensive equipment and the lightning. (I suppose you could also try knots in the phone cord.)

Troubleshooting

Communications troubleshooting can provide you with hours of mind-exercising delight, if you're the kind of person who likes puzzles. Let's see how to decompose the problem and isolate the bad component.

The Software First: Common Communications Software Problems. By far, the source of the greatest amount of communications trouble is the software. You must ensure that both parties in the communication have agreed on the *communication parameters:*

- Speed
- Parity (can be Even, Odd, or None)
- # data bits (can be 7 or 8)
- # stop bits (generally 1, could be 2)
- Local echo on/off

All communications packages have the ability to set these values. Don't worry about what the parameters mean, just be sure they match. Here are some common symptoms that can be software problems:

Cannot Connect. Check the parameters. If you cannot connect, or if you connect and see garbage ({ characters in particular), you've probably got a speed or data bits mismatch.

Cannot See Input. This is when you type but can't see what you're typing. Try a simple command, like whatever command you would use to get a file directory from the distant system. If the command gets a proper response from the other side, even though you can't see what you typed, the problem is that you must set your local echo to ON. *Local echo* tells your PC whether to display the characters you type or not. Sometimes you'll want to disable local echo, as the remote site will echo characters. In that case, you press a key, the key goes out to the remote site, the remote site echoes, and *then* you see the character you typed. Whether or not you need local echo is determined by whether or not the other site provides echoes.

Input is Double. You type a character, and two appear on the screen. Output from the other computer is normal. Answer: Set your local echo OFF.

Sometimes, there's no local echo command. In that case, the command has been misnamed (it's a common mistake) to *duplex*. (Duplex is something completely different, an engineering concern in data communications.) Then,

Half Duplex = Local Echo ON
Full Duplex = Local Echo OFF

Again, it's wrong terminology, but who cares as long as you can get the problem solved?

Is your software set up to talk to your modem? You instruct most modems to dial a number by sending the command ATD followed by the phone number. Some modems don't do it this way, however. (For a while, IBM sold an internal modem for their luggable PCs that used a strange command set.) As I said before, is your software equipped to talk to your modem?

Simple Hardware Problems. Besides software problems, basic hardware incompatibilities can keep your communications from successfully working.

Cannot Dial. You set up to dial the distant computer, but the modem doesn't respond. There are lots of possibilities:

- Is it plugged into the phone jack? It's common to share the modem's phone line with a regular phone and forget to plug the modem back in before using it.
- Is the modem plugged into the computer? Did the cable fall out? (It won't if you screw in the connectors.)
- Is the phone line working? Plug in a phone. Is there dial tone?
- Is it your phone system? If you have an in-house phone system, like a ROLM or Northern Telecom system, you might have to issue extra commands to dial out of your system (called a PBX). Check with your telecommunications manager.

Line Noise and Quality Problems. Sometimes it isn't hardware or software, it's the phone line itself. There are a few areas you can reasonably check:

- Quality of the communications provider
- The in-house wiring
- If call waiting is interrupting modem sessions

Controlling Which Long Distance Carrier You Use. Are you using a sufficiently high-quality carrier? If you're communicating at 2400 bps or faster, you might find that the only choice is (no, I don't own stock) AT&T. I know of only one modem (the US Robotics Courier HST that I've mentioned I use) that can handle 2400 bps over a non-AT&T line, and even then its success is sporadic. On the other hand, 1200 bps seems to work on *anything,* so I can use Joe Bob's Long Distance Service and Bowling Alley or whoever's cheaper at the time to save money on a minute-by-minute basis.

How do I do this? Simple. Equal access allowed us to pick our own long distance service (you remember, back in the early 80s, when the phone system went to pieces?). Most folks think they're stuck with what they've got, but that's not true at all.

You might be using an "off-brand" long distance service for your combined voice/data switched (dial) needs. You're not quite sure what long distance service you have? Simple. Dial (700) 555-4141 and you'll get a recorded message telling you. As I said, you'll find that 2400 bps and faster modems don't really do particularly well on a service other than AT&T. (That's not absolute, by the way: Some routes are well served by a number of carriers, and this is all based on my own subjective experience dialing into and out of Washington, D.C.) All isn't lost, however.

Rather than dialing long distance in the usual way:

1 (area code) (phone number),

dial instead

10288 1 (area code) (phone number)

to access AT&T.

Actually, there are codes for many of the big common carriers:

MCI	10222
Allnet	10444
Sprint	10333
ITT	10488

Please note that these codes are subject to change.

This also works for voice, by the way.

Suspending Call Waiting. Call waiting is a service whereby you can be talking on the phone but still be aware of incoming calls. A "beep" sound announces to you that someone is trying to get to you. You can tap the switchhook, and you're connected to the second caller.

That's great for busy people, but it's a problem for modems. The modem hears the beep as a suspension of carrier and drops the line. That's why the phone companies are in the process of reprogramming their phone switches to allow you to suspend call waiting for the duration of your conversation. How? Simple—just dial *70, then your phone number. The call waiting is suspended for the duration of the conversation. Once you hang up, the service is reestablished. Rotary phones users dial 1170.

Check The In-House Cable Plant. You might find that line noise is being created by your wiring in your building. You could have old wires that don't transmit as well as they once did, or someone may have run the wires near the high-voltage lines in the elevator shaft, or any one of a million things could go wrong with the in-house cable plant. Inspect your cable plant periodically. I had phone noise trouble in my building, so I restrung my phone lines and the problem went away. (I actually found that my termination block was made out of four wood screws driven into a rafter in the basement!)

Finally, did you check that the modem and the PC share a common ground? You may recall from the Power Protection chapter that plugging the PC and a peripheral into different outlets can lead to slight differences in the value of "electrical ground," leading to noisy communications.

The Port. The RS-232 port could be ill. As it's a bidirectional device (that is, it talks as well as listens), you can use a *loopback* to allow it to test itself. This involves putting a connector of some kind on the port to allow it to "hear" what it broadcasts; it can send out test messages and then compare them to what it receives. Serial ports do become ill. I don't know why. I presume it has something to do with the plugging and unplugging I do with my system (I do a large amount

of communications consulting, so I try a lot of equipment out on my system). For instance, I've had two Toshiba 1100+ laptop computers, and they both had something wrong with the serial port: Receive Data in the first one, Ring Indicate in the second. Probably 20 percent of the expansion boards I've worked with have had a serial problem. So it's worthwhile knowing how to diagnose such situations.

To test the port, you need to see what is happening on the various control lines. I recommend you get a *breakout box* to assist you in testing the communications port.

A simple, cheap, portable in-line breakout box is available from Hall-Comsec:

WireTap $42.50 plus $2.50 handling
Hall-Comsec, Inc.
2029 Manchester Dr.
Fort Collins, CO 80526
(303) 482-9905

Figure 18-2 A Typical Breakout Box

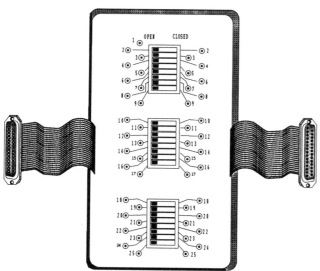

A breakout box allows you to proto-type a serial cable without soldering or pin crimping (the two most common methods of cable assembly). That's nice because you can then figure out what the correct cable configuration should be, even if you don't know how to solder or crimp, and then give that cable configu-ration to someone in your company or a technical service house to make the cable up for you. You see, getting the cable made (soldered) isn't too hard, once you've settled on a design. But making sure the cable's designed right is diffi-cult, so you'll want to do it yourself. A breakout box makes that possible.

Take a look at Figure 18-2. Regular 25-wire RS-232 type cables come in one side and go out the other. All 25 lines are represented on each side with large round metal posts. The breakout box comes with about a dozen wires that terminate in small plugs that mate with the posts. The way the box works is that you first design a cable, then run wires from post to post to make the connec-tions necessary for the cable, and plug in the breakout box (it serves as the cable) to the two devices you want to interface. The cable design either works or it doesn't.

Let's say you're trying to design a cable to allow your laptop to transfer data to your PC. The cables on either end are too short to connect the two devices, so first you'd run a couple of extension cables. Run a regular straight-through cable from the PC to one side of the breakout box, and a regular straight-through cable from the laptop to the other side of the breakout box.

Now you're ready to start proto-typing. First, figure to start your cable design with a cable that just connects 2 on the PC side to 3 on the laptop side, 3 on the PC side to 2 on the laptop side, and 7 on the PC side to 7 on the laptop side. (How did I know to try this? Hang on 'until the next section, when I de-scribe how to design an RS-232 cable.) To set this up, just run one of the wires from 2 on the PC side to 3 on the laptop side, and from 3 on the PC side to 2 on the laptop side. Actually, you don't have to run a wire from 7 to 7, as there are DIP switches for each of the 25 lines, and any time you want a "straight-through" con-nection all you need to do is to close the DIP switch for that particular line. (Make sure the others are all set to "open," or you'll have lots of "wires" in your cable that you didn't intend.)

Some breakout boxes have red and possibly green lights to indicate activity levels for various inputs and outputs in the RS-232 connection. Red lights indi-cate the presence of voltage in excess of $+3$ volts (interpreted as 0) and green lights indicate the presence of voltage below -3 volts (interpreted as 1). The 0 is the signal used to indicate *active* on the control leads.

How to Test a Serial Port Even if You Can't Spell RS-232. We'll use the public domain program PDIAGS.EXE found on lots of bulletin boards and a breakout box like the WireTap.

Any breakout box will do, as long as it has indicator lights. You could, alterna-tively, use a voltmeter, but the breakout box is a good investment.

1. Plug the breakout box directly into the serial connector on the back of the computer. Don't use a cable. You'll see activity on just three lines:

   line 2 = -3 volts (1)
   line 4 = $+3$ volts (0)
   line 20 = -3 volts (1)

2. Activate the diagnostics: PDIAGS. You'll see no change in the lights.

3. Get into the serial port diagnostic menu by pressing *S*.
4. Open the port: Alt-P followed by the letter *O* (not zero). Line 20 should reverse to value 0. If it does not, your *Data Terminal Ready* (DTR) line is defective.
5. Attach a jumper on the breakout box from line 20 to line 8. On the computer display, the word below CD should now be *YES*. It was *NO* before. If it does not, your *Carrier Detect* line is defective.
6. Now move the jumper so it runs from line 20 to line 6. On the computer display, the word below DSR should now be *YES*. (CD will be *NO* once more.) If it does not, your *Data Set Ready* line is defective.
7. Shut off local echo: Alt-P followed by *E*.
8. Move the jumper so it connects lines 2 and 3. Now press Alt-F. A "fox" message *(The quick brown fox jumped over the lazy dog 0123456789 times!)* should appear. If it does not, either your TXD (Transmit Data) or your RXD (Receive Data) lines are defective.
9. Quit by pressing Alt-Q, then *Q*.

If there's a problem, how can you fix it? Obviously, swapping the board is an alternative. But I've fixed a few serial ports when the wires connecting the printed circuit board to the connector were broken or when the main chips failed.

RS-232 interfaces (asynchronous ones, that is) are mainly designed around four chips:

• A large, easily identified chip called a *UART*, a *Universal Asynchronous Receiver/Transmitter*. It's often socketed (yay!), and it's often the problem circuit on asynchronous in-terfaces. There are two main UARTs:
  ▪ 8250, an older, more common model
  ▪ 16450, a faster improvement

These chips are upward compatible: you can remove an 8250 and put a 16450 in its place. By the way, that's handy information if you use OS/2. You see, in most applications you can't really see any difference between an 8250 and a 16450. But OS/2 won't recognize a serial port based on an 8250. A new 16450 is approximately $9, so if you're stuck with internal modems or multifunction cards that use 8250s but want to use OS/2, a chip swap could save the day.

• Two driver chips with model numbers 1488 and 1489. There are usually two 1488s and a 1489. When a power surge or lightning has damaged a serial port, it's often one of these two that have died. They're under $1 apiece, but sadly they're usually soldered, not socketed.

Again, there's no dishonor in choosing not to fix bad interface cards, so don't feel pressured to attempt such a fix. If, however, you do want to take a swing at it, try those three chips.

The Cable. If the port checks out okay, maybe the problem is the cable. Detach the breakout box from the computer, and then connect the cable you usually use to the computer. Connect the breakout box to the free end of the cable, and re-run the above tests. If one fails, you have a broken wire.

Remember that with cables, speed trades off for distance. If you have a hundred-foot RS-232 cable, you won't be able to run it at 38,400 bps. The exact same equipment and a two-foot cable might be able to run that speed. The only difference is in the length of the cable.

On the other hand, if you're reading this because the cable has never worked, turn to the later section, "Understanding RS-232 and Designing RS-232 Cables."

The Modem. Some modems have built-in loopback capabilities. (As you'll recall, this means they can send out test messages and then compare them to what they receive.) In that case, you can do simple loopback tests. If not, the best first procedure is just a modem swap. They're small and don't require much work to swap.

Do the front lights tell you anything? Put a breakout box in-line between the modem and the computer. You should see the following correspondences:

Table 18-1. Modem Front Panel Light/ RS-232 Line Correspondences

Modem Light	Red Light on Breakout Box
TR	20
MR	6
RD	3
SD	2
CD	8

When a specific modem light is on, the corresponding breakout box light should be on.

Are the connections correct? Many modems have two phone jacks: one to connect to the wall and one to pass through to the phone. Connect the "phone" jack to the wall, and you'll dial okay but disconnect as soon as the other side answers!

Do the modems match? Are you calling a 9600 bps modem with a 1200 bps modem? If so, is the 9600 smart enough to drop back to 1200? Is it an error-correcting modem, requiring another error-correcting modem in order to carry on a conversation?

The Phone Line. The phone line has four lines colored red, green, yellow, and black. Only the red and green ones are used. They should offer 48 volts DC power. If your phone varies greatly from this, call your repair office. Can you try the call on another line? Is it a multiextension phone—could someone be picking up the phone as your modem tries to dial?

Warning: The voltage on a normal phone line is enough to be felt. If you happen to measure the line while the phone is ringing, the voltage shoots up to almost 100 volts. Only do this test if you know what you're doing, please. We'd miss you.

The Other Side. Half of the possibility for problems comes from the folks with whom you're trying to communicate. Double check their parameters with them. Try calling out to another computer, if possible. Have they recently installed a new revision of *their* communication software or a new, "completely compatible" modem?

Going Further. Devices called *analog channel test units* exist that will actually test the phone line between you and the other party. They are, however, quite expensive. An *oscilloscope* can help you measure the frequencies being produced by your modem to see if they're within specification. Again, you might not want to go this far, as the required investment in test equipment isn't trivial.

Understanding RS-232 and Designing RS-232 Cables

You know, for a "standard," RS-232 sure provides a lot of headaches. Suppose you buy a device from vendor A with an RS-232 port on it, a device from vendor B with an RS-232 port on it, and try to hook them up. When it doesn't work (a common outcome), you start calling people.

Vendor A: "Trouble with our unit? Gosh, we don't really ever get bad reports on. . .wait! What are you trying to connect to? *Vendor B?* That's your trouble. That guy hasn't designed an interface that follows specs since the day he got into business."

So, reasonably, you're annoyed by the temerity of Vendor B and call him. He is jolly.

Vendor B: "Vendor A? Is that old rapscallion (not the actual word used) still lying about me? His problem is that he builds 'em to the standard, all right—the *1964* standard. He's building RS-232-A ports. We follow the 1984 conventions, and. . . ."

If you could get these two guys in the same room, you know what they'd say?

"Your problem is the cable; it's the wrong one." You wait expectantly for the solution, but they demur.

"Oh, no, we don't sell cables," they chorus, and then they leave.

You see, you'll probably face about two big RS-232 compatibility problems per year. You'll be a happier person if you can take a swing at fixing them. Look, if a simple country economist like myself can do it, so can you.

So here's the world's shortest course on what RS-232 is and how it works.

Why Is There RS-232? RS-232 basically exists so different vendors can offer equipment that can communicate with each other. I can buy a modem built before the PC was even designed and it'll work with the PC just fine, as they both use RS-232 to communicate. RS-232 is an example of a *physical interface*—an agreement among vendors about how to make equipment communicate.

For a simpler and more familiar example of a physical interface, think of the plug in your wall socket. It supplies 120 volts, 60 cycles per second (cps) alternating current. If you plug in something that uses, say, 200 volts, or 50 cycles per second, you'll get very unpleasant results, up to and including burning your house down. So when did you last check to be sure that something used 120 volt, 60 cps current? Probably never. You just figure that if you buy something with a regular power plug, it'll use the juice okay—and you're right. There's a standards agency, Underwriter's Laboratories, that concerns itself with power and safety, so you won't see a UL sticker on something you could plug into a wall socket and cause damage to yourself.

So the plug itself seems important. Can you, for instance, use your U.S. microwave in London? Nope, they have different power. The first problem you'd run up against is, again, the plug: your plug won't fit into any wall sockets. Can you just snip off the plug, install a British-type power plug, and use the wall current? No again: it's 220 volts, 50 cps.

Why use different plugs, then? Simple. The plug is a *reminder* about where the equipment can and cannot be used. The plug tells us something else, too: what devices *supply* power, and what devices *use* power. Female connectors indicate a device (like an extension cord) that supplies power. Male connectors indicate a device that uses power. This way, you don't plug a toaster into a microwave oven and think something will come of the marriage.

Behind the plug lies a lot of information about an interface standard. Know what plug you have, and you don't have to worry about things like the power's number of volts or cps. RS-232 does something similar.

Just as there are two members of the power interface, the user and the supplier, so are there two kinds of RS-232 interface. RS-232 was basically designed to allow computing devices called *DTEs (Data Terminal Equipment)*, to talk to communications devices called *DCEs (Data Circuit-terminating Equipment)*. So there's a DTE-type RS-232 interface and a DCE-type RS-232 interface. RS-232s use DB25 connectors: male DB25s go on the DTEs, female DB25s go on the DCEs.

DTE-type interfaces are most commonly found on PCs and printers. Devices with DCE-type interfaces include modems, mice, and digitizers. Remember that RS-232 is defined to allow DTE-type interfaces to communicate only with DCE-type interfaces.

How RS-232 Works. RS-232 is a digital interface, intended to communicate no more than 50 feet and at 20,000 bps. (Everybody uses it for greater distances and higher speeds, but 50/20,000 is the standard.) Communication is effected with 25 separate wires, each with their own task. RS-232 is defined for both synchronous and asynchronous communication, so there are a lot of lines in the 25 that we'll never use in asynchronous communications. As mentioned before, lines are either *on* with a voltage level of +3 volts or more, *off* below −3, or *neither* in between. *Flow control* is an important part of RS-232's purpose. Flow control allows a receiving device to say to a sending device, "STOP!!! My buffers (a small amount of memory in the printer itself) are overflowing—hang on a second and I'll get right back to you," and then allows it to print what's in its buffers and say, "Whew! I'm ready for more now."

There are ten important asynchronous lines in RS-232, as shown in Table 18-2. It's important to understand that each line is controlled by either one side or another. Line 2, for example, is viewed as an input by one side and an output by the other side. If both sides viewed it as an input, then both would be transmitting information that was never

received. So each line (except grounds, which are just electrical reference points) is controlled by one side or another. Note, by the way, that there's also a 9-pin version of the RS-232 connector. When I refer to pin numbers, I'm referring to the 25-pin numbers, not the 9-pin.

Here's the sequence of events for a normal RS-232 session.

1. **Both devices are powered up and indicate "power up" status.** The DTE powers up line 20 (DTR, Data Terminal Ready). The DCE powers up line 6 (DSR, Data Set Ready). A well-designed RS-232 interface won't communicate further until these two lines are activated. The DTE waits to see a signal on line 6, the DCE on line 20. Lines 6 and 20 are supposed to be *equipment check* signals that only indicate device power status, but they're sometimes used as flow control lines.

2. **The modem connects with another modem.** Data communication's no good without someone to communicate with, so next (in a modem/terminal situation, the situation envisioned by the RS-232 designers) a distant modem would be dialed. The modems exchange carriers (the high-pitched whine you hear when modems connect), and the modem (DCE) tells the terminal (DTE) about it over line 8, DCD (Data Carrier Detect). If you have a modem with red lights, by the way, you'll see the preceding in the lights: line 6 is attached to the light labeled MR, Modem Ready; line 20 is attached to line 20, Terminal Ready; and line 8 is attached to the light labeled CD, Carrier Detect.

3. **The terminal (DTE) asks the modem (DCE) if it's ready.** The terminal activates line 4, RTS (Request To Send). The modem, if ready, re-

Table 18-2. RS-232C Leads

Description	Pin # (25-pin)	Pin # (9-pin)	From	Abbreviation
DATA LEADS				
Transmit Data	2	3	DTE	TD
Receive Data	3	2	DCE	RD
POWER-ON INDICATOR LEADS				
Data Set Ready	6	6	DCE	DSR
Data Terminal Ready	20	4	DTE	DTR
LEADS THAT ANNOUNCE THAT AN OUTSIDE EVENT HAS TAKEN PLACE				
Data Carrier Detect	8	1	DCE	CD
Ring Indicator	22	9	DCE	RI
READY TO SEND/RECEIVE HANDSHAKE LEADS				
Request to Send	4	7	DTE	RTS
Clear to Send	5	8	DCE	CTS
GROUND LEADS				
Signal Ground	7	5	-	SG
Protective Ground	1	-	-	FG

sponds with line 5, CTS (Clear To Send). Now the handshake process is complete. Lines 4 and 5 are flow control lines

4. **Data is exchanged.** The terminal (DTE) passes information for the modem (DCE) to transmit along line 2. The modem passes information back to the terminal along line 3.

And that's all there is to RS-232.

A Note on Reality. The above description is nice and complete, so far as the standard goes. But most RS-232 interfaces aren't complete. Most PC software, for example, only looks at one handshake, such as 8 (Carrier Detect), 6 (Data Set Ready), or 5 (Clear To Send), and ignores the rest. Some software doesn't look at *any* control lines, so DTR, DSR, DCD, RTS, and CTS become irrelevant. That makes cabling easier but ignores the question of flow control.

The Simplest Cable. Let's start our cable discussion with the simplest cable: the straight-through. A straight-through cable connects a wire from line 1 on side 1 to line 1 on side 2, another wire from line 2 on side 1 to line 2 on side 2, another from line 3 on side 1 to line 3 on side 2, and so on. The standard PC-to-modem cable is an example of this cable. RS-232 was designed with this cable in mind.

A Simple Cable Problem. Let's say you have a modem with, it turns out, an unusual property: It never applies power to line 5, CTS. It powers up 6 (DSR) okay, and raises 8 when carrier is detected, but doesn't do anything on line 5. The PC side turns out to be "regulation" RS-232, and won't communicate without seeing a signal on line 5. Can a cable help?

Sure. The PC wants to see a signal on line 5, so let's give it one. Just construct a cable that's straight-through except for line 5. Then run a short wire (called a *jumper*) from line 8 on the PC side to line 5 on the PC side. Now when DCD (8) is raised, CTS (5) will also be raised, so line 5 shows activity, and the PC's interface is happy.

The Null Modem Problem: Designing Cables for Serial Printers and PC-to-PC Transfer. Many cables are just a variation on the straight-through cable. Of the rest, most are cables designed to solve something called the "null modem" problem. Recall that RS-232 is designed to connect DCEs to DTEs. Now ask, what kind of cable would connect a printer to a PC? Well, both the printer and the PC have DTE-type interfaces. According to the RS-232 standard, you can't directly connect two DTE interfaces. You're supposed to hook up a modem to the PC (recall that the modem's a DCE), hook up a modem to the printer, and then run the world's shortest phone wire between the modems. Of course, no one does this. A cable that allows us to avoid the two modems is called a *modem eliminator* or *null modem* cable.

What must be different to get two DTE's to talk to each other? First, both are trying to transmit on line 2 and receive on line 3. The answer here is pretty simple: just cross 2 and 3:

```
2-------------3
3-------------2
7-------------7
```

I included line 7 as it's the signal ground and must be present to ensure that both sides agree on what "+3 volts" means.

Now, even though this leaves all of the control leads out, it often works. Why? As I already mentioned, most software packages make only minimal use of the control leads, and most have no need of the control leads at all so long as flow control isn't needed—that is, so long as each side can keep up with the other. How do you know what control lines, if any, your software uses? Answer: You play around with it until you find out what works. Again, that's the beauty of a breakout box, it makes the "playing around" easier.

Next, we need to address the power status lines 6 and 20. As before, both are DTEs, so they're both activating line 20 and both looking for activity on line 6. As neither is activating 6, they'll wait forever. You can address this in one of two ways. One preserves the handshake, one doesn't.

The method that preserves the handshake is the crossover: 6 on side 1 to 20 on side 2 and 20 on side 1 to 6 on side 2. That brings our cable to this configuration:

```
2-------------3
3-------------2
6-------------20
7-------------7
20------------6
```

But there's another way. Consider that all each side wants is to see activity on line 6 about the same time that they provide a signal on line 20. Why not wrap the lines around on each side so each side is pushing its own buttons?

```
2-------------3
3-------------2
7-------------7
  6--|      |--20
 20--|      |--6
```

Which approach is better? It depends. If the equipment actually uses 6 and 20, and you need the handshake, use the crossover cable. If you're dealing with equipment that really doesn't use lines 6 and 20, it doesn't really matter. If you're running long cables and the number of wires in each cable is important cost-wise, the no-handshake approach is better. Sometimes you just want the silly thing to *work* and will worry about the flow control later.

There's a similar situation with RTS/CTS, so you can either cross 4 and 5 or jumper 4 to 5 on each side. I do the former in the following cable.

```
2-------------3
3-------------2
4-------------5
5-------------4
6-------------20
7-------------7
20------------6
```

Finally, don't forget the DCD line. Some software absolutely must see a DCD before it'll do anything. Since 8 is an input for both sides, we'll steal an active line to make it happy.

```
2-------------3
3-------------2
4-------------5
5-------------4
6--------- +-20
            |-8
7-------------7
8-- +
20-|----------6
```

Worrying About Flow Control. Once you've built your null modem cable, you should test that it handles flow control properly. Flow control is implemented either in hardware or software.

- Software flow control
  - XON/XOFF
  - ENQ/ACK
- Hardware flow control is done with one of the control lines, usually
  - DSR
  - CTS
  - DCD

The software approaches send *STOP!* characters back and forth when one side's buffers are overflowing. The hardware approaches just deactivate a line when the receiver needs a rest. Again, here's where your cable design is vitally important. If you neglect to include the particular handshake wire in your cable, there's no way for the computer to know that the printer is overflowing its buffer.

Another handshaking problem shows up when one side is using one method and the other side a different one, as when the PC is looking at CTS and the printer is using XON/XOFF.

You can test your handshake easily. Let's say you're hooking up a serial printer. Have the computer send a bunch of information to the printer to be printed; then do something like pulling the paper tray or taking the printer offline. See if the computer figures it out: does it stop sending information to the printer? Then put the paper tray back in, or put it back on line, and see if it picks up where it left off. Another way to force buffer overflows is to set the communications line at a high speed like 19,200 bps on a slow printer; the buffer will fill up fairly quickly.

Common Cables. Well, that's the RS-232 overview. Hopefully you're an RS-232 expert by now. But whether you are or not, here are a few basic cable diagrams. On the following pages, I present cables to connect:

- A PC (25-pin connector) to a modem
- An AT (9-pin connector) to a modem
- A PC (25-pin connector) to another PC, a printer, a PS/2
- An AT (9-pin connector) to another AT, a printer, a PS/2
- An AT to a PC, a printer, a PS/2

295

Figure 18-3   25-Pin DTE to 25-Pin DCE Cable Description

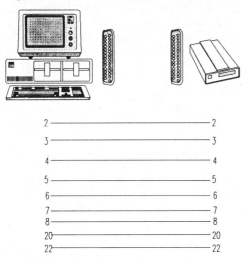

```
2 ——————————————————— 2
3 ——————————————————— 3
4 ——————————————————— 4
5 ——————————————————— 5
6 ——————————————————— 6
7 ——————————————————— 7
8 ——————————————————— 8
20 —————————————————— 20
22 —————————————————— 22
```

Figure 18-4   9-Pin DTE to 25-Pin DCE Cable Description

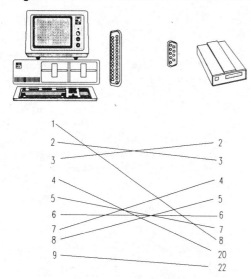

Figure 18-5   25-Pin DTE to 25-Pin DTE Null Modem Cable Description

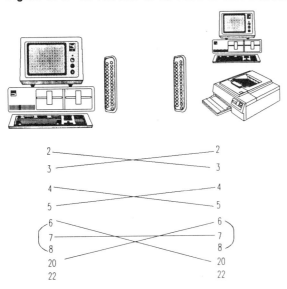

Figure 18-6   25-Pin DTE to 9-Pin DTE Null Modem Cable Description

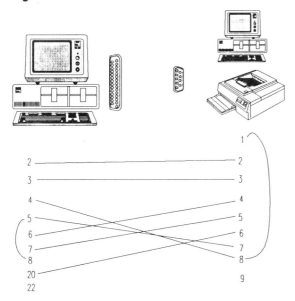

Figure 18-7   9-Pin DTE to 9-Pin DTE Null Modem Cable Description

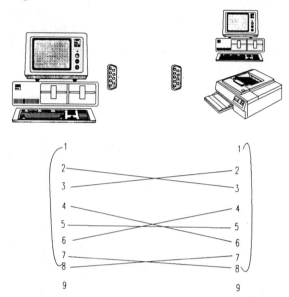

Chapter 19
Keyboards

The design of the PC keyboard has apparently kept IBM fairly busy since the original PC's inception. Every time a new PC is released, a new keyboard follows. They're all the same to troubleshoot, however.

Design and Components

Here's what makes them tick.

Keyboard Interfaces. There are four IBM-type keyboard interfaces, most incompatible with each other. They are:

- Original PC or XT keyboard (generally called the *XT keyboard)*
- Original AT keyboard (generally called the *AT keyboard)*
- The 101-key PS/2 keyboard (generally called the *enhanced keyboard*)
- 3270 PC keyboard

The XT and AT keyboards are different mainly because the XT keyboard puts the keyboard microprocessor in the keyboard, and the AT keyboard assumes the keyboard microprocessor is on the system board. They're generally incompatible: you can't use an XT keyboard on an AT or vice versa. Clone keyboards generally get around this by putting an XT/AT switch on the keyboard. The enhanced keyboard, on the other hand, will work on any machine without modification.

Switch/Contact Design. You'll find two basic kinds of keyboards:

- Switch-based
- Capacitive

The *switch-based keyboard* uses, as you'd imagine, microswitches for each key on the keyboard. The switches can become dirty. They can be cleaned sometimes, but often it's easier to just replace them. They're soldered, but it's an easy solder, as there are no delicate chips around. Then again, there's the fact (always hovering in the background with keyboards) that they're sufficiently cheap. Perhaps when a problem of this magnitude occurs, one should just throw away the keyboard and buy a new one. I've seen replacement keyboards for as little as $30. Clones tend to use this switch-type approach.

The IBM and AT&T keyboards are

capacitive. In the bottom of the keyboard is one large capacitive surface. Each keyboard key pushes a spring, which in turn pushes a paddle. The paddle makes an impression on the capacitive module. The capacitive module sends out signals, which are interpreted by the 8048 microprocessor in the keyboard. It sends the key's ID, called a *scan code,* to the PC. The PC then figures out what the key means.

This sounds more complicated (it is), but it involves one large capacitive module rather than a lot of prone-to-fail switches. Unfortunately, it limits you a bit as to what you can do to repair the keyboard.

As before, let's see what we can take apart and test.

The System Board Keyboard Interface. First is the interface between the keyboard cable and the system unit. This is a DIN plug, which has five pins, all odd-numbered. Figure 19-1 diagrams the connector on the system unit side.

Figure 19-1 Keyboard Interface Connector

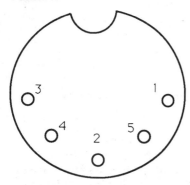

Test Voltages. Voltage between all pins and pin 4 should be in the range of 2–5.5 volts DC. If any of these voltages are wrong, the problem probably lies in the PC, the system board in particular. If they're okay, the problem is probably in the keyboard. Check the keyboard cable next.

The Keyboard Connector. The keyboard cable runs from a DIN connector, which attaches to the system unit, to a flat-jaw–type connector inside the keyboard housing. The cable has five wires and can be checked for continuity quickly with an ohmmeter. Disconnect the cable inside the keyboard and test each line.

Maintenance

The major item of maintenance for keyboards is *abstinence*. That is, abstinence from spilling things into the keyboard. The SafeSkin was discussed in Chapter 5 on maintenance; this is one protection approach. Another is to just be careful.

Periodically disconnect the keyboard and remove it from the general area of the PC. Pull the keytops off of it (be sure you have a similar keyboard nearby so you can put the keytops back in the right order). Then hold it upside-down and blow it clean with compressed air. The keytops aren't that tough to remove; I use one of those chip puller tools that comes with PC toolkits (recall that they're dangerous to use to actually pull *chips*) and find it to be just the tool for the job.

Troubleshooting

As with other items, you might want to view the keyboard as disposable. Replacement keyboards cost about $69 from discount houses. There are some simple things you can do before throwing out a keyboard, however.

Is It Plugged In? On the back of the IBM PC there are two identical ports, a cassette port and the keyboard port. Plugging the keyboard into the cassette port won't work. You could even destroy the keyboard if cassette instructions are sent to the cassette port. The ports should be labeled, but if they're not, the keyboard port is the one closer to the power supply.

Is It One Key or All Keys? If only one key is malfunctioning, check that key's spring. Remove the key by grabbing it with your fingers and pulling up. For the tough keys, fashion a hook from a paper clip or, again, use a chip puller. Under the key you'll see a spring. Replace the key cap and see if the problem goes away. If not, try pulling the spring out *just a little*. Then replace the key cap.

Checking the Cable Continuity. Next, test continuity of the cable. Turn the keyboard upside-down so the cable is coming out of the back of the keyboard, to the right. Remove the two screws. The bottom plate will swing back and up to remove.

You'll now see the cable splits to a single wire, which is grounded to the bottom plate, and a cable with a flat-jaw connector. Push apart the jaws of the connector to release. You can then test each of the five wires for continuity with your ohmmeter.

Completely Disassembling the Keyboard. This is not recommended for the fainthearted. You have a good chance of making things even worse, so don't do it unless there's no other hope. Warning: It'll take about four hours in total once you've taken the thing apart, put it back together wrong, figured out what you did wrong, taken it apart again, accidentally spilled all the pieces on the floor, and so on, before finally reassembling the keyboard.

Remove the main assembly from the keyboard case. With a vise or C clamps, set up a support for the keyboard assembly on the sides. If you don't support it on the sides, it will fall apart when you remove the back metal plate. (Remember those springs on each paddle?)

Alternatively, you can make your life easier by removing all the key tops. But, again, don't do it unless you have another keyboard around that you can use as a guide to replacing the keytops.

A printed circuit board with capacitive pads on it is held against a metal plate by ten metal tabs (five above, five below) and a hex screw. You must use a pliers to unbend the tabs enough to remove the plate. Position the assembly so the plate is on top (not the printed circuit board); then remove the metal plate.

The plate has been holding dozens of plastic paddles against the printed circuit card, one for each key. These are small, flat, easily-broken pieces of plastic shaped like the outline of a castle turret, or the rook piece in chess. You're looking for a broken paddle. Replace any broken paddles and replace the metal plate.

The other reason to attempt this is if you've poured hot coffee into the keyboard. Very carefully remove all of the paddles and clean them, as well as the brackets where they sit. Use alcohol to clean the capacitive PC board. Then reassemble and pray. I've seen this work, but only once.

Replacing the metal plate is a bit difficult. Position it correctly; then use clamps to hold one side together while you bend the tabs on the other side into place. Again, it's very easy to damage paddles at this point. Where do you get replacement paddles? I know of no one who sells them, so get them from the first keyboard that dies: it's good for 83 replacement paddles.

Replacement Keyboards

If you've gotten this far and no luck, don't despair. Many keyboard problems aren't solvable, and the things aren't that expensive anyway.

Keytronics, Datadesk, and Northgate make good replacement keyboards. Datadesk's are a bit cheaper, and they

301

have one that's programmable. What this means is that you can move that annoying ESC key somewhere else, set up your keyboard as a Dvorak keyboard, and the like.

Keytronics offers a keyboard with an online bar code reader. Other software allows you to print out bar codes with a dot matrix or laser printer. One firm I know of uses bar codes at the top of their document tracking forms so secretaries don't have to key (and sometimes miskey) a 12-digit document tracking ID every time they have to update the document tracking database.

Another interesting keyboard enhancer product is a touchpad. Keytronics offers the KB5153, which can be AT- or XT-compatible and includes a capacitive touchpad that doubles as a mouse emulator. It's considerably more expensive (about $280), but that, you'll recall, is the price IBM charged for the original simple PC keyboards, and you get a mouse in the process.

Chapter 20
Displays and Display Adapters

The display on a computer is the primary output device. It's the sort of thing people get opinionated about. Personally, I've had the cheapest video combination available for years, simple composite black-and-white monitor and color/graphics adapter, but some folks just gotta have high resolution displays. What's behind all this, and how much can we fix?

The display system has two components: a display and a display controller.

Displays

The first part of a display system is the display. Many options have grown up in the PC world. Some are cheap, some cost thousands of dollars. They all show at least 25 lines of 80-column text.

There are several basic kinds of monitors:

- Composite monochrome (around $75)
- Composite color ($200–$350)
- RGB ($350 +)
- EGA monitors (about $560 with adapter card)

- Direct drive TTL monochrome ($150)
- Multiscan ($500 +)

Table 20-1 helps you understand these monitors.

Table 20-1. PC Monitor Types

	Analog	Digital
Monochrome	Composite Monochrome	Monochrome TTL
Color	Color Composite	RGB:
		• CGA (640 × 200)
		• EGA (640 × 350)
		• VGA (640 × 480)

Composite monitors are a step better than a television set. They have greater resolution than a TV, but that's about it. Composites offer low expense and good quality. You see very few composite monitors in the PC world these days.

303

RGB (Red, Green, Blue) monitors offer better resolution for color text than do color composite monitors. The IBM Color Display and the Princeton Graphics HX12 are RGB monitors. RGBs are more expensive, with somewhat better quality than composite color. They attach to a display adapter with a nine-pin D-shell connector.

More expensive than regular RGB, *EGA (Enhanced Graphics Adapter) monitors* are RGB monitors with higher resolution. Characters are sharper and the display is steadier. In addition, these monitors can display 43 lines on a screen rather than the usual 25. This isn't as great as it sounds; most programs won't support the 43-line mode. Notable exceptions are *dBase* and the IBM Personal Editor, but more and more are joining the crowd. OS/2 even directly supports 43-line displays with the MODE command. An example of an EGA monitor is the IBM Enhanced Color Display. EGA has now been supplanted by *VGA (Video Graphics Array)*, an even higher resolution display standard (it can display 50 lines of text where EGA can only do 43).

Direct drive *TTL monitors* are monochromatic (generally amber and black or green and black) and offer high resolution, steady images. They're connected with nine-pin D-shell connector like the RGB, but don't plug one of these in where RGB is expected or vice versa. You honestly will get smoke. An example of this type is the IBM Monochrome Display.

Fairly expensive but most versatile are the *multiscan monitors*. These can serve as either an RGB or EGA monitor; they sense at what rate data is coming in and adjust their scan rates accordingly. The best-known example is the NEC Multisync monitor.

My personal favorite monitor these days is the *monochrome VGA monitor*. It is, as the name suggests, monochromatic, but it shows colors as shades of gray, the blue-gray of a black-and-white TV set. They're cheap: $170 to $300 for incredible resolution—better, in fact than color VGA for text. If you're word processing all day, you could do a lot worse (and spend a lot more money) than to buy a monochrome VGA. Of course, this requires a VGA board. Any VGA board will do, as the board doesn't know that its output is getting converted to shades of gray rather than colors. Again, take a look at this neglected market segment when shopping for monitors. It's much easier on the eyes than either monochrome direct-drive green screens or color screens.

Display Adapter Boards

The second part of a display subsystem is the controller board. There are quite a few in use currently, and they all have their characteristics. Table 20-2 summarizes them.

Since late 1988, there's been a revolution in video boards, and with good reason. *No-wait RAM, VRAM,* and *16-bit* are common adjectives when referring to today's video boards. Added to that are some old phrases, such as *interlaced* or *noninterlaced*. What does all this mean, and how important is it for you if you're buying a video board?

Video Memory Speeds. Memory in the PC is *memory mapped*. This means each location on the screen corresponds to a location in video memory. "Video memory," I hear you cry? Sure. Take a look at a video board. It has at least 4K and as much as one megabyte or more of memory chips on it—memory you can't put programs in, just video information. That means changing information on the screen is done by writing new information to this video memory.

Recall the discussion in Chapter 9 about memory speeds and wait states? I said that in order to increase the speed of

Table 20-2. Common PC Adapter Types

Adapter	Maximum Resolution/ Colors	Char. Box Size	Monitors Supported	Graphics Supported?
Color/Graphics (CGA)	640 × 200/2	8 × 8	● RGB ● Composite	√
Monochrome Display Adapter (MDA)	720 × 350/3	9 × 14	Mono. TTL	
Enhanced Graphics (EGA)	640 × 350/64	8 × 14	● RGB ● EGA ● Mono. TTL	√
Hercules Graphics Controller (HGC)	720 × 350/3	9 × 14	Mono. TTL	√
Multi Color Graphics Array (MCGA)	640 × 480/2	8 × 16	Analog RGB	√
Video Graphics Array (VGA)	640 × 480/ 262,144	9 × 16	Analog RGB	√
8514/A	1024 × 768/ 262,144	9 × 16	Analog RGB	√

the CPU, the designer must either increase the speed of the RAM in the system as well or insert *wait states*, clock ticks where the CPU just twiddles its thumbs. So how does the memory on video boards work in fast 286/386/486 machines? Well, you've never had to change the memory chips on a video board, have you? You guessed it; the video board inserts wait states when the machine is accessing video memory.

But *what* a pile of wait states. I once timed *29* wait states for each access in a generic EGA board. That means an operation that should take two clock cycles (the normal duration of a memory access) gets stretched out to *31* clocks. The machine is basically slowed down by a factor of 15 every time the video memory changes! That's why so many 386 machines don't update the screen much quicker than their XT counterparts.

What to do? Well, we're now seeing much faster video memories on the brand name video boards like Headlands

Technology, Paradise, or ATI. Faster video is also slowly filtering down to the clonemeisters. When buying video boards, ask for a *no wait state* video board, one with 100 nanoseconds (ns) or faster memory chips on it. But remember that the video board is sitting in an 8 Mhz bus slot, so it's *still* running at less than top speed. There's not much that can be done there: you can't make the bus run faster. (Look back to the bus discussion in Chapter 4 if you don't remember why the bus slots are 8 Mhz.) Some systems get greater speed by designing the video right into the motherboard. This is a feature that makes the PS/2s look faster than they really are.

Even faster than no wait state memory is *Video RAM, (VRAM)*. It's faster because the memory is *dual ported*: it can be read and written at the same time. This means the video circuitry can be interrogating the memory at the same time the CPU is altering it. That's not possible with normal RAM (such as is found on most video boards), and it introduces some delays on some systems. VRAM is nice, but it's expensive at the moment.

16-Bit and 8-Bit Video Boards. You know that more and more boards are becoming available in a 16-bit format usable only on AT-type machines. The 16-bit boards are faster than 8-bit boards, and speed is pretty important in the video department, so it seems logical that 16-bit video boards are appearing.

The 16-bit interfaces are desirable because when the CPU has to transport a lot of data onto the screen (such as when running Windows or some other graphical program), it can transport that data twice as fast. There is a downside, however. Some software is written with 8-bit boards firmly in mind, so much so that a 16-bit board's power is left unused. So don't be surprised if buying a 16-bit board doesn't do anything for your speed. Fast video memory will be noticeable in any case, however. Remember that just because today's software doesn't use the 16-bit interface, that doesn't mean tomorrow's won't. It can't hurt to "overbuy" a little today so as to be on track with the world tomorrow.

Which Video Board Should You Buy? If you're going to build a fast system, you'll need *all* your components to be fast, or you'll waste some time. There's no point in buying a 50 Mhz 486 with a video board with slow 250 ns video memory, and then trying to run Windows. The machine will spend most of its time in wait states generated by the video board. It's better to spend a little less on CPU speed and a little more on video speed. As I said before, VRAM is nice, but at this point the extra cost (in some cases more than doubling the price) isn't justified by the higher speed.

Is there a "ceiling" on video performance, a point of diminishing returns? The answer depends on the video mode your software uses. The answer is *yes* for text screens; however, it's *yes, but not for a long time* for graphics screens. Let's see why.

First, there are a fixed number of screens that the video board displays in a second (this is explained in the next section). Each screen is represented by some amount of video memory. In text mode, that amount of memory is fairly small, but in graphics mode it can be rather large. This means the top usable memory transfer speed is

Memory transfer speed = amount of video memory updated × screens shown/second

In text mode, VGA (or CGA or EGA or MDA, for that matter) uses 4000 bytes to represent a screen. The number of screens per second varies from 50 (for MDA) to 60 (CGA, EGA) to 70 (VGA). Assume that VGA is showing its usual 70 screens per second and changing each screen *completely,* so the CPU must transfer 70 80 × 25 screens in a second. That implies a data transfer rate of 4000 bytes/ screen × 70 screens/second = 280,000 bytes per second. 280,000 bytes per second implies that each byte transfer can take up to 1/280,000 second, or 3571 nanoseconds—*loads* of time, even for old video boards. Figure each transfer requires about eight clocks: two for the memory write and six for other overhead (those numbers are just an educated guess). Eight clocks fit easily into 3571 ns.

But what about graphics mode? Here, the computer controls the color of each dot on the screen, and high resolution graphics can be quite memory-intensive indeed. VGA uses 256K for its highest resolution graphics modes, and some "super" VGAs use 512K for even more colors and dots. Now we're looking at 70 screens of 256K apiece. 70 screens/ second × 256K bytes/screen = 22.5 megabytes/second. 22.5 megabytes/second implies that there are, then, up to 1/22.5MB or 44.4 nanoseconds for each byte transfer—not very much time! Eight clocks in 44 nanoseconds means a clock rate of 5.5 nanoseconds. If the clock ticks were only 5.5 nanoseconds wide, the PC's clock rate would be about 180 Mhz, a little faster than current offerings.

I use a 16-bit Compaq VGA board on one of my machines and am very happy with it. It has the dual virtue of no wait state memory *and* 16-bit connections, so I'd recommend it to anyone. No VRAM, but then I wanted to keep the prices in the three-digit range. If I were buying today, I might look at the ATI, Paradise, and Headlands (Video 7) offerings.

Vertical Trace Frequency. As you probably know, CRTs work by painting lines of dots on the screen. At any point in time, only one dot on the whole screen is being illuminated. You don't see this, fortunately, because (1) the phosphor coating on the CRT tube retains its brightness briefly, and (2) your eyes contain *visual purple*, which is responsible for what biologists call *persistence of vision*. To maintain the illusion of a steady screen, about 60 screens must be painted onto the CRT each second. Displaying significantly fewer screens per second will lead to flicker. Some people have very fast eyes and see flicker in normal screens. I'm thankful for slow eyes.

The rate of screens per second is called the *vertical trace frequency*. It's 60 hz for most screens, 50 for monochrome TTL monitors. The TTL monitors often combat the flicker problem by using high persistence phosphor on the inside of the CRT. This adds persistence, aiding your eye. This isn't called "screens/second," but hertz; it's not correct, but everybody does it. The high-persistence phosphor screens can get away with 50 screens/second without flicker because of the high persistence, but there's a price: high persistence means "ghosting" when the screen updates quickly.

The horizontal scan frequency is more interesting. The monitor must draw several hundred lines in order to display one screen. As stated before, it must also display around 60 screens per second. A composite monitor, for instance, uses 262 lines per screen. You can only use 200 lines; the rest are wasted. 262 lines/screen × 60 screens/second = roughly 15,700 lines per second. This is referred to as a 15.7 Khz *horizontal scan frequency*. Again, "hertz" isn't really being used correctly here; it should refer to *cycles per second*, not lines or screens. But everyone uses this phrase, so you and I will, too. Table 20-3 has the values for common monitor types.

Another monitor buzzword is *dot pitch*. This is how narrow each dot is. The

Table 20-3. Statistics for Common Monitor Types

Type	Screens/Second	Lines/Screen		Horizontal Scan Frequency
		Actual	Used	
Composite	60	262	200	15.7 Khz
RGB	60	262	200	15.7 Khz
TTL Direct Drive	50	368	350	18.4 Khz
EGA	60	363	350	21.8 Khz
Multiscan Monitors	depends	up to 500		up to 50Khz
VGA	70	525	480	35 Khz

narrower, the better: the characters can be sharper. Nowadays many manufacturers offer .31 mm or better.

Interlacing. Some computers, like the Commodore Amiga, seem to get unbelievable resolution out of regular composite monitors.

How is this possible? An EGA display needs 350 lines, and the absolute maximum that a composite has is 262 lines.

The trick is this: It actually shows each screen as *two* screens, one immediately following another. First come the even lines, then the odd lines. There's no free lunch, however; this means instead of 60 screens, we get 30 screens/second, as each "screen" requires two screen paints. This process of alternating odd/even to get greater resolution is called *interlacing*. The screen uses the top 175 lines to display 350 lines. Thus, it not only looks weird, it looks squat and weird, and makes the screen seem flickery. Adding a glare screen reduces this somewhat.

Maintenance

There's not much to say here. Treat the display board like another PC board. Ensure that the connectors are secured, as the little pins can bend over time. Be very sure not to plug RGB into monochrome and vice versa, even if they *do* use the same connector.

Clean the display when it gets too dust-filmed. There's one item to be careful about, however. I've heard of a case wherein a NEC Multisync monitor actually imploded when cleaned with a damp cloth while turned on. I'm not sure I believe it, but maybe you want to turn the monitor off before cleaning it.

Troubleshooting

Some of the dumbest monitor problems are the easiest to solve.

- Is it turned on?
- Is the brightness or contrast turned down?
- Is everything plugged in? Is it plugged into the right place?
- If you're using a multiple-display board, are the DIP switches and jumpers set for a mono display or RGB? If you set it for RGB and plugged in mono, throw away the mono monitor.
- Has someone cleverly convinced DOS to display black letters on a black background? Reboot.
- Did you hear a long beep and two short ones, indicating a bad video card?
- If using a multispeed computer, is it in Turbo mode? The display memory might not be fast enough in the higher speed mode. Drop back to the lower speed. If the problem goes away, you'll probably have to replace the memory on the display board. (Remember the ten Mhz bus problem.)
- There are non-video reasons for a display "malfunction," like when the power supply has killed the computer. If the display is dead, do you hear the power supply fan? Try typing *DIR* blind. If the computer is okay but the display is bad, you'll see the drive light come on. Use a sound-emitting program to see if the computer is functioning.
- Are the motherboard DIP switches set correctly for your display adapter?

The quickest test is a monitor swap. DO NOT DO THIS if you're working with a multidisplay (one that supports both RGB and mono TTL monitors) and are unsure about jumper settings. There's no sense in torpedoing *two* monitors today.

If that does nothing, swap the display cards and then the cable.

If the display card is the problem, do the usual easy stuff: Check the seating of the socketed chips. Clean the edge connector and the video connectors. Try again.

Still no luck? If you're courageous, you can attack the display board. Many simple monochrome or color/graphics-type display boards are based on a Mo-torola 6845 chip, a character generator ROM, and memory. If the memory is faulty, you'll only lose some of the display. If the ROM is bad, you'll get funny-looking characters on screen. If the 6845 is bad, just about anything could happen.

Don't try to service the monitor. As I've said before, you can hurt yourself doing that.

Chapter 21
The Most Common Problem: Software

Software is probably the most common PC problem. You can't usually "troubleshoot" software in the sense that you can hardware; it doesn't wear out a print head or need replacement after 10,000 uses. You *can* troubleshoot software in another way, though. You can determine what's causing the problem. This leads you to the right source for a solution.

There are basically two kinds of software problems, ones that are *your* fault and ones that are the *software vendor's* fault—bonafide bugs. You can't really do anything about bugs except either throw out the software or figure out a workaround. Often the problem boils down to a problem of interaction: some software in the system doesn't like other software in the system.

Tracking Down the Problem

Here are a few tips on solving a problem. Sometimes (hopefully), problems just go away. If they don't, you can at least try to fence them in, understanding what makes the bugs come out and what keeps them quiet. The first big question to ask is, "Have I ever seen this software run on this machine before?"

If the software has worked before:

1. Reboot. Sometimes, cosmic rays (I know, it's a weak excuse) or a power surge makes the computer temporarily brain-damaged.
2. If the problem persists, perhaps the program has been damaged on disk. Minor damage of a byte or so wouldn't incapacitate the program, it would just produce strange results in some cases. Reload the software from the backups. (You do back up your software, don't you?) Years ago, I wrote a lot of programs with a compiler called Turbo Pascal. When I wanted to customize TP, I would run a customizer program that came with TP. It read TP into memory, made changes, and then wrote it back out. One time, I made some minor customization changes and saved the newly-customized version of TP to disk. From that point on, I

couldn't get anything to compile. Eventually the problem turned out to be a bad memory chip up around the 640K level. The TP install program loaded TP up there around 640K while it was working on it, and didn't realize that the bad memory had made a hash of TP before the install program rewrote TP to disk. A lesson in the importance of backups.

3. However, don't try to restore regular backups of copy-protected software unless you've used a backup program made for copy-protected software, like Copywrite or Copy II PC. (Again, I'd recommend that you don't buy any copy-protected software at all.)

4. Has someone helpfully messed with your program? Many programs include an Install program to set information like screen type, printer type, and so on. Rerun it, just in case. You can generally see if someone has changed the settings by checking the date on the configuration or setup file.

5. Have you started using a new memory-resident program, like *Metro* or *SideKick*? Retry without the new software. In fact . . .

6. . . .reboot without *any* memory-resident programs. I only know of a few that have never given me any conflict problems.

7. Did you install another piece of software recently? If so, did it "helpfully" rewrite your CONFIG.SYS or AUTOEXEC.BAT files? I've started making a habit of backing up these two files before installing new software.

8. If you suspect memory residents, don't despair. You might be able to solve the problem by rearranging

the order in which the programs are called. Attack software troubleshooting as you would hardware troubleshooting: *isolate*. Remove the strange device drivers, the TSRs, and so on, and then read them one by one until the problem returns.

If You Are Installing New Software. If you've never seen this piece of software work on your machine, any of the preceding problems can pop up. Since it's never worked before, there are, in addition, several more possible problems.

1. First, of course, is the PC compatibility question. If you aren't using a 100-percent compatible IBM PC, there's the possibility that your compatible just plain can't run this program. Run it on an IBM PC with the same configuration. (If you don't have one, how about the local computer store?) If it runs, that's the problem; contact your computer manufacturer. Just in case, call the software folks and ask if they have, perchance, found a patch for your computer. If you have a clone, ask if there's a newer version of the BIOS. If so, get the latest ROM.

2. Check the version of DOS. Don't even think of using a version of DOS before 2.1. Use DOS 3.3 preferably. Some programs run only on either 2.1, 3.1, or 3.2. Obviously, network applications must run on 3.1, 3.2, or 3.3. The occasional program needs so much memory that it can't run in 640K unless you're using DOS 2.1, which is smaller than later versions. Another problem is running a secondary command processor from inside an ap-

plication. DOS 2.1 doesn't do it particularly well; try 3.X. Be careful with DOS 4.01, however. It can interfere with an application's use of LIM memory, and the user shell doesn't like TSRs very well.

3. Check memory. Some old oddball programs won't run in *more* than 512K. You actually have to run some memory-resident programs to cut down enough memory so the program will run. One answer is to reset the DIP switches or run the SETUP program so the computer thinks it has less than 640K. Alternatively, create VDISKs until there's less than 512K of RAM available. (VDISK.SYS is a program that comes with DOS, and is discussed in your DOS manual.)

4. What is required in the CONFIG.SYS and AUTOEXEC.BAT files? Check the installation notes. What must the FILES= and BUFFERS= values be? Does the program ship with a device driver? If so, it must be installed via CONFIG.SYS with the DEVICE= command.

5. Some (thankfully, fewer and fewer) programs assume the existence of a B: floppy and can only read data from there. Or they might require a subdirectory you haven't created. Some programs will warn you of this problem; others just offer an error number or a cryptic message, and then drop you back to DOS. Other programs start and then seem to "hang." A couple of these have fooled me until I realized that they're looking for a particular device, like a printer or a modem, and that they're trying to initialize that device. If it isn't around, they go out to lunch and stay there.

Reporting the Problem

Once you've isolated the problem, report it to the software manufacturer. In all probability, they'll be fairly skeptical. You'll have to prove that the problem exists.

A really annoying little game Microsoft and Ashton-Tate play is that they deny a problem exists, or won't warn you about it, until you can prove it; *then* they'll admit it exists and promise a fix in the next version. Don't believe me? Ask Ashton-Tate for a list of known bugs and workarounds in *dBase III+*, or Microsoft for the bugs in QuickBasic. They won't give it to you. I found a few problems in Microsoft's QuickBasic. They said they'd seen them in other programs, and other bugs existed also. When I explained that I was building a fairly large program with the QB product and could use the bug list to save some time, I was told by Product Support that the list couldn't be released to me.

It's unfortunate that some vendors charge you money for buggy software, then treat you like a deadbeat when you complain that the software doesn't do what it's advertised to do. In any case, report it to your local user group through whatever "user-to-user" type column the group has in its monthly newsletter. (You *are* a member of your local user group, aren't you?)

Once you determine the problem and what causes it to occur, produce the briefest possible example of it. Write up the problem and any workarounds in a letter to the software vendor. Include the brief example on a floppy disk, and send the floppy with the letter to the vendor. Here are details to include:

● Version number and serial number of the software

- The kind of PC you're using and ROM date
- If it's a multispeed PC, the speed at which you were working
- The version of DOS you use

When you call with a problem, vendors will sometimes ask, "What version are you using?"

You reply (let us say), "Version 2.3."

"Oh, ho," they respond. "You're *way* behind. We're up to 3.1" (I send in my registration cards. How is it that I was so uninformed?) "What's your name? I'll send you the upgrade."

At this point, you think the answer is in the mail. In my experience, new versions only fix about 50 percent of the problems. Ask, "Does the new version fix this problem? Have you ever heard of this problem before?"

Chapter 22

Buying New Systems and Upgrading Existing Systems: Balancing Your PCs

If you buy PC hardware or advise others who do, you live in an interesting time. There are lots of options, many of them good and some varying degrees of bad. Further, you might have an old system like an IBM XT or AT that you'd like to bring into today's world, power-wise. So this chapter draws on the previous ones and asks,

- How do I cheaply make an existing XT or AT faster?
- What *new* machines will allow me the greatest flexibility now and in the future at a reasonable cost?

It turns out that the same answers apply to both questions in most cases. I have some old XT-type systems that I'm slowly making tolerable speed-wise, and I'm always buying new systems, either for my business or myself. Here are the things I look for when buying so as to get the maximum bang for my buck and to correctly balance the system.

Balancing Major PC Subsystems

Your PC or compatible has just a few basic time-critical subsystems:

- CPU/memory subsystem
- Hard disk/disk controller subsystem
- Video subsystem

You're not going to crank up your floppy speed or install a newer and faster serial port. You might install a newer printer, such as a laser printer, that will speed your printing tasks, but I assume that's obvious. One more item, by the way, will speed up some applications:

- A numeric coprocessor.

Systems nowadays seem absolutely CPU-crazy. Sure, it's nice to have a 50 Mhz 486 system under the hood, but what good is it if the CPU experiences 50 wait states every time it accesses video memory, or if the hard disk has a 175 ms seek time and a 100KB/second data transfer rate? (Review the hard disk and video chapters if you don't remember why fast video memory is important, and that reasonable hard disk seek times and data transfer rates are 25 ms and 255 KB/second, respectively.)

You don't want a machine that's fast.

You want a machine that *seems* fast.

I've built a "faker" system that I use as a workstation when my 386 is busy. People sit down at it and think they're working on a 16 Mhz or faster 386. Its features include:

- 10 Mhz, 0 wait state 80286 CPU
- A 1:1 hard disk controller
- An 80 MB, 28 ms seek time hard disk
- A disk cache program using 1.5 MB of cache
- A 16-bit VGA board

I'm going to try to convince you *not* to buy 33 Mhz 386's, but instead to buy slower 386 machines and spend the money that you saved on CPU speed on better disk and video.

Snappier Disks

Recall that there are two components to your disk system: the disk and the controller.

- What disk you buy determines your system's *seek time* (how long it takes to move the head to an area of the disk).
- What controller you buy determines your system's *data transfer rate* (how long it takes to pull that data off the disk).
- A disk cache program can make any disk subsystem seem faster.

There's not much to say about improving seek time. Just buy a faster drive. As I've said, don't even look at drives with seek times worse than about 30 ms. Recall that smaller is better when it comes to seek times.

Your controller can be a fruitful (and cheaper) source of disk improvement. What controller you buy depends on the kind of system you have. Recall that XT-

type and AT-type systems use fundamentally different controllers.

XT systems may currently be working with an IBM/Xebec-type controller that supports no better than a 1:5 disk interleave—a data transfer rate of about 80 KB/second. Replace that controller with a Western Digital WD1002-WX1 or XT-GEN or a Data Technologies Corp DTC 5150CX, and you can reformat your disk to a 1:3 interleave and double your disk's throughput. Plus, XT controllers are cheap—about $70.

AT systems can step up to 1:1 interleave cheaply with the Western Digital WD1006 or DTC 7280. Common AT-type controllers can only handle a 1:2 interleave, for a maximum data transfer rate of 255KB/second. 1:1 doubles that to 510 KB/second, and the controllers are relatively cheap—I've seen them for as little as $115.

Next, take advantage of extra extended or expanded memory with a disk cache program. I've already mentioned *PC-Kwik Cache* from Multisoft in the hard disk chapters, and I recommend it highly. You can really speed up a slow XT-type system by adding a megabyte of LIM memory to it and running *PC-Kwik Cache* in that megabyte.

Making Video VROOOM!

Fast Video Hardware. I've already discussed video board do's and don'ts in Chapter 20 on displays and display Adapters, so I'll summarize the main points here and add a software consideration. No matter what system you're using, the video memory is no doubt slower than the system can utilize. So be sure that you

- Buy 16-bit interface if it's an AT-type; XT-types can't use 16-bit boards.

- Buy fast no-wait state RAM on the video board.
- If you're using a 386-family computer, relocate your video ROMs to RAM (see below).

If you're feeling flush, you can spend $500 more for a VRAM board.

An assistant I know was using a slow old 4.77 Mhz XT-type system in the office with an IBM CGA board in it, and I found myself with an extra EGA board and monitor. I had a little time, so I thought I'd treat her and put the EGA board in the system. Her reaction surprised me.

"Did you put one of those speedup boards in the system?" she asked.

"No, " I replied. "Why?"

"It seems a lot faster. Watch this," she said, and ran the communications program we use. It opens up with a graphic of a curtain dropping across the screen, then drawing open to the left and right. It usually takes a few seconds and is a pain to have to sit through. Now, however, the curtain went down, bang! and opened, bang!

"I'll be darned. . ." I said. Just putting a clone EGA board into a regulation IBM PC had speeded even *it* up! The difference was faster RAM. (Imagine how much faster a 16-bit board will be on your AT-type system.)

Remapping Video ROM. You can't cache video operations, but you can speed up video software.

You see, the video board (if it's an EGA or VGA) has a ROM on it with BIOS-type video software that's called each time a character goes on the screen. The screen is used a lot, however, and so this ROM is pretty important; its software is being executed all the time. There's a problem, however: ROM is slower than the slowest RAM in many cases. That means that once again we find video slowing up the show. Is there

an answer? Well, yes, but you need a 386 or 486 system to implement it.

The 386 family (the 386, the 386SX, and the 486) are blessed with the ability to *remap* memory. The 386 can actually copy the ROMs into some unused (formerly extended) RAM, readdress the ROM to some far-off address, and then readdress the RAM with the ROM contents to where the ROM originally was! This means the 386 can make RAM take over for slow ROM.

The 386 has the power, but how do you unlock that power? Memory managers for 386 (discussed back in the "Main Memory" section of Chapter 4) generally come with a remapping feature built in. I use either Qualitas' *386-to-the-Max* or Quarterdeck's *QEMM386* memory managers, and both include ROM remap as a standard feature. The difference is dramatic. If I boot my 386 without a memory manager and tell DOS to type this chapter, it takes DOS 26 seconds to put the entire chapter on screen, data scrolling off the top of the screen and all. If I boot with *386-to-the-Max*, it takes 15 seconds. Nearly a 50-percent decrease in time—pretty good for just a software fix. So if you have a 386, don't miss out on this cheap speedup: run a memory manager and remap your ROMs.

Replacing or Choosing Your Motherboard

The motherboard is the heart of a PC system. Whether you've got an old XT that you're looking to upgrade or you're putting together the pieces for a new system, here's what I'd look for in motherboards.

There are basically two classes of motherboards that I recommend for my clients:

- Cheap 10 Mhz XT motherboards
- 16-20 Mhz 386 motherboards (per-

haps SX motherboards, as they are getting cheaper)

The two classes represent the two types of PC-based workstations in use today. The first type, the turbo XT, is for those who are doing nothing more than word processing and perhaps a little spreadsheet work. These people aren't running Windows or *Lotus 1-2-3* version 3.0, they're running *PFS Write* or *WordPerfect* and *1-2-3* version 2.1. There are lots of users like them, too, and the machines that will serve them are dirt cheap. You can assemble a 640K turbo XT clone with a 130 watt power supply, monochrome monitor and MDA video board, 5¼-inch 360K and 3½-inch 720K floppy drive, parallel/serial adapter, and 40 MB hard drive for about $1,000 without looking too hard. (It took me five minutes to find that price in the Jameco catalog; *PC Week* advertisers don't even list XT-type machines any more.) If you have an old XT-type machine you want to speed up a bit, think about buying a 10 Mhz 8088 motherboard ($90 without memory from clonemeisters) or—the only 286 I'll ever recommend—an 8 Mhz "baby 286" motherboard. It lacks full 286 features, but then you're not buying it for the 286 features in this case; you're buying it for the speed. They're down around $140 in price, so think of it as a very fast 8088 turbo motherboard. It's called "baby" because it's sized to fit in an XT chassis.

The second type of PC workstation is the one that must:

- Run fast
- Accommodate advanced operating systems like OS/2 and UNIX
- Accommodate "DOS extender" products like Windows, *1-2-3* version 3.x
- Have a 16- or 32-bit bus

- Be able to address much more memory than 640K
- Have the hardware to support multitasking

Such a PC must, obviously, be built around a 286 or better chip. I'm going to argue in favor of *skipping the 286 altogether* and buying nothing below 386SX-based machines in a minute, but for now let's look at motherboard features. When shopping for an advanced motherboard, consider the following features:

- Size and slots
- Amount of memory that the on-board sockets or the special 32-bit memory board (if any) can accommodate
- BIOS maker
- Speed options
- CPU

Motherboard Size, Slots, BIOS, and Speed Options. Size is important because you have to know if it'll fit in your existing case, if you're upgrading an older system. The number of slots is important because you don't know what the market will demand in the next few years: maybe untold amounts of memory, perhaps SCSI controllers for WORM drives, perhaps everyone must have LAN cards, and so on. I'd steer clear of the machines with just three to five slots and concentrate on the machines with eight slots.

As I've said before, stick with Phoenix, Award, or AMI, but be wary of AMI BIOSes. I've had trouble running OS/2 on older AMI BIOSes, but people I trust tell me AMI has straightened out those woes.

It's nice to be able to slow down the clock to 8 Mhz with a switch. That means you can boot up the system in 8 Mhz mode if you suspect that a piece of software or hardware is malfunctioning because it's being used at a speed above the one for which it was designed.

Space for On-Board Memory. As I explained in Chapter 9, memory speeds are now faster than bus speeds for machines 12 Mhz and faster. This has forced manufacturers to either (1) provide a special high-speed slot for a proprietary memory card, (2) put high-speed memory sockets right on the motherboard or (3) just throw their hands up in the air and only put memories in the system that run at the speed of the bus, slowing down the whole system.

The 386 I use most of the time has a special 32-bit, 16 Mhz memory bus slot with room on the memory board for only 4MB. I've got more memory on the system than 4MB, but it must be memory on a board that's plugged into one of the (gag!) 8 Mhz, 16-bit bus slots, as I've filled the capabilities of the 32-bit slot's board. The memory over 4 MB works, but the system slows down whenever accessing it. Learn from my mistakes (*I* have, for subsequent systems). Ensure that when you buy a system there's a way to put a full 16MB in high-speed sockets, either on the motherboard or on a high-speed memory board. Believe me, you'll want 16MB by the mid-90s. Right now I'm running OS/2 version 1.2 on a machine with 7MB of memory and find that I *still* run out of memory sometimes.

CPUs: Go for the 386. The 286 was a quantum leap from the 8088, as it added to the 8088's powers a protected mode with access to 16MB of RAM. (If you've forgotten this, review the section on extended memory in Chapter 4.) But it's also in many ways a brain-damaged chip, one that promises much and delivers much less. The 286 was designed in 1978–1981 and was built to lead the world away from the 8088. Intel had no way of knowing that 8088 software (DOS

software, you'll recall) would be with us through the 90s and probably through the turn of the century. The 386, on the other hand, was designed in the early 80s, by which time DOS was firmly rooted in the marketplace, and the Intel designers knew they could not turn their backs on DOS and 8088 programs. The 386 is, then, better built to blend the old and the new. The 286 almost seems to be a rough draft of the 386.

Those are general indictments. Specifically, what's so great about the 386 family?

- Complete backward compatibility with earlier iapx86 chips (the 286 shares this but will not run 386-specific software)
- Programming support of large data structures to make writing large programs easier
- Smoother switching between real and protected mode
- Support of DOS multitasking
- On-chip limulation support to remove extended/expanded memory quandaries
- Memory remap feature to allow ROM remaps faster RAM
- Protection against obsolescence for years to come

Let's look at these in some detail.
The 386 Protected Mode. Look back to the discussion in Chapter 4 about memory to review the notion of *protected memory*. The 286 has support for the protected mode that gives it access to 16MB. The 386 has that protected mode as well and adds a second protected mode of its own.

The 386 protected mode is much more useful than the 286 one. Programs running on Intel CPUs are forced by the design of those CPUs to address memory not as one large pool of space, but as small areas called *segments*. The 286 protected mode won't allow a segment larger than 64K. The effect of this on 286 protected mode programs is to impose a "nuisance barrier" of 64K. Data structures or programs larger than 64K require special handling, so many software vendors have simply not offered large program or data capabilities.

The 386 has a protected mode that allows segments to be as large as *four gigabytes*. All of the existing code written for mainframes and minis, programs written in an environment without the 64K shackles, can be more easily ported to 386-based machines as a result.

386 Support of Mode Switching. A second argument for the 386 is *mode switching*. Let's say you're working in a 286 protected mode environment like OS/2 or *Lotus 1-2-3* version 3. DOS operates in *real mode*, the 8088 emulation mode. A 286 powers up in real mode. When OS/2 or *1-2-3* version 3.0 starts, it switches the 286 to protected mode. OS/2 has a *compatibility box* that runs DOS programs, so OS/2 must be able to return to real mode. *Lotus 1-2-3* version 3.0, similarly, must return to real mode to return to DOS. But there's a problem: There is a command to put the 286 in protected mode from real mode, but none to reverse the process. How, then, does OS/2 switch to real mode to run the compatibility box; how does *1-2-3* version 3.0 return to DOS? Believe it or not, they *reset the processor*—reboot the system, in effect. Since the processor is thrown back into real mode when reset, the compatibility box can now run. The downside is that the 286 is then deaf to external interrupts (communications, keyboard, and so on) for *30 ms*. The 386 improves matters. Intel included a command to switch the 386 from protected to real mode with-

out going through the reboot sequence. Result: no dropped interrupts.

386 Support of DOS Multitasking. The third argument for buying a 386 is that the 386 has a DOS multitasking mode called the *Virtual 8086 (V86) mode*. As the real mode DOS lives in involves no protection of resources, there's no way to write a bulletproof multitasking version of DOS for the 8088, 8086, or 80286. But the 386's V86 mode provides the hardware support to make DOS multitasking possible. Products like IGC's *VM/386*, Quarterdeck's *DESQview*, or Microsoft Windows/386 use the V86 mode. V86 is designed to coexist with protected mode, so it would be easy to support multiple compatibility boxes (that's how OS/2 version 2.0, the 386-only version, does it).

386 Memory Paging Finally Makes Extended Memory Useful. Remember all the worrying about extended versus expanded memory in Chapter 4? That worrying goes away with the 386. It has a *memory paging* feature that manifests itself in several ways. I've already mentioned 386 memory managers, so I won't go into detail again about what they do. Briefly, however, they use the 386 memory paging feature to:

- Remap software in slow ROMs to fast RAM.
- Add extra memory to DOS's 640K. *386-to-the-Max* and *QEMM386* allow you to stuff up to 160K of TSR programs up above the DOS 640K, giving the memory that they formerly took up back to DOS.
- Turn unused *extended* memory into *expanded* memory.

I'd say that you can buy the 386 without fear of obsolescence for years. Intel released the 486 four years after the

386, and it contains no major differences software-wise: it's just faster. Anything that runs on a 486 runs on a 386 or a 386SX. You might run slow but you won't have to worry about being stuck with a useless machine, such as you would if you wanted to run OS/2 version 2.0 on a 286, or Windows on an XT.

If I haven't convinced you yet, here's the topper: Clone 16 Mhz 386SX motherboards are going for about $350 at the moment (late 1989). That's only $100 more than the cost of a similar 286 motherboard. The price difference for IBM's corporate customers between the Model 50Z (a 286 machine) and the 55SX (a 386 SX machine) is only about $200. So do yourself a favor. Buy a 386 now and save yourself trouble later.

Summary: Speeding Up an XT

Let's review. Assuming you have an XT and you don't want to spend a lot of money jazzing it up, here's a laundry list of things to try to get better speed out of it. You can do any combination of these upgrades, so pick and choose as your budget permits.

- Install a disk cache (very cheap if you already have LIM memory) or think about getting a LIM board. If you *do* get a LIM board, stuff it with 100 ns memories so you can move them over to your 386 machine when you junk the XT and buy the next level up.
- If you have an IBM 1:5 hard disk controller, get a 1:3 controller ($70).
- Spend $120 and put an 8087 numeric coprocessor on the motherboard.

- Get a faster video board (price varies).
- Swap the motherboard for a 10 Mhz 8088 ($150 with 640K memory) or an 8 Mhz 80826 ($250 with 1 megabyte memory).

Summary: Outfitting an AT-type Machine

Whether you're upgrading an existing AT-type machine or configuring a new one, there are a few high points to be sure to hit.

- Buy 386. If you're buying 286, comparison-shop the 386SX machine from the same manufacturer. Remember that the decision you make today will be with you for years. (The boss went along with an upgrade from 8088 to 286/386, but he might not next time, particularly when the next quantum leap after 386/486 won't be for years.)
- Buy 1:1 hard disk controllers and install disk cache software.
- Buy only hard disks with seek times 30 ms and below, and buy at least 80MB drives. It doesn't cost that much more, and you'll be living with these drives for a good long time.
- Buy 16-bit video. If you need to save money, you can do that *and* buy your eyes some relief with a monochrome VGA monitor.
- Make sure the BIOS is written by a reputable software house and that you can put lots of memory on the motherboard or on a high-speed memory board.

Chapter 23
Advanced Projects: Safely Improving Your PC or AT

By now, you have the flush of power. No longer is the PC the daunting, mysterious device it once was. So you might be feeling brave. Here are a few parting projects: cheap improvements on the PC.

Speaker Volume Control

Here's one thing on the PC that could have been done a bit better: the speaker. It would be nice to turn it down, shut it off, or connect the output to another speaker.

The speaker is connected to the PC via a flat rectangular connector called a *Berg connector*. It has four connectors, but only two are used. It's a simple circuit: two wires attach to the leads of an 8 ohm speaker.

Some people disconnect the speaker to shut it up. This isn't a good idea, from what some engineers tell me. Apparently you need to replace the speaker resistance with some alternative of the same resistance, like a resistor. The circuit is a one-half–watt circuit, so don't use the smallest resistor available: get a one-half–watt power resistor. Then you want a *DPDT (Double Pole, Double Throw) switch* so one position connects the speaker wires to the speaker and the other one connects the speaker wires to the resistor.

A superior approach would be to put a variable resistor called a *potentiometer*, or *pot*, in line with the speaker. The speaker would always be in the circuit, but the potentiometer could produce enough resistance to make the speaker quiet or inaudible. You could run longer wires from the pot to the speaker so the pot could be mounted in the front of the case to serve as a volume control. A potentiometer with a maximum resistance of 100 to 300 ohms would serve well. (Minimum resistance on potentiometers is zero ohms.)

An Interface for an External Speaker

It could be that you use your speaker for something more than beeps, like tinny music or awful speech synthesis. In this case, you might want an external speaker jack so you can run it into your stereo or a recording device.

You could use a typical phone jack, but a better approach would be to use a two-position jack. When nothing is plugged into the jack, the internal speaker would be in use. When something is plugged in, the internal speaker is taken out of the circuit and the external is in the circuit.

Before plugging this into anything, be sure it's designed for one-half–watt power, 8 ohm resistance.

Installing a Hardware Reset Switch

Something many clones have that the PC doesn't have is the *hardware reset switch*. The Ctrl-Alt–Del combination is a software combination. If the processor meets a simple HLT (halt) opcode, no key combination will be of any use.

The chip that controls the microprocessor's RESET line is the RST line on 8284 (on XT-type machines) or the 82284 (on AT-type machines), the clock chip. Just hold its RST line to ground (you must be sure to hold it down for at least 810 nanoseconds), and the process is done. RST is pin 11, GND is pin 9. Just install a pushbutton switch between 9 and 11. And that's all there's to it.

Details on Installing a Reset Switch for Cowards. First, if you have a clone, you probably already have a reset switch, so don't bother. If you have a Compaq, a PS/2, or a Zenith, don't bother for another reason: They don't use the 8284/82284 line of chips, but instead use some other combination of electronics. I don't know how to make them reset.

Now, if you're going to try to do this, understand that there are two big hurdles (both of which I'll try to make easy to overcome):

- Soldering wires to lines 9 and 11 on the clock chip
- Drilling a hole in the back of the case to accommodate a pushbutton switch

Here's the basic sequence of events, with crib notes on how to make it easy. You do need very basic soldering skills.

1. Attach wires to legs 9 and 11 of the clock chip, the 8284 or 82284 (see Figure 23-1 for an example). Remember that you count chip legs counter-clockwise from the notch. You might have one of the motherboards that sockets the clock chip. If you do, a simple way to painlessly attach wires to legs 9 and 11 is to get *another* socket (make sure it's the correct size for the clock chip) from Radio Shack and solder wires to legs 9 and 11 of the socket. Now you can (1) remove the clock chip from its socket, (2) insert the socket *with the wires* in the socket that's on the motherboard, and (3) insert the clock chip into the wired socket (which is in the motherboard socket).

   If your clock chip isn't socketed, you can gracefully chicken out at this point if you're leery of directly soldering onto components on the motherboard (quite understandable, and not lacking in honor). Otherwise, solder a wire to line 9 and one to line 11 on your clock chip.

2. Now, to reset the system, you need only touch the wire from line 9 to the wire from line 11. You *could* just hang the two wires out the back of the box, but that would be inelegant. Instead, let's install a pushbutton switch between the two wires and then install the switch somewhere in the chassis.

   I don't know about you, but I got skittish at this point. I had a vision of using the drill on the case, the drill slipping, and ending up with a nice deep furrow through

Figure 23-1   Locating Legs 9 and 11 on the Clock Chip (XT)

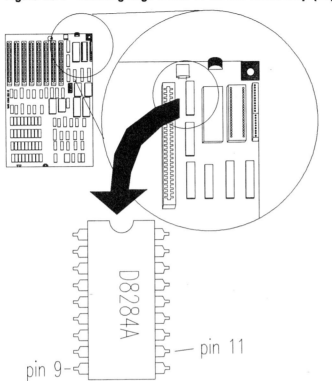

pin 9 —

— pin 11

the motherboard. So I devised the coward's way. I just removed the slot cover from an unused slot, took the cover far away to my workbench, and drilled a hole in the slot cover. Yeah, I slipped a few times, but all that happened was that I scratched the work table. Reinstall the slot cover, and you have a pushbutton-sized hole in the back of your machine.

3. Install a pushbutton switch. You can get one at Radio Shack for a couple of bucks. Now, be careful about what kind of switch you buy; there are *normally open* and *normally closed* switches. A normally closed switch would connect 9 and 11 all of the time *except for when you hold down the button*. This would mean you'd have to hold the button down all of the time, which would make typing difficult and disk changing virtually impossible. So get a normally open switch, and you're in business.

Appendix A
The Basic Survival Kit

What constitutes a basic troubleshooting toolkit? I have mentioned the following tools at various times:

- Small flashlight
- Hex nut drivers
- Offset screwdrivers (to take out PC/XT drives without removing circuit boards)
- Tweezers or hemostats
- Multimeter
- Digital temperature probe
- Compressed air
- Hair dryer or heat gun
- Tweaker screwdriver to pull chips
- AC circuit wiring tester
- Tasco AC monitor (reports voltage delivered by the power company and power spikes)
- Breakout box
- PARA Systems AC power meter (measures how many watts your system uses)

- Software:
  - The public domain disk
  - Mace Utilities Gold or
  - Norton Utilities Advanced Edition version 4.5.1 or later
  - Kolod hTEST/hFORMAT
  - A toolkit disk with:
    - DOS bootable (include any device drivers, like OnTrack Disk Manager's DMDRVR.BIN)
    - DOS FDISK
    - DOS FORMAT
    - DOS SYS
    - Some low-level formatter
    - HFORMAT, GETSEC, PUTSEC and XFDISK from hTEST/hFORMAT
    - DOS DEBUG
    - Some disk head parking program
    - Mace REMEDY or Norton's DISKTEST (DT) or DISKDOCTOR (NDD)
    - SETUP, if it's an AT or 386

Appendix B
Short Overview on Reading Hexadecimal

Throughout this book and in technical publications, you'll see numbers expressed not in *decimal,* the numeric system we're all accustomed to using, but in *hexadecimal,* a somewhat different system. This appendix is a quick guide to what you need to know about hex.

Decimal is based on the number 10 as we know it—the number of fingers on most people's hands. *Dec-,* a word root, permeates the language: *decathalon* refers to a contest with ten sporting events, *decimate* literally means to kill every tenth man, *December* is the name of what once was the tenth month. We write ten as 10, but that's really only correct if we base the numbering system on 10. Strictly speaking, the number that I wrote is "one zero," and it means different things to different number systems. Look at the sequence of how we write the first 11 numbers: 0, 1, 2, 3, 4, 5, 6, 7, 8, 9, 10. Why is ten written with *two* digits, not *one* as with all the numbers before? Because the system is based on 10. So 10 is written 10 pretty much by definition once you decide that you're using 10 as your number base. Next, look at 10 × 10, or 100: It's written 100, the first number with three digits. Ditto for the first number with four digits (1,000), which is 10 × 10 × 10. Why did we pick 10 as a basis for a number system? No one knows, but the obvious guess is that 10 is, again, the number of fingers most people have.

For reasons that aren't really worth pursuing here, it's easiest to talk about numbers in a computer system (memory or I/O addresses, for example) not in a number system based on 10, but rather on 8 or 16. A base-8 system is called *octal,* and a base-16 system is called *hexadecimal,* or *hex* for short. PCs tend to use hex, so I'll discuss that here. You don't even have to know hex in entirety, just a few salient points.

Counting in Hex. Recall that a base-10 system uses single-digit numbers up to, but not including, 10. A base-16 system, similarly, has single-digit numbers up to, but not including, 16. In order they're (Table B-1):

Table B-1. Hex Digits and Decimal Equivalents

Hex Digit	Decimal Value
0	0
1	1
2	2
3	3
4	4
5	5
6	6
7	7
8	8
9	9
A	10
B	11
C	12
D	13
E	14
F	15

The next number after F is 10, (which would be 16 in decimal), then 11 (which would be 17 in decimal). With decimal, the two-digit numbers increase up to 99, the last two-digit number. Hex goes up to FF. In hex, 100 isn't ten times ten but 16 × 16; that would be 100 in hex, 256 in decimal.

Reading Memory Hex Addresses. You'll recall that the typical PC, when running DOS, can address one megabyte of memory: 640K for user data and programs and 384K of reserved area for video memory, ROMs, and buffers. Let's look at how to read memory addresses in hex.

First, understand that one megabyte is composed of sixteen 64K *segments*. Conveniently, 10,000 in hex equals 64K.

640K is ten 64K segments, so the low 640K is the address range from 00000 to one short of A0000, or 9FFFF. All of the addresses in 64K increments are shown in Table B-2.

Table B-2. Memory Addresses in Decimal and Hex

Decimal Address	Hexadecimal Address	Preceding Hex Address
0K	00000	n/a
64K	10000	0FFFF
128K	20000	1FFFF
192K	30000	2FFFF
256K	40000	3FFFF
320K	50000	4FFFF
384K	60000	5FFFF
448K	70000	6FFFF
512K	80000	7FFFF
576K	90000	8FFFF
640K	A0000	9FFFF
704K	B0000	AFFFF
768K	C0000	BFFFF
832K	D0000	CFFFF
896K	E0000	DFFFF
960K	F0000	EFFFF
1024K	100000	FFFFF

So when you see that a VGA puts memory in addresses A0000–BFFFF, you know that the board uses the addresses starting just above 640K and going up to just short of 768K. Or when you see that the BIOS ROM is addressed from FC000 to FFFFF, you know it's right up against the top of the first megabyte.

You've endured enough theory for the moment. Right now, let's put it to good use. Here are a couple of examples.

Example 1: Counting in Hex—Determining the Size of a Range. If COM1 uses I/O addresses 3F8 to 3FF, how many I/O addresses does it use?

Count them: 3F8, 3F9, 3FA (remember that A comes after 9), 3FB, 3FC, 3FD, 3FE, 3FF. Eight addresses.

Example 2: Comparing Overlapping ROM Address Ranges. In Chapter 7 about installing new circuit boards, we were discussing where to address a ROM in the ScanJet interface card. I was concerned that the address of the ROM on the ScanJet card not conflict with the addresses of any other ROMs in the system and said something like this:

The only thing in the system with ROM is a VGA, but what is its ROM's address? Checking Table 7-4 (earlier in this chapter) gives us C0000–C4FFF. The scanner interface has a factory default of C4000–C7FFF. That would be okay for an EGA, as the EGA's ROM ends at C3FFF, just short of C4000. But note that the VGA's ROM goes all the way up to C6000, which tromps all over the range C4000–C7FFF.

You may have had some trouble following it, so let's review exactly what the quandary was:

1. **The factory default address for the ScanJet ROM is C4000–C7FFF.** Note that this is a *range* of values: C4001, C4002, and so forth up to C7FFF. There are *lots* of them—16K of addresses, in fact.
2. **The address range of the EGA ROM (if there is an EGA in the system) is C0000–C3FFF, and that range doesn't conflict with the ScanJet's range.** The last value in the EGA range is C3FFF; C4000 comes after C3FFF in hex. You

compare numbers in hex just like you do in decimal. (1) If they have the same number of digits, just compare the leftmost one. In this case, they've both got hex digits C in the leftmost position, so there's no difference. (2) If the leftmost digits are the same, look immediately to the right. The number 4 comes after 3, so C4000 is after C3FFF.

3. **The address range of the VGA ROM is C0000–C5FFF, and that conflicts with the ScanJet ROM range of C4000–C7FFF.** The top of the VGA ROM range is C5FFF. The bottom of the ScanJet ROM range is C4000, which is below C5FFF. Again, how do I know? Compare them: The C in the leftmost position is the same; the 4 and 5 are different. The C5FFF, then, is above C4000 (the starting point for the ScanJet ROM) and so the VGA range overlaps the ScanJet ROM range.

So we've briefly looked at how to use hex when looking at I/O address ranges and memory address ranges. If you'd like to get into the nitty-gritty details, like actually converting hex to decimal and back, read on. But you needn't know any more.

Converting Hex to Decimal. This isn't tough, but you can also live your whole life without having to know it.

First, look back at Table C-1. You'll need to know that F in hex is 15 decimal, 8 in hex is 8 decimal, and so on. Say you have a hex number like C801F. How do I convert it to decimal?

1. Start at the leftmost digit and con- **vert it to decimal. Multiply it by 16. That's your subtotal so far.** That's C in this case. C hex is 12

decimal, so multiply 12 by 16 to get our subtotal, 192.

2. **If the next digit to the right is the rightmost digit, convert it, add it to the subtotal, and stop. Otherwise, convert it, add it to the subtotal, and multiply the whole subtotal by 16.** The next digit is 8, which isn't the last digit, so add 8 to the subtotal to get 192 + 8, or 200. Multiply 200 by 16, and you'll get 3200.

3. **If you added the rightmost digit, stop. Otherwise, go to step 2.** Well, you haven't yet added the rightmost digit, so on to the next one. Rule 2 says "convert the next digit, add to the subtotal, and multiply by 16," so add 0 to 3200 and get 3200. Multiply that by 16 and you'll get 51,200.

There are still digits left, so keep going. Next is 1; 1 hex is 1 decimal, so add 1 and the subtotal is now 51,201. Multiply that by 16 and get 819,216.

The last digit is F, 15 in decimal. Add it to the subtotal and get 819,231. As it's the last digit, don't multiply by 16, and you're finished. C801F hex equals 819,231 decimal.

Converting Decimal to Hex. This is just about the reverse process. Let's convert 75,000 from decimal to hex.

1. Divide the decimal number by 16. **Convert the remainder to a hex digit and make that the RIGHTMOST hex digit. That's the first digit in the subtotal.** 75,000 divided by 16 yields a quotient of 4687 and a remainder of 8, which is just 8 hex, so the rightmost hex digit is 8.

2. **Divide the quotient by 16. Make the remainder the next hex digit; put it to the left of the subtotal.** Dividing 4687 by 16 yields a new quotient of 292 and a remainder of 15. The 15 decimal remainder is F hex, so the next hex digit is F, making the subtotal F8.

3. **If the new quotient is 0, stop. Otherwise, just keep dividing the quotient by 16 and putting the hex remainder to the left of the subtotal.** 292 divided by 16 yields a new quotient of 18 and a remainder of 4, so 4 goes on the subtotal. It's now 4F8.

Divide 18 by 16 and you'll get a quotient of 1 with remainder 2, so the subtotal becomes 24F8.

Finally, divide 1 by 16 and you get quotient 0, remainder 1, so the subtotal is now the final total— 124F8. 124F8 hex equals 75,000 decimal.

Appendix C
Information on the Centronics Interface

You won't generally have to worry about parallel (*Centronics*) cables. The much more likely trouble points are serial cables. But here's the background on parallel cables, just in case you ever need it.

Originally, a company named Centronics developed a cable interface for their printers. It was simple and cheap, but hampered by the fact that you couldn't really run the cables more than about 6–10 feet without the possibility of noise and error in the cables. That's not a bad constraint when considering printer-to-PC interfaces, so the cable's still pretty popular. When IBM started using it, however, they didn't use the then-standard 34-finger edge connector. Instead, they used a female DB25 connector. Table C-1 documents the lines in the interface.

- Is RS232-like: not a standard, just a guideline
- Uses TTL voltage levels:
  - 2.4V–5V = "high" (1)
  - 0V–0.8V = "low" (0)

Comments on parallel interface:

- Be careful about 18, +5. It's intended for inline buffers, serial/parallel converters, and the like.
- For those who are wondering, no, you don't need all of those signal grounds, but it helps.
- The 36-pin connector on Centronics is like a card edge (it *is* a card edge on some Radio Shack computers).
- A simple cable: With 25-wire cable, connect a push-on Centronics connector to a push-on DB25 connector, and then cut out line 15 (eliminates false faults).
- Signal levels for Centronics interface will damage RS-232, so don't mix them up. That means be careful about using breakout boxes to debug Centronics cables.

Comments about Centronics Handshaking:

1. Computer puts the data on D0 to D7.

Table C-1. The Centronics (Parallel) Interface

Pin # on 34 Pin Cable	Pin # on 25 Pin Cable	Abbrev	Description	Source: Printer or Computer
1	1	*STB	Data Strobe. Printer accepts data upon low-to-high transition	C
2	2	D0	Data bit 1	C
3	3	D1	Data bit 2	C
4	4	D2	Data bit 3	C
5	5	D3	Data bit 4	C
6	6	D4	Data bit 5	C
7	7	D5	Data bit 6	C
8	8	D6	Data bit 7	C
9	9	D7	Data bit 8	C
10	10	*ACK	H/L/H = ready for next char	P
11	11	BUSY	Low = can't receive data	P
12	12	PO	High = Paper Out	P
13	13	SEL	High = Printer is on, "online"	P
14	14	SG	Signal ground	
16		SG	Signal ground	
17		CG	Chassis ground	
18		+5	Voltage source for inline buffers. Should not be wired through from printer to PC	either or both
19	19	SG	Signal ground	
30	25	SG	Signal ground	
31	16	*IP	Low = reinitialize printer. (You know the "hiccup" printers do when you start some programs? *IP causes it.)	C
32	15	*Fault	Low = printer fault has occurred.	P

* Active when low

2. Computer indicates the data is ready by pulsing *STB: It starts out high and goes low for a short time, then back to high.
3. The printer responds by raising BUSY.
4. When printer has the character, it drops BUSY. Then it pulses *ACK: high to low, then back to high.

It's easier to understand this with some pictures. PDIAGS.EXE, distributed on the utility disk, contains a limited *(very limited)* oscilloscope-like display. Following are two screen shots, the first of a normal character print (note the activity of BUSY and ACK), and the next when trying to print when out of paper (note the level of P.E., the "paper out" line).

Figure C-1 PDIAGS Output with Normal Character Print

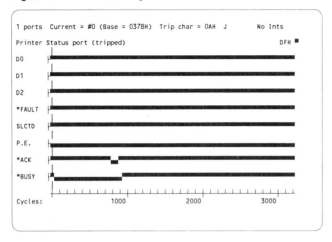

Figure C-2 PDIAGS Output with Printer Out of Paper

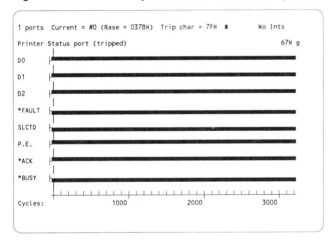

Appendix D

Switch Settings for 8086-based AT&T and Olivetti Computers

The Olivetti M24 and the AT&T 6300s have two banks of DIP switches for configuration, like other XT-type machines, but their switches do completely different things, so I've found having these switch settings around to be handy.

The AT&T 6300 has two switch banks labelled SW-0 and SW-1. SW-0 is closest to the front of the machine. The meaning of some of the switches have changed from ROM v1.21 to v1.43, and that is shown on the tables on the following pages.

Table D-1. AT&T 6300 DIP SW-0 Settings

Description	S1	S2	S3	S4	S5	S6	S7	S8
128K total RAM on motherboard (mbd) (ROM v1.21 only)	0	1	1	1	X	X	X	X
256K total on mbd, all 64K chips (ROM v1.21 only)	1	0	1	1	X	X	X	X
512K (4–64K bytes on mbd, rest on expansion board) (ROM v1.21 only)	1	1	0	1	X	X	X	X
640K (4–64K on mbd, 384 expansion) (ROM v1.21 only)	0	1	0	1	X	X	X	X
640K (all on mbd, 128K in bank 0, 512K in bank 1) (ROM v1.21 only)	0	1	0	0	X	X	X	X
640K (all on mbd, 512K in bank 0, 128K in bank 0) (ROM v1.21 only)	0	1	1	0	X	X	X	X
512K (all on mbd in bank 0) (ROM v1.21 only)	1	1	1	0	X	X	X	X
128K total RAM on mbd (ROM v1.43 only)	0	1	1	1	X	X	X	1
256K total on mbd, all 64K chips (ROM v1.43 only)	1	0	1	1	X	X	X	0

Table D-1. AT&T 6300 DIP SW-0 Settings, *continued*

Description	S1	S2	S3	S4	S5	S6	S7	S8
512K (4–64K bytes on mbd, rest on expansion board) (ROM v1.43 only)	1	1	0	1	X	X	X	0
640K (4–64K on mbd, 384 expansion) (ROM v1.43 only)	0	1	0	1	X	X	X	0
640K (all on mbd, 128K in bank 0, 512K in bank 1) (ROM v1.43 only)	0	1	0	0	X	X	X	0
640K (all on mbd, 512K in bank 0, 128K in bank 0) (ROM v1.43 only)	0	1	1	0	X	X	X	0
512K (all on mbd in bank 0) (ROM v1.43 only)	1	1	1	0	X	X	X	1
8087 not installed	X	X	X	X	1	X	X	X
8087 installed	X	X	X	X	0	X	X	X
8250 (asynchronous) communications installed	X	X	X	X	X	1	X	X
8530 (synchronous) communications installed	X	X	X	X	X	0	X	X
2732 ROMs on mbd (ROM v1.21 only)	X	X	X	X	X	X	X	1
2764 ROMs on mbd (ROM v1.21 only)	X	X	X	X	X	X	X	0

X = don't care 1 = on 0 = off

Table D-2. AT&T 6300 SW-1 switch settings

Description	S1	S2	S3	S4	S5	S6	S7	S8
Floppy drives are 360K	1	X	X	X	X	X	X	X
Floppy drives are 720K	0	X	X	X	X	X	X	X
Slow head settle time for floppy drives	X	1	X	X	X	X	X	X
Fast head settle time for floppy drives	X	0	X	X	X	X	X	X
Use built-in BIOS to control hard disk	X	X	1	X	X	X	X	X
Use BIOS on hard disk controller to communicate with hard disk	X	X	0	X	X	X	X	X
Fast scrolling (ROM v1.43 only)	X	X	X	1	X	X	X	X
Slow scrolling (ROM v1.43 only)	X	X	X	0	X	X	X	X
EGA installed, built-in video controller disabled (ROM v1.43 only)	X	X	X	X	1	1	X	X
40 × 25 color video	X	X	X	X	0	1	X	X
80 × 25 color video	X	X	X	X	1	0	X	X
80 × 25 monochrome	X	X	X	X	0	0	X	X

Table D-2. AT&T 6300 SW-1 switch settings, *continued*

Description	S1	S2	S3	S4	S5	S6	S7	S8
1 Floppy drive	X	X	X	X	X	X	1	1
2 Floppy drives	X	X	X	X	X	X	0	1
3 Floppy drives	X	X	X	X	X	X	1	0
4 Floppy drives	X	X	X	X	X	X	0	0
X = doesn't matter, 1 = on, 0 = off								

Appendix E
Information About Most Hard Disks

Notes on the table:

Size physical size (form factor)
- 5F = 5.25" full height
- 5H = 5.25" half height
- 3 = 3.5"

Cap capacity in megabytes

Cyls number of cylinders (tracks) in drive

H number of heads (surfaces, sides) in drive

RWC Reduced Write Current; first cylinder where reduced write current is applied

WPC Write Precomp Cylinder; cylinder to start write precompensation (Note for RWC and WPC: if indicated cylinder is greater than or equal to total # of cylinders, this drive does not need RWC or WPC.)

Enc encoding scheme, MFM (M), RLL (R), or ZBR (Z)

Rt data transfer rate in MB/second; B = buffered, can't directly measure

Seek seek time in MS

SPT Sectors Per Track

Drive/Interface	Size	Cap (MB)	Cyls	H	RWC	WPC	Enc	Rt	Seek (MS)	SPT
ALPS ELECTRIC										
ST-506 MFM										
DRND-10A	3	10	615	2	616	616	M	5	60	17
DRND-20A	3	20	615	4	616	616	M	5	60	17
ST-506 RLL										
RPO-20A	3	20	615	2	616	616	R	7.5	60	26
DRPO-20D	3	20	615	2	616	616	R	7.5	60	26
AMPEX										
ST-506										
PYXIS-7	5F	5	320	2	132	132	M	5	90	17
PYXIS-13	5F	10	320	4	132	132	M	5	90	17
PYXIS-20	5F	15	320	6	132	132	M	5	90	17
PYXIS-27	5F	20	320	8	132	132	M	5	90	17
ATASI										
ST-506										
3020		17	645	3	320	320	M	5		17
3033		28	645	5	320	320	M	5		17
3046		39	645	7	320	320	M	5		17
3051		43	704	7	359	350	M	5		17
3053		44	733	7	350	-	M	5		17
3075		67	1024	8	1025	1025	M	5		17
3085		67	1024	8	-	512	M	5		17
BASF										
ST-506										
6185		23	440	6	220	220	M	5		17
6186		15	440	4	220	220	M	5		
6187		8	440	2	220	220	M	5		17

Drive/Interface	Size	Cap (MB)	Cyls	H	RWC	WPC	Enc	Rt	Seek (MS)	SPT
BULL										
ST-506										
D-530		25	987	3	988	988	M	5		17
D-550		43	987	5	988	988	M	5		17
D-570		59	987	7	988	988	M	5		17
C. ITOH										
ST-506										
YD-3530		32	731	5	732	732	M	17		
YD-3540	5H	45	731	7	732	732	M	5	26	17
SCSI										
YD-3042	5F	43	788	4	789	789	R	8.5		26
YD-3082	5F	87	788	8	789	789	R	8.5		26
CARDIFF										
ST-506										
F-3053	3	44	1024	5	-	-	M	5	20	17
ESDI/SCSI										
F-3080	3	68								26
F-3127	3	68	1024	5	-	-	R/N	10	20	35
C D C										
ST-506										
BJ7D5A 77731614	5F	23	670	4	375	375	M	5		17
BJ7D5A 77731608	5F	29	670	5	375	375	M	5		17
94155-21	5F	21	697	3	698	698	M	5	28	17
94155-25		24	697	4	698	128	M	5		17
94155-28		24	697	4	698	128	M	5		17
94155-36	5F	36	697	5	698	698	M	5	28	17
94155-38		31	733	5	734	128	M	5		17
94155-48	5F	40	925	5	926	926	M	5	28	17
94295-51	5F	43	989	5	990	990	M	5	28	17

Drive/Interface	Size	Cap (MB)	Cyls	H	RWC	WPC	Enc	Rt	Seek (MS)	SPT
94155-57	5F	48	925	6	926	926	M	5	28	17
94155-67	5F	56	925	7	926	926	M	5	28	17
94155-77		64	925	8	926	926	M	5		17
94155-85	5F	71	1024	8	-	-	M	5	28	17
94155-86	5F	72	925	9	926	926	M	5	28	17
94205-51	5H	43	989	5	990	128	M	5	32	17
94335-55	3	46	-	5	-	-	M	5	25	17
94335-100	3	83	-	9	-	-	M	5	25	17
94355-55 SWIFT-2	3	46	-	5	-	-	M	5	16.5	17
94355-100	3	83	-	9	-	-	M	5	16.5	17
ST-506 RLL										
94155-135	5H	115	960	9	-	-	R	7.5	28	26
94205-77	5H	63	989	5	-	-	R	7.5	28	26
94355-150	3	128	-	9	-	-	R	7.5	16.5	26
94335-150	3	128-	9	-	-	-	R	7.5	25	26
ESDI										
94156-48		40	925	5	926	926	N	5	28	
94156-67		56	925	7	926	926	N	5		
94156-86		72	925	9	926	926	N	5		
94166-101	5F	86	969	5	970	970	N	10	16.5	
94166-141	5.25	121	969	7	970	970	N	10	16.5	
94166-182	5F	155	969	9	970	970	N	10	16.5	
94186-383	5F	383	1412	13	-	-	R/N	10	8.3	
94186-383H	5F	383	1224	15	-	-	R/N	10	14.5	
94186-442	5F	442	1412	15	-	-	R/N	10	16	
94216-106	5F	91	969	-	-	-	N	10	16.5	
94356-200 SWIFT 3	3	172	-	9	-	-	R/N	1 0	16.5	
WREN III	5H	106	969	5	-	-	R/N	10	18	
SCSI										
94161-86	5F	86	969	-	-	-	-	-	16.5	
94161-121	5F	121	969	-	-	-	-	-	16.5	
94171-300	5F	300	1365	9	-	-	R		16.5	
94171-344	5F	344	1549	9	-	-	Z	9-15	17.5	

Drive/Interface	Size	Cap (MB)	Cyls	H	RWC	WPC	Enc	Rt	Seek (MS)	SPT
94181-574	5F	574	1549	15	-	-	Z	9-15	16	
94211-91	5F	91	969	-	-	-	-	-	16.5	
94221-190	5H	190	1547	5	-	-	R	10	8.3	
94351-172 SWIFT 4	3	172	-	9	-	-	10	16.5		
WREN III	5H	106	969	5	-	-	R/N	10	18	
SMD										
386 SABRE 8'		386	-	10	-	-	1.8	18		
500 SABRE 8'		500	-	10	-	-	2.4	18		
736 SABRE 8'		741	-	15	-	-	1.8	16		
1230 SABRE 8'		1236	1635	15	-	-	2.4			

CENTURY DATA

ESDI

Drive/Interface	Size	Cap (MB)	Cyls	H	RWC	WPC	Enc	Rt	Seek (MS)	SPT
CAST-10203E	5F	55		3	1051	1051	R/N	10	28	35
CAST-10304	5F	75	1050	4	1051	1051	R/N	10	28	35
CAST-10305	5F	94	1050	5	1051	1051	R/N	10	28	35
CAST-14404	5H	114	1590	4	1591	1591	R/N	10	25	35
CAST-14405	5H	140	1590	5	1591	1591	R/N	10	25	35
CAST14406	5H	170	1590	6	1591	1591	R/N	10	25	35
CAST24509	5F	258	1599	9	1600	1600	R/N	10	18	35
CAST24611	5F	315	1599	11	1600	1600	R/N	10	18	35
CAST24713	5F	372	1599	13	1600	1600	R/N	10	18	35

SCSI

Drive/Interface	Size	Cap (MB)	Cyls	H	RWC	WPC	Enc	Rt	Seek (MS)	SPT
CAST10203S	5F	55	1050	3	1051	1051	R	10	28	35
CAST10304S	5F	75	1050	4	1051	1051	R	10	28	35
CAST10305S	5F	94	1050	5	1051	1051	R	10	28	35
CAST14404S	5H	114	1590	4	1591	1591	R	10	25	35
CAST14405S	5H	140	1590	5	1591	1591	R	10	25	35
CAST14406S	5H	170	1590	6	1591	1591	R	10	25	35
CAST24509S	5F	258	1599	9	1600	1600	R	10	18	35
CAST25611S	5F	315	1599	11	1600	1600	R	10	18	35
CAST24713S	5F	372	1599	13	1600	1600	R	10	18	35

Drive/Interface	Size	Cap (MB)	Cyls	H	RWC	WPC	Enc	Rt	Seek (MS)	SPT
C M I										
ST-506										
3426		20	615	4	616	256	M	5		17
5206		5	306	2	307	256	M	5		17
5205		4	256	2	128	128	M	5		17
5410		8	256	4	128	128	M	5		17
5412		10	306	4	307	128	M	5		17
5616		13	256	6	257	257	M	5		17
5619		15	306	6	307	128	M	5		17
6213		11	640	2	641	256	M	5		17
6426		21	640	4	641	256	M	5		17
6640		33	640	6	641	256	M	5		17
7660		50	960	6	961	450	M	5		17
7880		67	960	8	961	450	M	5		17
GITO										
ST-506										
CG-906		5	306	2	128	128	M	5		
CG-912		11	306	4	128	128	M	5		
PT-912		11	612	2	307	307	M	5		
PT-925		21	612	4	307	307	M	5		
CONNER PERPHER										
AT-BUS										
CP-342	3	40	805	4	-	-	R	7.5	29	
CP-3022	3	21	636	2	-	-	R	10	27	
CP-3102	3	104	776	8	-	-	R	10		25
SCSI										
CP-340	3	42	788	4	-	-	R	7.5	29	
CP-3100	3	104	776	8	-	-	R	10		25

Drive/Interface	Size	Cap (MB)	Cyls	H	RWC	WPC	Enc	Rt	Seek (MS)	SPT
CORE INTNL										
ST-506										
AT 32	5H	31	733	5	-	-	M	5	21	17
AT 30	5F	31	733	5	-	-	M	5	26	17
AT 40	5F	42	988	5	-	-	M	5	26	17
AT 63	5F	42	988	5	-	-	M	5	26	17
AT 72	5F	107	924	9	-	-	M	5	26	17
OPTIMA 30	5H	31	733	5	-	-	M	5	21	17
OPTIMA 40	5H	41	963	5	-	-	M	5	26	17
OPTIMA 70	5F	71	918	9	-	-	M	5	26	17
ST-506 RLL										
AT 32	5H	48	733	5	-	-	R	7.5	21	26
AT 30	5F	48	733	5	-	-	R	7.5	26	26
AT 40	5F	61	924	5	-	-	R	7.5	26	26
AT 63	5F	65	988	5	-	-	R	7.5	26	26
AT 72	5F	107	924	9	-	-	R	7.5	26	26
OPTIMA 30	5H	48	733	5	-	-	R	7.5	21	26
OPTIMA 40	5H	64	963	5	-	-	R	7.5	26	26
OPTIMA 70	5F	109	918	9	-	-	R	7.5	26	26
ESDI										
HC 40	5F	40	564	4	-	-	R/N	10	10	35
HC 90	5H	91	969	5	-	-	R/N	10	16	35
HC 150	5F	156	969	9	-	-	R/N	10	16	35
HC 260	5F	260	1212	12	-	-	R/N	10	25	35
HC 310	5F	311	1582	12	-	-	R/N	10	16	35
DISCTRON										
ST-506										
D-503		3	153	2	-	-	M	5		17
D-504		4	215	2	-	-	M	5		17
D-506		5	153	4	-	-	M	5		17
D-507		5	306	2	128	128	M	5		17

Drive/Interface	Size	Cap (MB)	Cyls	H	RWC	WPC	Enc	Rt	Seek (MS)	SPT
D-509		8	215	4	128	128	M	5		17
D-512		11	153	8	-	-	M	5		17
D-513		11	215	6	128	128	M	5		17
D-514		11	306	4	128	128	M	5		17
D-518		15	215	8	128	128	M	5		17
D-519		16	306	6	128	128	M	5		17
D-526		21	306	8	128	128	M	5		17

DMA

ST-506

306 remov.		11	612	2	612	400	M	5		17

ELCOH

ST-506

DISCACHE10		10	320	4	321	321	M	5		17
DISCACHE20		20	320	8	321	321	M	5		17

FUJI

ST-506 MFM

FK305-26	3	21	615	4	-	616	M	5	50	17
FK305-39	3	32	615	4	616	616	M	5	50	17
FK309-26	3	21	615	4	-	616	M	5	50	17
FK301		10	306	4	307	128	M	5		17
FK302-13		10	612	2	613	307	M	5		17
FK302-26		21	612	4	613	307	M	5		17
FK302-39		32	612	6	613	307	M	5		17
FK303-52	3	40	615	8	-	616	M	5	50	17

ST-506 RLL

FK305-39R	3	32	615	4	-	616	R	7.5	50	26
FK305-58R	3	49	615	6	-	616	R	7.5	50	26
FK309-39R		32	615	4	-	616	R	7.5		26

Drive/Interface	Size	Cap (MB)	Cyls	H	RWC	WPC	Enc	Rt	Seek (MS)	SPT
ESDI										
FK308S-58R	3	45	615	6	-	-	R	7.5	50	
FK308S-39R	3	32	615	4	-	616	R	7.5	50	
FK309S-50R	3	41	615	4	-	-	R	7.5	50	

FUJITSU

ST-506

Drive/Interface	Size	Cap (MB)	Cyls	H	RWC	WPC	Enc	Rt	Seek (MS)	SPT
2230 AS		5	320	2	321	321	M	5		17
2233 AS		10	320	4	321	321	M	5		17
2234 AS		15	320	6	321	321	M	5		17
2235 AS		20	320	8	321	321	M	5		17
2241 AS		26	754	4	755	755	M	5		17
M2226DS	3	30	615	6	-	-	M	5	35	17
M2227D2	3	40	615	8	-	-	M	5	3	17
M2242AS2	5F	43	754	7	-	-	M	5	30	17
M2243AS2	5F	67	754	11	-	-	M	5	30	17
M2243T	5H	68	1186	7	-	-	M	5	25	17
ST-506 RLL										
M2225DR	3	32	615	4	-	-	R	7.5	35	26
M2226DR	3	49	615	6	-	-	R	7.5	35	26
M2227DR	3	65	615	8	-	-	R	7.5	35	26
M2243R	5H	110	1186	7	-	-	R	7.5	25	26
ESDI										
2244E	5F	73	823	5	-	-	R/N	10	25	35
2245E	5F	120	823	7	-	-	R/N	10	25	35
M2246E	5F	171	823	10	-	-	R/N	10	25	35
ESDI/SCSI										
M2249		389	1243	15	-	-	R	10	18	
SCSI										
M244SA		73	823	5	-	-	R	B	25	35
M2245SA		120	823	7	-	-	R	B	25	35
M2246SA		171	823	10	-	-	R	B	25	35
M2344KS		690	624	27	-	-	R	B	16	

343

Drive/Interface	Size	Cap (MB)	Cyls	H	RWC	WPC	Enc	Rt	Seek (MS)	SPT
HITACHI										
ST-506										
DK301-1	3	10	306	4	-	-	M	5	85	17
DK301-2	3	15	306	6	-	-	M	5	85	17
DK511-3	5F	28	699	5	-	-	M	5	30	17
DK511-5	5F	40	699	7	-	-	M	5	30	17
DK511-8	5F	67	823	10	-	-	M	5	23	17
DK521-5	5H	51	823	6	-	-	M	5	25	17
ESDI										
DK512-8	5F	67	823	5	-	-	R/N	10	23	
DK512-12	5F	94	823	7	-	-	R/N	10	23	
DK512-17	5F	134	823	10	-	-	R/N	10	23	
DK514-38	5F	330	903	14	-	-	R/N	15	16	51
DK522-10	5H	103	823	6	-	-	R/N	10	25	36
SCSI										
DK512C-8	5F	67	823	5	-	-	R	10	23	
DK512C-12	5F	94	823	7	-	-	R	10	23	
DK512C-17	5F	134	819	10	-	-	R	10	23	35
DK522C-10	5H	88	819	6	-	-	R	10	25	35
IMI										
ST-506										
5006		5	306	2	307	214	M	5		17
5012		10	306	4	307	214	M	5		17
5018		15	306	6	307	214	M	5		17
JCT										
ST-506										
100	5H	5	-	-	-	-	M	5	110	17
105	5H	7	-	-	-	-	M	5	110	17
110	5H	14	-	-	-	-	M	5	130	17
120	5H	20	-	-	-	-	M	5	100	17

Drive/Interface	Size	Cap (MB)	Cyls	H	RWC	WPC	Enc	Rt	Seek (MS)	SPT
COMMODORE										
1000		5	-	-	-	-	M			
1005		7	-	-	-	-	M			
1010		14	-	-	-	-	M			
KALOK CORP										
AT-BUS										
KL343 OCTAGON 40		40	644	4	645	645	R	8	25	30
ST-506 MFM										
KL320 OCTAGON 20	3	20	615	4	616	300	M	5	48	17
ST-506 RLL										
KL330 OCTAGON 30		32	616	4	617	617	R	7.5	48	26
PS/2										
KL332 OCTAGON 30		40	615	4	-	-	R	8	48	30
SCSI										
KL341 OCTAGON 40		40	644	4	-	-	R	8	25	30
KYOCERA										
ST-506										
KC20A/B	3	20	616	4	-	-	M	5	65	17
ST-506 RLL										
KC30A/B	3	30	615	4	-	-	R	7.5	65	26
LAPINE										
ST-506 MFM										
3522		10	306	4	307	-	M	5		17
LT 10		10	615	2	616	-	M	5		17
LT 20		20	615	4	616	-	M	5		17
LT 200		20	614	4	615	300	M	5		17
LT 2000		20	614	4	615	-	M	5		17
ST-506 RLL										
LT 300		32	614	4	615	300	R	7.5		26

Drive/Interface	Size	Cap (MB)	Cyls	H	RWC	WPC	Enc	Rt	Seek (MS)	SPT
MAXTOR										
ST-506 MFM										
XT-1065	5F	56	918	7	919	919	M	5	28	17
XT-1085	5F	71	1024	8	1025	1025	M	5	28	17
XT-1105	5F	87	918	11	919	919	M	5	27	17
XT-1140	5F	113	918	15	919	919	M	5	27	17
XT-2085	5F	74	1224	7	1225	1225	M	5	30	17
XT-2140	5F	117	1224	11	1225	1225	M	5	30	17
XT-2190	5F	150	1224	15	1225	1225	M	5	30	17
ST-506 RLL										
XT-1120R	5F	104	1024	8	-	-	R	7.5	27	25
XT-1240R	5F	196	1024	15	-	-	R	7.5	27	25
ESDI										
XT-4170E	5F	157	1224	7	-	-	R/N	10	16	35
XT-4175	5F		-	7	-	-	R/N	10	27	35
XT-4380E	5F	338	1224	15	-	-	R/N	10	27	35
XT-8380E	5F	360	1632	8	-	-	R/N	15	16	54
XT-8760E	5F	676	1632	15	-	-	R/N	15	18	54
SCSI										
XT-3170	5F	146	1224	9	-	- •		15	30	48
XT-3280	5F		1224	15	-	-	R	15	30	
XT-3380	5F		-	15	-	-	R	15	27	
XT-4170S	5F	157	1224	7	-	-	R	10	16	36
XT-4280S	5F	338	1224	15	-	-	R	10	18	36
XT-8380S	5F	360	1632	8	-	-	R	15	16	54
XT-8760S	5F	676	1632	15	-	-	R	15	18	54
MEMOREX										
ST-506										
321		5	320	2	321	128	M	5		17
322		10	320	4	321	128	M	5		17
324		20	320	8	321	128	M	5		17
450		10	612	2	321	350	M	5		17

Drive/Interface	Size	Cap (MB)	Cyls	H	RWC	WPC	Enc	Rt	Seek (MS)	SPT
512		25	961	3	321	480	M	5		17
513		41	961	5	321	480	M	5		17
514		58	961	7	321	480	M	5		17

MICROPOLIS

ST-506

Drive/Interface	Size	Cap (MB)	Cyls	H	RWC	WPC	Enc	Rt	Seek (MS)	SPT
1302	5F	21	830	3	831	400	M	5		17
1303	5F	36	830	5	831	400	M	5		17
1304	5F	43	830	6	831	400	M	5		17
1323	5F	35	1024	4	1025	1025	M	5	28	17
1323A	5F	44	1024	5	1025	1025	M	5	28	17
1324	5F	53	1024	6	1025	1025	M	5	28	17
1324A	5F	62	1024	7	1025	1025	M	5	28	17
1325	5F	71	1024	8	1025	1025	M	5	28	17
1333A	5F	44	1024	5	1025	1025	M	5	30	17
1334	5F	53	1024	6	1025	1025	M	5	30	17
1335	5F	71	1024	8	1025	1025	M	5	30	17

ESDI

Drive/Interface	Size	Cap (MB)	Cyls	H	RWC	WPC	Enc	Rt	Seek (MS)	SPT
1353	5F	79	1024	4	1025	1025	R/N	10	23	35
1353A	5F	99	1024	5	1025	1025	R/N	10	23	35
1354	5F	119	1024	6	1025	1025	R/N	10	23	35
1354A	5F	139	1024	7	1025	1025	R/N	10	23	35
1355	5F	159	1024	8	1025	1025	R/N	10	23	35
1556-11	5F	248	1224	11	1225	1225	R/N	10	18	36
1557-12	5F	270	1224	12	1225	1225	R/N	10	18	36
1557-13	5F	293	1224	13	1225	1225	R/N	10	18	36
1557-14	5F	315	1224	14	1225	1225	R/N	10	18	36
1557-15	5F	338	1224	15	1225	1225	R/N	10	18	36
1566-11	5F	496	1632	11	-	-	R/N	15	16	
1567-12	5F	541	1632	12	-	-	R/N	15	16	
1567-13	5F	586	1632	13	-	-	R/N	15	16	
1568-14	5F	631	1632	14	-	-	R/N	15	16	
1568-15	5F	676	1632	15	-	-	R/N	15	16	

Drive/Interface	Size	Cap (MB)	Cyls	H	RWC	WPC	Enc	Rt	Seek (MS)	SPT
1653-4	5H	92	1249	4	-	-	R/N	10	16	
1653-5	5H	115	1249	5	-	-	R/N	10	16	
1654-6	5H	138	1249	6	-	-	R/N	10	16	
1654-7	5F	161	1249	7	-	-	R/N	10	16	
SCSI										
1373	5F	76	1024	4	-	-	1.25	B	23	
1373A	5F	95	1024	5	-	-	1.25	B	23	
1374	5F	115	1024	6	-	-	1.25	B	23	
1374A	5F	134	1024	7	-	-	1.25	B	23	
1375	5F	153	1024	8	-	-	1.25	B	23	
1576-11	5F	243	1224	11	-	-	1 .6	B	18	36
1577-12	5F	266	1224	12	-	-	1 .6	B	18	36
1577-13	5F	287	1224	13	-	-	1 .6	B	18	36
1577-13	5F	287	1224	13	-	-	1 .6	B	18	36
1578-14	5F	310	1224	14	-	-	1 .6	B	18	36
1578-15	5F	332	1224	15	-	-	1 .6	B	18	36
1673-4	5H	90	1249	4	-	-	R	10	16	
1673-5	5H	112	1249	5	-	-	R	10	16	
1674-6	5H	135	1249	6	-	-	R	10	16	
1674-7	5H	158	1249	7	-	-	R	10	16	
1586-11	5F	490	1632	11	-	-	R	15	16	
1587-12	5F	535	1632	12	-	-	R	15	16	
1587-13	5F	579	1632	13	-	-	R	15	16	
1588-14	5F	624	1632	14	-	-	R	15	16	
1588-15	5F	668	1632	15	-	-	R	15	16	

MICROSCIENCE

ST-506

Drive/Interface	Size	Cap (MB)	Cyls	H	RWC	WPC	Enc	Rt	Seek (MS)	SPT
HH-312		10	306	4	307	307	M	5		
HH-315		10	306	4	307	307	M	5		17
HH325		21	612	4	613	613	M	5	80	17
HH612		11	306	4	307	307	M	5		17
HH625		21	612	4	613	613	M	5		17

Drive/Interface	Size	Cap (MB)	Cyls	H	RWC	WPC	Enc	Rt	Seek (MS)	SPT
HH712	5H	10	612	2	613	613	M	5	105	17
HH725	5H	21	612	4	613	613	M	5	105	17
HH825	5H	21	612	4	613	613	M	5	65	17
HH1050	5H	44	1024	5	1025	1025	M	5	28	17
HH-1075	5H	62	1024	7	1025	1025	M	5	28	17
HH-1090	5H	80	1314	7	1315	1315	M	5	28	17
ST-506 RLL										
HH 330		32	612	4	613	613	R	7.5		26
HH 738	5H	32	612	4	613	613	R	7.5	105	26
HH 830	5H	32	612	4	613	613	R	7.5	65	26
HH 1060	5H	66	1024	5	1025	1025	R	7.5	28	26
HH-1095	5H	95	1024	7	1025	1025	R	28		26
HH-1120	5H	122	1314	7	1315	1315	R	7.5	28	26
ESDI										
HH-2085	-	-	-	-	-	-	R/N			
HH-2120	5H	121	1024	7	-	-	R/N	10	28	
SCSI										
HH1080	-	-	-	-	-	-	R			
HH-3120	5H	122	1314	7	-	-	R	7.5	28	

MINISCRIBE

Drive/Interface	Size	Cap (MB)	Cyls	H	RWC	WPC	Enc	Rt	Seek (MS)	SPT
8051A	3	42	745	4	-	-	-	8	28	
8425XT	3	21	615	4	-	-				
8425XT	3	21	615	4	-	-				
438XT	3	31	615	4	-	-				
ST-506 MFM										
1006		5	306	2	153	128	M	5		17
1012		10	306	4	153	128	M	5		17
2006		5	306	2	307	128	M	5		17
2012		11	306	4	307	128	M	5		17
3212	5H	11	612	2	613	128	M	5	85	17
3212 PLUS	5H	11	612	2	613	128	M	5	53	17
3412		11	306	4	307	128	M	5		17

Drive/Interface	Size	Cap (MB)	Cyls	H	RWC	WPC	Enc	Rt	Seek (MS)	SPT
3425	5H	21	612	4	613	128	M	5	85	17
3425 PLUS	5H	21	612	4	613	306	M	5	53	17
3053	5H	44	1024	5	1025	1025	M	5	25	17
3650	5H	42	809	6	810	128	M	5	61	17
4010		8	480	2	481	128	M	5		17
4020		17	480	4	481	128	M	5		17
5330		25	480	6	481	128	M	5		17
5338		32	612	6	613	306	M	5		17
5440		32	480	8	481	128	M	5		17
5451		43	612	8	613	306	M	5		17
6032	5F	26	1024	3	1025	512	M	5	28	17
6053	5F	44	1024	5	1025	512	M	5	28	17
6074	5F	62	1024	7	1025	512	M	5	28	17
6085	5F	71	1024	8	1025	512	M	5	28	17
6212		10	612	2	613	-	M	5		17
7426		21	612	4	613	613	M	5		17
8212		11	612	2	613	613	M	5		17
8412		10	306	4	307	0	M	5	68	17
8425	3	21	615	4	616	616	M	5	68	17
8425F	3	21	615	4	-	-	M	5	40	17
ST-506 RLL										
3438	5H	32	612	4	613	300	R	7.5	53	26
3438 PLUS	5H	32	612	4	613	613	R	7.5	53	26
079	5F	68	1024	5	-	-	R	7.5	28	26
6128	5F	110	1024	8	-	-	R	7.5	28	26
8434F	3	32	615	4	-	-	R	7.5	40	26
8438	3	32	615	4	616	-	R	7.5	68	26
8438F	3	32	615	4	616	-	R	7.5	40	26
ESDI/SCSI										
9230	5F	203	1224	9	-	-	R	10	16	
9380	5F	338	1224	15	-	-	R	10	16	

Drive/Interface	Size	Cap (MB)	Cyls	H	RWC	WPC	Enc	Rt	Seek (MS)	SPT
SCSI										
8425S	3	21	615	4	-	-	R	5	68	
8051S	3	42	745	4	-	-	1025	8	28	

MMI

ST-506										
M 112	3	10	306	4	-	128	M	5	75	17
M 106	3	5	306	2	-	128	M	5	75	17
M 125	3	20	306	8	-	128	M	5	75	17
M 306	3	5	306	2	-	128	M	5	75	17
M 212	5H	10	306	4	-	128	M	5	75	17
M 225	5H	20	306	8	-	128	M	5	75	17
M 312	5H	10	306	4	-	128	M	5	75	17
M 325	5H	20	306	8	-	128	M	5	75	17

N E C

ST-506										
D3126	3	20	615	4	616	256	M	5	85	17
D5124	5H	10	309	4	310	310	M	5	85	17
D5126	5H	20	612	4	613	-	M	5	85	17
D5126H		20	612	4	613	-	M	5	40	17
D5146	5H	40	615	8	616	-	M	5	85	17
D5146H	5H	40	615	8	616	-	M	5	40	17
ESDI										
D5652	5H	143	823	10	-	-	R/N	10	23	

NEWBURY DT

ST-506										
NDR 340	3	42	615	8	-	-	M		40	
NDR 1065	5F	55	918	7	-	-	M		25	
NDR 1085	5F	71	1025	8	-	-	M		26	
NDR 1105	5F	87	918	11	-	-	M		25	

Drive/Interface	Size	Cap (MB)	Cyls	H	RWC	WPC	Enc	Rt	Seek (MS)	SPT
NDR 1140	5F	105	918	15	-	-	M		25	
NDR 2190	5F	191	918	15	-	-	M		28	
ESDI										
NDR 4175	5F	179	1224	7	-	-	R/N	10	28	36
NDR 4380	5F	384	1224	15	-	-	R/N	10	28	36
SCSI										
NDR 3170S	5F	146	1224	9	-	-	R	7.5	28	26
NDR 3280S	5F	244	1224	15	-	-	R	7.5	28	26
NDR 4380S	5F	319	1224	15	-	-	R	10	28	34

OKIDATA

ST-506 RLL

Drive/Interface	Size	Cap (MB)	Cyls	H	RWC	WPC	Enc	Rt	Seek (MS)	SPT
OD526		31	612	4	613	613	R	7.5		26
OD540		62	612	8	613	613	R	7.5		26

OLIVETTI

ST-506

Drive/Interface	Size	Cap (MB)	Cyls	H	RWC	WPC	Enc	Rt	Seek (MS)	SPT
HD662/11		10	612	2	-	-	M	5		17
HD662/12		20	612	4	-	-	M	5		17

OTARI

ST-506

Drive/Interface	Size	Cap (MB)	Cyls	H	RWC	WPC	Enc	Rt	Seek (MS)	SPT
C 214		10	306	4	128	128	M	5		17
C 519		15	306	6	128	128	M	5		17
C 526		21	306	8	128	128	M	5		17

PANASONIC

ST-506

Drive/Interface	Size	Cap (MB)	Cyls	H	RWC	WPC	Enc	Rt	Seek (MS)	SPT
JU-116	3	20	615	4	616	616	M	5	85	17
JU-128	3	42	733	7	734	734	M	5	35	17

Drive/Interface	Size	Cap (MB)	Cyls	H	RWC	WPC	Enc	Rt	Seek (MS)	SPT
PRIAM										
ST-506										
V-150		42	987	5	988	988	M	5		17
V-160		50	1166	5	1167	1167	M	5		17
V-170		60	987	7	988	988	M	5		17
V-185		71	1166	7	1167	1167	M	5		17
502		46	755	7	756	756	M	5		17
504		46	755	7	756	756	M	5		17
514	5F	117	1224	11	1225	1225	M	5	22	17
519	5F	160	1224	15	1225	1225	M	5	22	17
ST-506 RLL										
V-130		39	987	3	988	988	R	7.5		26
V-170		91	987	7	988	988	R	7.5		26
ESDI										
617	5F	153	1225	7	1226	1226	R/N	10	20	
628	5F	241	1225	11	1226	1226	R/N	10	20	
638	5F	329	1225	15	1226	1226	R/N	10	20	
SCSI										
717	5F	153	1225	7	1226	1226	R	10	20	
728	5F	241	1225	11	1226	1226	R	10	20	
738	5F	329	1225	15	1226	1226	R	10	20	
PTI										
AT-BUS										
PT-238A	3	32	615	4	-	-	R	7.5		35
PT-251A	3	43	820	4	-	-	R	7.5		35
PT-357A	3	49	615	6	-	-	R	7.5		35
PT-376A	3	65	820	6	-	-	R	7.5		35
ST-506 MFM										
PT-255	3	21	615	4	-	-	M	5	35	17
PT-234	3	28	820	4	-	-	M	5	35	17

353

Drive/Interface	Size	Cap (MB)	Cyls	H	RWC	WPC	Enc	Rt	Seek (MS)	SPT
PT-351	3	42	820	6	-	-	M	5	35	17
ST-506										
PT-238R	3	32	615	4	-	-	R	7.5	35	26
PT-251R	3	43	820	4	-	-	R	7.5	35	26
PT-357R	3	49	615	6	-	-	R	7.5	35	26
PT-376R	3	65	820	6	-	-	R	7.5	35	26
PT-4102R	3	87	820	8	-	-	R	7.5		26
SCSI										
PT-238S	3	32	615	4	-	-	R	7.5		35
PT-251S	3	43	820	4	-	-	R	7.5		35
PT-357S	3	49	615	6	-	-	R	7.5		35
PT-376S	3	65	820	6	-	-	R	7.5		35

QUANIUM

Drive/Interface	Size	Cap (MB)	Cyls	H	RWC	WPC	Enc	Rt	Seek (MS)	SPT
AT-BUS										
PRO40	3	42	-	-	-	-	-	-	19	
PRO80	3	84	-	-	-	-	-	-	19	
PRO120	3	120	-	-	-	-	-	-	19	
PRO170	3	168		-	-	-	-	-	-	19
ST-506										
Q-510		8	512	2	256	256	M	5		17
Q-520		18	512	4	256	513	M	5		17
Q-530		27	512	6	256	513	M	5		17
Q-540		36	512	8	256	513	M	5		17
ESDI										
PRO100	3	102	-	-	-	-	-	-	19	
PRO145	3	145	-	-	-	-	-	-	19	
SCSI										
Q-250	5H	53	823	4	-	-	R	10		26
Q-280	5H	80	823	6	-	-	R	10		26
Q-160	5H	200	-	12	-	-	R	10		26
PRO-40	3	42	-	-	-	-	-	-	19	
PRO-80	3	84	-	-	-	-	-	-	19	

Drive/Interface	Size	Cap (MB)	Cyls	H	RWC	WPC	Enc	Rt	Seek (MS)	SPT
PRO-120	3	120	-	-	-	-	-	-	19	
PRO170	3	168	-	-	-	-	-	-	19	

RICOH SYS

ST-506

RH-5130		10	612	2	613	400	M	5	85	17
RH-5260 remov.		10	615	2	-	-	M	5	85	17

SCSI

RH-5261 remov.		10	612	2	-	-	M	5	85	

RODIME

ST-506

RO-101	5F	6	192	2	96	192	M	5		17
RO-102	5F	12	192	4	96	192	M	5		17
RO-103	5F	18	192	6	96	192	M	5	55	17
RO-104	5F	24	192	8	96	192	M	5		17
RO-201	5F	5	321	2	132	300	M	5	85	17
RO-201F	5F	11	640	2	264	300	M	5	55	17
RO-202	5H	10	321	4	132	300	M	5	85	17
RO-202E	5F	21	640	4	264	300	M	5	55	17
RO-203	5H	15	321	6	132	300	M	5	85	17
RO-203E	5F	32	640	6	210	210	M	5	55	17
RO-204	5F	21	320	8	132	300	M	5	85	17
RO-204E	5F	43	640	8	264	300	M	5	55	17
RO-251	5H	5	306	2	307	307	M	5	85	17
RO-252	5H	11	306	4	64	128	M	5	85	17
RO-351		5	306	2	307	307	M	5	85	17
RO 352	3	11	306	4	64	128	M	5	85	17
RO 365	3	21	612	4	613	613	M	5		17
RO 3045		37	872	5	873	-	M	5	28	17
RO 3055		45	872	6	873	-	M	5	28	17
RO 3065		53	872	7	-	-	M	5	28	17

Drive/Interface	Size	Cap (MB)	Cyls	H	RWC	WPC	Enc	Rt	Seek (MS)	SPT
RO 5065	5H	63	-	5	-	-	M	5	28	17
RO 5090	5H	89	1224	7	-	-	M	5	28	17
SCSI										
RO 652A		20	-	-	-	-	-	-	85	
RO 652B		20	306	4	-	-	R		85	
RO 752A	5H	25	-	-	-	-	-	-	85	
RO 3070S		71	-	-	-	-	28			
RO 3085S		85	750	7	-	-	R	28		
RO 3057S		45	680	5	-	-	R	28		
RO 5040		38	-	3	-	-	M	5	28	
RO 5075S	5H	76	-	-	-	-	-	-	28	
RO 5125S	5H	127	1219	5	-	-	R	28		
RO 5180S	5H	178	1219	7	-	-	-	-	28	

SEAGATE

ST-506

Drive/Interface	Size	Cap (MB)	Cyls	H	RWC	WPC	Enc	Rt	Seek (MS)	SPT
ST125	3	21	615	4	616	616	M	5	40/28	17
ST138	3	32	615	6	616	616	M	5	40/28	17
ST-206	5F	5	306	2	307	128	M	5		17
ST-212	5F	10	306	4	307	128	M	5		17
ST213	5F	10	615	2	613	307	M	5		17
ST225	5H	21	615	4	616	307	M	5	65	17
ST251	5H	42	820	6	821	410	M	5	40	17
ST-251-1	5H	42	820	6	821	821	M	5	28	17
ST-406	5F	5	306	2	307	128	M	5		17
ST-412	5F	10	306	4	307	128	M	5		17
ST-419	5F	15	306	6	307	128	M	5		17
ST-425	5F	21	306	8	307	128	M	5		17
ST-506	5F	5	153	4	128	128	M	5		17
ST-706	5F	5	306	2	307	128	M	5		17
ST-4026	5F	21	615	4	616	307	M	5		17
ST-4038	5H	38	733	5	734	367	M	5	40	17
ST-4051	5F	42	977	5	978	498	M	5	40	17

Drive/Interface	Size	Cap (MB)	Cyls	H	RWC	WPC	Enc	Rt	Seek (MS)	SPT
ST4053	5F	44	1024	5	1023	1023	M	5	28	17
ST4096	5F	80	1024	9	1023	1023	M	5	28	17
ST-506 RLL										
ST138R	3	32	615	4	616	616	R	7.5	40/28	26
ST157R	3	49	615	6	616	616	R	7.5	40/28	26
ST238R	5H	30	615	4	616	307	R	7.5	65	26
ST251R	5H	43	820	4	821	821	R	7.5	40	26
ST277R	5H	65	820	6	821	821	R	7.5	40	26
ST4077R	5F	65	1024	5	1025	1025	R	7.5	28	26
ST4144R	5F	122	1024	9	1025	1025	R	7.5	28	26
ESDI										
ST-4192E	5F	169	1147	8	1148	1025	R/N	10	17	36
SCSI										
ST138N	3	32	613	4	614	614	R	10	40/28	35
ST157N	3	48	613	6	614	614	R	10	40/28	26
ST225N	5H	21	615	4	616	616	M	5	65	17
ST-251-N	5H	43	818	4	819	819	R	7.5	40	26
ST-277N	5H	64	818	6	819	819	R	7.5	40	26
ST296-N	5H	85	818	6	819	816	R	10	28	34
ST-4077N	5F	67	1024	5	1025	1025	R	7.5	28	26
ST-4192N	5F	168	1147	8	1148	1148	R	10	17	36

SHUGART

ST-506

604		5	160	4	128	128	M	5		17
606		7	160	6	128	128	M	5		17
612		11	306	4	307	128	M	5		17
706		6	320	2	321	128	M	5		17
712		11	320	4	321	128	M	5		17

SIEMENS

ESDI

1200	5F	174	1216	8	-	-	R/N	10	25	

Drive/Interface	Size	Cap (MB)	Cyls	H	RWC	WPC	Enc	Rt	Seek (MS)	SPT
1300	5F	261	1216	12	-	-	R/N	10	25	
2300	5F	261	1216	12	-	-	R/N	10	25	
2200	5F	174	1216	8	-	-	R/N	10	25	
5710		655	-	15	-	-	R/N	15	16	
SCSI										
5720		655	-	15	-	-	-	-	16	

SYQUEST

ST-506

Drive/Interface	Size	Cap (MB)	Cyls	H	RWC	WPC	Enc	Rt	Seek (MS)	SPT
SQ 306RD remov.		5	306	2	307	307	M	5		17
SQ 312RD remov.		10	615	2	616	616	M	5		17
SQ 325F		20	615	4	616	616	M	5		17
SQ 338F		30	615	6	616	616	M	5		17
SQ 340AF		38	640	6	616	616	M	5		17

TANDON WD

ST-506

Drive/Interface	Size	Cap (MB)	Cyls	H	RWC	WPC	Enc	Rt	Seek (MS)	SPT
TM 252		10	306	4	307	307	M	5		17
TM 261		10	615	2	616	616	M	5		17
TM 262		21	615	4	616	616	M	5		17
TM 361		10	615	2	616	616	M	5		17
TM 362		21	615	4	616	616	M	5		17
TM 501		5	306	2	128	153	M	5		17
TM 502		10	306	4	128	153	M	5		17
TM 503		15	306	6	128	153	M	5		17
TM 703		10	733	5	734	734	M	5		17
TM 755	3	21	981	5	982	982	M	5		17
TM 3085		71	1024	8	1024	1024	M	5	37	17
TM 6025		10	153	4	128	128	M	5		17
TM 6035		10	153	6	128	128	M	5		17
TM 6025E		21	230	6	128	128	M	5		17
ST-506 RLL										
TM 244		41	782	4	783	783	R	7.5	37	26

Drive/Interface	Size	Cap (MB)	Cyls	H	RWC	WPC	Enc	Rt	Seek (MS)	SPT
TM 246		62	782	6	783	783	R	7.5	37	26
TM 262R	3	20	782	2	783	783	R	7.5		26
TM 264		41	782	4	783	783	R	7.5	85	26
TM 344	3	41	782	4	783	783	R	7.5	37	26
TM 346	3	62	782	6	783	783	R	7.5	37	26
TM 362R	3	20	782	2	783	783	R	7.5	85	26
TM 364	3	41	782	4	783	783	R	7.5	85	26
TM 702		20	615	4	616	616	R	7.5		26
TM 3085		104	1024	8	1024	1024	R	7.5	37	26
SCSI										
TM 2085		74	1004	9	1005	1005	M	5	25	
TM 2128		115	1004	9	1005	1005	R	7.5		25
TM 2170		154	1344	9	1345	1345	R	7.5		25

TEAC

ST-506

SD 510		10	306	4	128	128	M	5		17
SD 520		20	615	4	128	128	M	5		17

T.I.

ST-506

5F	5	153	4	64	6 4	M	5		17

TOSHIBA

ST-506

MK53FA	5F	43	830	5	831	831	M	5	30	17
MK 54FA	5F	60	830	7	831	831	M	5	30	17
MK 56FA	5F	86	830	10	831	831	M	5		17
MK134FA	3	44	733	7	734	734	M	5	25	17
ST-506 RLL										
MK53FB	5F	64	830	5	831	831	R	7.5	23	26
MK 54FB	5F	90	830	7	831	831	R	7.5	25	26
MK56FB	5F	130	830	10	831	831	R	7.5	25	26

Drive/Interface	Size	Cap (MB)	Cyls	H	RWC	WPC	Enc	Rt	Seek (MS)	SPT
ESDI										
MK153FA	5F	74	830	5	831	831	R/N	10	23	35
MK154FA	5F	104	830	7	831	831	R/N	10	23	35
MK156FB	5F	148	830	10	831	831	R/N	10	23	35
ESDI/SCSI										
MK250F	5F	382	1224	10	-	-	R/N	10	18	35
SCSI										
MK153FB	5F	74	830	5	831	831	R	10	23	35
MK154FB	5F	104	830	7	831	831	R	10	23	35
MK156FA	5F	148	830	20	831	831	R	10	23	35

TULIN

ST-506										
213		10	640	2	656	656	M	5		17
226		22	640	4	656	656	M	5		17
240		33	640	6	656	656	M	5		17
326		22	640	4	641	641	M	5		17
340		33	640	6	641	641	M	5		17

VERTEX/PRIAM

ST-506										
V130		26	987	3	988	988	M	5		17
V150		43	987	5	988	988	M	5	17	
V170		60	987	7	988	988	M	5		17

WESTERN DIGITAL

ST-506 MFM										
WD 262		20	615	4	616	616	M	5	80	17
WD 362	3	20	615	4	616	616	M	5	80	17
ST-506 RLL										
WD 344R	3	40	782	4	783	783	R	7.5	40	26

Drive/Interface	Size	Cap (MB)	Cyls	H	RWC	WPC	Enc	Rt	Seek (MS)	SPT
WD 382R/TM 262R	3	20	782	2	783	783	R	7.5	85	26
WD 384R/TM 364R	3	20	782	2	783	783	R	7.5	85	26
WD 544R		40	782	4	783	783	R	7.5	40	26
WD582R		20	782	2	783	783	R	7.5	85	26
WD 584R		40	782	4	783	783	R	7.5	85	26

XEBEC

SCSI

OWL II	5H	25	-	4	-	-	M	5	55	
OWL II	5H	38	-	4	-	-	M	5	40	
OWL III	5H	52	-	4	-	-	M	5	38	

Index